THE CRISIS OF EMPIRE IN MUGHAL NORTH INDIA

For Rizwana

THE CRISIS OF EMPIRE
IN
MUGHAL NORTH INDIA

Awadh and the Punjab, 1707–48

MUZAFFAR ALAM

OXFORD
UNIVERSITY PRESS

OXFORD
UNIVERSITY PRESS

YMCA Library Building, Jai Singh Road, New Delhi 110001

Oxford University Press is a department of the University of Oxford. It furthers the
University's objective of excellence in research, scholarship, and education
by publishing worldwide in

Oxford New York
Athens Auckland Bangkok Bogota Buenos Aires Cape Town
Chennai Dar es Salaam Delhi Florence Hong Kong Istanbul
Karachi Kolkata Kuala Lumpur Madrid Melbourne Mexico City Mumbai
Nairobi Paris Sao Paolo Singapore Taipei Tokyo Toronto Warsaw

with associated companies in

Berlin Ibadan

Oxford is a registered trade mark of Oxford University Press
in the UK and in certain other countries

Published in India
By Oxford University Press, New Delhi

First published in India 1986
Oxford India Paperbacks 1991
Fourth impression 2001

ISBN 0 19 563000 9

Printed in India at Pauls Press, New Delhi 110 020
and published by Manzar Khan, Oxford University Press
YMCA Library Building, Jai Singh Road, New Delhi 110 001

Contents

Maps

Acknowledgements

I have had the privilege of receiving help from a wide circle of friends and critics. I acknowledge with gratitude the affection and encouragement received from Professor S. Nurul Hasan and Professor Satish Chandra. They suggested the theme, helped in locating sources in the early stages of research and were generous with their time for guidance through the long period of the writing of this book. Their advice, together with Professor Irfan Habib's critical comments on an earlier draft have been invaluable in its subsequent revisions.

I have profited over a long period and in no small measure from the kindness of my colleagues and fellow researchers at the Centre. Professor B. D. Chattopadhyaya, Professor Harbans Mukhia and Professor Romila Thapar have given me useful suggestions to make improvements in the text and presentation. Professor Romila Thapar has been particularly helpful in resolving the problems which arose in the course of preparing the final draft. Dr N. Bhattacharya, Professor Bipan Chandra, Yogesh Sharma and Dr Majid Siddiqi have read part of an earlier draft. Professor S. Bhattacharya, Professor Satish Saberwal, Dr Madhavan Palat, Dr Chetan Singh, Dr Dilbagh Singh and Dr K. K. Trivedi have always been willing to advise me on many issues directly or indirectly relevant to this study. Amongst others, Professor Barun De and Professor Iqtidar Alam Khan have encouraged my early efforts. Dr C. A. Bayly, Gautam Bhadra, Dr Mike Fisher, Professor P. J. Marshall, Professor Burton Stein and Dr Andre Wink have seen this work and commented on it. I thank them all for their valuable comments and for useful discussions, all of which have helped to make this a more balanced and coherent work than it would have otherwise been. But responsibility for any errors and the views expressed in this work remains mine alone.

It is my pleasure to recall my debt to my Aligarh teachers who taught me the intricacies of the medieval Indian system. The structure of this book has drawn a great deal on their writings and it is in the knowledge that even where I have disagreed with them the strength, if any, in my argument comes from the first lessons I had from them in research on Mughal history. Amongst the fellow researchers and colleagues, I am thankful in particular to Dr Iqbal Husain and Dr S. Z. H. Jafari for bringing to my notice some important documents; and to Dr I. H. Zilli for helping me in various ways during my research in Aligarh. My intellectual debt to the authors of the recent writings on the eighteenth century will be clear from the footnotes, and call for no special mention.

Professor Irfan Habib and Dr Chetan Singh have helped me in preparing the maps. Mr Faiz Habib and Mr Zahoor Ali Khan have drawn Maps 1 and 7. The other five maps have been drawn by Mr O. D. Tyagi. I have followed Irfan Habib's *Atlas* in identifying in the maps the Mughal administrative divisions. Mr Gabar Singh prepared the typescripts. I must express my gratitude to them all.

Material in the early stages of research for this work was gathered from the Department of History Library and the Maulana Azad Library, Aligarh; the Uttar Pradesh Archives offices, Allahabad and Lucknow; the Asiatic Society of Bengal Library and the National Library, Calcutta; the Tagore Library, Lucknow; the Indian National Archives, New Delhi; the Khuda Bakhsh Oriental Public Library, Patna; the Raza Library, Rampur; and the Raghuvir Library, Sitamau. The School of Social Sciences, Jawaharlal Nehru University and the Indian Council of Historical Research financed my visits to these libraries. A Commonwealth Academic Staff Fellowship in 1981–2 gave me an opportunity to benefit from the rich oriental collections of the British Library, the India Office Library, the Royal Asiatic Society Library, London, the Bodleian Library, Oxford, and the Edinburgh University Library, Edinburgh. The Maison des Sciences de l'Homme, Paris provided material support for a month's stay in Paris to enable me to consult eighteenth century Indo-Persian MSS in Bibliotheque Nationale. My thanks are due to these funding institutions for facilitating my work; to the staff of the libraries for allowing me to use their collections; and to Dr Raghuvir Sinh and the authorities of the Maulana Azad Library for lending certain MSS/Rotographs to the Jawaharlal Nehru University Library for my use.

I should not fail to thank the Oxford University Press for careful editing and meticulous production.

Finally, I must record my sense of obligation to Rizwana, Adnan and Asiya. They have been an unfailing source of sustenance through the protracted stages of completion of this work.

MUZAFFAR ALAM

Centre for Historical Studies
Jawaharlal Nehru University
New Delhi

Note on Transliteration

The Persian and Indian terms not in common use in the English language have been italicized, and their plurals have been indicated by adding the letter *s*.

It was not felt necessary to use diacritical marks each time these terms (as also the names drawn from Persian, Arabic or Indian sources) appear in the text and footnotes. In doing so, my principal consideration has been the convenience of the reader and more than that a concern for error-free printing. Over-insistence on diacriticals, it has been observed, entails for printers a heavy task which they rarely carry out satisfactorily. However, I have used the Greek spiritus asper (') and spiritus lenis (') for *'ain* and *hamzah* respectively, where pronunciation of the words without these marks, I thought, would have been atrocious. Again, to serve the interests of exactness, all non-English words including technical terms, names of persons and the titles of books have been spelt with diacritical marks in the Index and Bibliography.

In spelling and transliteration of the Perso-Arabic and Turkish words, I have generally followed the system adopted by F. Steingass in his *Comprehensive Persian-English Dictionary*. A dot under "d", "r" and "t" as *ḍāk*, *wāṛa* and Jaṭṭ represents the harder sounds of these letters in Indian languages.

I have, however, diverged from Steingass' system in transliteration of the combined words. In Persian combined words I have preferred to put a hyphen (-) between the first word (*muẓāf/mauṣūf*) and the letter "*i*" indicating its combination with the second (*muẓāf-ilaih/ṣifat*). I have written, for instance, *dīwān-i khāliṣa* and *wakīl-i muṭlaq* while Steingass would have written them *dīwāni khāliṣa* and *wakīli muṭlaq*. I have also differed from him in transcribing the word *madad-i ma'āsh*, which he writes *madad-ma'āsh*. Besides, I have preferred simpler spelling for words like *khud* and *khurāk*. Steingass has written them *khwud* and *khwurāk*.

In Perso-Arabic combinations, the Arabic definite article *al* has been consistently transcribed *ul* placed between two hyphens (*-ul-*). This is apparently simpler than Stengass' "*u'l-*", is in keeping with the Indo-Persian pronunciation system and, above all, separates distinctly the three components of the combination, the two words joined together in *izāfat* by the article *ul*. I have followed the same pattern of transcription in combinatiohs when the article is followed by a word beginning with a certain consonant. In such combinations, according to classical Perso-Arabic phonetics, the first letter of the second word gains a double sound, dislodging both the letter and sound of *l* of the article. I have thus written, for example, 'Aẓīm-ush-Shān and Qamar-ud-Dīn whereas Steingass would have written 'Aẓīmu'sh-Shān and Qamaru'd-Dīn. Steingass' system appeared cumbersome and also failed to bring out clearly the three constituents of the combinations. Also, I have written simply Abul and Zulfiqār.

Abbreviations

Aḥwāl	*Aḥwāl-ul-Khawāqīn* by Muḥammad Qāsim Aurangābādī
Āʾīn	*Āʾīn-i Akbarī* by Abul Faẓl
ʿAjāʾib	*ʿAjāʾib-ul-Āfāq*
Akhbārāt	*Akhbārāt-i Darbār-i-Muʿallā*
Allahabad	Persian records preserved at the Uttar Pradesh State Archives, Allahabad
A. S. B.	Asiatic Society of Bengal, Calcutta
Āshūb	Muḥammad Bakhsh Āshūb, *Tārīkh-i Shahādat-i Farrukh Siyar wa Julūs-i Muḥammad Shāh*
Auṣāf	*Auṣāf-ul-Aṣaf* by Inʿāmullāh bin Khurram Shāh
Badāʾiʿ	*Badāʾiʿ Waqāʾiʿ* by Ānand Rām Mukhliṣ
Baḥr-ul-Mawwāj	*Baḥr-ul-Mawwāj* by Muḥammad ʿAlī Khān Anṣārī
Bayān	*Bayān-i Wāqiʿ* by Khwāja ʿAbd-ul-Karīm Kashmīrī
Br. M.	British Museum (now British Library), London
BS (following *Akhbārāt* in footnotes)	Bahādur Shāh
Chahār Gulzār	*Chahār Gulzār-i Shāh Shujāʿī* by Harcharan Dās
FS (following *Akhbārat* in footnotes)	Farrukh Siyar
Ḥadīqat	*Ḥadīqat-ul-Aqalīm* by Murtaẓā Ḥusain Bilgrāmī
IESHR	*The Indian Economic and Social History Review*
Ījād	Muḥammad Aḥsan Ījād, *Farrukh Siyar Nāma*
ʿImād	*ʿImād-us-Saʿādat* by Saiyid Ghulām ʿAlī Khān Naqawī

I. O.	India Office Library (now Commonwealth Relations Library), London
Irādat	Mīr Mubārakallāh, Irādat K̲h̲ān, *Tārīk̲h̲-i Irādat K̲h̲ān*
JS (following *Ak̲h̲bārāt* in footnotes)	Jahāndār Shāh
Kamboh	G̲h̲ulam Husain Kamboh, *Tārīk̲h̲-i Banaras*
Kāmwar	Muḥammad Hadī, Kamwar K̲h̲an, *Taz̲kirat-us-Salātīn Chag̲h̲ta*
K̲h̲izana-i-'Amira	*K̲h̲izāna-i 'Amira* by Mīr G̲h̲ulam 'Alī Āzād Bilgrāmī
K̲h̲ujasta	*K̲h̲ujasta Kalam* by Ṣaḥib Raı
K. K.	Muḥammad Hāshim, K̲h̲āfī K̲h̲ān, *Muntak̲h̲ab-ul-Lubāb*
Ma'ās̲ir-ul-Kirām	*Ma'ās̲ir-ul-Kirām* by Mīr G̲h̲ulam 'Alī Āzad Bilgrāmī
Ma'dan	*Ma'dan-us-Sa'ādat* by Saiyid Sulṭān 'Alī K̲h̲ān Ṣafawī
Maktūbāt	*Manṣūr-ul-Maktūbāt* by Lāla Awadhī Lāl
M. A. L.	Maulana Āzad Library, Aligarh
Mir'āt-ul- Haqa'iq	*Mir'āt-ul Haqa'iq* by I'timād 'Alī K̲h̲ān
M. M.	Mirzā Muḥammad bin Mu'tamad K̲h̲ān, *'Ibratnama*
M. U.	*Ma'ās̲ir-ul-Umara* by Ṣamṣām-ud-Daulah, Shāhnawaz K̲h̲an
Mubārak	Mīr Mubārakallāh, Iradat K̲h̲an(?), *Tārīk̲h̲-i Mubaraknama*
Patna	K̲h̲udā Bak̲h̲sh Oriental Public Library, Bankipore, Patna (Bihar)
PIHC	*Proceedings of the Indian History Congress*
Qāsim	Muḥammad Qāsim Lāhorī, *'Ibratnama*
Rampur	Raẓā Library, Rampur (U. P.)
Risāla	*Risāla-i Muḥammad Shah wa K̲h̲ān-i Dauran*
Roshan Kalām	*Inshā'-i Roshan Kalam* by Bhupat Rāi
Safarnāma	*Safarnama* by Anand Ram Muk̲h̲liṣ
Shāhanshāhī	*Tārīk̲h̲-i Shāhanshāhī* by K̲h̲wājā Muḥammad K̲h̲alīl
Shākir	Shākir K̲h̲ān, *Tārīk̲h̲-i Shākir K̲h̲ān*

Sharā'if	*Sharā'if-i U<u>s</u>mānī* by <u>Gh</u>ulām Husain Firshorī Bilgrāmī
Shivdās	Shivdās Lakhnawī, *Shāhnāma Munawwar Kalām*
Siyar	*Siyar-ul-Muta'a<u>khkh</u>irīn* by Munshī <u>Gh</u>ulām Husain Ṭabātabā'ī
T. Hindī	*Tārī<u>kh</u>-i Hindī* by Rustam 'Alī Shāhabādī.
T. Muhammadī	*Tārī<u>kh</u>-i Muhammadī* by Mirzą Muhammad bin Mu'tamad <u>Kh</u>ān.
T. Muẓaffarī	*Tārī<u>kh</u>-i Muẓaffarī* by Muhammad 'Alī <u>Kh</u>ān Anṣārī
Tabṣira	*Tabṣirat-un-Nāẓirīn* by Saivid Muhammad Bilgrāmī
Tuḥfa	*Tuḥfa-i Tāza* or *Balwant Nāma* by <u>Kh</u>air-ud-Dīn Muhammad <u>Kh</u>ān
Wārid	Muhammad Shafi' Wārid, *Mir'āt-iWāridāt*
Yaḥyā	Yaḥyā <u>Kh</u>ān, *Tā<u>z</u>kirat-ul-Mulūk*

Introduction

In 1707, the Mughal empire had reached its farthest physical limits. The frontiers of the empire, in a determined thrust, had reached the southern edge of the peninsula, encompassing the vast fertile tracts of the erstwhile Deccan kingdoms of Golconda and Bijapur. The imperial principle had been established over almost the entire subcontinent. Yet, together with the expansion, the authority of the central administration in northern India had weakened. Within the heartland of the empire, in the Mathura-Agra region, the Jat *zamindars* and the peasants had repeatedly challenged Mughal authority. The revolts of the *zamindars* in the early 1700s marked an assertion of the power of local 'despots' against the Mughal system and perhaps were symptomatic of a kind of social resurgence. In the Punjab, the Sikh movements were emerging as a significant force. The Rajput chiefs who had made crucial contributions to the consolidation of Mughal rule were becoming lukewarm in their support of the imperial cause.

These developments corroded the bases of imperial power. Disputes arose on the nature and scope of the powers and the positions of the governor, the *faujdar* (area commandant) the provincial *diwan* (revenue minister) and the other local officials. The central administration was subjected to serious strains and stresses. While on the one hand competition for good *jagirs* (revenue assignments to state officials) brought to the surface the tensions within the ruling class, on the other, the *jagirdars*, (revenue assignees) sought to maximize short-run incomes in an atmosphere of uncertainty and apprehension. This resulted in widespread discontent.

Thus, there were unmistakable symptoms of a crisis in the making. The cracks and fissions in the Mughal system developed into breaches and chasms and the imperial edifice collapsed within forty years after the death of Aurangzeb. But while there was chaos and anarchy in some regions, an emerg-

ing political order tended to be constituted in the form of
virtually independent principalities, which nevertheless continued broadly with the Mughal institutional framework.

Historiographical perspective on the Mughal decline

The history of this phase of the Mughal empire has generally
been written from the perspective of the decline of Mughal
power. William Irvine and Jadunath Sarkar who wrote the first
detailed histories of this period,[1] attributed the decline to a
deterioration in the characters of the emperors and their nobles.
As Sarkar examined the developments of this period in the
context of law and order, he held Aurangzeb to have been the
arch-culprit. Aurangzeb was a religious bigot, and therefore
failed. He discriminated against certain sections of the nobility
who had served the empire like members of a large joint family.
Aurangzeb's successors and their nobles, he suggested, were
mere shadows of their predecessors and were thus unable to set
right the evils of the legacy of Aurangzeb. This explanation did
not lead us beyond the perspective of the seventeenth and
eighteenth centuries' Persian chroniclers, with the difference
that Sarkar also read evidence of a 'Hindu reaction' in the
Rathor, Bundela, Maratha and Sikh wars against the Mughal
empire. On the contrary, in contemporary sources the rebels
and 'disturbers' had been identified in terms of either their
class, namely, *zamindars*, or their caste, clan and region.[2]
Sarkar's views and like them, the views of many other historians,[3] are to be seen against the ambience of the times which
lent legitimacy to communal interpretations of Indian history

[1]W. Irvine, *Later Moghuls,* reprint, New Delhi, 1971, particularly the sections where
he assesses the characters of the emperors and nobles. Jadunath Sarkar, *Fall of the
Mughal Empire,* I, Calcutta, 1938; 3rd edn, Calcutta, 1964. *History of Aurangzeb,* I–V,
Calcutta, 1912, 1916, 1919 and 1924, in particular III and V.

[2]Like, *Rajputan, Jatan, Gujaran, Afghanan, Rohilaha,* or *Zamindaran-o-mufsidan-i Katehar*
or *Fitna-pazohan-i Baiswara* or *Shaikh-zadagan-i Lakhnau* and so on and so forth.
The Sikhs, however, are identified as such or as 'the worshippers of Nanak' or 'the
followers of Guru'.

[3] See, for example, S. R. Sharma, *The Religious Policy of the Mughal Emperors,* Oxford,
1940; 2nd edn, Bombay, 1962; Ishwari Prasad, *The Mughal Empire,* Allahabad, 1974,
pp. 584–608; Jagdish Narayan Sarkar, *A Study of Eighteenth Century India,* Calcutta,
Saraswati Library, 1976, pp. 173–392.

in the late-nineteenth and twentieth centuries.[4] They rightly emphasized Aurangzeb's attempt to associate the Mughal state with Muslim orthodoxy; but the conclusion that this engendered problems for the empire only from the Hindus and that the 'Hindu reaction' was the major cause of the decline is unsatisfactory, since Muslim nobles and officials also reacted to such policies. In addition, as this study will show, Muslim *madad-i ma'ash* holders independently created problems of comparable magnitude for the empire.

In 1959 the publication of Satish Chandra's *Parties and Politics at the Mughal Court, 1707–40*[5] from Aligarh marked the first serious attempt to study the structural flaws of the Mughal system with a view to understanding the decline of the empire in the eighteenth century. To Satish Chandra, the stability of the empire as a centralized state in the seventeenth century depended on an efficient working of the *mansab* and *jagir* system. The nobles (*umara*) were the core state officials whose position and status in the hierarchy corresponded to their rankings designated in numbers (*mansabs*) and who were paid generally in assignments of land revenue (*jagirs*). Availability of the revenues to be assigned and the ability of the Mughals to collect them thus became two crucial prerequisites for an effective working of the system. Towards the end of Aurangzeb's reign the Mughal failure to maintain the system had become too evident to be concealed any longer.[6]

In 1963, Irfan Habib from Aligarh attempted an in-depth analysis of the collapse of the empire in his seminal work, *The Agrarian System of Mughal India*. According to Habib, the mechanism of collection of revenues that the Mughals evolved was inherently flawed. If on the one hand the imperial policy was to set the revenue at the highest rate possible so as to secure the greatest military strength of the empire, the nobles, on the

[4] For a discussion of this aspect, see Romila Thapar, *et al.*, *Communalism and the Writing of Indian History*, New Delhi, 2nd edn, 1977; Bipan Chandra, *Communalism in Modern India*, New Delhi, 1984, pp. 209–36; Romila Thapar, Irfan Habib and P. S. Gupta, Symposium on 'The Contributions of Indian Historians to the Process of National Integration', *PIHC*, 24th Session, 1961, Delhi, pp. 345–61.

[5] Aligarh, 1959; 2nd and 3rd edns, New Delhi, 1972 and 1979.

[6] Satish Chandra, *Parties and Politics at the Mughal Court, 1707–1740*, Introduction and concluding remarks.

other, tended to squeeze the maximum from their *jagirs*, even if it ruined the peasantry and destroyed the revenue-paying capacity of the area for all time. The noble, whose *jagirs* were liable to be transferred frequently, could never follow a far-sighted policy of agricultural development. In some areas the peasants were even deprived of their means of survival. By the late 1700s, the burden on the peasants, thus, became unbearable. In many areas, they took to flight or refused to pay the revenue and were up in arms against the Mughals.[7] Habib argued that the working of the Mughal authority structure proved disastrous also for the pre-colonial economy. The Mughal system left little with the peasantry to invest in improvement of agriculture and to provide a market for the tools, techniques and goods of others.[8]

In 1966, also from Aligarh appeared yet another major study of the subject in M. Athar Ali's excellent work on the nobility and their politics in the late-seventeenth century.[9] Athar Ali provided quantitative support to Satish Chandra's study. In these two studies, the problems attending the annexation of the Deccan states, the absorption of the Marathas and the Deccanis into the Mughal nobility, and the subsequent shortage of *jagirs* have the pride of place.

In a recent symposium on the decline of the Mughal empire, J. F. Richards, M. N. Pearson and P. Hardy also give a pivotal position to the Mughal involvement in the Deccan and the Maratha land.[10] But the participants of this symposium also try to modify the explanations offered by the Aligarh historians. Pearson notices a basic flaw in the Mughal system. Mughal rule, he argues, was 'very indirect' and it was not state control but local ties and norms which governed 'the lives of most people most of the time'. It was only for the nobles that the concept of the Mughal empire outweighed other 'primordial attachments'; and the nobles were bound to the empire only by 'patronage' which depended on the 'constant military success' of the emperor. Pearson emphasizes the absence of an im-

---

[7] Irfan Habib, *The Agrarian System of Mughal India*, Bombay, 1963, pp. 317–51.

[8] Irfan Habib, 'Potentialities of Capitalistic Development in the Economy of Mughal India', *Enquiry*, New Series, III, 3, Winter 1971, pp. 1–56.

[9] M. Athar Ali, *The Mughal Nobility under Aurangzeb*, Bombay, 1966, reprint, 1970.

[10] *Journal of Asian Studies*, Vol. XXXV, No. 2, February, 1976, pp. 221–63.

personalized bureaucracy, its consequences for the Mughal state and thus reaffirms an oft-repeated explanation for the absence of successful states in Asia and Africa in pre-modern times.

There is no denying the fact that the personal achievements and failures of the emperors and their declining military fortunes weighed considerably with the nobles. Pearson's formulation, however, is not borne out from the details of the history of our period. My study shows that not only the small group of nobles (*umara*) but also the *zamindars*, the village and *qasba*-based *madad-i ma'ash* holders and a very large number of lower-level officials drawn from various regional and local communities were all integrated intimately into the framework of the empire. The Mughal empire rested on a balancing of these diverse interests. But it is true that the imperial system could not fully override, let alone obliterate the landholders' primary attachments to local groups, in particular those of kin, clan and caste. The empire signified a coordinating agency between conflicting communities and the various indigenous sociopolitical systems at different levels. The basis of the empire, in a measure, had been negative; its strength had lain in the inability of the local communities and their systems to mobilize beyond relatively narrow bounds.

Political integration in Mughal India was, up to a point, inherently flawed. It was conditional on the coordination of the interests and the political activities of the various social groups led by local magnates. This, in turn, was dependent on the latter realizing that they could not make fortunes by themselves. The nobles were dependent for their position and power directly on the emperor who appointed them. They had no hereditary estates to consolidate or bequeath to their successors. Their resources were scrutinized and regulated by the state. They were, in substance, salaried civil and military servants; and they represented the emperor in various capacities at different levels. Yet the nobility had its tensions. The principle of the *jagir* transfer, by checking the noble's ambition to build a personal base, was meant to strengthen the imperial organization; but it implied an inconvenience for the nobles who resisted its enforcement, and therefore it was left unimplemented in a number of cases in the seventeenth century.

Thus, the thrust of the nobles' actions in our period, and their endeavour towards independent political alignments with the *zamindars* in order to carve out their own fortunes, were not absolutely incompatible with earlier developments.

The leaders of the local communities, generally identified as *zamindars* in our sources were hereditary local potentates. Their position, strength and resources were, in origin, independent of the state. But they were sharply divided among themselves on caste, clan and territorial lines and were perpetually at war with each other. Each group feared the other; each had to be constantly on guard against the actual or threatened encroachment of the other. The social conditions of the period rarely allowed the various local communities to stand together, they could always be subjugated by a power that was able to stand above kin, clan, regional and religious connections. Such a paramount power also promised to keep in check the threats to the various groups' individual positions. Thus the very nature of local social and political conditions had facilitated and legitimated imperial Mughal penetration. In almost every Mughal victory over a local community, the support of one or other local chief had proved crucial in the sixteenth and seventeenth centuries.

The basis for the integration of the local communities into the empire was narrow and negative. The submission of *zamindars* to the imperial state depended not only on a demonstration of the latter's political and military power, but also on creation of conditions of security. The *zamindars* were frequently the virtual rulers of the region; and the terms on which their relations with the state were worked out depended on the strength or weakness of the people and the areas they controlled. The regions under examination, as we shall see, did not remain stagnant; they experienced economic growth in the seventeenth century, and so the *zamindars* and their followers in the community felt increasingly confident and strong enough to stand on their own. Much of their earlier feeling of insecurity was neutralized. It is thus incorrect to explain the instability of the Mughal system merely in terms of the personal and military failures of the emperor or his nobility.

By contending that the shortage of usable *jagirs* in the Deccan in the 1690s was artificial, J. F. Richards[11] makes a valuable

---

[11] See also his book, *Mughal Administration in Golconda*, Oxford, 1975, pp. 135–214 and 306–16.

contribution to an explanation of the problems of Mughal administration in the late-seventeenth and early-eighteenth centuries. He demolishes the long-held belief that the Deccan was a deficit area from which had sprung the belief that *be-jagiri* (absence of *jagirs*) was the major cause of the decline of the Mughal empire. Considering newly discovered archival sources, Satish Chandra makes a clear distinction between *be-jagiri* and the crisis in the *jagirdari* system in a review of his explanation of the decline of the Mughal empire.[12] Central to the growth of the crisis of the *jagirdari* system, as he suggests in this study, was its non-functionality—not the growth in the size of the ruling class and the corresponding decline in the revenues earmarked to be assigned in *jagirs* (*paibaqi*). Richards is right in stressing the role of 'the local warrior aristocracies' for any analysis of the problems of the Mughal administration in the late-seventeenth and early-eighteenth centuries. Satish Chandra hints at the possibility of a 'tripolar relationship' between the *jagirdars, zamindars,* and the *khudkashtas* (resident cultivators) having been the principal factor in the stability of the Mughal empire. Nowhere, however, has the dynamic of these relationships been linked to the social conditions of those constituting them: the *jagirdars,* the *zamindars* and the peasants. Richards sometimes explains 'the imperial crisis' in terms of the emperor's decisions and policies.

An examination of some of the problems of these 'tripolar' relationships is necessary. In addition, the role of the *madad-i ma'ash* holders and of a large number of the indigenous elements (Shaikhzadas in Awadh and Khatris in the Punjab) in Mughal administration must be taken into account, not as dependents and officials of the state or as associates of the big nobles, but as elements embedded within local communities and groups.

The Mughal decline has also been explained in terms of participation in eighteenth-century politics of groups conventionally regarded as non-political. Karen Leonard argues that 'indigenous banking firms were indispensable allies of the Mughal state', and that the great nobles and imperial officers 'were more than likely to be directly dependent upon these firms'. When in the period 1650–1750 these banking firms began 'the

---

[12] Satish Chandra, *Medieval India: Society, the Jagirdari Crisis and the Village,* Delhi, 1982, pp. 61–75.

redirection of [their] economic and political support' towards nascent regional polities and rulers, including the British East India Company in Bengal, this led to bankruptcy, the ensuing series of political crises and the 'downfall of the empire'.[13] The premises on which Leonard builds her conclusions do not get adequate support from the existing studies of Mughal polity and economy; yet her explanation is worth considering and cannot be dismissed summarily.

Philip Calkins was the first to take serious note of the role of merchants and bankers in his analysis of political formation in the eighteenth-century Bengal.[14] In Pearson's study of Gujarat there is some convincing evidence of the merchants' participation in politics.[15] Still, Pearson refrains from suggesting that the Mughal finance system was dependent on merchants' credit. Calkins also limits his generalization to the period and the region he examines and refrains from attributing the stability of the empire to merchant participation in earlier periods or in other regions. Without any fresh evidence to support her contention, Leonard extends further what Calkins and Pearson have suggested with rather unfair and exaggerated emphasis on the role of bankers.

It is difficult to pinpoint the exact nature of the political participation of the merchant, for the Persian sources on which this study rests contain little information about the conventionally non-political urban groups. However, some references to the Khatris as 'nobles' (*umara*) and 'notables' (*a'yan*) are worth considering. Big merchants (*sahukars*) and some artisans in the Punjab supported the Mughal drive against the Sikhs in the early-eighteenth century. This indicates that, at least in some parts of Mughal India, the trading community had a tradition of political participation. But it is possible that the merchant interests were tied to the prosperity and stability of the ruling class and the markets they had encouraged. They appear to

[13] Karen Leonard, 'The "Great Firm" Theory of the Decline of the Mughal Empire', *Comparative Studies in Society and History*, Vol. 21, No. 2, April, 1979, pp. 161–7.

[14] Philip C. Calkins, 'The Formation of a Regionally Oriented Ruling Group in Bengal', *Journal of Asian Studies*, Vol. XXIX, No. 4, August, 1970, pp. 799–806.

[15] M. N. Pearson, *Merchants and Rulers in Gujarat*, California, 1976; see also his article, 'Political Participation in Mughal India', *IESHR*, Vol. IX, No. 2, June 1972, pp. 113–31.

have begun to take active part in politics when their fortunes were in danger in the wake of imperial decline. It may be presumed that a class with a tradition of political participation would certainly not remain passive onlookers if they thought regional stability might be possible with their support.

Societal 'crisis' is the dominant note in the writings of Cantwell Smith, K. M. Ashraf, Irfan Habib and Athar Ali.[16] The Mughal empire, according to them, declined as society failed to produce enough surplus to sustain a vast all-India polity. In other words, economic failures, at least, coincided with, if they did not actually precede, political decline. The belief that the phase of decline was predominantly a period of chaos and disorder receives nourishment even in the writings of those who have recently tried to replace the term 'decline' with 'decentralization'. My study confirms that society in the early-eighteenth century was disturbed; old relationships between the different constituents of the empire were, willy nilly, undergoing political realignments. But the connection between this disturbance and failures in the spheres of production and market is far from obvious.

The eighteenth century in Indian history, particularly its first half, was unfortunate in that it was sandwiched between the political glory of the Great Mughals and the humiliation of colonial rule. Further, the British who wrote the first modern histories of India's past had their own interests in presenting a bleak portrayal of the period. A virtually uncritical acceptance of the British depiction is implicit in a number of modern writings on the eighteenth century. The fact that most contemporary Persian chroniclers have also projected the period as one of total chaos and failure not only suited the interests of the British writers but also lent strength to their interpretations. This factor still conditions our appreciation of the circumstances that led to the imperial decline and the ensuing developments in the regions. But we have to be on guard against the prejudices of these chroniclers, who, in most cases, were pro-

---

[16] Cantwell Smith, 'Lower Class Uprisings in Mughal Empire', *Islamic Culture*, 1946, pp. 21–40; K. M. Ashraf, 'Presidential Address to the Medieval Indian Section', *PIHC*, 23rd Session, Aligarh, 1960, pp. 143–52; Irfan Habib, *Agrarian System*, pp. 317–51; M. Athar Ali, 'The Passing of Empire: The Mughal Case', *Modern Asian Studies*, Vol. 9, No. 3, 1975, pp. 385–96.

teges of the nobles, the premier beneficiaries of the Mughal
imperial structure. They suffered as the regions resisted imperial control and obtained some independence from Delhi. The
decline of their fortunes has been portrayed in these chronicles
as the decline and decay of the entire society. We may also bear
in mind that the Mughal throne and the person of the emperor
was central to their vision and the decline of the imperial edifice
was tantamount to a total collapse of all society.

Empire and the province

Eighteenth-century India needs to be studied in terms of its
own structure, disregarding for a moment perhaps what pre-
ceded and followed this period. This has already been recognized in the writings on the late-eighteenth and the early-
nineteenth century by scholars who have not been over-
whelmed by the fate of the Mughal power.[17] Most studies of the
earlier phases of the eighteenth century appear to have been
largely conditioned by the trajectory of the Mughal empire.

Richard Barnett has considered briefly political formations
in Awadh against the backdrop of imperial disintegration. But
his interest seems to be more in the latter half of the eighteenth
century.[18] The process of the subordination of all offices and
authorities within a region to the governor and, simultaneously,
the governor's acquisition of a practically independent and
hereditary position needs to be studied in greater depth. Local
political and administrative problems were reflected in changes
in the actions and positions of the various social groups, particularly, the *zamindars*, the *madad-i ma'ash* grantees and the *man-*

[17] Besides Hermann Goetz's 'The Crisis of Indian Civilization in the Eighteenth
Century' (Calcutta University Lecture Series, reprint 1938), in recent years there have
been some serious and comprehensive studies of different parts of India casting grave
doubts about the validity of an unqualified 'crisis' and 'bleak-century' perspective. See,
for example, C. A. Bayly, *Rulers, Townsmen and Bazaars: North Indian Society in the Age of
British Expansion, 1770–1870*, Cambridge, 1983; Richard B. Barnett, *North India between
Empires, Awadh, the Mughals and the British, 1720–1801*, Berkeley, 1980; Andre Wink,
'Land and Sovereignty in India under the 18th Century Maratha Swarajya',
unpublished Ph. D. thesis, University of Leiden, 1984.

[18] In *North India between Empires*, Richard B. Barnett, raises the questions relating to
the governor's bid to control the provincial finance in his Introduction; but he sums up
'the developments of autonomous political goals' of Burhan-ul-Mulk and Safdar Jang
in Chapter I without considering their antecedents.

sab holders, which in turn compelled governors to adopt new policies that could only be implemented at the expense of imperial authority or of those sections of the nobility which remained outside the province. While examining political realignments in the provinces, it can be seen that local and regional social groups were emerging as powerful forces. I have thus tried to study the history of the period in the context of the Mughal imperial centre, namely, the emperor, the nobles posted at the court or outside the provinces under review on the one hand and the region, on the other. The interaction of these elements have also been scrutinized.

The stages of the breakawav from the centre—of individuals, of social groups, of communities, and of regions—have been studied with a view to understanding the nature of political transformation in the eighteenth century. My primary purpose is not only to explain the Mughal imperial decline. Several aspects of the history of the eighteenth century tend to be overlooked when one examines the problems of the period solely with the objective of explaining the decline of the Mughal empire. This perspective has often prevented us from going out of the precincts of the Mughal empire into the regions to look for the causes of turmoil or stability in different parts of the empire. One remains imprisoned within the narrow confines of Delhi to the exclusion of significant developments eleswhere.

No study of the eighteenth century can, however, overlook the debate regarding the causes of the decline of the Mughal empire which has been briefly reviewed in the preceding pages.

The focus of this book is on the interplay of the forces of the centre and the region in twn north Indian provinces, Awadh and the Punjab. Both these provinces were extremely impor- tant to Mughal India. They lay in close proximity to the capital and were fully integrated into the empire at the beginning of the period of our study. The Punjab linked the Mughal empire, through commercial, cultural and ethnic intercourse, with Persia and Central Asia. Control over the Punjab was necessary not only for its own rich agricultural and non-agricultural production but also because Central Asian and Persian horses, Kabuli fruits and Kashmiri shawls passed through the pro- vince, on their way to Delhi and Agra and thence to different parts of the empire. The province was of strategic importance for watching the movements of armies beyond Kabul and Qandahar, as well as the hill chiefs in control of the Himalayan range from Kishtawar and Jammu to Srinagar Garhwal.

On the other hand, Awadh—together with the northern parts of the Mughal province of Allahabad—was the gateway to the eastern provinces. As the routes through and along the Yamuna became vulnerable by the late-seventeenth and the early-eighteenth centuries, in the wake of the Maratha and the Bundela risings, the roads from Delhi *via* Bareilly, Lucknow, Jaunpur and Benaras to Patna, Murshidabad and Hugli acquired special import. Moreover, a large number of smaller *mansabdars*, petty commanders of the troopers and the associates of the nobles came from the *qasbas* of Awadh.

Both the Punjab and Awadh registered unmistakable economic growth in the seventeenth century. In the early-eighteenth century in both provinces, politics and administration appear to have moved along similar lines. The local officials faced stiff resistance from the *zamindars* and the peasants to the exercise of imperial control. The governors sought wide powers in order to bring provincial finance and all other offices eventually under their own control. During the later phases of our period, however, developments in these provinces began to diverge. In Awadh the governor could mobilize local social groups around his own banner and was thus able to place *nawabi* rule on firm ground; in the Punjab the new *subadari* (governorship) collapsed and there was total chaos and confusion towards the end of our period. Given this divergence the history of these provinces appears to be especially amenable to an examination of issues concerning both the decline of the imperial authority and the circumstances that caused and accompanied emergent political formations in the provinces.

My purpose here is to assess the nature of the problem facing the Mughal administration; and given the limitations of my sources, I am able only to offer some details about the Himalayan chiefs, Jat Sikhs, Rajput and Afghan *zamindars*, Khatris, the Muslim *madad-i ma'ash* holders, and the Shaikhzadahs—together with instances of defiance of imperial regulations by local Mughal officials.

The zamindars, *the* jagirdars *and imperial decline*

A close examination of the Persian sources brings to light a large number of rebel *zamindars* besides the well-known categories of so-called *mufsids* (disturbers) of the early-eighteenth century: Sikhs, Jats, Marathas and Afghans. *Zamindars* of different denominations mounted the rural uprisings (each with its own logic) but all sought greater share in power over, and thus in the revenues of, their region. In some cases, it was a strong landholding community seeking to establish some form of dominance over its region. In several cases in Awadh rural pressure took the form of the *zamindar* beseiging a fortress (*ihdas-i qilacha*) and mobilizing his kinsfolk and an armed retinue (*jami'at-o-sipah*). One or more *zamindars* would thus proclaim the central position of their clans and villages in the area—*pargana* or a group of *parganas*—where they had *zamindaris*.

These revolts were organized and led by powerful *zamindars*. But their goals were limited. The scale of their mobilization against imperial power could not transcend the divisions of their caste and community. The Mughals could handle the Awadhi *zamindars* either by a show of strength, using the other local elements against them or by extending concessions to the powerful rebels. Rural resistance in the Punjab, however, was less tractable. This difference has been examined in terms of the history of the two regions, including the nature of their relationships with the centre.

Even though not always directed against the state, these uprisings corroded the basis of imperial authority, sometimes through linkages with imperial court politics. In the emerging political situation, service and loyalty to *imperial* authority ceased to count, for it was not the emperor but the nobles in the region who began to dictate state actions. Thus, the imperial assistance available to provincial nobles and the local officials for coping with local problems depended more on their individual influence with powerful nobles at the centre, and less on their loyalty to the emperor. Thus were the beginnings of the new *subadari* in Awadh and the Punjab made.

In the context of rapidly diminishing imperial authority at local levels, I have examined certain administrative developments which had originated with a view to enabling the nobles to meet local challenges effectively. Among such developments were the *jagir-i mahal-i watan* and the long-term *jagir* holdings aimed at augmenting the strength of the nobility. These developments violated the classical Mughal concept of imperial authority, as seen in the seventeenth century, undermined the prospects of its survival, and reinforced the course of provincial autonomy.

Social and political base of eighteenth century provincial states

As the play of various factors is examined the period of my study separates into four phases, 1707–13, 1713–*c*. 1722, *c*. 1722–39 and 1739–48. In the first two phases, the issues are those of imperial authority *vis-á-vis* the governors and the local potentates, and the slow pull to provincial independence; in the latter two phases, the issues relate to the working of the new *subadari*, sometimes called the 'successor state', the extent of its independence from the imperial centre and its relations with the emerging system of regional powers.

The period of our study appears to have witnessed an emerging sense of regional identity which buttressed both political and, to a degree, economic decentralization. This sense of identity or provincial obduracy followed and accompanied economic prosperity in the regions. Different regions of the empire gained in strength in the wake of relative peace and political stability under the Mughal system in the seventeenth century. Intra-region as well as inter-region trade in local goods, artifacts and foodgrains sustained a network of towns and money markets of varying sizes throughout the empire, linking some of the regions together with strong ties of economic interdependence. Conditions were thus generated for economic unity among these areas, irrespective of their political and military relations with each other. In a measure, the economic developments of the regions took a course independent of their political detour, even though their political unification under the Mughals had a bearing on this course.

The provinces of Awadh and the Punjab were among such regions. Economic developments in these provinces, as we shall see later, resulted in not only a rise in the revenue figures but also in the emergence and affluence of a number of towns, with a chain of routes to link them to the long-distance trade. The prosperity of these regions was to the obvious advantage of the *zamindars* who enjoyed a dominance in rural production; it also benefited the merchants who controlled and regulated the markets. The *zamindars* in our period, as 'local despots', were in an almost uncompromising conflict with the imperial authorities. They had allied with the Mughals and accepted their subordinate position either in the face of the fear of the invincible Mughal or with an objective of protecting and promoting their individual interests *vis-á-vis* the others within the region. Since they now found themselves strong enough, they were up in arms. But as their goal was narrow and parochial, they failed to incorporate the interests of other regional groups in their programmes and thus fight the imperial power. They relied on support from peasants and smaller *zamindars* of their own castes and in many cases their interest remained limited to their kinsfolk in the villages; the townsmen and traders also became victims of their fury.

In addition, the enrichment of the region generated conflict among the various local groups, as they each tried to maximize their profits at the expense of the other. The *madad-i ma'ash* holders made a bid to turn their grants into *zamindaris*, without forefeiting their existing privileges and perquisites. The *jagirdar* too aspired to a permanent holding so that he could build his own base in the region.

Conflict and absence of coordination between the local elements enabled the Mughal nobles to establish their hegemony over them and to mobilize the regional resources to emerge as a focus of power in the region. The political formations in these areas remained within the Mughal institutional framework.

However, it would appear that Awadh and the Punjab differed radically from each other in the social and economic bases of the problems in the period under review. In fact even earlier the leaders of the agrarian uprisings in these two provinces did not have the same programmes, slogans and perspectives. Besides, the *jagir* holdings in the Punjab were large in size and the *jagirdars* were powerful nobles who were unwilling to accept the authority of the governor. Further, the location of the Punjab— exposing it to developments in and invasions from Persia and Afghanistan—did much to shape the course of its history. These factors in combination with the nature of its relations with the centre and the interest of the *wazir* and a number of his Turani associates in the province constricted the growth of the new *subadari* in the Punjab. In contrast, the governor of Awadh was able to make fresh arrangements both with the local potentates and the petty *jagir* holders in the province, providing a new social basis for his rule, and thus establish the new *subadari* on firm ground.

Governorship during this period was consolidated at the initiative of the then incumbent; the office became hereditary ultimately and the province began to be designated as the 'home province' (*suba-i mulki* and *dar-ul-mulk*) of the governor. It, however, remained a *suba* (province), part of empire, replete with imperial symbols. The governor, despite his attempt, was unable to shake off the Mughal centre completely. These powerful new *subadars* continued to seek links with one or the other group at the court.

The imperial court in the eighteenth century

One may ask why the new *subadar* wanted this support from the imperial court or, in other words, why the symbols of empire continued to be persuasive, even though the power which had promoted them decayed. We shall see that the social and political realities of the eighteenth century continued to require reference to at least a semblance of an imperial centre. Our period saw not only the collapse of central government, but also a restabilization in certain regions and this was achieved almost wholly within the Mughal institutional framework. Disintegration of the empire did not mean the drying up of all sources of growth in society. But no region was in a position to maintain itself in complete isolation of other areas. Despite decentralization and the regional rulers' war against each other, the regions remained integrated through trade and monetary transactions.[19] Again, in the conditions of unfettered political and military adventurism which accompanied and followed the decline of imperial power, none of the adventurers was strong enough to be able to win the allegiance of the others and then replace the imperial power. All of them struggled separately to make their fortunes and threatened each other's

[19] See Chapter I, n. 56.

position and achievements. Only some of them, however, could establish their dominance over the others. When they sought institutional validation of their spoils, they needed a centre to legitimize their acquisitions.

The Mughal emperor and his court provided the safest such centre, since it had long been generally accepted as a source of all political power and authority; but now it was too weak and ineffective to resist the adventurers' ambitions and was also unable to restrict regional developments. It is significant that even after the total collapse of the central government, the governors of the virtually independent provinces continued to make serious efforts to obtain offices at the Mughal court. Considered from the perspective of the Mughal court, this phase of politics has been seen either as mere factionalism in the nobility,[20] sometimes attributed to the 'crisis' of the period,[21] or as a kind of recurrence of an earlier pattern.[22] This study suggests that court politics in the 1740s, the last phase of our period, could well be linked to the conditions emerging in the provinces, particularly the ambitions of political and military adventurers who sought a standing at the centre, in order to secure firmly *their positions in the regions*. Ambitious individuals, like the governors of Awadh, or groups like the Marathas, looked for positions at the court after they had established their dominance over local groups in the regions in order to reinforce and secure their regional bases. This shift from control of peripheries by the centre in the seventeenth century to control of centre by the provinces is significant. But such was the myth and influence of Delhi that no regional power could replace it as the centre in the eighteenth century.

[20] Jadunath Sarkar, *Fall of the Mughal Empire* I, pp. 1–25.
[21] Z. U. Malik, *Reign of Muhammad Shah*, Bombay, 1977, pp. 182–9.
[22] Satish Chandra, *Parties and Politics*, p. xviii.

CHAPTER I
Breakdown of Imperial Organization

Political unification in Mughal times signified the successful working of a range of offices and institutions meant to be a mechanism of 'checks and balances'.[1] The Mughal imperial system in operation not only delimited the spheres of activity of the various social groups but also ensured a balance of their interests for the maintenance and promotion of political integration. This imperial principle was, in a very large measure, the result of particular patterns of relationships between the emperor, the nobility, minor officials, local potentates and petty assignees of land revenue, specially the *madad-i ma'ash* holders. Through a series of conflicts and adjustments under the Sultans of Delhi and the early Mughals these patterns were worked out and were finally evolved during the reign of Akbar (1556–1605). Akbar had ruthlessly rejected the high pretensions of the Chaghtai nobles and the Mirzas (princes claiming descent from Timur). He also tackled the threat from the local potentates who were entrenched throughout the empire with tact and determination. He was able, however, to provide enough opportunity to the nobility to feel reasonably satisfied by a system of lavish *jagir* assignments and other symbols of rank and authority. He also tried to accommodate the claims of the local magnates from the village headmen to the chieftains by integrating them, in different degrees, into the imperial

[1] Modern historians have used the terms 'checks and balances' in the context of their discussion of the theory and the functioning of the Mughal government. Cf. Ibn Hasan, *The Central Structure of the Mughal Empire*, reprint, New Delhi, 1970, pp. 291–301; P. Saran, *The Provincial Government of the Mughals*, reprint, Bombay, 1973, pp. 157–9, 174–7 and 183–91; Satish Chandra, *Medieval India: Society, the Jagirdari Crisis and the Village*, Delhi, 1982, p. 63. The use of the terms is intended to highlight the accountability of the Mughal officials, which Abul Fazl repeatedly emphasizes. Indeed, the terms are almost the literal translation of the words Abul Fazl uses. However, the terms may not be taken to suggest any bureaucratic formalism in its modern sense.

framework.[2] Thus a sort of equilibrium to contain conflicts and promote interdependence between the emperor, the nobility and the local elements was established on some kind of institutional basis. The coordination of all these complex relationships determined the existence of the imperial structure and political stability in Mughal India.

In the given power structure, however, the norms and the institutions governing the relationship between the emperor and the nobility were crucial for the imperial organization. In the actual working of Mughal polity the valour, the vigour, the courage, the morale and the efficiency of the individual nobles carried no value, unless they were made to act in unison conforming to the imperial system. The Mughals, therefore, made special efforts to achieve and maintain some kind of unity in the nobility. They devised numerous restrictions on the tendencies of the heterogeneous, and also conflicting, elements of the nobility to dislocate the equilibrium that secured and reinforced the overriding authority of the emperor.

Thus, the emperor in the Mughal system was placed in a position of supreme awe, buttressed by an elaborate paraphernalia of court etiquette and royal prerogative. Central authority came to be identified ultimately with the person of the emperor. In order to make the central government work, the emperor was

---

[2] Almost every good modern research work on the Mughal state-structure has taken note of the problems which the early Mughal Emperors, Humayun and Akbar, had to face with the Turani nobles. The measures and the policies adopted by Akbar to meet these problems and build his empire are also now widely known. For a pioneering major work on the nobility, however, see S. Nurul Hasan, 'New Light on the Relations of Early Mughal Rulers with their Nobility', *PIHC*, 1944. The problem has been examined in detail by Iqtidar Alam Khan in his *Mirza Kamran, A Biographical Study*, Bombay, 1964, and *Political Biography of a Mughal Noble: Mun'im Khan, Khan-i Khanan, 1497–1575*, New Delhi, 1973, Introduction, pp. IX–XX. See also his 'The Turko-Mongol Theory of Kingship', *Medieval India—A Miscellany*, Bombay, 1972, Vol. II, pp. 8–18. How the Mughals accommodated the local potentates has been examined by Irfan Habib, *Agrarian System*, pp. 136–89, S. Nurul Hasan, 'Zamindars under the Mughals' in R.E. Frykenberg, *Land Control and Social Structure in Indian History*, Madison, 1969, pp. 17–31 and A.R. Khan, *Chieftains in the Mughal Empire during the Reign of Akbar*, Simla, 1977, *passim*. For the position of the *madad-i ma'ash* holders who were no less a significant local element and their relationship with the Mughal state see Irfan Habib, *Agrarian System*, pp. 298–316; N.A. Siddiqi, *Land Revenue Administration under the Mughals, 1700–1750*, Bombay, 1970, pp. 123–34 and Shaikh Abd-ur-Rashid, 'Suyurghal Lands under the Mughals', in H.R. Gupta (ed.) *Essays Presented to Sir Jadu Nath Sarkar*, Punjab University, 1958, pp. 313–22.

expected to be able to resolve the conflicts of these sections. Factional strife among the nobles and the emperor's inability to be, or at least to appear to be, above these factions meant (as actually happened in our period) a grave danger to imperial unity. Such a situation threatened not only the balance in the relationship between the emperors and the nobility, but also acted upon, as it was determined by, their relations with the different regional and local elements. Satish Chandra has discussed at length the problem of the nobility in the eighteenth century. N. A. Siddiqi in the context of his study of the revenue system of the first half of the eighteenth century and Z.U. Malik as a background to his comprehensive history of the reign of Muhammad Shah, have also examined factional politics at the court and its consequences for the Mughal administration.[3] In the following pages which set the scene for discussing the problems of imperial power and political formations in the regions under review, I notice some more evidence of such developments at and around the centre in the post-Aurangzeb period. By examining these developments, analysing their interaction with factional politics and the administrative relapse at the centre in four phases, I intend to highlight the gradual but steady alienation of the nobles, the smaller government officials and the local magnates from the Mughal state, both at the centre and in the provinces. The problems and the shifts of social and political alignments in the provinces leading finally to their virtual breakaway from the imperial centre followed closely the chronological order of these developments.

I 1707–12

The nobility

Towards the last years of Aurangzeb's reign (1658–1707) the older problems of conflict between imperial authority and certain groups of the nobility began to reappear, though in a very different form. In a number of cases, the nobles began to seek avenues to build their fortunes in obvious disregard of the

[3] Compare Satish Chandra, *Parties and Politics, passim;* N.A. Siddiqi, *Land Revenue Administration,* pp. 65–72, 96–101 and 115–23; Z.U. Malik, *The Reign of Muhammad Shah,* pp. 56–115.

principles defining their powers and positions.[4] Aurangzeb had to constantly warn his nobles against the consequences of a tendency among them to flout Mughal norms and royal prerogatives.[5] Bahadur Shah (1707–12) thus inherited a difficult situation. Moreover, a large section of the nobility, particularly that which had supported Prince Muhammad Azam, his erstwhile opponent in the contest for the throne, was uncertain and apprehensive.

Bahadur Shah tried to solve the problem by encouraging some new elements and by imposing certain constraints on the ambitions of the dominant sections of the nobility, as well as by extending some concessions to some of them. In accordance with the usual tradition, he appears to have decided to give *mansabs* to the nobles with a liberal hand,[6] more so because Prince Muhammad Kam Bakhsh, another claimant to the throne, was still to be dealt with in the Deccan. A change is, however, also discernible in Bahadur Shah's attempt to tackle the dilemma of the nobility. He showed restraint in promoting the interests of the members of the old and the established families (*khanazads*) and favoured high positions for the relatively new and obscure elements in the imperial service. He did not accept the high claims of the two powerful groups of the nobility—led by Asad Khan and Zulfiqar Khan, Iranis, on the one hand and by Chin Qilich Khan (Nizam-ul-Mulk), a Turani, on the other—for the office of *wazir* (chief revenue minister) and other special privileges. He appointed as *wazir* Mun'im Khan, an Indian born Turani, who was outside the charmed circle of the privileged groups and had not held a high position at the time of Aurangzeb's death. After Mun'im Khan's death (28 February 1711) Bahadur Shah did not appoint any eminent noble to the office of the *wazir*, even though both Zulfiqar Khan and Chin Qilich Khan reasserted their claims. Instead, Prince Azim-

---

[4] Satish Chandra, *Parties and Politics*, p. 4; J. F. Richards, *Mughal Administration in Golconda*, pp. 224–5 and 233; see also Jadu Nath Sarkar, *History of Aurangzeb*, Calcutta, 1924, Vol. V, pp. 68 and 74 for disaffection of some Deccani nobles.

[5] Compare *Ahkam-i Alamgiri*, edited and translated by Jadu Nath Sarkar, pp. 81 and 116–18. For an account of the prerogatives of the emperor see J. N. Sarkar, *Mughal Administration*, reprint, Bombay, 1972, pp. 89–98.

[6] Compare K.K., II, p. 600; Kamwar, pp. 16–36 entries of the 1st and the early 2nd R. Ys.

ush-Shan was allowed to control and supervise affairs of the *wizarat* with Sadullah Khan, a Kashmiri Indian, to practically carry on the work.[7] It is significant to note that Chin Qilich Khan and a number of the other Turanis resigned their *mansabs* and decided to live in retirement, protesting at the neglect of the old nobles and the rise of the new nobles to high position.[8]

In this connection the appointments and promotions of the Indian Shaikhzadas who find little mention in the better-known Persian histories of the period are significant. Shaikh Ilahyar of Bilgram who joined the imperial service through Prince Azim-ush-Shan seems to have held an important position under Bahadur Shah. Later in 1715 in the reign of Farrukh Siyar he rose to a rank of 6000 *zat* with the high sounding titles of Mubariz-ud-Daulah, Rustam Zaman Khan.[9] In another instance, Ruh-ul-Amin Khan of Bilgram is reported to have entered state service through Mun'im Khan, the *wazir*, with only sixty horsemen and foot soldiers. Soon, however, he became a close associate of the *wazir* and on his (*wazir's*) recommendation obtained a *mansab* of 6000/2000.[10] Further, a number of Indian Afghans appear to have risen in favour with Prince Azim-ush-

---

[7] K.K., II, pp. 677–8; *M.Ū.*, II, pp. 98, 831, 504.

[8] Compare Ghulam Ali Azad Bilgrami's explanation for Chin Qilich Khan's resignation from the *subadari* of Awadh. *Ma'asir-ul-Kiram*, II, p. 174. Though the evidence of *Ma'asir-ul-Kiram* is a little late, it may be noted that Azad Bilgrami had close links with the family of Nizam-ul-Mulk around the middle of the eighteenth century. In this connection, Khafi Khan's account may also be taken into consideration. Khafi Khan was an associate of Nizam-ul-Mulk. He therefore characterizes Bahadur Shah's policy of favouring the non-*khanazads* as a result of the emperor's weakness and ignorance. Similarly Khafi Khan describes with utter contempt certain steps taken by Mun'im Khan. In actuality, Khafi Khan and a number of other eighteenth-century historians such as Mirza Muhammad and Muhammad Bakhsh 'Ashub' believed the rise of the new nobles to be a major cause of the decline of the Mughal empire. Since Bahadur Shah granted high *mansabs* even to petty officials and clerks (cf. Bhimsen, *Nuskha-i Dilkusha*, Ms., Br. M. Or. 23, f. 167a) he is described by these historians as the first Mughal Emperor responsible for having set in the process of the decline. Their explanation may be taken as an illustration of their treatment of history. Cf. K.K., II, pp. 628 and 675–6. The word 'new nobles' (*umra-i jadid*) is apparently intended by these historians to indicate that section of Mughal officials who did not belong to the dominant Irani and Turani clans and yet moved to higher positions, e.g., *wazir* and *mir bakhshi*.

[9] *Sharaif*, pp. 255–7 and *Hadiqat*, p. 131.

[10] *Sharaif*, p. 232.

Shan in Bahadur Shah's reign. Some of them from Awadh were among those who sided and died with the prince in the Civil War at Lahore in 1712.[11]

Bahadur Shah's appreciation of the problem of the nobility and the efforts he made remained within the limited confines of some of the experiences of his predecessors. In the demands and protestations of the old nobles he saw the reappearance of the ambitions and pretensions of some of the sections of the nobility, namely, the Turanis and also the Iranis. The solution of the problem, the emperor believed, lay in the statement of the loyalty of the nobles to his person which he thought he could do by bringing to the fore the relatively obscure sections.

The old families seem to have appreciated the emperor's concern and tried to meet the threat they saw to their fortunes, by reiterating their loyalty to the emperor. It is significant that the contemporary Persian chroniclers have portrayed the rise of the non-Turani-Iranis in terms of a conflict between the *khanazads* and the *umara-i jadid* (new nobles). The use of the term *khanazads* for the Turani-Iranis, which asserted the age old servant-master ties between them and the emperor, and the term or adjective of *jadid* (new) for the others, which emphasized the notion of the upstart, are to be specially noted in the context of both the emperor's emphasis on loyalty to his person and the Mughal system. The *khanazad* position or long tradition of service involved an assertion of trustworthiness and loyalty to the salt, and legitimized their claims to privileges. These attributes—loyalty and trustworthiness—assume special importance in a milieu in which the noble was theoretically in the position of a slave (*banda*) of the court (*dargah*).

However, the disaffection was no longer limited to one or the other family group of the nobility. It involved both the organization and the emoluments of this institution, namely, *mansab* and *jagir* systems, and thus the whole nobility as well as lower sections of the Mughal officials were affected. The problem of the nobility was closely linked to a number of challenges that

---

[11] Qasim, f. 41a. Bahadur Shah's refusal to concede to the demands of Rajas Jai Singh and Ajit Singh as indeed his decision to take away the *zamindari* of Amer from Jai Singh and award it, though to no avail, to his younger brother, Bijay Singh perhaps acquire additional meaning when seen in this context.

For Jai Singh and Ajit Singh's relations with Bahadur Shah, see Satish Chandra, *Parties and Politics*, pp. 28–38.

the Mughal state began to encounter from the *zamindar* and peasant uprisings. The threat from these uprisings, however, assumed a serious form in the wake of the widening gap between the emperor on the one hand and the nobility, the core of the empire, and the petty revenue assignees and the *madad-i ma'ash* holders on the other.

Problem of jagir *administration and finance*

Khafi Khan reports how the nobles were greatly agitated over the deductions from their emoluments for feeding the royal animals (*khurak-i dawab*), till these were virtually remitted altogether.[12] That the new *mansabs* and *jagirs* carried little weight is also amply borne out from our sources. We will notice below some more evidence to show how the emperor's orders for assignment of *jagirs* and *mansabs* had become ineffective. The problems of the realization of revenues from the *jagirs* by *jagirdars* and their resistance to the principle and practice of frequent transfer of *jagirs* require a little more attention. Since the inception of the *jagir* system, the *jagirdars* encountered difficulties in their *jagirs*. Even under Akbar, the *jagirdars* were not expected to realize in full the revenues assigned against their *mansabs*. In the course of the seventeenth century a number of measures including the Rule of Proportion and the Monthly Scales were taken to adjust the actual collections of the *jagirdars* (*hasil*) to their income on paper in the exchequer (*jama*).[13] We cannot say if it would be fair to account for the gap between the *jama* and the *hasil* in the seventeenth century in terms other than the tendency of the exchequer to assess the revenues at an inflated rate. This tendency which also thrived on the *jagirdars'* urge to have a large income, even if on paper, commensurate with their status, must have been a major factor responsible for the gap, in addition to the influx of bullion and the subsequent price rise.[14] For the eighteenth century, however, we have some evidence to

---

[12] K.K., II, pp. 602–3; see also W. Irvine, *The Army of the Indian Moghuls*, reprint, New Delhi, 1962, pp. 20–2; Satish Chandra, *Parties and Politics*, pp. 58–9. For *khurak-i dawab* and other deductions from the pay of the nobles, see M. Athar Ali, *Mugal Nobility*, pp. 50–3.

[13] Cf. M. Athar Ali, *Mughal Nobility*, pp. 53–9.

[14] See also Irfan Habib, 'The Mansab System 1595–1637', *PIHC*, 29th Session, Patiala, 1967, pp. 221–42.

suggest that the difference between the *jama* and the *hasil* had a close bearing on the *jagirdars'* ability/inability to mobilize strength to collect the revenues. In this connection it is interesting to note that in some regions of the Mughal empire, at least, the actual yield increased without a corresponding rise in the *jama*.[15] This was a symptom of a decline of imperial control over these regions and proved to be to the obvious advantage of the intermediaries who steadily gained in power resulting in the increase in number and magnitude of their resistance to the *jagirdars*. The *jagirdars'* military power had declined following the reforms in the *mansab* and *jagir* systems in the seventeenth century. With a rise in the strength of the intermediaries their position further weakened and they were in greater need of help and protection from the centre. But as almost the entire central power was harnessed against Kam Bakhsh, the Marathas and the Sikhs, one uprising following the other, little resources were left to defend the interests of the *jagirdars* all over the empire.

We can conjecture how in these conditions the *jagirdars* could have begun to manipulate, first, to cling to their *jagirs* for a longer period and then to make them their life-term holdings. The genesis of the *jagirdars'* resistance to the frequent transfer of the *jagirs* can be traced back to the days of the Great Mughals.[16] With long-term *jagirs*, the *jagirdars* may have expected to build local roots by playing one group against another, for instance. A long-term *jagir* would obviously eliminate the lurking fear of encountering a new set of difficulties each time the *jagirdar* came to his new *jagir*.

The rise in strength of the intermediaries further jeopardized the income of the smaller *jagirdars* who expressed their anguish by disregarding the state regulations even in and around the imperial centre. In a number of instances, the local officials of Delhi violated the rules and became responsible for hardships to 'the traders and wayfarers'.[17] Indeed total chaos seems to

---

[15] See Chapters III and VII.

[16] Irfan Habib, *Agrarian System*, pp. 267–8.

[17] For example in 1711, the *faujdars* in the vicinity of Delhi realized an unlawful road toll (*rahdari*) from the dealers of foodgrains and oil. Subsequently, the prices of foodgrains and oil began to rise. In another instance they forced the Hindu and the Muslim traders to pay the cesses on their merchandise at the exorbitant rate of 15 per cent and 10 per cent respectively. In yet another case the deputy *faujdar* of Delhi exacted unlawful cesses from the *banjaras* and thus caused a scarcity of foodgrains in the city.

have prevailed in Mathura, a town not very far from the Mughal centre. The 'ruffians', as our source puts it 'plundered the grain stores and put the town at ransom'. Subsequently, foodgrains became scarce and the price of wheat rose to 5 *sers* a rupee. The riot may have been confined to the region of Mathura and may have occurred, as our source implies, due to the absence of the *faujdar* from Mathura,[18] but it probably indicated the existence or the beginning of a problem of a much wider dimension. In the following chapters we will notice more instances of this development which impaired local administration.

All this led to an atmosphere of increasing uncertainty which in turn further exacerbated the strains on royal finance. If the chroniclers are to be believed we can presume that the reign of Bahadur Shah began upon a note of relief. 'Food was in abundance, trade prospered and the opportunities for the artisans, traders and the troopers were so much that they were hardly pressed by the necessities.'[19] Thus the emperor, as Khush-hal Rai reports, regulated and stabilized the prices of foodgrains which had been lately fluctuating due to the political disturbances.[20] Further, strict orders were despatched to the *faujdars*

Akhbarat BS. 5th R.Y., pp. 298 and 420 (18 August and 20 October 1711); 6th R.Y., II, p. 559 (11 January 1712). For similar cases in Jahandar Shah's reign, see, ibid., JS, pp. 6, 8, 128, 275 and 318, 19 March and 30 October 1712.

[18] *Akhbarat*, BS, 6th R.Y., p. 592, 23 January 1712. Shamsher Khan the *faujdar* was ·immediately ordered to leave the court for Mathura.

[19] Qasim, f. 22a.

[20] According to Khush-hal Rai, the price-rate in Delhi in December 1707 was as follows:

	In sers per rupee	In rupees per man
Wheat	8 *sers*	5.00
Barley	27 ,,	1.48
Gram	25 ,,	1.60
Sukhdas	10 ,,	4.00
Mung	15 ,,	2.67
Mash	18 ,,	2.22
Moth	20 ,,	2.00
Arhar	18 ,,	2.22
Ghee	3 ,,	13.33
Mustard oil	7 ,,	5.71
Red sugar	12 ,,	3.33

posted in the vicinity of Delhi, urging them to maintain an uninterrupted and regular supply of a sufficient amount of foodgrains to the capital.[21] The extent to which the *faujdars* carried out these orders is a matter of conjecture. However, within a period of two years, the imperial camp on the emperor's way back from the Deccan to Hindustan is reported to have been hit by a shortage of foodgrains. This shortage may have followed drought and epidemic in addition to the inter-mediaries' resistance. We have some such references in our sources which are also supported by the rise in the prices of foodgrains in the areas in close proximity to the imperial route.[22]

The Deccan expedition and the shortage of supply in the royal camp must have drained the treasury. The empire was thus faced with the crisis of money. 'To sum up', as Chhabele Das, the agent (*vakil*) of Raja Jai Singh at the court commenting on the progress of the preparations for the imperial campaigns against the Sikhs in 1711, observed, 'the battles are fought with army and the provision of army requires money, but money is not seen anywhere. Let us see how God wills.'[23]

Cf. Khush-hal, p. 298. As we do not have the price figures of the previous years for the Delhi market, we are not in a position to make out the magnitude of the rise in the prices of these commodities. In 1702 at Lahore, the rates of some of these were, however, substantially low:

Wheat	1.4	per *man-i Shahjahani*
Sukhdas	2.0	,,
Mung	1.0	,,
Moth	1.0	,,

(Compare Irfan Habib, *Agrarian System*, p. 83). In relation to these three rates, the prices of wheat were over 4¼ times, of *sukhdas* two times, of *mung* nearly 2⅔ times and *moth* twice as high at Delhi in the end of 1707.

[21] Khush-hal, p. 298.

[22] Compare Yahya, f. 115a; *Ahwal*, f. 39a. For the two-fold rise in the prices of wheat, barley, gram, *moth*, urad and *mung* in certain *parganas* of eastern Rajasthan in 1708 compared to the immediate past years, see S. Nurul Hasan and S.P. Gupta, 'Price of Food-grains in the Territories of Amer', *PIHC*, Patiala, 1967, I, pp. 354–66.

But shortages in the military camp did not necessarily always indicate non-availa-bility of foodgrains. In 1761, the Marathas in Karnal encountered a severe food crisis mainly because over 4,00,000 oxen loaded with provisions for them from Kalpi could not reach them. The man in charge of the caravan was overpowered and killed by an Afghan *sardar* and the oxen were driven away to the Afghan Camp. Cf. Ghulam Qadir Khan Jaisi, *Tarikh-i Imad-ul-Mulk*, I. 0.4000, f. 27a.

[23] Miscellaneous Papers on Administration, I, Sitamau transcripts, p. 245. Financial difficulties were also probably a factor which prompted the emperor to make

Under the circumstances, the emperor was compelled to take certain steps which provoked discontent and rancour among yet other sections of the nobility and state functionaries. It has been pointed out earlier that Bahadur Shah's failure also stemmed from his inability to come out of the frame of the previous traditions. This is also illustrated from his orders discriminating against the Hindus on religious grounds in the wake of imperial campaigns against the Sikhs. On suspicion of some Hindu clerks' sympathy with the Sikhs of Banda, he issued an order requiring all Hindu officials to shave off their beards to prove their loyalty to Mughal authority. Simultaneously, the Hindu *waqai'nigars* (news-reporters) were ordered to be replaced by the Muslims.[24] It is not unlikely that Bahadur Shah took these steps in a desperate bid to mobilize the *khanazads* for a Sikh expedition. That these orders further alienated the emperor from the nobility and the other officials is, however, beyond doubt.

Further in view of the financial difficulties, certain promises seem to have been left unfulfilled. Ghazi-ud-Din Khan, the governor of Gujarat, received nothing against the emoluments of 4000 soldiers of the army which he had temporarily raised to realize the revenue from the local *zamindars*. The amount had been sanctioned by the emperor over two months earlier. On 13 September 1711, Imad-ud-Din Khan complained that he was still to receive the amount of Rs 10,000 which were ordered to be paid to him in advance as loan (*musa'ada*).[25]

Thus, the imperial order tended to carry little weight even with the state functionaries at the centre. Much worse, in this

---

a compromise with the Rajputs in 1710. When Bahadur Shah knew of the Sikh revolts, he rushed towards the Punjab, having summarily dealt with the Rajput question. With the existing resources, the Mughals were probably not in a position to fight on two major fronts.

The terms of settlement with the rajas were 'far above their status' and 'inconsistent with good policy as well as the dignity of the sovereign. Since the Rajputs were old allies of the Mughals and had been used to obey [the Mughal Emperor] for generations, Bahadur Shah did not consider it likely that they would commit further aggression if left in possession of their hereditary lands.' Cf. M.M., 58b.

[24] *Akhbarat*, BS, 4th R.Y., p. 200; 5th R.Y., p. 292. See also Chapter IV.

[25] Ibid., BS, 3rd R.Y., p. 166 (16 September 1709); 5th R.Y., p. 363 (18 September 1711); Imad-ud-Din Khan whose name was Mir Murtaza Husaini was an Iranian noble. He died in 1712. For him and his relatives in the Mughal service see *T. Muhammadi*, pp. 31 and 122.

context, was the order to control promotions and the award of new *mansabs*. On 31 May 1710, Hidayat Kesh Khan, the chief news writer was directed to refrain from accepting, making entry of and issuing a memorandum (*yaddasht*) for any new *mansab* or promotion (apparently to the new elements) without confirmation from the offices of the *bakhshis* (heads of military departments). This was to be done even if the candidate carried an order with the special signature of the emperor.[26]

The directive was purportedly to regulate the *mansab* system. But it also had a bearing on the nobles' (in this particular case certainly the old nobles) urge for extended powers. The offices of the *bakhshis* were still with the *khanazads*. A greater control of the *bakhshis* over the grant of *mansabs* would imply a check over the emperor and also over his queens who were 'recklessly' awarding favours to the 'upstarts'. Another order intended to set right the administration could not be implemented, as it affected the position of the *khanazads*. It had to be withdrawn for the same reason later in Jahandar Shah's reign.[27]

Thus was the beginning of the widening gap between the Mughal emperor and the different sections of the state officials. Till this point, however, there was no substantial change in the relationship of the province with the imperial authority. The nobles in charge of the provinces were content with a few additional offices under their control in the province. It was a measure of Bahadur Shah's success in that his successor, Jahandar Shah immediately after his accession to the throne received *arzdashts* (letters of obeisance) along with plenty of treasures and precious presents from the chiefs, the governors and the other nobles posted in the provinces.[28]

Yet, in Bahadur Shah's time some unmistakable symptoms of the decline of the imperial edifice could be noticed. Cracks

---

[26] Ibid., 4th R.Y., p. 98. Hidayat Kesh Khan (Bhola Nath) a neo-Muslim held a rank of 700/100 under Bahadur Shah. He retained his position in Jahandar Shah's reign. He caught Prince Muhammad Karim who had run away after the death of his father, Azim-ush-Shan in 1712 and the prince was later killed at the instance of Khan Jahan Kokaltash. Farrukh Siyar, therefore, ordered him to be strangled to death. Kamwar, 337a, 341b and 342a; *M.U.*, II, p. 507; *T. Muhammadi*, p. 32.

For *bakhshis, mir bakhshi* and the rule and procedure of the grant of *mansab*, see, W. Irvine, *The Army of the Indian Moghuls*, pp. 36–44.

[27] Ibid., BS, 4th R.Y., p. 51 (8 April 1710) and JS, pp. 36, 60.

[28] Qasim, ff. 45b, 46b and 47a.

had appeared in the emperor-noble-other officials relationship. The emperor attempted to mend these but without changing or modifying the rules governing the existing structure of the relationships. None of the measures he took to straighten the administration could rectify the structural flaw of the existing framework in which power and authority, in a large measure, depended on the individual achievements and the capabilities of the emperor. The emperor calculated that the loss incurred to the prestige of the empire following military failures against the local 'disturbers' could be compensated merely by an exaggerated demonstration of the myth that he was the source of all power and patronage. He thought that he would restore the imperial aura by emphasizing his authority and ostensatious display of pomp and eclat at the court.[29] This is also illustrated from the way he decided to deal with the growing power of the Sunni Muslim theologians. Of late, they had acquired some strength which occurred from their privileges as *madad-i ma'ash* holders. But Bahadur Shah did not touch the rules governing their holdings. Instead, he followed the example of Akbar and invited the *ulama* to debate with them to emphasize his supreme position in religious matters.[30] Against the nobles, he seems to have been concerned more with his prerogatives. At best, he tried to streamline the central official structure, while the problem had its roots in the dislocation of the relationships at the local level which sustained this structure.

Again, the developments of Bahadur Shah's own time, namely the Deccan expedition, the Rajput problem and the Sikh uprisings imposed serious constraints on the emperor's efforts. In the sixteenth century Akbar had been enormously assisted by favourable circumstances in his success against the pretensions of the Chaghtais and the Mirzas. The Mughal empire was still growing then. With prospects of expansion and avenues unfolding increasingly, Akbar could easily venture to enlist the support of the other sections, e.g., the Iranis and the indigenous

---

[29] *Iradat*, ff. 31b and 32a; *Mubarak*, f. 47a.

[30] Contrary to common Sunni custom, he wanted to have the word 'wasi' (heir) inserted after the name of Ali in the sermon preceding the Friday prayers (*khutba*). He called the *ulama* at Lahore for the purpose and asserted his right as king and, like Akbar, as a *mujtahid* (interpreter of Islamic law and theology), not confining himself to the tenets of any one of the schools of *Sharia*. Cf. *Ahwal*, f. 37b; *Iradat*, f. 32a. For the *khutba* incident see also W. Irvine, *Later Moghuls*, I, pp. 129–31.

elements to bolster his position without thwarting the legitimate claims of the older nobility. With little scope for further
expansion after 1707, the mechanism to keep the state machinery intact and in effective working order had to be sought
much beyond the contours of territorial and military adventure.
Further, multiplying financial difficulties, in the wake of
famines and recurring rural disturbances, did not allow the
emperors, in our period, to take adequate stock of the situation.
Their individual failings as compared with those of their predecessors further aggravated problems in our period. The following details of the second phase of our period provide ample
illustration of the extent to which developments at the centre
were interconnected with those in the periphery.

II 1713–19

Famine and zamindar *uprisings*

According to our sources the reign of Farrukh Siyar (1713–19)
opened with two disastrous famines. In the beginning of
Farrukh Siyar's reign, 'the calamities of death and fire and the
scarcity of foodgrains reached a limit that nobody had ever seen
or heard of in the past'.[31] A widespread epidemic raged in the
wake of the famine. Scarcity of rain, shortage of food and the
epidemic took hundreds and thousands of lives of men and
animals. 'In and around the towns, the cities, the wards and the
villages in the whole kingdom', as a contemporary chronicler in
his typical Persian style observes, 'there was nothing to see and
think about save the heaps of bones and the human skulls.'[32]
Owing to the great famine and the severe epidemic, 'scores of
common people and imperial troopers died in Delhi for want of
bread and became carrion feed of kite and crow'.[33]

   Although the chroniclers generalize the bleak situation for
almost the whole of the empire, the severity appears to have
been confined to Delhi and its surroundings alone.[34] The prices
of foodgrains in Delhi seem to have become twice as high as
those of 1707.[35] Subsequently, the superintendents of the grain

---

[31] Yahya, f. 122b.   [32] *Ahwal*, ff. 62b–63a.   [33] Kanwar, f. 340a.
[34] *Ahwal*, f. 63a.
[35] Wheat had so far been sold in Delhi at the rate of about 7 to 8 *sers* a rupee. At the
beginning of Farrukh Siyar's reign, even 4 *sers* of wheat were not easily available for one

markets and grain dealers were ordered by the emperor to see to
it that foodgrains were available in Delhi at fair prices. Cultivators were exempted from paying revenues on foodgrains.[36]
We do not know if these measures, if at all implemented,
mitigated the suffering of the people. Even if they eased the
distress,[37] the relief was short-lived. In 1717, Delhi was hit by an
another severe famine. 'The people were in the grip of great
distress, commotion broke out all around and they brought the
leaves of *karyal* from the jungle, boiled them and ate them.
When that too was exhausted, they encountered death [lit. it
was the turn of death]. One to two hundred people died daily in
the towns and villages. *Scores of them vacated their houses and left for
other territories* while most of them sold women and children for
little.'[38]

---

rupee. Cf. Kamwar, f. 344a. According to Yahya (f. 122b) only 3 *sers* of wheat could be
had for a rupee and rice, gram, *moth* and *mash* all were sold at the same rate. According
to the *Ahwal* (f. 63a), the *nan* of wheat, nay even of barley disappeared from the market
and the stingy and small wheat was rated at no more than four *sers* a rupee. *Khar-muhra*,
black-*til*, white and red rice were to be seen only in the imperial stores and in the
establishments of big nobles who had excellent *jagirs* or in the shops of big *sahukars*.

[36] *Akhbarat*, FS, 1st R.Y., I, p. 55, 2nd R.Y., II, p. 30.

[37] According to Yahya (f. 122a) within one or two years the situation was under
control and one could get wheat and rice of good quality in open market at the rate of 8
sers a rupee.

[38] Mubarak, ff. 89; Kamwar, ff. 354b and 355b. While the severity of the drought was
limited to Delhi and the surrounding *parganas*, the famines of 1712 and 1717 seem to
have been widespread and extend to quite a large part of northern India. Our
assumption is based on the available prices of foodgrains in Delhi, Allahabad and
eastern Rajasthan. Prices in Delhi in 1712 and 1717 were much higher than those of the
earlier years. In Chatsu, for instance, in eastern Rajasthan in the same years, the prices
were again unusually high while the prices of certain commodities at Allahabad in the
7th R.Y. of Farrukh Siyar (1718–19) which are fortunately available to us were the least
flattering.

PRICES IN RUPEES FOR *MAN* OF 40 *SERS*

	Delhi 1717	Allahabad 1717–18	Chatsu 1712	Chatsu 1717
Wheat	6.67	—	2.98	3.18
Gram	5.33	—	2.83	3.20
Mash	6.15	—	—	—
Mung	—	5.00	2.34	4.66
Urad	—	—	2.01	2.66
Arhar	—	2.86	—	—
Ghee	26.67	8.69	—	—

Famines following the failure of the monsoons were not unprecedented in Mughal India. The Mughals had also dealt with them with some amount of success. Farrukh Siyar, too, showed the will to encounter the consequences of the droughts. The widespread agrarian uprisings, aggravating the problem of the nobility and the *mansabdars*, however, seem to have rendered his efforts ineffective. Of more serious consequence for the empire was the dislocation in the balance of the state's relations with the intermediaries. Apart from the provinces, the *parganas* (administrative divisions, districts) all around the vicinity of the imperial capital were rocked by the *zamindar* uprisings. So long as the Mughals could maintain the aura of their might, the *zamindars*, either in fear or to further their own interests, remained subservient. The Sikh uprisings in the beginning of our period had noticeably exposed the myth of Mughal military supremacy. The news of the defeat of the Mughal Emperor, Jahandar Shah, at the hands of a prince (Farrukh Siyar) at Jaju in January 1713 further encouraged the *zamindars* in the vicinity of Agra and Delhi.[39] A hurried survey of the *Akhbarat*, keeping in view the references to such uprisings in the earlier records, enables us to appreciate the magnitude of the *zamindar* revolts during the period. Disturbances in *chakla* Etawah of Agra province which lay on the grand highway from Delhi to Agra and on to Allahabad, Benaras, Patna and Bengal and occupied an important economic, political and military position, are, for instance, a case in point. The Rajputs and the Afghans seem to have been the major source of threat in the *chakla*.[40] It is signi-

---

(Compare Khush-hal, p. 406 for Delhi; *Mirat-ul-Haqaiq*, f. 135b for Allahabad, and S. Nurul Hasan and S. P. Gupta, 'Price of Food-grains' pp. 354, 357 and 363–5, for Chatsu. We have picked up Chatsu for our purpose because only Chatsu out of the six *parganas* listed in the table contains the price figures of these commodities for 1712 and 1717. Since we have no information about the seasons, let alone the months, of these prices, they are not comparable. But they do show a trend.

[39] Cf. Warid, p. 315.

[40] *Akhbarat*, FS, 3rd R.Y., II, p. 125, 26 November 1713 for Nahar Rohilla's revolt. Subsequently an army of 4000 under the command of the younger brother of the *faujdar* could force the Rohilla rebel to retire to one of his other fortresses; p. 140, 15 December 1713, for the development of an army of 4000 *sawars* under Mardan Ali Khan and Nasir Khan to chastise the recalcitrant *zamindars* in the vicinity of Etawah town.

A *chakla* was a territorial division and was often identical with a *sarkar*, but in general a *chakla* was a smaller unit than a *sarkar*. In Bengal, however, a *chakla* consisted of a group of *sarkars* in the eighteenth century.

ficant to note that the *zamindar* uprisings in Awadh, assumed serious proportions in Farrukh Siyar's reign.

Admittedly, the situation deteriorated due to the famines and the politics of intrigues and counter-intrigues at the court. The *zamindars* were emboldened to rise in arms in the face of the steadily weakening centre. The central government failed to provide adequate military assistance to the nobles—governors, *faujdars*, etc.—posted in these regions to quell these disturbances. These nobles some of whom gradually broke away from the centre repeatedly ascribed the centre's failure to the dominance and machinations of one or the other faction. The intensity of the revolts in drought years may also be explained in terms of scarcity.

It is difficult to explain these disturbances in terms of the poor peasants' predicament. It is also difficult to suggest that the initiative for these came from the hard-pressed cultivators and that the *zamindars* joined the fray to provide leadership in their battle against the Mughals. Details from different regions militate against any interpretation common to all cases, all regions. While in some cases the *zamindars* and the peasants fought hand in hand against the Mughals, in some others there was no coordination in their actions, even if these were directed against the Mughals. In still other cases, the *zamindars'* fury was directed against the other *zamindars* and the peasants. Out of the four cases of *zamindar* disturbances in *chakla* Etawah taken randomly from the *Akhbarat*, for instance, two basically represented an inherent social conflict among the various *zamindar* groups themselves rather than their antagonism as a class against the Mughal state. In such cases, Mughal officials and the army were expected to defend and protect the *zamindars* who became victims of the ravages of the bigger *zamindars*. Dalpat Singh, the *zamindar* of the village of Chharoli, *pargana* Deokali invaded a village in the *zamindari* of one Kunwar Sen. The *faujdar* of Sikandra came to the rescue of Kunwar Sen and Dalpat Singh died fighting in the battle. In an another instance, the *zamindar* of the village Atha in *pargana* Jalesar was killed and his women and children were forced to leave the village as a result of their clash with another *zamindar* of the same *pargana*.[41]

[41] Ibid., FS, 3rd R.Y., pp. 213 and 275 (3 December 1713 and 3 March 1714). See also Chapters III and IV.

Further evidence to prevent us from making any unqualified generalization about these rural disturbances has been discussed in some recent studies of the different regions of the empire.[42]

In this connection it is interesting to note that Churaman, the leader of the Jat *zamindars* offered a sum of Rs 8,00,000 to Saiyid Abdullah Khan to win a peace with the Mughals in Farrukh Siyar's reign. Notable also, is a report about a trading caravan with 1300 cartloads of *ghee* which was plundered (possibly by the *zamindars*) near Hodal in the vicinity of Delhi.[43] The rebel *zamindars* were thus not so weak and indigent. It would appear that it was the strength and the money that the *zamindars* had acquired in the long period of stability which enabled them to rise to secure still more. The differential impact of the price rise of the seventeenth century provided them with opportunities to gain in power. This they acquired at the cost of both the weaker elements of their own class as well as state officials whose claims to revenue they felt had been superimposed over their rights. We will examine below in the chapters on Awadh and the Punjab some evidence to this effect, namely, the prosperity and rise in strength of the local magnates leading to their resistance to imperial prerogatives.

Jagir, Ijara *and the economy*

Whatever the nature of *zamindar* uprisings and whosoever the target of their attack, these revolts threatened the social security which a stable government means in different degrees for state functionaries. In this event Mughal officials preferred to have their *jagirs* in and around their homelands, and also for a long, preferably, life term. In sharp contrast to the established Mughal practice, these two features, namely, a *jagir* in or around one's own *watan* (homeland) and for a long tenure, became *de facto* a part of *jagir* administration in almost the whole of north India. This caused further damage to the imperial

---

[42] Compare Muzaffar Alam, 'Sikh Uprisings under Banda Bahadur, 1709–1712', *Studies in History*, Vol. I, No. 2, July–December, 1979, pp. 197–213; R.P. Rana, 'Agrarian Revolts in Northern India during the late 17th and early 18th Century', *IESHR*, V, XVIII, Nos. 3 and 4, July–December, 1981, pp. 287–326; André Wink, 'Land and Sovereignty in India under the Eighteenth Century Maratha Swarajya'.

[43] Cf. Shivdas, English translation by S. Hasan Askari, Patna, 1980, pp. 21–2.

organization as it demonstrated the nobles' distrust of the ability of the state to defend their interests.

It may however, be noted that the central authorities were still struggling to maintain the empire in the existing framework. In this context some reforms intended to satisfy the state functionaries are significant. As the *jagirs* in most of the disturbed regions especially for the *mansabdars* of lesser stature began to decline in value and as it became impossible for them to make payments in time to their contingents, Lutfullah Khan Sadiq, who was in charge of *jagirs* as a revenue minister at the centre, (*diwan-i tan*), converted the *jagirs* against the ranks indicating the strength of their armed contingents (*sawar mansabs*) into cash payments (*naqd*) with a fixed monthly pay of Rs 50 for each horseman (*sawar*). This was applicable to the contingents of only those who held the rank of 200 to 900 *zat*. But the measure proved to be of little help. The regular contingents of the *mansabdars* began to break up and the practice of *sih-bandi* came into vogue.[44] 'What provisions can a servant make and how can he take any initiative when he is paid Rs 50 only *per mensem* in both the situations when he is at home and also when he has set out for an expedition and is on a journey? What should he do with such a small amount? Should he meet family expenses or prepare for a fight? The army of Hindustan, thus, is suspended from the service of His Majesty and added to this is the calamity of the [soaring] prices of foodgrains.'[45]

The payment in cash ensured, even though only theoretically, regularity in the payment of emoluments. But it did not have the advantages of payment in *jagir*, namely, the prospects for defalcation and concealment of excess receipts, especially when the cash payment was the same to all in all circumstances. It appears that the *mansabdars* did not approve of a uniform cash

---

[44] Cf. Khush-hal, p. 373–4; The passages in K.K., II, p. 769 and *T. Muzaffari*, f. 118a who copies K.K. are confusing and may be read along with Khush-hal's account. *Sih-bandi* was the name for the armed men hired for the occasion by local officials for enforcing revenue-collection. This was to be distinguished from the troops permanently employed and the regular contingents of the *mansabdars*. The practice of *sih-bandi* was an old one. Babur characterized the Indian levies of Ibrahim Lodi as *sih-bandis*. We have evidence for the employment of *sih-bandis* by the *khalisa* officials in the seventeenth century. (Cf. W. Irvine, *Army of the Indian Moghuls*, p. 166; Irfan Habib, *Agrarian System*, p. 276 and n.) Khush-hal bewails the fact that even permanently employed troops were practically turned into *sih-bandis*.

[45] Khush-hal, p. 374.

rate. Further, the cash payment did not have the semblance of landed property as a *jagir* had. But even if it satisfied the *mansabdars*, its implementation was difficult for more than one reason. Its successful functioning required, in the first place, adequate arrangements for the collection of revenues in the lands reserved for the imperial treasury (*khalisa*); secondly, an unbroken flow of the bills of exchange (*hundis*) from the provinces and, thirdly, their immediate encashment at the capital. But there was little surety even of the *khalisa* sum, the proportion of which must have gone up following the change in the mode of payment,[46] reaching the imperial treasury. Whatever *hundis* for the amount were despatched from the *khalisa*, the money-changers in Delhi were reluctant to cash these and submit the sum to the office of the *wazir*. The money-changers suppressed the news of their receipt of the *hundis* from the *khalisa*, possibly because they were not sure if the collection in the *mahals* had actually been made. The central government thus began to substantially expend the accumulated treasury.[47] In 1707 the imperial treasury at the fort of Agra contained at least over nine crores of rupees in addition to valuables and unminted gold and silver. By 1720 the cash at the fort of Agra

[46] According to K.K., II, p. 769 the order for the payment in cash (at the rate of Rs 50 per unit) was also applicable to the *wala shahi mansabdars*. The *wala shahis*, according to W. Irvine (*Army of the Indian Moghuls*, pp. 40 and 43–4) comprised the personal and household troops of the emperor, paid by him out of his privy-purse (*khalisa*). This definition which seems to have been uncritically accepted, however, needs re-examination. For the evidence of K.K. conclusively proves that the *wala shahis* were paid in *jagir* as well and that the arrangement of the payment in cash was simply for a period when they were not provided with *jagirs*.

[47] *Akhbarat*, FS, 3rd R.Y., II, p. 73. The incident indicates that perhaps the bankers were necessary to the state organization and also the consequences for the state of their non-cooperation. But it is difficult to make any generalization about their political role in Mughal India. Karen Leonard however, contends that the stability and decline of Mughal state, may be explained in terms of its relationships with the banking firms. Karen Leonard, 'The "Great Firm" Theory of the Decline of the Mughal Empire'. Significantly the network of the money transactions remained apparently unimpaired throughout the empire in our period. Evidence for the *hundi* transactions for the latter half of the eighteenth century even through regions, politically different and sometimes hostile to each other, is available in *I'jaz-i Arsalani*, a collection in two volumes of Persian letters of Polier, dated 1187–1193 A.H./1773–1779, Blochet, Nos. 713 and 714. For western India's contact with Agra see G.T. Kulkarni, 'Banking in the 18th Century: A Case Study of a Pune Banker', *Artha Vijnan*, XV, 2 June 1973, pp. 180–200.

had been reduced to only one crore and eighty thousand rupees.[48] Consequently in 1716, the contingents which were promised a monthly payment of Rs 50 per unit were ordered to be disbanded.[49]

It is interesting, however, to note that in contrast to the general plight of the *mansabdars* and the crisis of the imperial treasury, some of the nobles' personal coffers only were marginally affected by the financial difficulties of the court. The extravagant affluence of those who were in service of Husain Ali Khan, the *mir bakhshi*, is an example. 'The purse [lit. the money belt] of each of his (Husain Ali Khan's) troopers was full of gold and silver coins. Nay, the agents of his establishment [*sarkar*] at every stage insisted upon the soldiers coming to the court and collecting their emoluments. Most of them said in reply that 'our houses [lit. resources] are replete with gold and silver. We have no room left [for any further amount]'.[50] Again, the governors of the provinces were directed by Husain Ali Khan to make, on his behalf, offerings of Rs 111 and Rs 112 in the name of Saikh Abd-ul-Qadir Gilani and the Prophet on the eleventh and twelfth days of each lunar month in the towns all over the empire.[51] Two bags full of gold coins (*ashrafis*) and a sum of Rs 1,800,000 were among the cash and the valuables captured by the loyalists following the assassination of Saiyid Husain Ali Khan in 1719. In contrast, only Rs 200,000 out of Rs 600,000 sanctioned could be paid by the imperial treasury to Saiyid Muzaffar Ali Khan when he was appointed governor of Ajmer replacing Ajit Singh in 1726. The amount was too big for the exchequer to pay in one instalment.[52] The factions of the nobles like Husain Ali Khan had large followings among the state functionaries, at times even larger than the emperor could singly muster up on his own. It is not surprising that a strong

[48] Cf. K.K., II, pp. 568 and 837; *Risala*, f. 59a; Mubarak, f. 108b. According to K.K. the cash at Agra fort in 1707 was nine crore while *Risala*, says 'at least over nine crore'.

[49] Cf. K.K., II, p. 769 and *T. Muzaffari*, f. 118a.

[50] *T. Hindi*, ff. 235b–236a.

[51] Ibid., f. 236a.

[52] Shivdas; For some details of the wealth of the Saiyid brothers, see also Saiyid Roshan Ali Khan Barha, *Saiyid-ut-Tawarikh* (a mid-nineteenth century Urdu family history) 1.0., 423, ff. 48a–40a. From *Lauh-i Tarikh* of Munawwar Ali Khan Farrukhabadi (1.0 U134, ff. 54a, 62b–63a) glimpses can be had of the wealth of Muhammad Khan Bangash who founded Farrukhabad, a major commercial and industrial centre of eighteenth-century north India, together with a number of other *ganjs* in upper India.

alliance of these nobles dethroned the emperor in 1719 and emerged as king makers.

The question of how a section of the nobility both at the centre and in the provinces, as we shall see later, continued to thrive in spite of the increasing difficulties of the empire, is worth considering. No answer to this question can be given in definitive terms till the production conditions of the areas under the control of such nobles are fully investigated. But it is significant to note that the prosperity or decay of a number of areas coincided with the transfer of the persons who controlled these areas. The political and economic position of the nobles perhaps depended on a demonstrated ability to live with the practice of *ijara* (revenue farming). As *ijara* implied involvement of a new man in the collection of the revenue, it tended to increase support for the state. In the case of the *zamindar* himself being the *ijaradar* it meant his autonomy and also the third man's share for him in the surplus produce, while if a merchant or moneylender (*mahajan*) contracted an *ijara*, it associated a new social group with the government. By generating profits for these two major social classes, *ijara*, thus, reduced the magnitude of the problems of the *jagirdars*.

The growth of the *ijara* practice in our period has been seen in the perspective of the decline and decay of the Mughal administration. It has been suggested that *ijara* came to be a major factor in the excessive and unbridled exploitation of the peasantry and thus the ruination of the country. The *ijara* practice, has also been seen to have caused dislocation in agrarian relations, with many ancient hereditary *zamindaris* having been dislodged by bankers and speculators from the cities.[53] While it is not possible to comment on how drastic a change in the land relations the countryside witnessed in the wake of the extension of *ijara* in the early-eighteenth century, the extension of this practice cannot be fully explained in terms of mere laxity

[53] Compare N.A. Siddiqi, *Land Revenue Administration*, pp. 96–101; Satish Chandra, *Parties and Politics*, pp. 81, 109 and 174. But recently Dilbagh Singh ('Ijarah System in Eastern Rajasthan (1750–1800)', *Proceedings of Rajasthan History Congress*, 6, 1973, pp. 60–9), Richard Barnett (*North India between Empires, Awadh, the Mughals and the British, 1720–1801*) and André Wink ('Maratha Revenue Farming', *Modern Asian Studies*, 17, 4, 1983, pp. 591–628) have tried to demonstrate the *ijara* as an organizational means of agrarian restoration and expansion.

in the rules and regulations of the Mughal revenue administration and the greed of Ratan Chand and the Saiyid Brothers. The extension of this practice indicated a very high level of monetization in which everything, including a government office, came to be regarded as a saleable commodity. This is to be seen against the background of the developments under the Great Mughals.

Even if the growth of the money economy in Mughal India followed upon state taxation,[54] economic development appears to have gradually taken an almost independent course during the seventeenth century. The processes of monetization implied the development of extensive commodity production in the countryside and of markets to which the peasants had access. Influx of silver and the rising prices helped the merchant to strengthen his position. It has been suggested that the decline in value of silver 'discouraged hoarding and encouraged lending at interest, thus increasing the supply of money capital and cheapening credit for the merchant.' The differential impact of price inflation on the agricultural and industrial sectors might have also augmented the 'mercantile capitalist operations and "putting out" enterprises.'[55] Several sophisticated monetary and financial institutions developed in the wake of new peasant settlements and accelerated urban growth at all levels, from the small market towns to major cities. These institutions, and together with them the merchant, had come to be part of a general development of the society, no longer tied so closely to the Mughal imperial edifice.

By the 1720s when the symptoms of political distintegration were all too evident, the different parts of the empire were economically integrated by inter-regional trade along the coastal as well as the inland routes. These economic links and the monetary institutions that evolved in earlier times survived the collapse of the Mughal empire. Distant credit markets remain

---

[54] Compare Irfan Habib, 'Potentialities of Capitalistic Development in the Economy of Mughal India' *Enquiry*, Winter 1971, pp. 1–56; Satish Chandra, 'Some Aspects of the Growth of a Money Economy in India during the Seventeenth Century' *IESHR*, Vol. III, No. 4, 1966, pp. 321–31.

[55] Compare S. Bhattacharya's Review of Tapan Raychaudhuri and Irfan Habib (eds.), *The Cambridge Economic History of India*, I, *Economic and Political Weekly*, 1 October 1983.

connected despite political turmoil during the eighteenth century.[56]

In addition to the merchants, the intermediaries and the bigger peasants or small *zamindars* were also among the beneficiaries of the growth in the seventeenth century. With their wealth and strength, the merchants now perhaps endeavoured to control government offices, while on the other hand, the *zamindars* aspired to a greater share in the revenues as well as in the administration of their holdings. The increasing *ijara* practice did not, thus, imply a drying up of trade prospects. It showed that investment in land was still profitable.[57] While in certain areas, as in Awadh, the *zamindars* had sufficient wealth and political strength to establish their dominance and acquire new powers through *ijara*, in certain other regions traders and money changers were strong enough to stand surety for payment in time, of the stipulated revenue, from the *jagir*. The challenges to the Mughal system thus appear to have been in connection with the pattern of collection and distribution of the revenue resources. When the land grew in profitability why should the bulk of its produce go only to the *jagirdars*. This was perhaps how the local magnates argued. *Ijara* was to form part of a broader process of 'localization' in the distribution and organization of power. In a large measure, therefore, the state

[56]Cf. B.M. or. 9876 (a collection of Shah Alam II's letters to the nobles and the officials of the East India Company) ff. 39b–40, 48b, 54a–61b for Benaras, Allahabad and Kora's links with Agra and Delhi. *I'jaz-i Arsalani*, I, ff. 53a, 119b, 123a, f. 180a, 288a; II, ff. 67a, 140b; 173b, 177a, for trade and monetary links between Delhi, Agra, Etawah, Farrukhabad, Faizabad, Kheir (Aligarh), Lucknow and Benaras and of these northern Indian towns with Hugly and Calcutta. See also Makrand Mehta, 'Indian Bankers and Political Change: A Case Study of the Travadis of Surat, c. 1720–c. 1820', *Studies in History*, IV, 1, January–June 1982, pp. 41–55 for the connection between, Benaras in north India and Ahmedabad in western India through the Travadis; Tapan Raychaudhuri's article in Dharma Kumar and Meghnad Desai (eds.), *The Cambridge Economic History of India*, II, Cambridge University Press, 1983, pp. 3–35; Frank Perlin makes a good analysis of the recent writings on the subject in his articles, 'Proto-Industrialization and Pre-Colonial South Asia' *Past and Present*, No. 98, February 1983, pp. 30–95, and 'The Pre-Colonial Indian State in History and Epistemology: A Reconstruction of Societal Formation in the Western Deccan from the 15th to the Early 19th Century', in H.J. M., Classen and Peter Skalnik (eds.), *The Study of the State*, the Hague, Mouton, 1981, pp. 275–302.

[57] Despite a backward farming technology and obvious shortcomings in agricultural prices, yield per acre was very high. Cf. Dharma Kumar and Meghnad Desai (eds.), *The Cambridge Economic History*, II, pp. 15–17.

could have possibly met the challenges, as it happened in Awadh, by institutionalizing the *ijara* practice and by accepting the *ijaradars* (revenue-farmers) as an official category of revenue collectors. Raja Ratan Chand who hailed from a trading community and held a key position during the years of the Saiyid Brothers' ascendancy in Farrukh Siyar's reign, appreciated the problem, and appears to have made attempts at institutionalizing the *ijara* practice. But he was accused by the old nobles of having converted state craft into shopkeeping (*baqqaliat*).[58] And in an atmosphere of distrust at the court, the accusation carried credibility with the emperor.[59]

In effect, *ijara* implied a greater burden on the lower categories of the revenue payers. *Ijara* implied fiscal and administrative control over the revenues of men motivated by gains, without any checks and supervision to which a government official, albeit theoretically, was subjected. An instance from Etawah would probably illustrate the implications of the *ijara*. The *qazi* (judge) of *pargana* Jalesar pressed upon the grain dealers to sell foodgrain (wheat) at the rate of 12 *sers* a rupee. In protest the grain dealers closed their shops and expressed their inability to follow the *qazi*'s directive. For 'the deputy of Kalyan Singh', as they are reported to have presented to the *qazi* 'has farmed out the *rahdari* (road toll) on Rs 6000 to Jagat who is tyrannically levying 4 *annas* per ox-load'.[60] Of whatever benefit to the individual nobles, the *ijara* practice thus also tended to alienate revenue payers from the Mughal government, until it was reformed by some new *subadars* (governors) and evolved as an institution with such responsibilities as those of a government office.

Towards the close of the second phase of our period it was not only the nobility but also minor state officials, *zamindars*, traders

[58] According to Khafi Khan the people of the country belonging to every class hated the Saiyid Brothers and Ratan Chand as they patronized only the Saiyids of Barha and the *baqqals* (shopkeepers), K.K., II, p. 902.

[59] Khafi Khan reports that whenever Saiyid Abdullah Khan appointed an *amil* he took from the appointee an undertaking and realized money from his banker and that Saiyid Abdullah's *diwan*, Ratan Chand leased out even the *khalisa* lands in *ijara*, and that this practice accentuated the rift between the *wazir* and the emperor. K.K., II, p. 773; See also N.A. Siddiqi, *Land-Revenue Administration*, p. 96; Satish Chandra, *Parties and Politics*, p. 109.

[60] *Akhbarat*, FS, 6th R.Y., II, p. 212 (8 January 1718).

and money changers who had almost lost faith in Mughal government. While the nobility's indifference to state affairs further impaired the imperial organization, the *zamindar* revolts and subsequent developments caused an irreparable blow to the credibility of the government. The challenges to the Mughal state—*zamindar* revolts and increasing practice of *ijara* probaby indicated the beginning of a trend towards a transition in political power. These challenges could not be solved militarily. The situation could perhaps have been brought under some control if there was no aversion to change in the pattern of government. To the majority of the dominant ruling sections of the Mughals state craft still meant swordsmanship and a benevolent despotism. The factional politics at the court also contributed to the atmosphere in which any drift from the existing institutional structure of the government was resisted.

The nobility

Against this backdrop it becomes perhaps more meaningful to examine the nobles' struggle for unprecedented control of imperial offices at the court as well as in the provinces. During his viceroyalty of the Deccan, Husain Ali Khan is reported to have paid little respect to imperial orders. He appointed his own men to the offices of the *qiladars* (fort commandants) which had so far been under the control of the emperor.[61] The revolts of Nizam-ul-Mulk and Chhabele Ram in Malwa and Allahabad and the defiance of the governor of the Punjab indicated the emerging change in the attitude of the provincial governors to the central government.

A measure of the alienation of the nobles from the emperor is also illustrated from the disappearance of the personal element in their relationship. The Mughal emperors were markedly different from their contemporaries in Persia in their attitude towards the nobility. Whatever the stand of the nobles may have been during the wars of succession, once a Mughal prince occupied the throne, he treated them with equal magnanimity. This convention was laid aside first in Jahandar Shah's reign. The reign of Farrukh Siyar began with an indis-

[61] K.K., II, p. 773.

criminate elimination of even those nobles whom his friends
and supporters among the nobility suspected to be a potential
threat to their position and ambition. In Jahandar Shah's reign,
Rustam Dil Khan and Mukhlis Khan, for instance, were killed
at the instance of Zulfiqar Khan while a number of the other
nobles were ordered to be put in prison. On Farrukh Siyar's
accession, Zulfiqar Khan, Hidayatullah Khan and Saiyidi Qasim
were killed and many others were imprisoned. Contemporary chroniclers ascribe a number of executions and the
severities to the influence of Mir Jumla.[62] Farrukh Siyar's alleged letters to Ajit Singh in 1713 and to Daud Khan Panni in
1715 showed how the emperor was also implicated in the cons-
piracies against the nobles.[63] 'The fear of [being strangled by]
the thong was so much ingrained in the heart of the nobles that
whenever they intended [to go to] the court, they bade adieu to
their wives and children'.[64] In consequence, the traditional ties
of mutual confidence and affection between the emperor and
the nobles were further broken. The emperor was almost totally
isolated. It was only after a violent shock in the unprecedented
deposition and brutal killing of Farrukh Siyar that they were
again bound to the person of the emperor. This was, however,
on their own terms and permitted only the symbolic existence of
the imperial framework.

III 1729–39

The emperor and the nobility

By the time Muhammad Shah came to power the nature of the
relationship between the emperor and the nobility had almost

[62] Cf. Kamwar, pp. 159 and 181; K.K., II, p. 732; Yahya, f. 121b. See also W. Irvine,
Later Moghuls, I, pp. 275–80. For the Mughal emperors' approach to their nobles see
M. Athar Ali, 'Mughal Empire in History', *PIHC*, the 33rd Session, Muzaffarpur,
1972, pp. 175–88.

[63] In 1713 when *Amir-ul-Umara*, Husain Ali Khan, was deputed to lead an expedition
against Ajit Singh, the emperor is reported to have written to the raja to kill the
Amir-ul-Umara. Again in 1715 when Husain Ali Khan, after a kind of compromise with
Mir Jumla and the emperor, left for the Deccan, Daud Khan Panni, the deputy
governor of the Deccan, was allegedly instigated by the emperor to eliminate the
Amir-ul-Umara. Subsequently in a battle with Husain Ali Khan, near Burhanpur, Daud
Khan was killed. For details see W. Irvine, *Later Moghuls*, I, pp. 285–6 and 303.

[64] *T. Muzaffari*, f. 112a.

changed totally. Individual interests of the nobles had openly guided the course of politics and state activities. The end of the ascendancy of the Saiyid Brothers meant only a decline in their power and the ascendancy of the 'Turani' faction, and not the assertion of imperial authority. In 1720, the replacement as *wazir* of Saiyid Abdullah Khan by Muhammad Amin Khan, the leader of the Turanis at the court, was decided not by the emperor but Muhammad Amin Khan himself. After Amin Khan's death (27 January 1720), the office of *wazir* was occupied by Nizam-ul-Mulk, a cousin of his, for a brief period, till his (Amin Khan's) son Qamar-ud-Din Khan (appointed on 22 July 1724) held the office almost on account of hereditary right. But since no faction of the nobility, nor for that matter the nobility as a whole, was in a position to rule on its own, due to either a continuation of the myth of the paramountcy of the Mughal dynasty or the inherent inability of the nobility to act in unison, the symbols of imperial power together with the dynasty and the person of the emperor had to be retained with a rather exaggerated emphasis. The nobles in control of the central offices still had an all-empire outlook, even if they were more concerned with the stability of the regions where they had their *jagirs*. *Farmans* to governors, *faujdars* and other local officials were sent in conformity with tradition, in the name of the emperor. The emperor's routine seems to have been carefully followed till at least the end of 1722.[65]

Gradually a sort of functional, rather dysfunctional, mutuality emerged in the wake of the emerging powers of the nobles while sustaining the symbolic position and role of the emperor. As a result, a position at the Mughal centre no longer depended on administrative ability, office or military achievements. This is amply illustrated from Koki Jio's influence on Muhammad Shah and the rise of her relations and associates, better known

[65] Compare Shakir, f. 25a for *farmans* to the governors and *faujdars* in the name of the emperor and *Sahifa-i Iqbal*, f. 35a, for the emperor's routine and court etiquette in the early 1720s. Describing the routine of the emperor, the author of the *Sahifa-i Iqbal* notes that a large number of the people (lit. slaves) received *mansabs*, promotions and the other favours through the *bakhshis* in the *Diwan-i 'Am* (audience hall); while the ambassadors from the neighbouring countries were given audience and the officials in the provincial service were sent off in the same place (*Diwan-i 'Am*). And at night, after the recitation (of the Qur'an) and the fulfilment of the ends of the people the emperor put his seal and signature on the papers relating to the governors.

as the emperor's favourites, to high offices. One of Koki Jio's brothers, Ali Ahmad Khan, looked after the service seekers' renewed petitions and the ensuing confirming orders (*darogha* of *arz-i mukarrar*), while her other brother, Ali Hamid Khan, was superintendent of postal department (*darogha* of *dak*) and her third brother, Ali Asghar Khan, possibly held the *faujdari* of the Doao in the Punjab. Notwithstanding the emperor's signature and recommendation, no new *mansab* or promotion could be procured without offering a bribe to Ali Ahmad Khan. Similarly, Ali Asghar Khan came into direct conflict with the governor of the Punjab over *jagir* questions. How the information and news channels began to deteriorate under Ali Hamid Khan is a matter of conjecture. Roshan-ud-Daulah, Zafar Khan, the third *bakhshi* and the *bakhshi* of the gentlemen troopers under the direct command of the emperor (*ahadis*) was one of Koki's confidants. Since he was very close to the emperor, he became the agent (*vakil*) of some nobles and governors of distant provinces, such as, Bengal, Kabul, Thatta and Kashmir, secured *mansabs*, promotions and other favours for them and thus accumulated crores of rupees. Hafiz Khidmatgar was another confidant of the emperor whose opinion weighed heavily in the appointment and dismissal of the governors. Nobles with ability and strength thus sought to build a base for themselves in a province.

The emperor's favourites were little concerned with the problems of the empire; their main endeavour was to amass wealth and to keep their positions on a secure footing. Zafar Khan is reported to have been in possession of a treasury 'beyond the imagination of even the Pharaoh'. According to Warid, whatever revenue came from the provinces, the emperor's favourites, namely Zafar Khan, Koki Jio and Abd-ul-Ghafur, instead of depositing it with the imperial treasury, took it themselves. The amount so misappropriated can be gauged from the fact that when Abd-ul-Ghafur was censured, over twenty lakh rupees were discovered from his house. Half of the sum of Rs 12,00,000 which was handed over to Zafar Khan each month for the emoluments of the imperial army in Kabul were misappropriated by him. In 1732 it was discovered that over two crore rupees had till then been embezzled by him.[66]

[66]Cf. Ashub, ff. 45, 47 and 48; Shakir, f. 38b; Warid, p. 383.

Imperial decline and the province

The decay in imperial administration was exacerbated by the adverse circumstances which followed the droughts in the 1720s and also by the increase in number and intensity of the *zamindar* risings. According to the author of the *Tarikh-i Muzaffari*, 1134/1721–2 was a year of good harvest and the prices of foodgrains which had been soaring spirally for the last few years came down.[67] This statement is to be accepted with certain reservations. The author of the *Tarikh-i Muzaffari*, not unlike many other chroniclers of the period, has obvious prejudices against the Saiyid Brothers and describes the conditions that followed the eclipse of their power and which brought relief to a section of the nobility as a general relief for all. On the contrary, the plight of the people and disruption all over the country were given as major reasons for the proclamation abolishing the *jizya* in 1722.[68] Towards the middle of the third decade, the food shortage in and around Delhi seems to have become very acute.[69] Though this unusual situation did not continue, from a general statement of the *Mirat-ul-Haqaiq* it can be inferred that the prices of foodgrains in quite a large part of northern India in the late 1720s and the 1730s continued to rise.[70] Further, the Maratha raids in the 1730s must have caused considerable dislocation of agrarian production.

Moreover, it is not only that we have new categories in the list of *zamindars* who spearheaded rural disturbances, according to our sources, the chief targets of these disturbances were now the Mughal revenue collectors (*amils*). The Gujars of *chakla* Etawah, for instance, are for the first time mentioned as rebels

[67] *T. Muzaffari*, f. 123a. No further details, apart from a general statement are available in the sources. It seems that after the last year of Farrukh Siyar's reign (1718–19) prices began to fall. According to Yahya, wheat in Delhi at the end of Farrukh Siyar's reign was sold at 10 to 11 *sers* a rupee.

[68] Cf. K.K., II, p. 936; *T. Muzaffari*, f. 171a; Kamwar, f. 376.

[69] According to Shakir around 1723, wheat in Delhi was sold at the rate of 2 to 3 *sers* a rupee. Within a year of two, however, the price of wheat fell to 7 to 8 *sers* a rupee. The relief is ascribed by the chronicler to the mystic influence of Shah Bhika. Shakir Khan states that Roshan-ud-Daulah, Zafar Khan who was a devoted follower of Shah Bhika asked the emperor to make an offering of Rs 1,00,000 in the name of the Shah. The emperor did accordingly and then the rain came. Compare Shakir, ff. 74b and 75a.

[70] *Mirat-ul-Haqaiq*, f. 139a where the author states that prices in Bengal and Bihar were rising and gives the prices of certain commodities at Agra in 1137/1724–25 as follows:

in 1722.[71] The *ri'aya* of the *jagirs* of the Saiyids of Barha who had hitherto been cowed down so successfully, dispossessed the *amils* and misappropriated the revenue of the *kharif* crop.[72]

Irregularities in the offices and the institutions which had direct connections with provincial and local government bore more disastrous consequences for imperial unity than did even the decay in the office of the *wazir*. The gap between the provincial and local officials and the centre must have increased enormously when 'the emperor's favourites' occupied offices crucial for provincial government. As *darogha* of *dak*, Koki Jio's brother, Ali Ahmad Khan had control over the channels of information from the provinces. On the other hand Zafar Khan, another favourite of the emperor, was *vakil* of many nobles posted in the provinces while Hafiz Khidmatgar Khan, a personal attendant of the emperor, influenced the fortunes of the provincial governors. Added to it was the fact that Zafar Khan also held the charge for the maintenance of the army on the ever vulnerable north-western borders.

These factors together with the steadily increasing vulnerability of the centre in the face of the *zamindari* unrest combined to set in motion a new type of provincial government. The court

Rice (*basmati*)	5	*sers* per rupee	= Rs	8.00 per *man*
Rice [*sondi* (?)]	6	„ „	= Rs	6.67 „
Rice [*dosiali* (?)]	7	„ „	= Rs	5.71 „
Gram	7½	„ „	= Rs	5.33 „
Flour (wheat)	7	„ „	= Rs	5.71 „
Mung	6½	„ „	= Rs	6.15 „
Ghee	4	„ „	= Rs	10.00 „
White sugar	2½	„ „	= Rs	16.00 „
Red sugar	5½	„ „	= Rs	7.27 „
Black sugar candy (fine variety)	6	„ „	= Rs	6.67 „
Black sugar candy (lower variety)	7	„ „	= Rs	5.71 „

For the prices of some of these commodities at Agra in the seventeenth century see Irfan Habib, *Agrarian System*, pp. 83–6.

The statement of the *Mirat-ul-Haqaiq* is also supported by a list of the price of coarse rice which Brij Narain quotes: One could have only 35 *sers* for a rupee in 1722 and 1723, while the situation was little better when the price fell down only marginally to 40 and 45 *sers* a rupee in 1724 and 1725 respectively. Cf. Brij Narain, *Indian Economic Life Past and Present*, Lahore, 1929, p. 96.

[71] *Mirat-ul-Haqaiq*, f. 209b.

[72] *T. Muzaffari*, f. 154a.

needed money from the governors to maintain both its functional structure and the necessary pomp and majesty. As militarily it was not in a position to enforce its regulations in the empire, different provinces in proportion to their internal conditions, geographical distance from Delhi and ambition and the capacity of their governors gave a new shape to their links with the court. The Mughal court's chief concern at this stage was to ensure that the flow of the necessary revenue from the provinces and the maintenance of at least the semblance of imperial unity were not disrupted. Not surprisingly then, one or two governors who obtained governorships on the payment of a heavy sum as *peshkash* (present) to the court, gave these on *ijara* to someone else.[73]

Towards a new imperial framework

It is interesting to note that at this stage a sizeable section of the nobility appreciated the changing situation and tried to adapt the Mughal imperial framework to it. They thought in terms of a basic modification in the nature and extent of the Mughal paramountcy over the *zamindars*. Samsam-ud-Daulah who in his capacity as *mir bakhshi* was in constant touch with the provincial and local *bakhshis* and news-reporters, was the chief exponent of this idea. 'The Rajput rajas and the small and big *zamindars*', as Samsam-ud-Daulah argued, 'had been the rulers of Hindustan who, because of their ill-fortune, could not withstand the blow of [the swords of] the Mughal emperors and had to accommodate with them by accepting their overlordship in all humility. We should therefore be content with this, for any deliberation for their chastisement would amount to putting our hands into the hornets' nest.'[74] Samsam-ud-Daulah illustrated his plea by referring to the repercussions of Aurangzeb's policy towards the Marathas in the late-seventeenth century. Samsam-ud-Daulah tried to conciliate almost all the *zamindars* who could individually collect, on whatsoever account, even a

[73] In 1740, Mir Munnu, the governor of Ajmer, for instance, farmed out the *suba* to Raja Jai Singh. Mir Munnu, son of Qamar-ud-Din Khan, the *wazir*, was appointed the governor of Ajmer in the same year. Due to the discontented and rebellious rajas, however, he was unable to control the *suba*. This unusual case of *ijara* was as per the instruction of the *wazir*. Cf. *T. Hind*, f. 295b.

[74] Ashub, f. 79a. As it was difficult to translate it literally, I have taken some liberty in translating the passage.

small army of peasants to rise against the Mughals. His agents, spread all over the empire, tried to persuade the *zamindars* to accept *mansabs* and titles, *jagirs* and the *zamindaris* of their *watans* (home districts) along with some additional favours from the Mughal court. When the *zamindars* reached the court, an important friend or associate of the *mir bakhshi* escorted him to the audience hall.[75]

Samsam-ud-Daulah's plea was probably for a formal accept-ance of decentralization. He advocated giving away of fiscal rights, as it was in an ordinary case of *ijara*, and also some administrative rights by local Mughal officials to the *zamindars*. The plea did not find a ready response at the court. But the rationality of such a policy was well appreciated by some nobles in the provinces which emerged as 'successor states'.[76] The arrangement with the *zamindars* in these states meant addi-tional power to them and also their participation in the government.

On the eve of Nadir Shah's invasion of India the major institutions and the norms that regulated the Mughal system had reached almost a total collapse. At the centre it was not the emperor but the nobles who dictated the terms of their services to the state while in the provinces the governors had been emerging as virtually autonomous rulers. Their association with the imperial court or loyalty to the emperor and the Mughal system was effected on their own terms and in their own interest.

However, the decline of imperial authority did not mean the disappearance of the imperial frame. The semblance of the empire had to be guarded, for it suited all the elements who had hitherto constituted the substance of the empire. It appears that the decline of the Mughal empire was accompanied by a rearrangement of the state structure based perhaps on a redis-tribution of imperial resources. Nadir Shah's invasion of India in 1739 gave a final blow to the emperor's authority by creating conditions for these developments to take firm root. The battle against the Persian invaders in Karnal was lost before it actu-ally started. Two nobles, Samsam-ud-Daulah and Burhan-ul-Mulk entered the fray while Nizam-ul-Mulk, the *wazir* and the

---

[75] Ashub, f. 79b.
[76] See Chapter VI for Awadh.

entire 'Turani' group preferred to stay away. And the emperor, the supreme commander, was a mere helpless onlooker.

IV 1739–48

Financial collapse and restatement of the imperial myth

The Persian invasion in 1739 substantially drained the wealth of the Mughal empire. Whatever was left in the imperial treasury was distributed among those *mansabdars* and *risaladars* (commanders of small army units) who had not received their emoluments for years. It was promised that their debts to the traders would be cleared after the victory over Nadir Shah.[77] Again, in the wake of the invasion, foodgrains became scarce.[78] This was followed by an indiscriminate massacre and the sack of Delhi by the Persian soldiers. Noted *ganjs* and *mandis* (grain markets) of the city, namely, Azimganj, Ganj Shahdara, and Ganj Khas Mahal were turned into ruins. After that prices in Delhi soared so high that even one or half a *ser* of foodgrains could not be had at a rupee.[79]

Though the Mughal empire is reported in a contemporary account to have a *jama* (assessed revenue) of over 40 crore of rupees in our period, the imperial treasury at Delhi possessed little in 1740.[80]

In 1741 when Nadir Shah sent his agents to collect the effects of Shuja-ud-Daulah and Sarfaraz Khan, the governors of Bengal, the revenue that was sent from this province to the court

---

[77] Ashub, ff. 171.

[78] According to the *Tarikh-i Ali* (f. 88b) one could obtain only one *ser* of ordinary rice (*shali* and *sathi*) for Rs. 5.00 and that, too, was not available to most of the people. According to the *Tazkira Mukhlis* the price of flour rose to Rs 4.00 a *ser*. A letter of the Maratha *vakil* at the court probably narrates the plight of the camp most vividly. 'Five or six days passed and then no food could be had in the camp. Grain could not be had even at six or seven rupees the *ser*. The country was desert, nothing could be had (from the neighbouring villages). For five days the men went without food.' Quoted by J.N. Sarkar in W. Irvine, *Later Moghuls*, II, p. 357.

[79] *Tarikh-i-Ali*, f. 88b.

[80] *Risala*, f. 146a. The evidence of *Risala* regarding the *jama* is interesting, but is certainly to be accepted with reservations. The *jama* figures of the provinces as given in different sources of our period do not support so high a *jama* as over 40 crore of rupees at any point of time in the earlier half of the eighteenth century. Compare N.A. Siddiqi, *Land Revenue Aaministration*, Appendix E, pp. 164–71.

was very small and the emperor was advised to write to Nadir Shah for an exemption so that he could spend the Bengal treasury on the *necessities* of the court. It is, however, to be noted that the emperor managed *to secure some amount in debt from Sita Ram and the other traders of Delhi and handed over twenty lakh rupees to the agents of Nadir Shah.*[81] After that the Mughal empire headed towards total financial collapse. In the wake of the Maratha inroads into Bengal, the revenue of the province which had so far been the mainstay of the imperial economy ceased to come. Excessive rain causing heavy damage to the standing *rabi* crops in 1747 further complicated the difficulties.[82] In 1748 when Muhammad Shah died the empire was totally bankrupt.[83] But Safdar Jang, the governor of Awadh, could still afford to spend over Rs 40,00,000 on the marriage of his son, Shuja-ud-Daulah in 1745,[84] while the Delhi merchants continued to be able to help the emperor in need.

It is true that Nadir Shah's invasion, on the one hand shook Delhi to its foundation, on the other it also awakened the emperor and a section of the nobility to the need of recouping the central army to avoid such humiliation in future. They made some attempts in this direction, but in vain. This is illustrated, among other things, from the pathetic failure in raising a new royal army. The raising of the army began with ten thousand *sawars* (cavalry) and *piyadas* (infantry) with a monthly payment of Rs 50 to each trooper. Soon the strength of the army increased and a number of eminent nobles, such as Sad-ud-Din Khan, Hafiz-ud-Din Khan, Muhammad Sa'id Khan, Azam Khan and his sons and Bairam Khan and Sarbu-land Khan were given the commands of its different units. As the sword (*shamsher*) was the mark of the branding (*dagh*) of the horses of the army, it came to be known as the *risala-i shamsher dagh*. In the meanwhile, the old troopers who had dispersed in 1739 also collected together and reformed the old imperial army (*risala*). Since Delhi did not receive enough revenue from the provinces to pay the emoluments of the new recruits and the old troopers together, the strength of the new *risala* was reduced to 50 per cent. Yet the central exchequer could not meet the

---

[81] *Tazkira Mukhlis*, pp. 104–6.   [82] *T. Muzaffari*, f. 270b.   [83] Shakir, f. 36b.

[84] Compare, A.L. Srivastava, *First Two Nawabs of Awadh*, Second edn., Agra, 1954, p. 112.

pay-claims of the troopers of the new *risala*. In 1743 Amir Khan, therefore, convinced the emperor of the futility of spending such a sum on a standing army. The *risala* was subsequently disbanded without the payment of the arrears of nine months to the soldiers. Eventually, Asad Yar Khan, the noble-in-charge of the *risala*, had to dispose of some of his own assets and thus paid the arrears of the mutinous troopers.[85]

The emperor's order to Safdar Jang to lead an expedition to assist Ali Virdi Khan against the Marathas probably again represented an assertion of the centre's authority over the province in the 1740s. According to some contemporary accounts, Safdar Jang was deputed by the emperor primarily to collect the revenue that had been withheld by Ali Virdi Khan in Bengal.[86] The Rohilla campaign in 1745 at the instance of Safdar Jang and Amir Khan was also an expression of the same endeavour. In this context it may also be noted that the emperor was an active party in court politics in the 1740s. His attempt to reorganize the army, recall Amir Khan, his favourite, from Allahabad, together with the appointment as *mir atish* (imperial artillary chief) of Safdar Jang, who was a friend of Amir Khan, and finally his connivance at the assassination of Amir Khan, all indicated an effort towards the restoration of the pivotal position of the emperor.[87]

Nonetheless, these steps could hardly help in restoring the imperial power. A major reason for the dismal result was obviously the financial crisis of the imperial centre. However, the unusual part taken by the nobles, who had staked their interests principally in one or another province, in court politics is worth considering. In 1745 it was Safdar Jang, the governor of Awadh, who emerged as the chief supporter of the emperor. But ironically, Safdar Jang, virtually as an independent ruler of Awadh, himself represented one of the agencies of disintegration of the imperial structure. The ambivalence inherent in Safdar Jang's position is revealed in the case of the Rohilla campaign. Safdar Jang, as *mir atish* at the centre advocated the policy of coercion as against compromise, while in Awadh, as its

---

[85] *Chahar Gulzar*, ff. 373a, 375a and 382b; *Siyar*, III, p. 856.

[86] *Ruqa-i Mutafarriqat*, Patna MS., ff. 43b–44a.

[87] See for details Chapter VII. See also Jadu Nath Sarkar, *Fall of the Mughal Empire*, I, pp. 1–25.

governor, he extended the privileges to the as yet new categories of local magnates in order to conciliate them and build up his power base.

The case of Safdar Jang's interest in the centre highlighted the necessity of maintaining the imperial framework. Those who had greater ambitions in the regions aspired for higher offices at the court, since it was still the only source of legitimate political authority. Awadh, the Punjab, Farrukhabad, Anola and Benaras, as we shall see later, had emerged as virtually autonomous principalities in north India. But 'legally' these principalities were tied with the Mughal court. Whatever the nature of the forces of disintegration, the person of the Mughal emperor represented order and authority, albeit symbolically. The news of the death of Muhammad Shah in 1748 led to a breakdown of 'law and order'.[88] Thus, even in the 1740s, not only the nobles who had carved out their principalities, but also the Marathas vied with each other in securing office at the Mughal court.

The necessity of emphasizing imperial symbols was inherent in the kind of power politics that emerged in different parts of the erstwhile Mughal empire in the eighteenth century. As the emergence of the new power structures in the provinces followed the decline of the long accepted legitimate imperial organization of the Mughals, each of them, in proportion to its strength, looked for and seized opportunities to establish its dominance over the others in its neighbourhood. But each of them also resisted any such attempt by the other. For legitimacy, they sought the 'hegemony' of the Mughal central government which had come to coexist with their ambitions. In one of the regions of our study, for example, which we shall see in detail in Chapter VII, the rise of the Benaras *zamindari* synchronized with the emergence of the new *subadari* of the governor of Awadh, the latter being obviously more powerful and capable of suppressing the former. In a bid to avert such a danger, the *zamindar* of Benaras tried to establish direct access to the emperor. Similarly, the Afghans of Farrukhabad and Anola on the western borders of Awadh tried to protect their interests in the region by seeking legitimacy from Delhi. In the absence of a new paramount power it served regional interests

[88] *Siyar*, III, p. 868.

to sustain the myth of Mughal imperial authority. This feature of political developments in our period not only provided continued nourishment to the symbols of imperial authority, but also reactivated politics at the Mughal court in the 1740s. The nobles who had carved out principalities for themselves in the provinces attempted to obtain high offices at the centre in order to sustain their local/regional positions. This, however, represented also a failure of developments in these areas which could not evolve anything other than the Mughal paradigm within a limited context.

CHAPTER II
The Changing Position
of the Governor

I Awadh

While the nobles' urge for additional powers at the centre implied that the principle of the king as the real core and the source of authority was no longer tenable, its extension to those posted in the provinces marked a virtual rejection of the centre itself. The unwillingness of the governors to function with their erstwhile military and executive powers had a bearing on the existing imperial framework. In this chapter we will examine the stages of the evolution in Awadh and the Punjab of the new *subadari* which signified the subordination of all the military, executive and financial authorities within these provinces to the governors.

The chapter again illustrates Bahadur Shah's failure to appreciate the conditions in which the governors began to ask for extended powers. The emperor saw the problem in the perspective of the pretensions and high claims of the old nobles and acceded some privileges to the governors in view of their eminence and stature. He allowed them to govern with these privileges not to enable them to meet the difficult conditions in the provinces, but because he wanted them away from, and was not prepared to allow them to be in key positions at, the centre. In a bid to assert his authority, the emperor still encouraged the checks on the governors within the old pattern of the centre-province relations. Later, under Farrukh Siyar a process of institutional change in the position of the governors seems to have begun. However, the governors' claim for control over provincial finance in particular clashed with the concept of the new *wizarat*. The factional politics at the court were then extended to the provinces resulting in further deterioration of the administration. Thus, the course of the developments in the provinces in which originated the nobles' difficulties was also affected by the developments at the centre.

The position of subadar

An account of the classical position of the Mughal *subadar* (governor) is provided by Abul Fazl in the chapter on *sipahsalar* *(ain-i-sipahsalar)* in the *Ain*. But it is understandable that in practice the powers of the governor did not accord exactly with the *Ain*, as indeed it was not possible to maintain the theoretical position through the vicissitudes of a vast period of over a hundred eventful years between the compilation of the *Ain* and the death of Aurangzeb. In the course of the seventeenth century, however, there evolved a consensus regarding the functions and powers of the governor. The governor's authority under no circumstances was to extend beyond the geographical limits of his province, which he held normally for not more than four to five years. On the strength of his high *mansab*—4000 to 5000 in the case of a large province and 3000 if the province was small—the governor had direct access to the emperor, but in several provincial matters he was under close surveillance of some central authorities. The revenues, the administration of *jagir* and *khalisa* and the provincial offices for branding of horses and verification of horsemen *(dagh-o-tashiha)* were under the control of the *diwan* and the *bakhshi* of the province who in turn were accountable to the *diwan-i a'la* *(wazir)* and the *mir bakhshi* at the centre. The *diwan*, in particular, acted as a check on the governor. Similarly, the *faujdars*, the *waqai'nigars* (news writers) and the *amils* and the *diwans* in the *sarkars* were independent of the governor. The governor was also not allowed to go on a big military expedition on his own discretion.[1]

The period of our study, however, saw definite changes in the position of the governor. The process of these changes are discernible in certain regions right from the beginning of the eighteenth century, even though their pattern was not uniform throughout the empire. The developments in Bengal and the

[1] Compare *Ain*, I, Nawal Kishore, (1882), pp. 195–6 for the governor's theoretical position. For the provincial *diwan*'s powers and duties in the seventeenth century, see *Khulasat-us-Siyaq*, Subhanallah Collection *(zamima)*, F, 900/15, Muslim University Library, Aligarh, ff. 16b–17a; *Nigarnama-i Munshi*, Abd-us-Salam Collection, 362/132, Muslim University Library, Aligarh, ff. 160b–165a. For the local officials' direct responsibility to the emperor and the central authorities see the specimens of appointment letters to the various officials in *Nigarnama-i Munshi* (ff. 122b–160b *bab-i chaharum*); see also its Part II which includes *arzdashts* of the local officials to the emperor. See also, P. Saran, *The Provincial Government of the Mughals, 1526–1658*, pp. 144–91.

Deccan, for instance, which are known to have set the pace of struggle for a new form of provincial administration had little similarity with each other. In the case of the former the *diwan* assumed the dominant position,[2] while in the Deccan it was the *subadar* who accelerated the processes of a new pattern of relationship between Delhi and the provinces. In Awadh and the Punjab, which we propose to examine in some detail, it was the *subadar* who emerged eventually as a virtually independent provincial ruler. Besides this similarity, the nature of the relationship of these provinces with the imperial centre was influenced by the political developments at the court as well as by the necessity for the extension of the governor's control over certain important provincial offices.

Extension of the governor's power

Our sources record some additional powers of the Governor of Awadh in Bahadur Shah's reign. In early November 1707, Chin Qilich Khan (later Nizam-ul-Mulk) combined his governorship of Awadh with a number of *faujdaris* in the province and the *faujdari* of Jaunpur which lay on the borders in Allahabad province in the neighbourhood.[3] Later, on 25 January 1708, when he resigned protesting, among other things, for a *mansab* of

[2] In 1700 when Kartalab Khan, later Murshid Quli Khan, was appointed to the *diwani* of Bengal, the empire, its treasury having been substantially drained out in the Deccan war, was in need of money. The *diwan* of Bengal, a rich and prosperous *suba*, was therefore given full authority which included even executive powers over about half of the revenue-yielding districts of the province. He enjoyed the full confidence of the emperor to the extent that on his report, Aurangzeb reprimanded the ablest of the princes, Muhammad Azim-ud-Din (Azim-ush-Shan) who was the governor of Bengal and on a number of questions at variance with Murshid Quli Khan. It was perhaps peculiar with Bengal that the headquarters of the *diwani* were permitted to be established far from the provincial capital. Compare *Akhbarat* BS, 1st R. Y., 25th Rabi II and 22nd Rajab, pp. 17 and 210; Abdul Karim, *Murshid Quli Khan and his Times*, Dacca, 1963, pp. 18 and 22–4; Ghulam Husain Salim, *Riyaz-us-Salatin*, Bib. Indic. Calcutta, 1898, pp. 243 and 247–50; J. N. Sarkar (ed.), *History of Bengal*, II, second impression, Dacca, 1972, p. 403.

[3] *Akhbarat* BS, 1st R. Y. pp. 311, 362, 389 and 417; Yahya, f. 115a; *M. U.*, II, p. 839 and Kamwar, f. 307b. Kamwar and *M. U.* do not give correct dates of Chin Qilich Khan's posting in Awadh. According to *M. U.* he was the first, while actually he was the third governor of Awadh in the time of Bahadur Shah. Kamwar gives 15 Ramzan/29 November 1707 as the date of his appointment which is the date of Chin Qilich's securing of *faujdari* of Khairabad. Cf. *Akhbarat*, p. 311.

7000/7000, he was persuaded to withdraw his resignation by no less a person than Mun'im Khan, the *wazir*. Chin Qilich returned to Awadh with a *mansab* of 7000/7000 together with all his earlier *faujdaris*, barring, of course, Jaunpur which still remained in his family as it was given to his uncle, Qilich Muhammad Khan.[4]

But these additional offices were not meant to strengthen the position of the governor and enable him to encounter the problems of the local administration forcefully. *Subadari* with more than one *faujdari* was simply an additional privilege for Chin Qilich Khan, more as a mark of special consideration for his eminence and stature than as an index of any change in the institution of governorship. Chin Qilich's claim to a high rank of 7000/7000 was also conceded because he was a leader of an important group at the court. Besides, his father, Ghazi-ud-Din Khan Firoz Jang was the governor of Gujarat while a number of his associates were posted in the Deccan where the emperor had yet to meet the challenge of another claimant to the throne, Prince Muhammad Kam Bakhsh. Thus, when Chin Qilich Khan came to Awadh in 1708 he was made to recognize the fact that his special position as governor by no means implied additional power in matters related to *subadari*. The emperor did not approve of his recommendation that one of his friends be appointed to the *faujdari* of Bahraich. Instead, the post was given to an associate of Zulfiqar Khan, his arch-rival at the court.[5] Also when Chin Qilich Khan disapproved of the compromise that the emperor effected with the Rajputs,[6] he lost the *faujdaris* of Khairabad and Lucknow to the *diwan* of the pro-

[4] Ibid., BS, 2nd R. Y., pp. 14 and 82; Kamwar, f. 308a. Chin Qilich Khan's resignation followed his removal from the *faujdaris* as a punishment for his indifference to the provincial affairs. Compare Yahya, f. 115b; *Akhbarat* BS, 1st R. Y., p. 389.

[5] Ibid., 2nd R. Y., p. 16 (10 February 1709). He was Saif Khan, the son of Amir Khan (d. 1698) who through his mother, Hamida Bano was the first cousin of Zulfiqar Khan. Hamida Bano's mother, Malika Bano and Zulfiqar's mother Mehr-un-Nisa Begum were the daughters of Asaf Khan. Compare *M. U.*, I, pp. 277–78, 311 and II, p. 93.

[6] On 27 March 1709, Chin Qilich Khan was ordered to join Asad Khan and assist him in the proposed expedition against the Rathors of Jodhpur. But Chin Qilich Khan and Asad Khan held divergent views on the Rajput question. Asad Khan advocated a policy of reconciliation with the Rajputs while Chin Qilich Khan was for total war against them. Kamwar, f. 312b; M. M., f. 58a; *Dastur-ul-Amal*, f. 188a.

vince.[7] The *diwan* was again an associate of Zulfiqar Khan and
thus independent of and a check on Chin Qilich Khan .[8] Since
these privileges did not suggest any institutional change in the
position of the governor, his successors were not allowed to
combine these with their governorships of Awadh.[9]

Chin Qilich Khan perhaps calculated that since a difficult
and 'thorny' (*khardar*) province was entrusted to him, his position as governor would be, at least, *on par* with the powers of
Zulfiqar Khan in the Deccan,[10] if he was not to be given an
important office at the centre.[11] Bahadur Shah not only saw
Chin Qilich's claims in the context of the old nobles' ambitions
and ignored his plea for a high position at the centre, but also
failed to take note of the developments in the province. He tried
to play, as is illustrated from the appointment of Zulfiqar
Khan's associates to some of the key offices in Awadh, on the
rivalry between the two factions. It seems that Chin Qilich was
appointed governor and was able to combine additional pri-

---

[7] *Akhbarat* BS, 4th R. Y., pp. 103 and 146. Correspondingly, the *sawar* rank of the *diwan*
was raised from 400/300 to 1400/300 2–3h which implied a proportionate decline in the
conditional *sawar* rank of Chin Qilich Khan.

[8] Ibid., 1st R. Y., p. 118; Yahya, f. 115a.

[9] Abu Nasr Khan and Shamsher Khan had preceeded Chin Qilich Khan as governors in Awadh under Bahadur Shah. Though Abu Nasr Khan (4 August 1707) was an
important member of a powerful group, the family of Asad Khan, he hardly obtained
any additional privileges as governor. He had not held any *faujdari* and his *mansab* at his
death had only been 3000/2000/500 2–3h. Shamsher Khan had held the *faujdari* of
Gorakhpur as well, but his appointment was a temporary arrangement. In fact it was a
case of a *faujdar* ordered to look after the affairs of the *suba* temporarily. *Akhbarat*
BS, 1st R. Y., pp. 18, 48 and 53. For Abu Nasr Khan's relations with the family of Asad
Khan see *M. U.*, I, pp. 292 and 814; II, pp. 93 and 690; *T. Muhammadi*, pp. 14, 22 and
137. For Chin Qilich's successors, Ali Quli Khan and Muhammad Amin Khan's
appointments see Kamwar, ff. 308 and 326b; *Akhbarat* BS, 4th R. Y. , p. 339 and *M. U.*,
III, pp. 627–32.

[10] In 1708 Zulfiqar Khan was made governor of the Deccan with full authority in all
revenue and administrative matters pertaining to the Deccan. Moreover Zulfiqar
Khan was allowed to remain at the court and to combine his viceroyalty with the office
of *mir bakhshi*. Cf. Satish Chandra, *Parties and Politics*, pp. 43–4.

[11] Chin Qilich had an eye on the office of *wizarat* which explains his close relations
with Prince Azim-ush-Shan even during his retirement. Azim-ush-Shan used to see
him frequently and promised him that, if ever he became emperor he would make him
his *wazir*. It seems that the prince had marked him out as a man whose personality and
influence could well be used against Zulfiqar Khan whose overweening authority he
regarded with intense dislike.' Cf. Yusuf Husain, *The First Nizam*, reprint, Bombay, p.
41.

vileges precisely because the emperor wanted to keep, at least some of the old nobles with high pretensions away from the centre. Bahadur Shah was not prepared to allow any change in the existing frame of the province's relations with the centre. As for the case of Zulfiqar Khan, it was in an altogether different situation that unprecedented powers were granted to him as governor of the Deccan. Bahadur Shah had been in the Deccan and had had first hand experience of its problems. He had opposed the annexation of Golconda.[12] After his accession, he had agreed to give Bijapur and Golconda to Prince Muhammad Kam Bakhsh on the condition that coins should be struck and the *khutba* read in the name of the Mughal Emperor.[13] In Bahadur Shah's assessment, the Deccan, thus, had a special position and was to be only loosely integrated into the empire. On the other hand, the case of Awadh was entirely different. Bahadur Shah had never been in Awadh. Again, he seems to have regarded the northern provinces which formed part of the division of the empire bequeathed to him in the famous will of Aurangzeb,[14] as the core of the empire and therefore believed in having full control over them. For this reason he was probably more concerned with the Rajput and Sikh questions than that of Marathas.

Chin Qilich Khan thus again resigned, this time even from the imperial service.[15] But significantly this time his resignation followed his dismissal from the governorship of Awadh. Chin Qilich's resignation created disaffection among his associates. With him therefore a number of his associates also resigned.[16] In

[12] J. N. Sarkar, *History of Aurangzeb*, Calcutta, 1919, Vol. IV, pp. 362–5.

[13] K. K., II, p. 608. It appears that it had also become difficult to bring under control the Deccan governors, some of whom had set about entrenching their positions in the province. Compare J. F. Richards, *Mughal Administration in Golconda*, pp. 237–40 for Rustam Dil Khan's ambitions in Hyderabad.

[14] For the will of Aurangzeb for the partition of the empire, see W. Irvine, *Later Moghuls*, I, pp. 5–6.

[15] Kamwar, ff. 322b and 324a; M. M., f. 100a; K. K., p. 674; *Akhbarat* BS, 4th R. Y., p. 254. In the meanwhile, however, some changes in the *faujdaris* seem to have been made to accommodate Chin Qilich Khan. Mirza Muhammad Khan and Qilich Muhammad Khan, for instance, replaced Saif Khan and Mir Abul Qasim as *faujdars* of Bahraich and Khairabad respectively. Cf. Ibid., 4th R. Y., pp. 165 and 301. But the order of his promotion to 7000/7000 was not implemented. Cf. Ibid., 4th R. Y., p. 254 and M. M., f. 100a which mention him as *shash hazari* (rank of 6000) the day he resigned.

[16] K. K., II, p. 665.

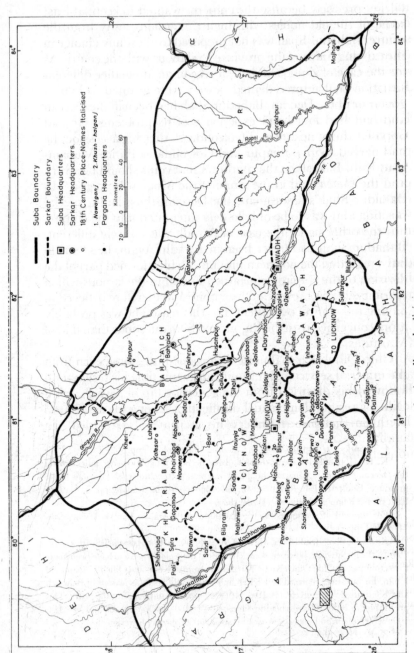

1. Awadh and adjoining areas

the face of the Sikh threat in the vicinity of the capital, the empire could not afford their withdrawal from the imperial service. It was also difficult to satisfy Chin Qilich Khan. A compromise seems to have been worked out in the grant of a *mansab* of 5000/5000/1000 2–3h to his cousin, Muhammad Amin Khan on 14 October 1709.

The developments following the dismissal of Chin Qilich Khan showed that it was no longer possible for the emperor to assert his authority in the old framework of the emperor-noble relationship. In the case of the appointment of Muhammad Amin Khan, it was a faction of the nobility which, for all practical purposes, coerced the emperor to choose him as gover-nor of Awadh,[17] even though he had no additional powers. He was still allowed to stay at the court,[18] in obvious disregard of the requirements of the province. Chin Qilich Khan's indiffer-ence to, or his failure to get adequate help from the centre to deal with, *suba* affairs and Amin Khan's absence from Awadh, however, aggravated the problems for the provincial administ-ration in Awadh.

The beginnings of the new subadari

After the death of Bahadur Shah there seems to be some appreciation of the difficulties of the provincial government. During Muhammad Amin Khan's absence, Mir Musharraf,[19] a local Afghan of Malihabad deputized for him in the province. The appointment of a local man was perhaps because of his familiarity with local problems. In such a situation it was not. unlikely that the privileges which had specially been given to

[17] Especially when initially the name of Shamsher Khan, the erstwhile *faujdar* of Gorakhpur was proposed to succeed Chin Qilich. Cf. Kamwar, f. 324a.

[18] Kamwar, f. 324b; *Akhbarat* BS, 4th R. Y., p. 339. Muhammad Amin Khan did not lose his position at the court. He accompanied the emperor in his campaigns against the Sikhs and governed the province through his deputies. On 7 January 1711, one Zia Khan was ordered to deputize for him in Awadh. Later, he was replaced by Abd-ur-Rasul Khan who was also *faujdar* of Gorakhpur and Khairabad. on 21 October, following a report about the irregularities of Abd-ur-Rasul Khan, he was replaced by a new *naib*. Cf. Kamwar, ff. 326b and 327a; *Akhbarat* BS, 4th R. Y., p. 24; 5th R. Y., pp. 48 and 421. For further favours of Muhammad Amin Khan see *Akhbarat* BS, 5th R. Y., p. 29; Kamwar, f. 328a.

[19] For Mir Musharraf see Chapter VI.

Chin Qilich Khan would become (as indeed they did), part of the governorship of Awadh. Thus, Muhammad Amin Khan's successors, Qilich Muhammad Khan and then Sarbuland Khan held the governorship of Awadh with more than one *faujdari* and some additional authority.[20]

Thus set in, the process of the changes in the position of the governor in the early-eighteenth century. These changes are to be seen in the light of developments both at the court as well as in the province. Sarbuland Khan and after him Chhabele Ram were appointed governors with additional authority as they were close associates of Farrukh Siyar. Still the former's links with the Shaikhzadas of Awadh and the latter's familiarity with the province weighed considerably in their appointments. Sarbuland Khan was expected to use the support of the Shaikh-zadas in meeting the threat of the *zamindar* revolts.[21] Sarbuland Khan, however, failed, despite his efforts to ensure stability in the province by extending some favours to a section of the Shaikhzadas, namely, the *madad-i ma'ash* holders.[22] On 3 July 1714, therefore, he was replaced by Raja Chhabele Ram with an addition of 3000 conditional (*mashrut*) *sawar* to his existing rank of 5000/5000. His nephew, Girdhar Bahadur also came with him and was given the *faujdari* of Bahraich,[23] an important trans-Ghagra *sarkar* of Awadh.

These additional privileges of the new governor were evidently to equip him to deal with the *zamindars* more effectively. However, the prevalent political atmosphere at the court, together, of course, with his growing acquaintance with the nature of provincial problems compelled him to make continued demands for sources of power. A man of the emperor, Chhabele Ram was openly the *wazir's* foe and was fully involved

---

[20] Kamwar, ff. 341; M. M., f. 25a; K. K., II, 693; *Dastur-ul-Amal*, f., 200b; *Akhbarat* BS, 1st R. Y., pp. 103 and 172; *Ajaib*, f. 68a. Qilich Muhammad Khan was appointed in March 1713 and within a few months in October 1713 he was ordered to join Nizam-ul-Mulk in the Deccan while Sarbuland Khan replaced him in Awadh.

[21] For *zamindar* revolts see Chapter III. For Sarbuland Khan's association with the Shaikhs and Saiyids of Bilgram see Chapter VI.

[22] He confirmed all the *mu'afis* indiscriminately, without even asking the grantees to present themselves to the *kachahri*. *Hadiqat*, p. 152.

[23] *Akhbarat* FS, 3rd R. Y., I, pp. 141, 186 and 191; Kamwar, ff. 345b and 346a; *Ajaib*, f. 34b.

in court intrigues.[24] When Chhabele Ram was appointed governor, the *wazir* had conceded him additional powers, since he did not want him to be in power at the court. Now that the rift between the *wazir* and the emperor widened, Chhabele Ram also secured the office of the provincial *diwan* for one of his close relations, Anand Ram Brahman,[25] This was an obvious case of erosion of the centre's authority over the province, even if the emperor perhaps only intended to contain the *wazir*, the *diwan* in the province who represented the *wazir* had usually been an important check on the governor.

Chhabele Ram led more than one successful expedition against the *zamindars*, but the province does not seem to have been restored to stability. In order to maintain orderliness in the *suba*, he wanted his governorship extended and a few more *faujdaris* added to it. Chhabele Ram also expected to combine with his existing offices the governorship of Allahabad and an increase in his *mansab*.[26] But his petition, notwithstanding the emperor's support, was accepted only marginally.[27] After about one and a half years of struggle for additional power and longer tenure, Chhabele Ram was then transferred to Allahabad.[28]

[24] In this connection it is interesting to note the developments at the court that attended Chhabele Ram's appointment in Awadh. It seems that the governorship of Awadh was given or at least promised to him as early as 1712 when he deserted Prince Azz-ud-Din and joined Farrukh Siyar at Kora. (Shivdas, f. 3a; Mubarak, f. 77b and *Tarikh-i Shahanshahi*, Buhar MS, f. 14b). Later, however, the situation took a new turn at Agra and relations between the emperor and Saiyid Abdullah Khan, the *wazir*, began to deteriorate. At this juncture Farrukh Siyar asserted his authority and appointed his dependable followers—Afzal Khan and Chhabele Ram—to the offices of *sadr* and *Diwan-i tan-o-khalisa* respectively. Saiyid Abdullah Khan objected to these appointments on the grounds that they were a violation of his power as *wazir*. A compromise was finally reached. Chhabele Ram got the *subadari* of Agra but he seems to have remained at the court and governed the province through his deputy. He was deputed to accompany Saiyid Husain Ali Khan in the imperial campaign against the Rathors of Jodhpur. The antagonism between the emperor and the *wazir* became more acute during the campaign. According to some of our sources, Ajit Singh, the Rathor chief, was secretly directed by Farrukh Siyar to kill Husain Ali Khan. Chhabele Ram's send off to Awadh was thus an attempt by the *wazir* to keep the emperor's followers at a distance from the court. For details see Satish Chandra, *Parties and Politics*, pp. 103–4 and W. Irvine, *Later Moghuls*, I, pp. 286 and 292.

[25] *Akhbarat* FS, 3rd R. Y., I, p. 240. Within a month the *faujdari* of Lucknow was also assigned to Anand Ram. Anand Ram moved with Chhabele Ram to Allahabad and finally with Girdhar Bahadur to Malwa where he died fighting against the Marathas in the battle of Amjhara in November 1728. *T. Muhammadi*, p. 70.

The governorship of Chhabele Ram (July 1714–October 1715) has much significance for our argument. For the first time in our period, the governor by having his loyal supporter as *diwan* of the province tried to be virtually supreme in Awadh. Again, it was he who first made an attempt to secure the governorship for a longer term. It was done largely with a view to securing greater strength so that he might govern the province effectively. It is also not unlikely that he thus sought a base in case of his and his master's defeat in their battle against the *wazir*. This was what he later tried to do as the governor of Allahabad.[29] Further, his attempt to govern both Awadh and Allahabad together may not be construed as the mere ambition of an individual. In view of disturbances in Baiswara region which extended to Allahabad *suba* as well, it was an administrative necessity. Later Burhan-ul-Mulk and Safdar Jang made every possible effort gradually to acquire the whole of the province of Allahabad.[30]

Chhabele Ram attempted a major break from established Mughal convention. He failed, but his governorship set a precedent. An incident of conflict between his successor, Muzaffar Ali Khan,[31] and the *diwan* over the *sair* (taxes other than land revenue) of the areas earmarked for *jagir* assignment (*paibaqi*) in

---

[26] *Ajaib*, ff. 36–7.

[27] Thus while the *faujdari* of Khairabad was given to him, the *faujdari* of Lucknow was taken away from Anand Ram and was awarded to Mir Musharraf. This was done at the *wazir*'s instance, for Mir Musharraf had close links with the Saiyid Brothers. Subsequently, on Chhabele Ram's protest Farrukh Siyar cancelled Mir Musharraf's appointment. The emperor's plea was that since the beginning of his reign the governorship of Awadh included the *faujdari* of Lucknow as well. But ironically within a few weeks, one Hashim Khan was appointed to the *diwani*, *amini* and *faujdari* of Lucknow. Akhbarat FS, 4th R. Y., I, pp. 97, 155; Allahabad 1316; *Ajaib*, ff. 67b–68.

[28] Kamwar, f. 350a; *Ajaib*, f. 42a.

[29] In 1719, after the deposition of Farrukh Siyar, Chhabele Ram refused to submit to the Saiyids. He instigated an uprising at Allahabad and compelled the Saiyids to negotiate with him. Cf. W. Irvine, *Later Moghuls*, II, pp. 6–16, Satish Chandra, *Parties and Politics*, pp. 145–7.

[30] See Chapter VII.

[31] He was appointed on 28 October 1715, Kamwar, f. 349b. Saiyid Muzaffar Ali Khan is to be distinguished from Muzaffar Khan, the brother of Samsam-ud-Daulah and Saiyid Muzaffar Khan Barha. Later in the 4th R. Y. of Muhammad Shah, Saiyid Muzaffar Ali Khan, then *faujdar* of Gwalior, was appointed deputy governor of Agra. Compare Kamwar, 378b.

early 1716 shows the governor's endeavour to control matters relating to the finance of the province. The incident also records the governor's resentment over the possession of executive powers by the *diwan*. The *diwan* in this case held the *faujdari* of Lucknow and in his capacity as *faujdar* he appointed the *kotwal* (police officer) of the city. And yet the governor appointed his own *kotwal* under the pretext of the maintenance of law and order. The emperor when he heard about the dispute, rejected the pleas of both the governor and the *diwan* and directed Samsam-ud-Daulah to nominate the *kotwal* from the centre as was the rule.[32]

The incident illustrates how the provincial governor began to make encroachments into an area which had hitherto been theoretically under the imperial centre. But this was incompatible with the notion of imperial control over the province, and also clashed with the concept of the new *wizarat* of Saiyid Abdullah Khan, the *wazir* of Farrukh Siyar. The *wazir*, therefore, tried to prevent the process from gaining further ground, which in the cases when the governor was not his associate also reinforced the province's estrangement from the centre. During the tenure of the next governor (July 1716–December 1717), his personal presence in Awadh notwithstanding the *diwan* held the deputy governorship of the *suba* as well.[33] The arrangement was intended as a check on the governor. For, in this particular case the governor was Aziz Khan Chaghta[34] who was not only opposed to the *wazir*[35] but was capable of successfully defying him. Aziz Khan was a leader of the Afghans of Shahabad, a *pargana* town in the *sarkar* of Khairabad.

The *wazir* virtually tried to retard a process which was developing in the provinces in response to internal conditions. His attempt provided nourishment to the agencies that weakened imperial control over the province. The attempt far from being aimed at restoring imperial authority was actually geared to promote the interests of a section of the nobility. With the widening gap between the emperor and the *wazir* and his

---

[32] *Akhbarat* FS 5th R. Y., II, p. 258.

[33] Ibid., 6th R. Y., I, pp. 201 and 86.

[34] Kamwar, f. 351b.

[35] Compare Kamwar, p. 318. Aziz Khan Chaghta was one of those nobles who congratulated the emperor on the death of Saiyid Husain Ali Khan in 1720.

faction, the latter apprehended a threat to their position from a powerful local chief being in control of the province with a rank of 6000/6000. Aziz Khan Chaghta was thus transferred (December 1717) to be replaced in quick succession by two of the *wazir*'s associates.[36] Again, in November 1718, when a confrontation between the emperor and the Saiyid brothers was imminent, the governor of Awadh was recalled to the court.[37] This was at the instance of the *wazir* and formed part of his preparations for a final showdown with the emperor. In the meantime Mir Musharraf who had been appointed *faujdar* of Lucknow on 7 September 1718, controlled the province as its deputy governor.[38] On 11 January 1719, Muhammad Amin Khan was directed to go to Awadh and take charge of the governorship of the province.[39] But he did not comply with the imperial order. The *wazir*, instead of pressing ahead, utilized the situation to strengthen his own position.[40] Consequently, for over three months, Awadh remained without

---

[36] They were Khan Zaman and Mahabat Khan. Khan Zaman was appointed on 4 December 1717. He was followed by Mahabat Khan on 12 February 1718. *Akhbarat* FS, 6th R. Y., II, p. 122, 7th R. Y., p. 55; Kamwar, ff. 355; M. M., f. 84a. In 1128/1715–16. Khan Zaman had deputized for the *wazir* in the *suba* of Multan. Mahabat Khan, who had been interned by Zulfiqar Khan in the time of Jahandar Shah, was reinstated by Farrukh Siyar on the recommendation of the Saiyid Brothers. On 13 December 1715, he was appointed *darogha* of the *gurzbardars* with a *mansab* of 4000/3000. On 12 February, 1718, however in the wake of the emperor's bid to remove his adversaries from the court and have loyalists in key posts, Mahabat Khan was replaced by Muhammad Murad Kashmiri, better known as Itiqad Khan. Kamwar, ff. 350a and 355b.

[37] Kamwar, f. 359a; M. M., f. 115b.

[38] Ibid., f. 357b; *Akhbarat* FS, 6th–8th R. Ys., p. 169.　　　　[39] Ibid., f. 359b.

[40] Muhammad Amin Khan's refusal to leave for Awadh can again be appreciated when it is considered against the background of the conflict between the emperor and the *wazir*. In 1714–15 Muhammad Amin Khan had been fully involved in the court intrigues against the *wazir*. He had aspired for the *wizarat*. At length by the end of 1717 he fell under imperial displeasure, was divested of his office of the second *bakhshi* and appointed *subadar* of Malwa. In the meantime, Farrukh Siyar had intensified his pursuits to eliminate the *wazir*. In December 1718 at the suggestion of Nizam-ul-Mulk, Muhammad Amin Khan was recalled to the court. The emperor, however, changed his mind before he arrived at Delhi. Subsequently, orders were sent to him directing his immediate return to Malwa. Amin Khan still proceeded and, on 11 January 1719, he was reported to have camped outside the capital. At this juncture, the *wazir* managed to secure the imperial order for his appointment in Awadh which the latter blatantly turned down. Saiyid Abdullah Khan took full advantage of this incident. Muhammad Amin Khan was deprived of his *mansab* and his son Muhammad Qamar-ud-Din Khan

a full-fledged governor.[41] Again in 1718, for almost the whole year, Awadh was governed by an absentee governor. After their ascendancy, the Saiyid Brothers appointed one of their associates, Mir Musharraf to the governorship of Awadh. But since they feared a strong reaction against the excesses they had committed against Farrukh Siyar, Mir Musharraf was asked to stay at the centre. His young and inexperienced son, Mir Asad Ali Khan *alias* Mir Kallu deputized for him in Awadh.[42]

Thus, developments at the court apart from reflecting the nobles' alienation from the emperor also had a bearing on the province's links to the centre. Factional politics allowed the province to drift from the control of the centre. The circumstances that attended the appointment of the next governor of Awadh are of particular import in this connection. In 1719 Chhabele Ram, the governor of Allahabad, and after his demise his nephew Girdhar Bahadur, revolted against the Saiyids. According to the author of the *Tarikh-i Hindi* Girdhar Bahadur was finally forced to submit to Ratan Chand, the *vakil* of the Saiyids.[43] But significantly enough it was Girdhar who dictated the terms of agreement. He handed over the fort of Allahabad to Ratan Chand on condition that he be appointed to the *subadari* of Awadh along with the office of the *diwan* and the *faujdaris* of the entire province.[44] It is not unlikely that the Saiyids agreed to concede Awadh to Girdhar with unprecedented powers in order to remove him, at whatever cost, from Allahabad. For, an undisturbed control over the road passing through Benaras, Chunar, Allahabad, Kara and Bindki, etc., was indispensable

---

lost his office of *bakshi* of the *ahadis*. Thereafter on 20 January the *wazir* established his own rapprochement with Muhammad Amin Khan and thus secured at least his neutrality in the coming conflict. According to some sources Muhammad Amin Khan was one of those who advised Husain Ali Khan to depose Farrukh Siyar. Cf. Satish Chandra, *Parties and Politics*, pp. 111–16 and 141; W. Irvine, *Later Moghuls*, I, pp. 294–302 and 365–7.

[41] On the day of Farrukh Siyar's deposition, even Mir Musharraf, the deputy governor of Awadh is reported to have been present in Delhi. Kamwar, f. 362a.

[42] Shivdas, ff. 35b and 36a.

[43] *T. Hindi*, ff. 240a–240b.

[44] Shivdas, f. 35b; K. K., p. 946; Mubarak, f. 110b. Also Rs 3,00,000 were paid to Girdhar as war indemnity.

to ensure safe passage of the Bengal treasury to the Mughal court.[45]

In this case it was not the emperor nor even a faction of the nobility but the governor himself who chose the province. This was certainly not inconsistent with developments at the centre where nobles endeavoured to dictate the course of state action.[46] However, the method of Girdhar's posting was irreconcilable with sixteenth-seventeenth century Mughal convention when governor's appointment followed unfettered from the will of the emperor, even though initiatives for it sometimes came on the recommendation of certain nobles. Girdhar's governorship was self-earned which included the rights of *diwani* and *faujdari* as well. This was the beginning of the new *subadari* in Awadh. But even though Girdhar was the first new *subadar* in Awadh, the chief constituents of the new *subadari*—long tenure, full authority in financial, administrative and military matters were evident in the aspirations of Chhabele Ram and possibly Muzaffar Ali Khan.

Subadari along with *faujdari* was not an absolutely new phenomenon in the history of the provincial administration of the Mughals. The governor in a few cases in the late-seventeenth and the early-eighteenth centuries, combined his office with one or the other *faujdari*.[47] In Awadh in this period, however, more than one important *faujdari* consistently remained under the control of the governor. A phenomenon which began as a privilege developed in the wake of the *zamindar* disturbances into an administrative necessity, as an essential part of

[45] See Chapter VII. Control over the road from Benaras to Delhi passing through Lucknow and Bareilly was also a factor which later enabled Burhan-ul-Mulk to shape his relations with the centre on his terms.

[46] See Chapter I, Section II.

[47] In 1690 Himmat Khan, the governor of Awadh, held the *faujdari* of Gorakhpur as well. Compare *Maasir-i Alamgiri*, Eng. tr. by Jadunath Sarkar, Calcutta, 1947, p. 202. Himmat Khan's successors, however, did not combine any *faujdari* with their governorship. Cf. Ibid., pp. 223, 241, 279 and 307. However, in 1702, the *faujdari* of Jaunpur (a *sarkar* of *suba* Allahabad) was assigned to Murad Khan, the then *subadar* of Awadh, for a short period. Also Sipahdar Khan, the governor of Allahabad (1696–1702) held the *faujdaris* of Benaras (1696), Rae Bareli (1701) and Jaunpur (1702). Cf. S. N. Sinha, *Subah of Allahabad, under the Great Mughals*, Delhi, 1974, pp. 89–90; Chetan Singh examines this at length in 'Socio-Economic Conditions in Panjab during the Seventeenth Century', an unpublished Ph. D. thesis submitted to the Jawaharlal Nehru University, New Delhi, 1984, pp. 59–118.

the *subadari*. The governor's endeavour was to keep *faujdaris*, if not under his own charge, at least in the control of his associates.

The governor's urge for a change in his position may also be seen in the light of a new practice which seems to have gained ground towards the close of the seventeenth century. In the last years of Aurangzeb's reign, a number of *jagirdars* of Baiswara had *faujdari* rights over their *jagir mahals*. As the perspectives of these *jagirdars*-cum-*faujdars* were very narrow, their chief aim having been to assure themselves of undisturbed realization of the revenue of their *jagirs*, they did not hesitate to come to terms with the *zamindars*. This imposed certain constraints on the exercise of powers by the regular *faujdars* and even the *subadar* and this amounted to legitimizing dual authority in the province.[48] The governor, by arrogating *faujdaris* for himself or to his dependable associates, sought to restore stability and orderliness in the province. This, the governor believed, would meet the substance of the *jagirdar's* demand too. For, it was in an atmosphere of uncertainty and inefficiency that the practice of combining *faujdari* with *jagirdari* rights had begun to evolve. Similarly, with his control over the office of the *diwan*, the governor intended to keep a check on the distribution of revenues and *jagirs* in the province.

It may also be noted that in Awadh it was the governor and not the *diwan*, as in Bengal, who gave a new direction to the links between the province and the imperial centre. It is true that the *diwan*, at least for a brief period in Farrukh Siyar's reign, tried to assume a dominant position. The conflict between Saiyid Muzaffar Ali Khan and the *diwan* showed the latter's endeavour to emulate the example of Murshid Quli Khan, the *diwan* of Bengal. But not even by equipping him with executive and military rights over certain areas (deputy governorship and *faujdari*) could the *wazir* help him succeed, as did the *diwan* of Bengal, in his bid to reduce the stature of the governor. For, it

[48] Compare *Roshan Kalam*, p. 7. How this created difficulties for the regular officials is evident from the following passage from a letter of Rad Andaz Khan which gives the details of the problems he was faced with in the *parganas*: 'The *jagirdars* who possess *faujdari* rights over their *jagirs* have given shelter to the robbers in their *mahals*. These robbers are playing havoc in and around these places, especially in the *jagir* of Aziz Khan whose agent, Mahmud is (a leader of) robbers. What is the remedy?' Ibid., p. 22.

was not merely the question of the ambition of one or the other individual. The *diwan*'s unprecedented powers in Bengal grew out of the restructured revenue administration in that province. By transferring most of the *jagirs* to Orissa and by introducing and encouraging a new pattern of revenue administration, Murshid Quli Khan managed to exercise exclusive control over provincial administration in Bengal.[49] On the other hand, no attempt was made to convert the *jagirs* on a large scale into *khalisa* in either Awadh or the Punjab. A large part of the revenue of the Mughal empire including these provinces, had been in *jagirs*. In Awadh, the proportion of *jagir* land to the *khalisa* seems to have gone up in the early-eighteenth century. Towards the end of our period the *khalisa* certainly suffered heavy reductions till its *jama* fell to even less than three per cent of the total *jama* of the province. In the Punjab the proportion of the *khalisa* to the *jagirs* was comparatively high (30 per cent of the total *jama* of the province) in the early-eighteenth century. By the end of Muhammad Shah's reign, however, it declined considerably (about 22 per cent of the total *jama* of the province).[50]

Indeed in Awadh and the Punjab quite a few problems of the provincial administration related to *jagir* administration. The

[49] Cf. Philip C. Calkins, 'Revenue Administration in Bengal' and 'The Revenue of Bengal and the Method of Assessment, 1700–1757', mimeographed.

The extent of Murshid Quli Khan's control over, and his indispensibility in handling the affairs of the *suba* of Bengal can be gauged from the following. In 1708 when Azim-ush-Shan dominated the court, he managed to get Murshid Quli transferred to the Deccan. In 1710, however, Murshid Quli was sent back to Bengal as the *diwan* and the deputy *subadar* of the *suba*. Again, in 1712 when Farrukh Siyar made a claim to the throne at Patna, Murshid Quli proved to be most hostile to his aspirations, yet Farrukh Siyar had to confirm him in his existing office. Moreover, he was made deputy governor to Farkhunda Siyar, the infant princely governor of Bengal and finally in September 1717 he gained the full *subadari* while the office of the *diwan* remained under the control of his relatives. Compare *Akhbarat-i Bahadur Shah*, Sarkar Collection, 19 January 1708 and 20 February 1712; Kamwar, ff. 307b and 320b; Abdul Karim, *Murshid Quli Khan and His Times*, p. 30. Ijad, f. 113b; Salimullah, *Tarikh-i Bangala*, Aligharh transcript, pp. 45, 53, and 68; Ghulam Husain Salim, *Riyaz-us-Saltain*, pp. 263 and 274; Farrukh Siyar sent a detachment under Rashid Khan to march against Murshid Quli and bring back either his treasure or his head. In May 1712 Rashid Khan was killed in a battle outside Murshidabad and his army was routed. J. N. Sarkar, *History of Bengal*, II, pp. 406–7.

[50] Cf. I. O. 4489 and 4506 Pt. II for Awadh. In the mid-eighteenth century in Awadh only 70,60,325 *dams* out of the total *jama* of the province (37,46,74,559 *dams*) remained in

governor in Awadh must have discouraged the continuation of at least some of the *khalisa* lands. For, the *karoris (khalisa* officials) in Awadh were by and large defiant local Shaikhzadas who barely recognized the authority of the governor or the *faujdars.* It is interesting to note that Rad Andaz Khan the *faujdar* of Baiswara in the early-eighteenth century, repeatedly reported to the centre the threat which the arrogant *karoris* posed to the local administration.[51]

The *jagirs* in a measure, also created conditions to the advantage of a resourceful governor. Although the administration of *jagirs* was largely under the control of the provincial *diwan,* political stability, without which no *mansabdar* could assure himself of his due from his *jagir,* depended on the efficient and effective operation of the governor's authority. In the wake of weakening imperial authority, the *jagir* thus also enabled the governor to deal with the *jagirdars* on his own terms. This, among other things, facilitated the emergence of the circumstances in which the governor in Awadh effectively took contract of the *jagirs* of all the outsiders in his province. Further, as a rule no *tankhwah jagir* could be made without the signature and seal of either the emperor or the governor.[52] The governor and not the *diwan* would thus command a superior position in the province, so long as the revenue of Awadh remained predominantly in *jagirs* of the *mansabdars.*

---

khalisa (66,28,125 *dams* from the *mal* and 432,200 *dams* from the *sair*). These *dams* were spread in the following *parganas*: Amethi, Bangar Mau and Jahangirabad in Lucknow *sarkar; Haveli* Khairabad, Bharwara(?), Laharpur, Hargam and Kherigarh in Khairabad *sarkar;* the town of Awadh (Ayodhya) in Awadh *sarkar; Haveli* Gorakhpur and Ramgarh-Gauri in Gorakhpur *sarkar.* Four *mahals,* namely, Behra, Rajhat, Sujauli and Dang-Dun, in Bahraich *sarkar* were earmarked for *sarf-e khas.* It may also be noted that five of six *sair mahals* were unassessed (*bila qaid-i dami*) and therefore the *jama* of these five *mahals* is not available.

For the Punjab two *jama* figures of the *khalisa* are available. According to one figure, apparently of the early years of Muhammad Shah's reign (1720s), 30,31,90,415 *dams* of the total *jama* of the province (1,06,64,19,937 *dams*) were in *khalisa.* By the 1740s, only 22,14,19,492 *dams* of the total had been left in the *khalisa.* These *dams* were spread over 91 *mahals* (31 *mal mahal* and 60 *sair mahals*) in the five Doabs and the *Biruni Panjnad.* Cf. I. O. 4488 and 4506 Pt. I. See also Irfan Habib, *Agrarian System,* pp. 271–3 for the general proportion of the *khalisa* to the *jama* of the empire in the seventeenth century.

[51] *Roshan Kalam,* pp. 6, 11, 15 and 19–20.

[52] *M. U.,* II, p. 61 in the context of the Deccan where developments towards provincial autonomy occurred on similar lines. It may be noted that the *jagirdars* demanded

II The Punjab

The issues and the institutions over which the conflict between
the central and the provincial authorities arose in Awadh and
the Punjab had some similarities during the earlier phase of our
study, even though the Punjab had three governors in the
period under review as against fifteen in Awadh. But the long
tenure of the governor in the Punjab at this stage did not signify
any institutional change in the pattern of provincial administration. It shows merely the strength of the governor's lobby at the
court and the extension of the infighting among the nobility to
the province. Towards the end of this phase, however, the
events in the Punjab began to take a different course which we
shall see later in Chapter V.

The Punjab and the case for imperial control

For various reasons, from the beginning of our period, the
dominant but mutually hostile sections of the nobility were
actively interested in retaining a measure of control over one or
the other area of the Punjab. In 1707 Prince Muhammad
Muazzam (Bahadur Shah) was the governor of the Punjab and
Kabul, and Mun'im Khan was his *naib* in the Punjab. Mun'im
Khan also held the post of *diwan* of the province.[53] After
Bahadur Shah's accession to the throne, Mun'im Khan, being
the chief architect of the new emperor's victory was made *wazir*
and for Asad Khan, erstwhile *wazir* of the empire, the old office
of *vakil* was revived. In the face of a strong *wazir*, the office of
vakil carried little weight and its revival, as we know, was
primarily motivated by the necessity for conciliating the leaders
(Asad Khan himself and his son, Zulfiqar Khan) of a powerful
group of the old nobility at the court.[54] Asad Khan's appointment to the *subadari* of Lahore (26 July 1707), in addition to his

---

faujdari rights over their *jagirs* as and when the provincial administration became
unable to keep order and enforce revenue collections. See J. F. Richards, *Mughal
Administration in Golconda*, pp. 196–8 for an explanation for such developments in the
Hyderabad province at the end of the seventeenth century.

[53] *M. U.*, III, p. 668.

[54] For details see Satish Chandra, *Parties and Politics*, pp. 25–6, W. Irvine, *Later
Moghuls*, I. pp. 37–40.

office of *vakil*, which had so far been under Mun'im Khan very
likely formed part of the conciliation. It is also possible that the
emperor tried, even though it was not so evident as in the case of
Chin Qilich Khan, to divert Asad Khan's attention from the
centre to a province.

As Asad Khan aspired to hold a key position at the court and
was too old to govern the province in person, the struggle for
power in the Punjab initially centred around the office of the
deputy governorship (*niyabat*). Further, a number of important
faujdaris, e.g., Jammu, Beth Jalandhar and *chakla* Gujarat were
also at issue between the *wazir* and Asad Khan. Some of the
major offices in the Punjab were under the control of the governor's associates.[55] This was, however, in consideration of Asad
Khan's personal status.

When Asad Khan tried to maintain actual power both at the
centre and in the province, he was ordered to stay away from
the court in Delhi and Mun'im Khan, the *wazir* was allowed to
impose a check upon him. Asad Khan's associate[56] who held the
office of *niyabat* and the *faujdari* of Jammu was replaced by an
associate[57] of the *wazir*. Later when Asad Khan tried to mollify
the emperor, his associate was reinstated to the *niyabat*.[58] But
the *faujdari* of Jammu and for that matter even some other
important *faujdaris* of the province like Beth Jalandhar, *chakla*
Gujarat, Emanabad and Wazirabad remained outside the control of Asad Khan. It may be noted that Jammu and Jalandhar
were not only large in size but also occupied a special position as
a number of the chieftains in the Punjab came under the
jurisdiction of these *faujdaris*, while the revenue of *chakla* Gu-

[55] Compare *Akhbarat* BS, 1st R. Y, p. 132 and 3rd and 4th R. Ys., pp. 2 and 75 for the
office of *kotwal* of Lahore to Mir Abd-us-Salam and Sultan Ali Khan, associates of Asad
Khan's son, Zulfiqar Khan.

[56] Kamwar, f. 311b. He was Mir Khan, a son-in-law of Bahramand Khan who was a
son-in-law of Asad Khan. *M. U.*, I, pp. 456–7.

[57] He was Dil Diler Khan, a brother of Lutfullah Sadiq who had risen under the
patronage of Mun'im Khan. In the reign of Jahandar Shah when Zulfiqar Khan, Asad
Khan's son, came to power Lutfullah lost his position and even his house was confiscated. Later, however, he managed to regain his position under Farrukh Siyar.
Compare *M. U.*, III, p. 177.

[58] *Akhbarat* BS, 4th R. Y., p. 445 and 4th–5th R. Ys., p. 435. For Asad Khan's two
arzdashts to the emperor in 1709 see, Kamwar, ff. 311b and 317a.

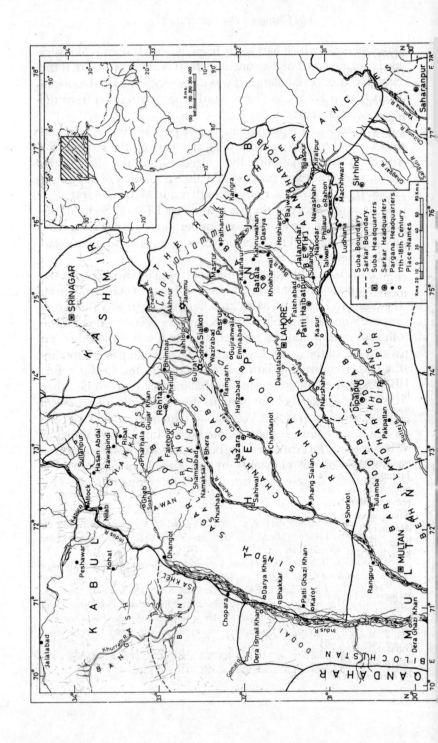

jarat, Emanabad and Wazirabad sustained a substantial part of the imperial expenditure in Kabul.[59]

The imperial policy of not allowing the privileges of the governor to grow into a new source of strength is further illustrated from the appointments in the province in 1711, when following the death of Mun'im Khan (28 February 1711), Prince Muhammad Azim-ush-Shan assumed supreme position at the centre. Asad Khan's associates in the province seem to have been gradually replaced by persons who for one or the other reason were attached to the prince, then the real authority behind the emperor.[60] Besides, some replacements at different levels took place in the office of the *bakhshi waqai'nigar*.[61] The office of the *bakhshi waqai'nigar*, not only formed part of the imperial intelligence but also maintained the provincial army's connection with the centre and was thus a major check upon the local officials.

These changes may be seen in the light of the emperor's

[59] *M. U.*, I, p. 205; *Akhbarat* BS, 3rd R. Y., p. 193, 3rd–4th R. Ys., p. 15 for Beth Jalandhar; for *chakla* Gujarat, Wazirabad and Emanabad, see *Akhbarat* BS, 1st R. Y., pp. 97. 103 and 143; 3rd–4th R. Ys., p. 116 in the volume entitled Aurangzeb I; 4th R. Y., p. 116; 4th R. Y., pp. 369 and 448; Kamwar, 307b, 324b and 330. The *faujdar* of Gujarat belonged to the family of an eminent orthodox Hanafi theologian of Agra (*T. Muhammadi*, pp. 21 and 75; *Majma-un-Nafais*, Rampur MS., f. 326b) and the *faujdar* of Emanabad was related to Inayatullah Kashmiri who had quarrelled with Asad Khan's son, Zulfiqar Khan. *M. U.*, I. pp. 319–20, II, p. 830.

[60] For example, Jahandar Shah who had good relations with Asad Khan was replaced by Hoshdar Khan, an associate of Mun'im Khan, in the *faujdari* of Beth Jalandhar. (October 1711). In January 1712, Rustam Dil Khan who had been appointed to the *qiladari* of Kangra on the recommendation of Zulfiqar Khan, was removed from office. The office of the *kotwal* of Lahore, hitherto held by Sultan Ali Khan, an associate of Zulfiqar Khan, was ultimately assigned to Muttalib Khan. *Akhbarat* BS, 5th R. Y., I, p. 259; II, pp. 318, 342, 441 and 476; Kamwar, f. 330a. For biographical notices of Rustam Dil Khan and Muttalib Khan's association with Mun'im Khan and Azim ush-Shan, see, Kamwar, ff. 329b and 336b; *M. U.*, II, pp. 650–1.

[61] In July 1711, for instance, Latatat Khan *Azim-ush-Shani* was made *bakshi waqai'nigar* of Lahore while Rahimullah Khan was appointed the *waqai'nigar* of the province. Within three months, Fakhr-ud-Din, was transferred from Delhi to Lahore as the *bakhshi waqai'nigar* of the entire Punjab. *Akhbarat*, BS 5th R. Y., I, pp. 235, 238 and 396; *T. Muhammadi*, p. 96. Fakhr ud-Din was a brother of Qutb-ud-Din, the *faujdar* of Gujarat, and thus disliked Asad Khan. Rahimullah Khan was a maternal nephew who was imprisoned at Zulfiqar Khan's instance in Jahandar Shah's time. *T. Muhammadi*, p. 75; Kamwar, p. 159.

attempt to keep the ambition of the nobles in check. Asad Khan's son, Zulfiqar Khan had again staked his father's claim to the *wizarat*. He thus aspired to combine in his family the two highest offices of the centre—the *wizarat* and the *mir bakhshi*-ship together with the viceroyalty of the Deccan and the gover-norship of an important northern province. However, the grow-ing Sikh menace also had obvious connections with these at-tempts. Asad Khan and Zulfiqar Khan were inclined to deal with the Sikh question cautiously and tactfully. Asad Khan had failed to give a prompt and efficient response to a *farman* from Bahadur Shah in early 1711. The emperor, therefore, struck at his control over the intelligence and the army organization in the province, and wrested from his associates, the *faujdari* and the *qiladari* in the areas affected by Sikh activities.

It will be seen that during the first phase of our period, namely, Bahadur Shah's reign, the governorship of the Punjab, as of Awadh, was vested in the leader of a powerful but dis-satisfied faction of the nobility. In both cases, the emperor tried to control the ambitions of the governors even though they had certain privileges. Two peculiar factors, however, distinguished the case of the Punjab. In the first place, Mun'im Khan, the *wazir*, keenly followed developments in the Punjab, since he had served there and recognized the importance of Delhi's control over the province for the north-western frontiers of the empire. Indeed, with a view to retaining imperial authority over the province, Mun'im Khan tried to win over some powerful nobles with a local base in the Punjab, and place them in authority in or around the province.[62]

Towards provincial independence

However, Mun'im Khan's attempt at encouraging the regional magnates as important officials in the locality is also to be

---

[62] For example Iradat Khan, a son-in-law of Mir Sanjar of Lahore was appointed *faujdar* of Beth Jalandhar on Mun'im Khan's recommendation. Iradat Khan's son Hoshdar Khan held the *faujdari* of Nur Mahal. Also, for Ibrahim Khan who belonged to Sodhra, a town in the Punjab, Mun'im Khan secured from the emperor the title of Ali Mardan Khan and the governorship of Kabul. Ibrahim Khan had specially been helped by Mun'im Khan when he had been asked to give explanation for certain irregularities he had committed in Bengal. *M. U.*, I. pp. 205 and 300; III, p. 833. Bindraban Das 'Khushgo', *Safina-i Khushgo* (ed. A. Rahman, Patna, 1959), p. 84. Mir

viewed against the background of the cases of the successful defiance of imperial directives by certain domiciled *jagirdars*.[63]

The geographic and economic position of the province was the second phenomenon, obviously not peculiar to any one phase of our period, which influenced the pattern of the Punjab's relations with the imperial centre. The Mughal province of the Punjab occupied a central place in the entire region beyond the Sutlej which had an access to the sea or led to Central Asia through trade routes. For a fuller authority over the Punjab, the provinces of Multan, Kashmir and Kabul had to be protected from occupation by hostile forces. The route from Kabul and Kashmir to Delhi passed through the Punjab and the latter had vital commercial links with these provinces, while any *zamindar* revolt in Multan might well disturb the south-western districts of the Punjab. In a period when the nobles had begun to look for avenues to build their own bases in the provinces the passing of any one of these provinces into the control of a powerful noble was likely to be a serious threat to imperial control of the Punjab. Asad Khan resisted the appointment of Ibrahim Khan, an associate of the *wazir*, to the governorship of Kabul. Prince Jahandar Shah, a friend of Zulfiqar Khan, was governor of Multan throughout the reign of Bahadur Shah while Jafar Khan *alias* Kamgar Khan, a maternal cousin of Asad Khan, held the governorship of Kashmir until his death on 22 August 1709.[64] Interestingly, Asad Khan and Zulfiqar Khan prudently withdrew from the Punjab in Jahandar Shah's reign when the governors of Multan, Thatta and Kashmir were appointed on Khan Jahan Kokaltash's sug-

---

Sanjar of Mashhad was a *Naqshbandi* sufi and yet is reported to be a Shi'a. He died in Lahore in 1105 A. H. *T. Muhammadi*, p. 5.

[63] The case of Muhammad Athar Khan of Wazirabad illustrates the tendency. In 1711, Athar Khan continued to be the *faujdar* and *jagirdar* of *pargana* Wazirabad, even though he had been officially replaced by Qutb-ud-Din Khan and his *jagir* converted into *khalisa*. An imperial order of 8 July 1711, eventually had to legitimize his *de facto* position in the *pargana*. Athar Khan could successfully flout the imperial order because he had strong social ties in the locality. He was the son of Hakim Ilm-ud-Din, entitled Wazir Khan, an eminent noble of Aurangzeb's reign. Wazir Khan hailed from Chanaut, a *qasba* in the Punjab, in the neighbourhood of which he founded the town of Wazirabad. *Akhbarat* BS, 5th R. Y., I, p. 92. For Hakim Ilm-ud-Din see *M. U.*, III, pp. 933–6; see also *T. Muhammadi*, pp. 90 and 126.

[64] *M. U.*, III, p. 833; see also II, p. 90; Kamwar, ff. 307b, 315a and 318a; *T. Muhammadi*, p. 27; III, p. 159.

gestion.[65] These were no ordinary changes, as Kokaltash was a favourite of the emperor and, having long held the deputy governorship of Multan and Thatta, had developed interests in the region. Since Zulfiqar Khan had high access in the new regime, he managed to secure Gujarat province for his father, possibly to strengthen his own position as viceroy of the Deccan.[66]

Asad Khan's withdrawal from the Punjab was also forced by the growing realization of his inability to deal with the Sikhs. At whatever cost, the emperor and a host of the nobles, unlike Asad Khan, were for an all out war against the Sikhs. This is illustrated from the appointment of Abd-us-Samad Khan by Farrukh Siyar. Zabardast Khan who had succeeded Asad Khan in Jahandar Shah's time did not fail to express his loyalty to the next Emperor, Farrukh Siyar.[67] Nonetheless, he was replaced by Abdu-us-Samad Khan[68] while Saiyid Abdullah Khan, the *wazir*, secured for himself the provinces of Multan

[65] *Akhbarat*, miscellaneous, II, p. 46; Kamwar, f. 337a.

[66] *M.U.*, III, p. 802; Kamwar, f. 337a; *Akhbarat*, JS, p. 22. It is interesting to note that Zulfiqar Khan as well as Husain Ali Khan and Nizam-ul-Mulk who aspired for more than a mere *subadari* in the Deccan, manipulated to have Gujarat, very likely due to its richness and strategic importance, under the control of their own men. Sarbuland Khan was first chosen by Kokaltash to deputize for Asad Khan in Gujarat. But he was soon replaced by Daud Khan, a protégé of Zulfiqar Khan. When Saiyid Husain Ali Khan held the viceroyalty of the Deccan, Ajit Singh, an associate of the Saiyid Brothers, governed Gujarat, with a brief break in 1717 when Khan Dauran held it. In the wake of the appointments and promotions following the decline of the Saiyid Brothers, Haidar Quli Khan, one of those who had planned to assassinate Husain Ali Khan replaced Ajit Singh, as governor of Gujarat. But as soon as Nizam-ul-Mulk, the viceroy of the Deccan, had his way, he managed to secure the governorship of Gujarat for himself. Later, even after the appointment of Shuja'at Khan, Hamid Khan who deputized for Nizam-ul-Mulk in Gujarat resisted handing over the *suba* to the new governor. Cf. Kamwar, ff. 342, 348b, 354a and 379a; W. Irvine, *Later Moghuls* II, pp. 169–89.

[67] As soon as the government of Farrukh Siyar was proclaimed, he sent 500 *ashrafis* to the new emperor. Kamwar, f. 341b.

[68] Abd-us-Samad Khan was a protégé of Zulfiqar Khan. He had served and fought against Azim-ush-Shan with a strong army of 10,000 'Mughals' in the Civil War in 1712 in Lahore. Zulfiqar Khan had reciprocated magnanimously. He raised Abd-us-Samad Khan from obscurity to the high rank of 7000/7000. But Abd-us-Samad Khan escaped the wrath of Farrukh Siyar. Though he could not retain his existing office and the *mansab* he soon managed to reach the highest rung of the nobility under Farrukh Siyar. The 'Mughal' nobles' neutral attitude at Samugarh and much more than that, the necessity of a governor of high military and administrative calibre in the Punjab accounted for Farrukh Siyar's favours to Abd-us-Samad Khan. Cf. Warid, p. 290; *Tarikh-i Shahanshahi*, f. 21a.

and Thatta.[69] For, vigorous military operations were necessary to quell the Sikhs and with Abd-us-Samad Khan who commanded a large Mughal armed contingent, eminent Mughal generals like Muhammad Amin Khan and Aghar Khan were expected to fight. Suppression of the Sikhs is mentioned as the chief objective of Abd-us-Samad Khan's appointment in the Punjab.[70]

We are not sure if Abd-us-Samad Khan came to Lahore with any additional powers. It is, however, interesting to note that by the time of Farrukh Siyar governorship with extended authority had emerged as a major issue of conflict between the governor and the imperial centre. For over two years Abd-us-Samad Khan was engaged in Sikh campaigns and had little time to look after the government of the province.[71] By 1715 when Banda Bahadur, the Sikh leader, had been captured and executed, he was relatively free to attend to the administration. In view of the peculiar problems of the province, he asked for greater control over the province. He failed in his bid, since he belonged to a faction at the court openly opposed to the *wazir* who as governor of Multan and Thatta had his own interests at stake in the region. The *wazir* tried every possible effort to contain the governor. He even overlooked the cases of violation of imperial rule by his associates who were, in consequence, emboldened to neglect their duties under one pretext or another.[72]

The *wazir* also made a bid to place the province in a more amenable hand. Samsam-ud-Daulah, a friend of the *wazir* and

[69] *Ijad*, f. 131a; K. K., II, p. 762; Warid, p. 291; M. M., f. 24b; also see Nur-ud-Din Faruqi, *Jahandar Nama*, Br. M. Or. 3610, f. 62a. *Siyar's* account is confused Cf. II, p. 402. Zabardast Khan died on 23 May 1713, and subsequently his property was escheated. Compare Kamwar, ff. 341b and 343b.

[70] Compare *Ijad*, f. 131a; K. K., II, p. 762; Warid, p. 291 and *Jahandar Nama*, f. 62a.

[71] For his relations with the centre during this period, see, Kamwar, ff. 344a and 345; *Akhbarat* FS, 3rd R. Y., I. p. 239.

[72] In February 1715, for example, Iradatmand Khan was reported to have colluded with the Sikhs in their ravages of the *khalisa* villages in *pargana* Emanabad. The Sikhs had promised him half the booty. Earlier, he had misappropriated half of the revenue of *pargana* Shamsabad. And yet the emperor's order to sack him remained unimplemented, apparently with the *wazir's* connivance. In May 1715, Iradatmand Khan and Mir Muhammad Khan, the *amins* of *khalisa*, paid little attention to a petition of the governor for the payment of Rs 8,00,000 against the pay-claim of a section of the army. *Akhbarat* FS, 4th R. Y., I, p. 131.

the deputy *mir bakhshi*, is reported to have advised the emperor to replace Abd-us-Samad Khan by his brother, Muzaffar Khan and to appoint as deputy governor Isa Khan Mein, a powerful Ranghar Rajput *zamindar* of Beth Jalandhar. But for the protest by the family members of Abd-us-Samad Khan, Samsam-ud-Daulah's scheme would have been carried out. Muhammad Amin Khan resigned from his *mansab* and ceased to visit the court. Subsequently, the emperor, afraid of losing the support of a powerful group of the nobility, persuaded Samsam-ud-Daulah to withdraw his proposal. Samsam-ud-Daulah, however, managed to secure Isa Khan the *faujdari* of Beth Jalandhar.[73] Abd-us-Samad Khan could meet this threat on account of the support of yet another local potentate. Some time in the beginning of 1716 he secured the *faujdari* of *sarkar* Beth Jalandhar for his son, Zakariya Khan and selected Shahdad Khan, a powerful Afghan chief of the province, as the deptuy *faujdar* of the *sarkar*. Isa Khan resisted the new arrangement and in an encounter with Shahdad Khan he was defeated and killed.[74]

The rupture between the centre or the *wazir* and the governor is also illustrated from the *wazir*'s abortive attempt to replace Abd-us-Samad Khan by Mir Jumla.[75] As a result of these developments, Abd-us-Samad Khan grew apprehensive and began to plan, strengthening his position in the province. This

[73] *M. M.*, ff. 50b–51b; K. K., II, p. 767. Isa Khan Mein who had lately risen to power was closely associated with Jahandar Shah. In recognition of his services to Bahadur Shah in the battle of Jaju in 1707, he was given a *mansab* and thus incorporated in the Mughal imperial service. In the reign of Jahandar Shah when he rose to the rank of 5000/5000 and got the *faujdari* of Lakhi Jungle and Jalandhar, he spared no effort to expand his *zamindari* and influence in the Punjab. After Jahandar Shah's defeat, Isa Khan lost his position and became *zortalab*. No *jagirdar* could realize the revenue from his territory which extended from the bank of the Beas to the town of Thara in *sarkar* Sirhind. Besides, he began to plunder the revenue of the neighbouring *parganas* and the caravans that passed through his territory. In a number of encounters, he defeated the armies of the *faujdars*. In the meanwhile, he approached Samsam-ud-Daulah and the latter seems to have further encouraged him in his spoliations. *M. U.*, II, pp. 825–8; M. M., ff. 50b–51b; Warid, pp. 287–8.

[74] Kamwar, f. 350a; *M. U.*, II, pp. 825–28. For Shahdad Khan see *M. U.*, pp. 711–15. Shahdad Khan's victory greatly enhanced the prestige of the governor and a number of refractory *zamindars* are reported to have then surrendered to him.

[75] Khush-hal, p. 386; K. K., II, p. 771; Kamwar, f. 350a. In 1714, as we know, it was decided that Mir Jumla and Husain Ali Khan who never agreed on any issue, would

probably constituted the first major stage in the breakdown of the existing pattern of relationship of the Mughal centre with the Punjab.[76]

Our sources record a number of cases that show the governor's utterly disrespectful attitude to the centre. In one case, the *waqai'nigar* of Jammu who had long been transferred is reported to have refused to hand over the charge to the deputy of the *waqai'nigar*, at the instance of the governor.[77] In an another instance, the *diwan* expressed his inability to maintain the provincial treasury, as the revenue realized from the *parganas* was either misappropriated by the governor or was sent off to Kabul.[78] In a third instance, the governor tried to shirk his responsibility for the maintenance of law and order in those areas of which he had perhaps wanted but failed to obtain the *faujdaris*.[79]

Abd-us-Samad Khan's attitude to the questions of the suc-

---

leave for Bihar and the Deccan respectively. Mir Jumla, however, either at the emperor's instance or on his own, soon returned to Delhi, but the emperor, primarily to appease the *wazir*, had to order him to withdraw to Lahore. For a different version of the context of these orders see Satish Chandra, *Parties and Politics*, pp. 107–12, 118, 119 and 138.;W. Irvine, *Later Moghuls*, I, pp. 301, 330–1 and 352. We have depended mainly on the evidence of Khush-hal which seems to have been overlooked. Mir Jumla, however, did not proceed beyond Sirhind. He probably wanted to avert any conflict with Abd-us-Samad Khan, for he did not want to lose the backing of the Turani nobles who were equally resentful of the rise of the Saiyids and were thus his allies. He realized that his appointment in the Punjab was at the instance of the *wazir* and that the *wazir*'s aim was to create a rift between him and the Turani nobles.

[76] This phase of the governor's relations with the centre is interpreted by a chronicler, whose prejudices are avowedly in favour of the *wazir*, as the governor's love for pleasure and a state of confusion and disorderliness in the *suba*.

[77] *Akhbarat* FS, 4th R. Y., II, p. 54.

[78] Ibid., p. 62.

[79] Thus, in September 1716, the *gurzbardars* (mace-bearers) who were carrying a *khilat* (robes of honour) and some precious presents for Nasir Khan, the governor of Kabul, were robbed of their belongings somewhere near Lahore. Thereafter the *gurzbardars* were directed by the centre to realize as compensation from Abd-us-Samad Khan the *khilat* and the presents and carry them to Kabul. To the subsequent petition of the *gurzbardars*, the governor reacted as follows: 'If His Majesty orders me, I pay the compensation from my own house, otherwise the presents, etc., were plundered in the territory of the *faujdari* of the sons of the late Amir Khan and (hence) they should be interrogated for it.' Subsequently, Amin Khan was directed to write to Abd-us-Samad that his response to the *gurzbardars'* petition was a lame excuse and that as governor he was responsible for whatever happened in the *suba*. He should therefore recover the stolen goods or do something in compensation. *Akhbarat*, FS, 5th R. Y., II, p. 74.

cessor and the left-over assets of Isa Khan is yet another example of how the governor threw the centre's directives overboard.
Isa Khan held a rank and in accordance with the rules his
property was escheated. But the confiscated property of the
deceased, instead of being deposited at the office of the *diwan*,
was reportedly seized by Shahdad Khan, the governor's protégé. Again, the son, the officials of the estate (*peshkar* and
mutasaddi) of the deceased were ordered to be escorted to Delhi.
But the governor, as it was reported on 10 August 1716, refused
to hand them over to the stewards (*sazawala*) of the *diwan*.[80]

The governor thus made attempts to extend his control over
the office of the *diwan*. The *diwan*, as we can presume, was no
longer adequately assisted by the centre in the performance of
his duty, it is not surprising then that he also tried to act as
independently as the governor. Sometime in the beginning of
1717 the *diwan* spent up to Rs 15,000 from the revenue of the
Salt Range, which was according to regulations, reserved for
the emoluments of the soldiers and local officials of Kabul. He
had also begun to neglect his duties and held the *kachahri* only
once a week. However, the *diwan* of the Punjab, unlike his
counterpart in Bengal, could not afford to act on his own
discretion. He lost his position in the province and was summoned to the court.[81]

Since Abd-us-Samad Khan also had the backing of his faction at the centre, Saiyid Abdullah Khan, the *wazir* and
Samsam-ud-Daulah, the deputy *mir bakhshi* could not dislodge
him from the province altogether. Yet they made consistent
efforts to contain him by keeping their own henchmen in control
of important offices in and around the Punjab. Among the

[80] *Akhbarat*, 5th R. Y., II, pp. 3 and 13. According to convention, imperial orders to
high officials in the province were normally communicated through either the
wazir or the *mir bakhshi*. The *hasb-ul-hukms* to Abd-us-Samad Khan therefore were
usually despatched through the Saiyid Abdullah Khan, the *wazir*, and Samsam-ud-
Daulah, the deputy *mir bakhshi*, for the *mir bakhshi* (Husain Ali Khan) had left for the
Deccan. In the existing situation, the emperor probably realized the futility of despatching *hasb-ul-hukms* to Abd-us-Samad Khan through either the *wazir* or Samsam-
ud-Daulah. Muhammad Amin Khan therefore was ordered to intercede and urge the
governor of the Punjab to immediately send the effects of Isa Khan to the court. This
also shows the extent of the influence of court politics on the functioning of provincial
government.

[81] Ibid., 6th R. Y., I, pp. 203, 213; II, p. 139 (14 April 1717).

significant provincial offices we know of, only the *faujdaris* of Jammu and Beth Jalandhar could be placed under the charge of the governor's men.[82] *Diwans* of the province, *faujdars* of Gujarat, Sialkot and Emanabad, *qiladars* and *kotwal* of Kangra and Lahore, all were in one way another associated with the *wazir* or Samsam-ud-Daulah.[83]

The *wazir* retained the governorship of Multan and governed it, through his deputies, throughout the period of his ascendancy.[84] He seems to have taken utmost care in choosing his deputies and assured himself of the absence of any association between them and the governor of the Punjab. It was only after the death of Saiyid Abdullah Khan, when 'Turani' nobles commanded supreme authority at the court that Muhammad Amin Khan, a supporter of Abd-us-Samad Khan, the governor

[82] Even Jammu was once taken away from Zakariya Khan. But the new *faujdar* failed in administering the area and Zakariya Khan had to be reinstated. Earlier, in 1715, the appointment of Ikhlas Khan *walashahi* had imposed a check on Zakariya Khan. *Akhbarat*, FS, 4th R. Y., I, p. 47; 6th R. Y., II, p. 115. *Walashahis*, literally of the exalted king, have been described as the body-guard or defenders of the imperial person. Cf. W. Irvine, *Army of the Indian Moghuls*, pp. 43–4.

[83] Saif-ud-Din Barha (appointed on 2 March 1713) and Abd-un-Nabi Barha (appointed on 16 March 1713) were *faujdar* of Gujarat and *qiladar* of Lahore respectively, while the *faujdari* of Emanabad was held by Saiyid Iradatmand Khan (appointed on 26 February 1713 on the recommendation of the *wazir*) and following him by Khiradmand Khan of Hansi (appointed on 24 September 1717), an associate of Samsam-ud-Daulah.

Sa'adat Kar Khan, *kotwal* of Lahore, (appointed on 15 April 1713), Altaf Khan, *qiladar* of Kangra, (appointed on 30 June 1713) being Indian Muslims had links with the *wazir* and Samsam-ud-Daulah. Ghulam Husain, *faujdar* of kalbhalak (appointed on 5 May 1714), Muhammad Husain, *amin faujdar* of Sialkot (appointed on 13 July 1714), and Ikhlas Khan, deputy *faujdar* of Jammu, all *walashahis*, were under the influence of Samsam-ud-Daulah who held the office of the *bakhshi* of the *walashahis*. *Akhbarat*, FS, 1st R. Y., I, pp. 127, 170 and 322; 2nd R. Y. I, p. 147; 3rd R. Y., I, pp. 103, 210; 4th R. Y., I, p. 47; II, p. 207; 6th R. Y., I, pp. 203 and 286; II, p. 139; Kamwar, ff. 329a and 341a; *T. Muzaffari*, f. 209; *T. Muhammadi*, p. 84.

We have information in our sources about three *bakhshi waqai'nigars* of the Punjab in Farrukh Siyar's reign, namely Qasim Khan (appointed on 2 May 1715), Ashraf Khan (appointed on 28 March 1716). None of them seems to have an amicable association with Abd-us-Samad Khan. Qasim Khan and Mahdi Yar Khan were Iranis and Ashraf Khan was an Indian Muslim. *Akhbarat*, FS, 4th R. Y., p. 36 (Sarkar Collection, National Library, Calcutta); 5th R. Y., I, p. 49; 7th R. Y., p. 8; *T. Muhammadi*, pp. 24, 29, 56 and 65.

[84] Dil Diler Khan (16 September 1714 to 29 October 1715), Khan Zaman son of Mun'im Khan (30 October 1715 to 3 November 1716), Aqidat Khan son of Amir Khan (1 December 1716 to October 1719) and Saiyid Hasan Khan Barha (October 1719 to 13 November 1720) deputized for the *wazir* in Multan. Kamwar, ff. 346b, 350a.

of the Punjab, was appointed the governor of Multan.[85] Abd-us-
Samad Khan deputized for him in Multan. Earlier he had
succeeded in securing for Muhammad Amin Khan, the governorship of Thatta, but only for a brief period of about five
months (16 June 1716–11 November 1716). For the rest of the
period Thatta was under the governorship of Raja Ajit Singh
and subsequently Muhammad Azam Khan and Mahabat
Khan, all associates of the *wazir*.[86] The *wazir*, also tried to
replace Nasir Khan, the governor of Kabul, by one of his own
associates, Aizz-ud-Daulah, Khan-i Alam. The arrangement,
however, did not work successfully and Nasir Khan had to be
recalled to Kabul. After his death, however, the *wazir* managed
to appoint Sarbuland Khan as governor of Kabul.[87] The governorship of Kashmir was initially given to Sadat Khan with
Muhammad Azam Khan as his *naib*. With Inayatullah Khan's
return to power in 1716–17, Kashmir came into his possession
and remained so for the rest of this period.[88]

The *wazir*'s endeavour to contain the governor assumed the
guise of establishment of institutional order, but the factional
politics at the court gave it a strong personal dimension. In 1719
when the *wazir* was at the height of his power, he plotted to
eliminate Abd-us-Samad Khan along with his other associates,
such as Muhammad Amin Khan and Nizam-ul-Mulk. Husain
Khan Khweshgi, an Afghan chief of Qasur, was promised a
rank of 7000 *zat* and the governorship of the Punjab, if he
prevailed over and killed Abd-us-Samad Khan.[89] Subsequently,
Qutb-ud-Din Khan, the *amil* of Abd-us-Samad Khan's *jagir* in
and around Qasur, was killed in an encounter and Husain
Khan with an army of about 9000 devastated the villages in the

[85] Kamwar, f. 376a.

[86] Ibid., ff. 347a, 351b, 352a and 365a; *T. Muhammadi*, p. 44.

[87] Ibid., ff. 347b, 359b and 360a. Sarbuland Khan's appointment in Kabul was also a
result of the *wazir*'s compromise with him and formed part of Saiyid Abdullah's scheme
to isolate the emperor from every section of the nobility. For details see Satish
Chandra, *Parties and Politics*, p. 138; W. Irvine, *Later Moghuls*, I, pp. 345–7.

[88] Ibid., ff. 342a, 345a, 354 and 371a.

[89] Qasim, f. 103a. In the wake of disturbed conditions in the late-seventeenth and
early-eighteenth centuries, Husain Khan Khweshgi had consolidated his position in
the Punjab. He expanded his *zamindari* at the expense of numerous weak *zamindars*. In
the reign of Farrukh Siyar he even drove out some of the *amils* of the *jagirdars* from his
territory. Compare Warid, p. 289; K. K., II, p. 861 and *M. U.*, I, pp. 602–3.

parganas of the *jagir* of the governor. In an encounter with the governor at Chhoni, 97 kms from Lahore, Husain Khan was ultimately defeated and killed.[90]

By the beginning of Muhammad Shah's reign, the governor of the Punjab was almost completely estranged from the centre. The congratulatory letters from the *wazir* to Abd-us-Samad Khan on the latter's victory over Husain Khan Khweshgi[91] were simply to allay the apprehensions of the governor. The *wazir* regarded Abd-us-Samad Khan and also Nizam-ul-Mulk as the instigators of the revolts by the old nobility (*khanazads*) in the Punjab and the Deccan respectively.[92]

We have no evidence for any open revolt of the nobility in the Punjab, but Abd-us-Samad Khan had tried to obtain a degree of independence from the centre in administering the province. This engaged his attention to such an extent that he could not give more than a lukewarm response even to the imperial *farman* sent to him after the death of the *wazir*'s brother, Husain Ali Khan, urging him immediately to reach the court and help the emperor overpower the *wazir*, Abd-us-Samad's arch enemy at the court. Abd-us-Samad Khan probably was still apprehensive of the strength of the *wazir*. He therefore thought it more prudent to remain in the province and consolidate his authority.[93] A portion of the letter (*arzdasht*) he sent in reply to the *farman* explaining his inability to arrive at the court, shows the nature of the relations that were to evolve between the Mughal centre and the *suba* of the Punjab:

> ... the army that was raised for the purpose (suppression of Husain Khan Khweshgi) clamoured for their pay that came to over Rs 4,00,000. This

[90] K. K., II, p. 862; Kamwar, f. 370a; *M. U.*, I, *pp. 602–3; T. Muzaffari*, f. 131a and *Siyar*, II, p. 425.

[91] K. K., II, p. 865.

[92] Compare Shivdas, f. 54b. Saiyid Abdullah Khan, the *wazir*'s *arzdasht* sent to the emperor after the assassination of Saiyid Husain Ali Khan. For the details of Nizam-ul-Mulk's revolt against the centre and the subsequent march of the emperor and Husain Ali Khan towards the Deccan and the latter's assasination at the hands of the Turani nobles, see W. Irvine, *Later Moghuls*, II, pp. 16–56; Satish Chandra, *Parties and Politics*, pp. 154–62. As for the Punjab we have no evidence for Abd-us-Samad Khan's revolt apart from his conflict with the *diwan* and the *wazir* and the consequent breakdown of law and order in the province. Saiyid Abdullah Khan might have referred to Abd-us-Samad Khan's march against Husain Khan Khweshgi, a friend of the Saiyids, as the governor's revolt.

[93] Ibid., ff. 50b–53a.

old slave repeatedly asked the *diwan* for the amount and gave the *qabz* (pay-bill) for it under my own seal, [but] he did not accept it nor did he pay the sum. Had the *diwan* released the sum from the imperial treasury this slave would have been free from [the responsibility of] the pay of the people who were recruited to the service of His Majesty and reached the victorious imperial camp. [This slave] thus could not help staying behind. If an imperial order is issued to the *diwan* regarding the payment of the amount after taking the *qabz* under the seal of this slave, this devoted servant would finish (the work of) the pay of these people and rush to the miracle-performing court. In future, either this slave [himself] would pay back [the sum] in cash from the revenue of the *jagir* or the imperial *mutasaddis* would deduct proportionately from the *jagir* of this slave.[94]

The governor made his departure for the court virtually conditional upon the emperor's order to the *diwan* for payment. Whether his condition was fulfilled or not is unknown to us, but Abd-us-Samad Khan did not miss the opportunity to witness the final eclipse of the power of the *wazir*. On 16 November 1720, Abd-us-Samad Khan along with his son Zakariya Khan arrived at the court and exchanged the customary rich presents with the emperor during their three-month stay in Delhi.[95] It is interesting to note that his statement of the financial difficulties in his *arzdasht* is not supported by the quantity of presents he offered the emperor during his stay in Delhi. He exaggerated his difficulties chiefly to secure the office of the *diwan* in his own name; Abd-us-Samad Khan seems to have succeeded as no *diwan* separately appointed by the centre is mentioned in the sources we have used.[96]

[94] Ibid., ff. 53.

[95] Abd-us-Samad Khan presented to the emperor 1000 *muhrs* and Rs 1000 while his son offered 100 *muhrs*. Both were reciprocated by the emperor with special *khilats* and other favours. On 22 November, Abd-us-Samad Khan's associates, Saiyid Mahmud Khan and Faizullah Khan received *khilats* from the emperor. In January 1721, in the wake of the celebrations of victory over Saiyid Abdullah Khan, Abd-us-Samad Khan offered Rs 1,00,000 to the emperor. After about a three-month stay in Delhi, on 9 February 1721, Abd-us-Samad Khan left for Lahore. Kamwar, ff. 376 and 377a; K. K., II, pp. 935–6 and 938; Shivdas, ff. 63a and 67a; *Siyar*, II, pp. 444 and 451. Saiyid Mahmud Khan of Sonepat, died in 1724. Cf. *T. Muhammadi*, p. 51. We could not identify Faizullah Khan. *T. Muhammadi*, however, notices two Faizullah Khans in our period, pp. 49, 93 and 101.

[96] Although Kauramal and Lakhpat Rai have been mentioned as *diwans* of the Punjab, they, like Atma Ram in Awadh and Rai Durlabh in Bengal, were totally subordinated to the governor and were practically little more than assistants to the governor in both personal and provincial financial matters.

By 1721, the governorship of the Punjab involved not only the highest executive and military power in the province but also an unchecked control over the provincial finance. However, the governor's clash with the *wazir* and the provincial *diwan* and his defiance of imperial rules on a number of occasions impaired the imperial power in the province. The governor's action set the example for the others. The fact that it was the governor's conflict with only a faction at the court and that throughout the period of his estrangement with this faction, the governor remained loyal to the person of the emperor[97] did not minimize the magnitude of the problem. The emperor was no longer the centre of the court. He was a mere member or at best a leader of a faction. Abd-us-Samad Khan's loyalty to the emperor was motivated by a desire to protect himself, and also to mobilize the emperor against the opponent faction. Indeed, the emperor also became a party to the process of the breakdown of the imperial structure. The emperor was not only involved in the factional fight of the nobility, but also became directly responsible for the violation of the time-honoured conventions that had governed the centre-province relations. In 1716 he sent an important order (*hasb-ul-hukm*) to Abd-us-Samad Khan through his (Abd-us-Samad's) associate at the centre, namely, Muhammad Amin Khan.[98]

The case of the Punjab also shows how the problems of the province and the governor's attempts at an acquisition of additional powers were tied to the old nobles' ambitions in Bahadur Shah's time. Initially, in the *wazir*, Mum'im Khan's efforts to associate the local elements in provincial administration there seems to be some reason why the governor asked for the extended powers of *faujdaris* and other local offices. It may be mentioned here that Mun'im Khan had governed the Punjab as Prince Muhammad Muazzam's (Bahadur Shah) deputy and was thus familiar with the problems of the province in 1710. Yet, even then Mun'im Khan's efforts were largely intended to be a check on the governor, Muhammad Asad Khan and his son, Zulfiqar Khan who had resented his rise to the office of the

---

[97] At the beginning of 1717, for example, in response to a *farman* asking him to join the Jat campaigns, Abd-us-Samad Khan arrived at the court and exchanged the usual rich presents with emperor. Kamwar, ff. 353a and 354a; M. M., f. 76a.

[98] See above, footnote 80.

wazir, totally thwarting their claims. Later in Farrukh Siyar's time too, the fact that the governor did not belong to the faction of the *wazir* added notably to the former's difficulties. Only two important *faujdaris*—Jammu and Beth Jalandhar—appear to be in control of the governor.

Because of the peculiar economic and geographic position of the Punjab, there were still more issues to strain the relations between the province and the centre. The *wazir* kept Multan, Thatta, Kashmir and Kabul under the control of his own associates, especially in the circumstances when he tried but failed to have his own man as the governor of the Punjab. For, the effective maintenance of the centre's authority in these provinces noticeably crippled the freedom of the governor of the Punjab. Again, the problem of the maintenance of the army on the north-western frontiers influenced the course of the developments leading to the changes in the position of the governor in the Punjab. The centre attempted to control effectively the local administration and the revenues of the *parganas* reserved for Kabul. The efforts of the central authorities to control, and the governor's resentment over, the appointments of the *faujdars*, the *diwans* and the other local officials in Gujarat, Emanabad, Shamsabad and Sialkot have to be considered also in this light. Under the circumstances when the governor of Kabul was a protégé of the *wazir*, a kind of conflict between the governor of the Punjab and the centre was unavoidable.

Moreover, the immediate interests and the ambitions of the individual and the groups concerned and the governors' estrangement with the centre represented a conflict between two views of administration. Saiyid Abdullah Khan, an advocate of the 'new *wizarat*', believed in and accordingly tried for the *wazir*'s complete control over the finance of the empire. He therefore fought to regulate appointments, transfers and dismissals of the revenue officials whose functioning had any bearing on finance. Notwithstanding the plight of the local soldiery in 1715, the *diwan*, as he was directed by the *wazir*, refused to grant to them anything from the revenue of the *pargana* of Sialkot which was reserved for Kabul.[99] Such were precisely the cases which convinced the governor of the necessity to establish

---

[99] *Akhbarat*, FS, 4th R. Y., II, p. 62.

his control over the revenues. In the face of steady increase in number and intensity of the local problems, the directives from Delhi were not available for immediate action. The lines of communication between the provinces and the centre were breaking down; the central authorities were unable to act promptly. In 1717, for instance, when the *diwan* acted on his own discretion and spent part of the revenues reserved for Kabul on an item which he thought of greater urgency, he was dismissed for violation of the rules. As the governors were confronted with local challenges and with the task of consolidating the power and prestige of the Mughal throne in the provinces, they demanded freedom to control the revenue resources and the important local offices. In the circumstances, the *wazir*'s effort or the new *wizarat* under Saiyid Abdullah turned out to be merely a device of his faction for the purpose of increasing its own power at the expense of the others.

CHAPTER III
The *Zamindars*, the *Madad-i Ma'ash* Holders and Mughal Administration in Awadh *c.* 1707–22

Internal strife among the nobility accelerated the decay of Mughal power and was the first grave manifestation of the chain of events leading to the breakdown of the imperial structure. But the problem of the nobility was, in a very large measure, symptomatic of rather than causal in the process of the disintegration. As a major source of the empire's strength in the sixteenth and seventeenth centuries lay in its success against the local roots of power and, no less than this, in its ability to coordinate its interests with those of the local elements, its weakness in our period is to be seen in the perspective of its failure to resolve its conflicts with them.

By the time the Mughals established their power in India, the land and its wealth had come to be in full control of the large and small family and kin groups. These groups constituted the local political and administrative elites and were also agencies through which the countryside was integrated into the larger outer world. They all enjoyed claims over the surplus produced by the peasants in accordance with a structure of graduated proprietary rights over the land. The power of these groups had by and large been identified with territories.[1] In the Mughal sources they have been referred by the generic term of *zamindars* (the holders [of the rights over the produce] of the land). This term implied a range of highly variegated dominant rural classes and was inclusive of even the so-called rajas who had an 'autonomous' control over the territories under their jurisdiction.

The origins of the power of the *zamindars* were independent of

---

[1] Compare, Tapan Raychaudhuri and Irfan Habib, (eds.), *The Cambridge Economic History of India*, pp. 53–60.

the Mughal system. But the *zamindars* who were integrated into the empire evidently grew in strength and influence in the wake of the political and economic unification under the Mughals. They were an important constituent of the Mughal state power which in turn also depended, in a very large measure, upon their absorption into the Mughal system. As they aligned with the Mughals they increased their position both by acquiring additional assigned rights over their territories and outside and also by depressing the rights of those who failed to come to terms with the paramount Mughal power.[2]

However, the *zamindars* also competed with the empire even after they had been a part of it. They were ever ready to shift alignments provided there was no threat to their hereditary properties or assigned positions. The different elements of the ruling class likewise the *zamindars* in the region served the empire as long as they recognized that only under the hegemony of a political paramount and through political unification could they promote their interests. As the region developed and its economic ties with other regions appeared to be strong enough to be sustained, the regional elements began to struggle for greater exercise of power. Against this background is to be seen the internal strife among the nobility at the centre as also the governor's endeavour for additional authority. For the governor had to encounter and adjust to the demands of the region under his jurisdiction.

The zamindar *uprisings*

According to the general observations of the Persian chroniclers, Mughal Awadh, in the earlier years of the eighteenth century, was mutinous and, therefore, very difficult to govern.[3] In a large part of the province, the *zamindars* had taken to armed resistance against Mughal authority. We are told by the author of the *Tarikh-i Hindi* that one of the reasons for Chin Qilich

---

[2] For the *zamindars'* alignment with the Mughals and their interdependence upon each other, see S. Nurul Hasan, 'Zamindars under the Mughals', Irfan Habib, *Agrarian System*, pp. 136–89; A.R. Khan, *Chieftains in the Mughal Empire, passim*; See also Richard G. Fox, *Kin, Clan, Raja and Rule: State Hinterland Relations in the Pre-industrial India*, Berkeley, 1971, *passim*.

[3] *M. U.*, I, p. 565; *Burhan-i Awadh*, p. 22.

Khan's resignation from the governorship was his inability to cope with the difficulties that an administrative assignment in Awadh, implied,[4] especially when he felt that he possessed no more power than an ordinary governor did in normal circumstances. The *Ajaib-ul-Afaq* records a letter from Chhabele Ram to the emperor beseeching the latter to supply him with adequate arms and ammunitions, 'for the seditious elements (*mufsids*) in the province which possesses a strong fortress in almost every village require proper chastisement'.[5]

A closer examination of the sources, however, shows that the insurrection, with the possible exception of the Baiswara region, assumed a serious magnitude only after 1712, and that a substantial number of the *zamindars* still supported the Mughals in the areas afflicted with the uprisings.

The *zamindaris* in Awadh were very largely shared by the various clans of Rajputs. In a number of *parganas*, the Muslims (including the Afghans), the Brahmans, and certain other castes are also recorded in the *Ain* as dominant *zamindars*.[6] Among them no single group were exclusively contumacious. While in certain *parganas* the Rajputs and the Afghans together or separately were regarded as the chief hostile elements, in the others *zamindars* of divergent castes together seem to have posed the main threat to imperial authority. The *zamindars* of Baiswara, the Gaurs of the *parganas* of Sadrpur, Laharpur and Sandi and the Kanhpurias of *pargana* Ibrahimabad, however, posed a major threat to Mughal power.

Since the reign of Aurangzeb the *zamindars* of Baiswara had constantly threatened imperial power in Awadh. A number of villages and *mahals* in Baiswara such as Bijnaur, Ranbirpur, Harha, Unao, Deori, *mauza* (village) Baliamau, Sadauli, *mauza* Parinda, Jhalotar and Dondia Khera were disturbed by *zamindar* revolts at the time of Aurangzeb.[7] By the time of Farrukh Siyar, Mardan Singh, the *zamindar* of Dondia Khera and Amar Singh, the *zamindar* of Jagatpur, had assumed the leadership of the Bais. In 1714, the Bais *zamindars* along with a large number of their clansmen collected in the *garhi* (fortress)

---

[4] *T. Hindi*, f. 217.   [5] *Ajaib*, f. 35a.

[6] *Ain*, II (Jarrett), pp. 184–90, see also S. Z. H. Jafari, 'The Land Controlling Classes in Awadh, 1600–1900', *PIHC*, (43rd Session, Kurukshetra, 1982).

[7] *Roshan Kalam*, pp. 6–7, 12 and 36–7.

of Mardan Singh in Dondia Khera. Although they had to submit to the Mughal forces under Chhabele Ram after a three-day-long battle,[8] their submission was only temporary. Within one and a half years, the Bais were again unified under the joint leadership of Mardan Singh and Amar Singh and demonstrated a more effective use of their strength against the Mughals. In May 1715, Amar Singh mobilized the Bais and established his clansmen and the armed bands one at a time at different places, namely Jagatpur, Bhika and Shankarpur. Mardan Singh along with his followers was among the various powerful Bais *zamindars* who joined Amar Singh, on 23 July, at Jagatpur.[9]

Besides the collective defiance of the Bais under these two leaders, our sources also register some individual revolts in Baiswara. These individual revolts were no less a threat to Mughal authority than the joint Bais resistance. In 1714, the *ta'alluqadar* of *pargana* Bar, in Baiswara, for instance, had built five strong fortresses and raised an army of 2000 horsemen. It was to a strong army under the command of Sarbuland Khan, the governor, that the *ta'alluqadar* was forced to surrender.[10]

Durgmal Gaur, a *ta'alluqadar* of *pargana* Katesar, is mentioned as the leader of the Rajput rebels of the *sarkar* of Khairabad. No less than twenty-five fortresses were under the control of the refractory Rajput *zamindars* of the region. Both Sarbuland Khan and Girdhar Bahadur are reported to have led military expeditions against these rebels.[11] The *garhi* of Tiloi in

---

[8] *Akhbarat* FS, 3rd R. Y., II, p. 143.

[9] Ibid., FS, 4th R. Y., I, p. 121; *Ajaib*, f. 18b. Amar Singh is no more mentioned in our sources. It seems that Chhabele Ram succeeded in totally crushing the leadership of Amar Singh. According to Benett, it was about twenty years after Chhabele Ram that Amar Singh's grandson resumed the lead of his clan levies and 'engaged' for the four villages of Khajurgaon, Sareli, Bajpaipur and Hajipur. Cf. W. C. Benett, *A Report on the Family History of the Chief Clans of Roy Bareilly District*, Lucknow, 1895, p. 36.

[10] Ibid., FS, 3rd R. Y., I, p. 149, (17 June 1714).

[11] In 1715, the Gaur Rajputs collected in a fortress at Kanha which belonged to the *ta'alluqa* of Katesar. Girdhar Bahadur, the governor's nephew, was deputed to chastise the rebels. The battle that took the lives of 300 Gaurs and of over fifty Mughal soldiers ended in the victory of the latter. Twenty-five fortresses in the neighbourhood subsequently fell to the Mughals and the Gaurs fled to the jungles. Girdhar then moved towards Katesar with a view to subjugating the remaining fortresses of the *pargana*. The fortress of Noner, an important centre of the Gaurs in Khairabad which had earlier been reduced by Sarbuland Khan after about a month's siege, also fell to Girdhar. Compare, *Ajaib*, f. 36a; *Tabsira*, f. 55a.

pargana Ibrahimabad of *sarkar* Awadh which belonged to a Kanhpuria Rajput *zamindar*, was another refuge of the Rajput rebels. In March 1715, an expedition against the *zamindar* of Tiloi was led by Girdhar.[12] Again in 1716, subsequent to a report about its *zamindar*'s refusal to pay revenue to the *jagirdars*, Saiyid Muzaffar Ali Khan, the governor, sent a detachment to Tiloi.[13] Both the campaigns failed to contain the *zamindars* of *pargana* Ibrahimabad, and Tiloi continued to be a major source of disturbance, to the government of Burhan-ul-Mulk as well.

No less disturbing were the Afghan *zamindars* of *sarkar* Lucknow. In September 1713, one of the Afghan fortresses in *pargana* Mandiaon was captured and a Mughal *thana* (police post) was established there. The rebel, however, managed to escape and took shelter in another fortress and within a month he remobilized the Afghans of the *pargana* for armed resistance against the Mughals.[14] In 1715, the *garhis* of Zafarabad and Jahangirabad were the centres of the Afghan resistance in *pargana* Dewi of *sarkar* Lucknow.[15]

A news-letter of 9 May 1714, probably offers a convincing example of the combined resistance of the *zamindar* clans against the Mughals in Awadh. The Rajput *zamindars* of almost the entire *sarkar* of Awadh assembled in certain fortresses in the *sarkar*. Though the campaign under the command of the governor ended, as the news-letter reports it, in his victory, about a thousand soldiers from his side were slain in the battle.[16]

The incident probably formed part of the circumstances which necessitated or rather precipitated the deputation of a person like Chhabele Ram to Awadh. Chhabele Ram governed the province, as we have seen earlier, with some military achievements. Again, an *arzdasht* of Chhabele Ram dated 4 December 1714, records his victory over the fortress of Hindalgarh in *sarkar* Lucknow.[17] In January 1715, he received a special *khilat* (robes of honour) from the court for his successful expedition to Selabhar.[18] In 1715, Dakhini Ram, the *faujdar* of

---

[12] *Akhbarat*, FS, 4th R. Y., I, p. 7.   [13] Ibid., 5th R. Y., II, p. 122.

[14] Ibid., 2nd R. Y., II, pp. 99, 130 and 154. Subsequently, the governor with a strong army, under the *thanadars*, tried to capture all the fortresses belonging to the leader of the Afghan rebels but he could subjugate only four of the Afghan *garhis* in the *pargana*.

[15] Ibid., 4th R. Y., I. p. 7.   [16] Ibid., 3rd R. Y., I, p. 147.

[17] Ibid., 3rd R. Y., II, p. 159.   [18] Ibid., p. 221.

Khairabad led another successful expedition against the *ta'allu-qadar* of Chandrapur, in *pargana* Karat, *sarkar* Khairabad.[19] The appointment of Aziz Khan Chaghta and the institution of the *naib-i suba* (deputy governorship) also seem to have increased the military strength of the Mughals against the *zamindars*. It is not unlikely that Aziz Khan, a local Afghan, was made governor with a view to containing the rebellious Afghans in the province. Subsequently, the Mughals scored quite a few victories over the armed bands of the rebels.[20]

But these successes showed only a marginal military superiority of the Mughals over the *zamindars*. We have no evidence to suggest that those *zamindars* who ran away and were still capable of reorganizing their strength offered total submission. Again, the Mughals did not attempt to make any new arrangement with the *zamindars* and thus contain their aspirations. The *zamindars* continued to look for opportunities which could provide them with sufficient strength to defy the Mughals, even though they had formally surrerendered to the latter's military superiority. In May 1717, for instance, a Bais *zamindar* petitioned the governor and asked to be forgiven for his earlier offences. In response, the *zamindar* was asked to present himself before the office (*kachahri*) of the *diwan*. Soon, however, the *zamindar* changed his mind, reorganized his clansmen and the troopers and took to armed resistance.[21]

Thus, the Mughals were not strong enough to restore stability in the province. On the basis of the sources we have used, it is not possible for us to say whether the Mughals could ensure an uninterrupted realization of the revenue in this period. From a letter of Chhabele Ram, however, we know that, in 1715–16, the *diwan* despatched Rs 30,000 to Delhi.[22] We do not know if this was the entire amount despatched from Awadh to the centre in those years.[23]

The *zamindars'* strength lay in their social ties with the armed

[19] Ibid., 4th R. Y., I, p. 121

[20] Ibid., for a successful military campaign against the *zamindars* of *pargana* Sadauli, *sarkar* Lucknow, in April, 1715. *Sharaif*, p. 245 for an expedition under Ruh-ul-Amin Khan, the deputy governor, against the *zamindars* of *pargana* Shahabad. *Akhbarat* FS, 6th R. Y., II, p. 86 for Nur Muhammad's chastisement of the *zamindars* of *pargana* Salas in November 1717.

[21] Ibid., 6th R. Y., I, p.   [22] *Ajaib*, f. 36a.   [23] See also Chapter VI.

bands which they led against the Mughals. They also had the advantage of the topographical conditions. In a number of cases, the Mughals, in their reports to the emperor, appear to have rationalized the inconclusive expeditions in terms of their inability to penetrate into the *zamindars*' hideouts in the jungles. These revolts may not, however, be taken as instances of the conflict of the entire locality against the Mughal state. A major advantage that the Bais *zamindars*, for example, took of their increased strength in the region was the extortion of a higher share from the peasants. This is borne out by the *qanungos*' report to Burhan-ul-Mulk about the rent-rolls in Baiswara.[24] In another instance, the small peasants (*reza ri'aya*) and the revenue grantees (*shurafa*) are reported to have suffered heavily at the hands of the rebel Gaur *ta'alluqadars* of the *parganas* of Kheri and Laharpur.[25] In yet another instance, the clansmen of the *zamindars* of *tappa* Marahta in the neighbourhood of *pargana* Daryabad committed atrocities on the peasants (*ri'aya*) of the *pargana*.[26]

The strength that the *zamindars* achieved, through their unified resistance to the Mughals, was often impaired by their own internal contradictions. In 1721, Singha Gaur, the *zamindar* of Kheri and Laharpur misappropriated the entire revenue including the shares of the *zamindars* of a number of *parganas* in *sarkar* Khairabad.[27] Indeed, there are instances of a clash among the *zamindars* of the same category. In 1714, the *ta'alluqa* of Bandha, a *zamindar* in *sarkar* Gorakhpur, was forcibly appropriated by 'recalcitrant' *zamindars*, Kesar Singh and Hindu Singh. The *ta'alluqa* was later restored by the governor to Bandha.[28] In 1717, the *zamindar* of *mauza* Girdhara, in *pargana* Amethi-Dongar, *sarkar* Lucknow plundered and took away the animals of the *zamindars* of the neighbouring villages.[29]

The revolts and the consequent disturbances reflected the social differences amongst the various constituents of the rural populace, were a menace to the local *zamindars* and the *ri'aya*, and also posed a threat to the imperial administration. It may be noted that in August 1721, when Girdhar Bahadur marched against the Gaurs of *sarkar* Khairabad, his army included a

---

[24] See Chapter VI.　　[25] Shivdas, ff. 72b–73a.　　[26] *Ajaib*, ff. 66.
[27] Shivdas, f. 73a.　　[28] *Akhbarat* FS, 3rd R. Y., II, p. 87 (27 October 1714).
[29] Ibid., 6th–8th R. Ys., p. 16 (14 June 1717).

large number of the local *zamindars*' contingents.[30] Again, the *zamindar* of *pargana* Majhauli in *sarkar* Gorakhpur always defended the imperial cause against the Ujjainiyas of *suba* Bihar.[31] It may, however, be noted that the *zamindars* of the southern part of Gorakhpur on the northern bank of the Ghagra had revolted against Aurangzeb's rule. They were contained only with the help of the *zamindars* of *pargana* Nizamabad. The Gautam Rajputs of the *pargana* on the southern bank of the river seem to have been encouraged by the imperial administration to subjugate the turbulent *zamindars* and impose levies from them across the river in Gorakhpur.[32]

Among the regions of Awadh worst affected by the *zamindar* uprisings in our period were the southern part of *sarkar* Khairabad and the southern and south-western *parganas* of *sarkar* Lucknow. A very large part of this region, namely, Baiswara, the land of the powerful Bais and the other Rajputs, had been disturbed by *zamindar* uprisings since, at least, the last years of the seventeenth century.[33] These uprisings appear to have been symptomatic of significant demographic change. The Bais Rajputs expanded out from the core of their respective original twelve settlements (*dwazdah dih*) and began to make encroachments into the *zamindari* areas of the others.[34] In the course of this, set in a process of extension of agriculture and the consequent growth in the region. A number of settlements like Ajgain, Murtaza Nagar, Husain Nagar and Ghaffar Nagar, assumed eminence in the seventeenth century while a number of others like Dondia Khera, Jagatpur and Shakarpur, as we noticed earlier, emerged as important *zamindari* centres in the early-eighteenth century. The nature of these settlements and the extent of the growth is illustrated, for instance, from the case of an Afghan raid on Husain Nagar which has been mentioned in our sources as a *qarya* (lit. a village) in the late-

---

[30] Shivdas, f. 73a.   [31] *Akhbarat* FS, 6th–8th R. Ys., p. 169.

[32] *Tarikh-i Azamgarh*, I. O. 4038, f. 15a.

[33] *Roshan Kalam*, pp. 6–7, 12 and 36–7.

[34] Ibid., pp. 6 and 14 and 27 for Jethi, Rajsahi and other *mufsids*' raids on the fortresses of the Saiyid *zamindars* of Murtaza Nagar and Ghaffar Nagar, etc., *pargana* Harha. Rad Andaz Khan, the *faujdar*, helped restore the old *zamindars*, and also tried to contain the turbulent Rajputs by replacing the new *zamindars* in existing Rajput strongholds (pp. 18, 3). This seems to have boomeranged, accentuating and accelerating the disturbances.

seventeenth century. The Afghans killed 600 male and female residents of this *qarya*, captured 700 members of the communities of the traders, money-lenders and the artificers (*mahajan* and *muhtarifa*) and plundered cash and goods worth Rs 2,00,000.[35]

It is interesting to note that the disturbances encompassed largely the areas wherein lay the eighteenth-century routes which linked Khairabad and Lucknow through southern and southwestern Awadh with important trading centres across the Ganga, namely, Farrukhabad and Bithur, in *sarkar* Qanauj of Agra *suba* and Jajmau, Kora, Khajua and Bindki of *sarkar* Kora of Allahabad *suba*.[36] Apart from these routes there was the major seventeenth-century road which passed through Awadh connecting Benaras on the east with Bareilly, Moradabad and Sambhal on the west. In the late-eighteenth century, Rennell showed two roads which passed through Baiswara region up to the Ganga on the southern borders of Awadh. One of these connecting Lucknow with Jajmau certainly existed in the seventeenth-century, even though it has not been noticed by Sarkar and Habib.[37] Ajgain, an obscure village which had hitherto had a *jama* of only Rs 600, seems to have emerged to be an important station on this route. The person in control of the *sarai* at Ajgain reportedly fleeced a big sum (*mubligh-i khatir*) in the name of *chaukidari*, *rahdari* and the other prohibited cesses from the traders (*beoparis*).[38] Some time towards the end of the 1730s or the early 1740s, 'a fine and massive bridge' was built across the river Sai at Mohan on this route.[39] The construction

[35] Ibid., p. 10. Of 24 places which acquired importance in our period, 18 were located in Baiswara and its immediate neighbourhood in south Awadh, See Map 1, p. 62.

[36] Compare James Rennell's map of 'Oude and Allahabad' with part of Agra and Delhi in *Memoir of a Map of Hindoostan* or the Mogul Empire, reprinted with his *Bengal Atlas*, Patna, 1975.

[37] Compare J. N. Sarkar, *India of Aurangzeb*, and Irfan Habib, *An Atlas of the Mughal Empire*, Delhi, 1982, Maps 8A and 8B and also notes pp. 26–33.

[38] *Roshan Kalam*, p. 37. Ajgain (Ojgein) figures in Rennell's map of 'Oude' and on the route between Lucknow and Jajmau and is a station on the modern railway connecting Kanpur with Lucknow.

[39] Cf. *Gazetteer of the Province of Oudh*, Vol. II, Allahabad, 1877, p. 500. In 1841 in the half-yearly report on the construction of Public Works in the Territory of Oude, Alexander Cunningham said of the bridge which was on the existing road to Kanpur as having been built 'upwards of one hundred years'. Compare R. G. Varady, 'The Diary

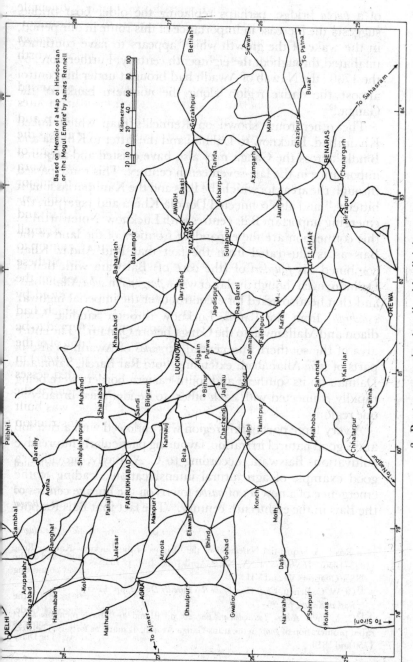

3. Routes connecting Awadh with adjoining areas

Based on 'Memoir of a Map of Hindoostan or the Mogul Empire' by James Rennell

Kilometres
20 10 0   20   40   60   80   100

of a *pucca* bridge, perhaps replacing the older boat bridge, suggests the increase in importance of this route in our period, in the wake of the growth which appears to have continued unabated throughout the eighteenth century. Furthermore, by the 1730s the Nawab of Awadh had brought under his control almost the entire region along the northern banks of the Ganga.[40]

The other route shown on Rennell's map which linked Khairabad, Lucknow to Dalmau and the latter to Khajua and Bindki across the Ganga may also have existed and acquired importance in the late-seventeenth century. This route passed through the areas for which the Bais and the Kanhpurias fought bitterly,[41] and also connected Dondia Khera and Jagatpur, the emerging important Bais centres with Lucknow. Noteworthy in this connection are the expanding frontiers of the land of the Bais as is illustrated from the fact that Rad Andaz Khan combined his *faujdari* of (the core of) Baiswara with that of Dalmau, even though the latter was a *pargana* in *suba* Allahabad, and that he also asked for a control over the imperial highway (*shahrah*) from Rai Bareli, Lucknow through Sandila, Mandiaon and Mallanwan to the Ganga before Qanauj.[42] The entire area of the southern and central *parganas* of Awadh as also of parts of *suba* Allahabad, extending upto Rai Bareli, Salon and Dalmau on its southern and south-eastern borders were being rapidly connected with each other, to be identified broadly as one region.

A very large part of this region was endowed with a rich soil and a good natural irrigation, favouring particularly impressive cultivation. Baiswara, according to C. A. Bayly, provided 'a good example of agricultural intensification', leading to the emergence of a new set of *qasba* towns on the lineage centres of the Bais in the eighteenth century.[43] The fact that Bais Rajputs

of a Road: A Sequential Narration of the Origins of the Lucknow-Kanpur Road (1825–1856)', *IESHR*, Vol. XV, No. 2, April-June, 1978, p. 153.

[40] See Chapters VI and VII.

[41] Cf. W. C. Benett, *Chief Clans of the Ray Bareilly District*, pp. 44–5.

[42] *Roshan Kalam*, pp. 26–7.

[43] C. A. Bayly, *Rulers, Townsmen and Bazaars*, pp. 81 and 96–9. Bayly mentions a very rapid proliferation of *ganjs* in the trans-Ganga Awadh, as many as forty-two between 1750 and 1819.

themselves emerged as merchants, linking Baiswara with some distant major commercial centres by 1790, shows the extent of monetization in the region.[44] A measure of the growth of the region was the establishment of new *mandis* and *puras* in Lucknow, resulting in the increase in the income from *khalisa mahal* of the city. The setting up of three *faujdaris*, Bilgram, Baiswara and Dalmau in the region also indicated the strength and importance of its local magnates.[45]

In this connection the rise in the *jama dami* (assessed revenue in *dam*) of the region which had almost doubled since the time of the *Ain-i Akbari* is also to be noted. The aggregate rise in the *jama* of the province, according to an eighteenth-century revenue roll, was by over 85 per cent since the late-sixteenth century, the maximum, 267.37 per cent, being in *sarkar* Gorakhpur, followed by 116.14 per cent in *sarkar* Khairabad, 82.66 per cent in *sarkar* Lucknow, 55.16 per cent in *sarkar* Bahraich and 43.40 per cent in *sarkar* Awadh.[46] A very large part of Gorakhpur was under forest in the sixteenth century, and its exceptionally good performance apparently owed to the special attention the Mughals paid to habilitate the *sarkar* under the new name of Muazzambad.[47] The *faujdar* of the *sarkar* in the late-sevente-

[44] Ibid., p. 97.
[45] *Roshan Kalam*, p. 12 for the new *mandis* and *puras* of the Shaikhzadas in Lucknow and p. 26 for the *faujdaris*.
[46] I. O. 4489.

Sarkar	Jama in dams in the Ain	Jama in dams in the 18th century (c. 1755)
Awadh	4,09,56,347	5,87,31,515 (rose by 1,77,75,168)
Bahraich	2,41,20,525	3,74,25,644 (rose by 1,33,05,119)
Gorakhpur	1,19,26,790	4,38,16,237 (rose by 3,18,89,447)
Khairabad	4,36,44,381	9,43,35,608 (rose by 5,06,91,227)
Lucknow	8,07,16,160	13,99,33,358 (rose by 6,67,22,825)

[47] Irfan Habib, *An Atlas of the Mughal Empire*, Map 8B and notes p. 29 for the new name of the *sarkar*.

enth century was often a noble of high rank, sometimes also holding charge of the province.[48]

The rise in *jama* may have reflected a mere readjustment of the revenue figures to the rising prices following the influx of silver in the seventeenth century. But it is well nigh impossible to work it out, as we have no information on the prices of the region. The increase in prices, over a span of 150 years since *c.* 1600, has been calculated by about 300 per cent,[49] while in no region of Awadh did the *jama* rise so spectacularly. The differences in the rate of the rise in *jama* figures of the contiguous areas of the same *sarkar* and *dastur* (revenue rate) circle, as also some evidence of urban developments, suggest that the rise in *jama* had a bearing on the actual production of the region. There was a difference of over 20 per cent in the increase in the *jama* of Saipur (47.26%) and Jhalotar (68.45%) which lay in close proximity with each other in the same *dastur* circle south of the river Sai in *sarkar* Lucknow, while about 64 kms to the south-east in the same area, *pargana* Panhan differed from Saipur in this respect by 69.31 per cent, the rise in *jama* there being 116.57 per cent. Panhan also differed radically from its close neighbours, Ranbirpur for instance, which lay at a distance of about 16 kms to the north.[50] A major factor in the difference in the rate of the rise of the *jama* of closely placed *parganas* seems to have been the availability or otherwise of good irrigation due to their location in relation to the rivers of the area. This suggests that the revenues of our period reflected the state of agriculture. Even if we assume that the rise in *jama* did not have any relationship with production and speculate a complete correspondence between it and the prices, this meant there was no actual rise in the state demand, to the obvious benefit of the intermediaries.

In this context, it is interesting to note the remarks of the *qanungos* in the early-eighteenth century when Burhan-ul-Mulk visited Baiswara to estimate the state of agriculture in the region. According to one tradition, early in Muhammad

---

[48] M. Athar Ali, 'Provincial Governors under Aurangzeb' in *Medieval India, A Miscellany*, Vol. 1, Bombay, 1669, pp. 96–133.

[49] Tapan Raychaudhuri and Irfan Habib, (eds.) *The Cambridge Economic History of India*, Vol. I, p. 376.

[50] I. O. 4489 for the *jama* figures, and Irfan Habib *Atlas* Map 8A for location of these places.

Shah's reign when Burhan-ul-Mulk took over the charge of
Awadh as its governor, he made a tour of Baiswara in a bid to
deal with the turbulent *zamindars* and set right the revenue
administration. When he summoned the local *qanungos* and
asked for the revenue-roll, the latter enquired as to which
revenue roll the Nawab wanted, 'the man's' or 'the coward's'.
On being asked the meaning of their answer, they explained
that there were two figures which a *qanungo* could give. In a
'coward's roll', against every land owner's name was written
only the sum which had been fixed for him at the last assessment but in the 'man's roll' every one's rent was indicated on
the basis of what it should have been, taking into account the
improvement that had taken place in land. Burhan-ul-Mulk
asked for the 'man's roll' and on that basis reportedly doubled
the assessment.[51]

The rural disturbances thus showed the strength of the
region in relation to the Mughal state, amply demonstrated in
the establishment of fortresses (*ihdas-i qila/qilacha*) and the
raising of armed bands of kin folks and mercenaries (*sipah-o-
jami'at*) by the *zamindars*. Rich and resourceful as they were,
they now aspired to have a greater share in power and authority over the territories under their *zamindaris*. In this, however, only those *zamindars* who had a large clan strength in
their *zamindaris* or at least readily available support from the
neighbourhood on caste and kin ties, could afford to launch a
sustained resistance against the imperial power.

It appears that in some cases, the local upheavals also
represented a powerful *zamindar* clan's struggle to bring under their hegemony the entire territory of their residence.
Their antagonism, in such cases, was directed not only against
the state but also the *zamindars* of other denominations who
may have been settled and encouraged by the Mughals with a
view to corroding the bastion of a given *zamindar* caste and
clan. In this connection it is interesting to compare, as we have
done for some *parganas*, the dominant *zamindar* castes as
given in the *Ain* and the leaders of these revolts whom we can
identify in terms of caste and clan. It would appear that in
eight out of ten cases the revolts were led by those castes

---

[51] Charles Alfred Elliot, *Chronicles of Oonao: a District in Oudh*, Allahabad, 1862, p. 73.

	Parganas	Dominant *zamindar* castes in the *Ain*[52]	Leaders of revolts in the early 18th-century
1.	Ibrahimabad, *sarkar* Awadh	Ansari	Kanhpuria Rajputs
2.	Kheri, *sarkar* Khairabad	Bisen, Rajput, Janwar	Gaur Rajputs
3.	Laharpur "	Brahman	Gaur Rajputs
4.	Bijnaur, *sarkar* Lucknow	Chauhan	Bais
5.	Ranbirpur "	Bais, Brahman	Bais
6.	Harha "	Bais	Bais
7.	Unao "	Saiyid	Bais
8.	Deora '	Rajput	Bais
9.	Jhalotar "	Chandel	Bais
10.	Dewi "	Rajput	Afghan

which were not accorded a noticeable position in the hierarchy of *zamindars* in the given *parganas* in the late-sixteenth century. In such cases, it was not surprising that the erstwhile *chaudhuris* like the Saiyids of Baiswara, for example, with their caste and community following sided with and also sought help from the Mughals against the so-called *mufsids* (disturbers).[53]

It may be noted here that the political recognition of 'the chiefs of stratified lineages' by the central government in the *parganas* in the sixteenth century did not, in all cases, buttress the cohesion of *only* these lineages. In a number of cases the other kin groups who could not obtain a superior position in revenue administration also acquired eminence during the course of Mughal rule in Awadh in the seventeenth century. This had a bearing on the developments that entailed changes in the caste composition of the *zamindars*. It is not perhaps fair to suggest that in pre-industrial India the dominant clan territories strictly coincided without any change with the ad-

[52] *Ain*, II (Jarrett), pp. 184, 188–90.
[53] *Roshan Kalam*, pp. 14, 18, 27 and 36.

ministrative and revenue units.[54] The state and more than it, certain conditions—a money economy and land market which emerged in the seventeenth century broke the continuity between the government boundary and kin territory. Indeed, the *pargana* organization of Akbar who tried to weaken and liquidate the solidarity of the kin and clan groups at local levels did not succeed in all cases in all regions. The failure, in a measure, is reflected in the fact that the revenues of a very large number of the *parganas* in Awadh, which had so thoroughly been brought under the imperial regulation, are given in round figures in the eighteenth-century roll.[55] For example, the rounding up in thousands of the revenues of 27 out of 54 and 13 out of 25 *parganas* in Lucknow and Khairabad respectively in our period as against only one *mahal* in both these *sarkars* in the *Ain* indicates how effectively the *zamindars* had resisted imperial regulations. But the political and economic integration of the regions and the localities under the Mughal empire certainly reduced the prospects of the local systems to emerge as viable political entities in our region.

While it is true that the revenues in round figures in a large number of the *parganas* suggest a reassertion of the *zamindars'* power, it is not correct to presume that these *parganas* were in control of the 'autonomous chiefs'. It is also incorrect to characterize the rebel *zamindars* as rajas,[56] implying their autonomous control over the territories under their *zamindaris*. The appellation of raja was adopted by some of them much later in the early years of the nineteenth century when their descendants under a different organization of agrarian relations obtained new powers and privileges. Even the so-

[54] Richard G. Fox, *Kin, Clan, Raja and Rule*, pp. 14–30. For his opinion that the political recognition of the lineages helped them buttress their self-definition, see pp. 76–7.

[55] I. O. 4489. For the revenue administration of Awadh see Irfan Habib, *Agrarian System*, pp. 4, 11–13, 22, 202n, 212n, 220 and 223; see also *Ain's* tables, pp. 184–90.

[56] A. L. Srivastava, basing himself exclusively on the evidence of *District Gazetteers* characterized these *zamindars* as 'the independent and semi-independent barons of Awadh'. See, for instance, A. L. Srivastava, *First Two Nawabs of Awadh*, pp. 31, 34–41, 43–9, 90–3 and 183–5, where he discusses the revolts of the so-called rajas of Awadh during the time of Burhan-ul-Mulk and Safdar Jang.

called raja of Tiloi 'the boldest spirit' who 'did not easily stoop
to submit' is mentioned in our records as '*malguzar*',[57] while a
number of the rebel *zamindars* have been characterized as
'*ta'alluqadars*'.[58] Again, one of the expressions of their defiance of imperial authority is given as 'the refusal to pay the
mal-wajib'[59] which shows that the rebels were by no means
rajas or tributary chieftains. They were the old and the new
intermediary *zamindars* who endeavoured to acquire an independent òr at least semi-independent status. How many of
their village kinsmen and the peasants turned over to their
side in the hope of escaping 'the excessive taxation' is a matter
of conjecture. The disturbance not infrequently meant the
zamindars' refusal to pay to the Mughals the revenues already
collected from the peasants.

The existing social conditions did not allow the entire region
to be mobilized by the *zamindars* against the central government. It was well nigh impossible for the *zamindars* and peasants
of different castes and kin groups to fight together against the
Mughals. The traders and artisans saw little to gain from these
battles which apparently hit their interests as well.[60] Thus the
solution to the problem, in a large measure rested, as it actually
happened in the case of Burhan-ul-Mulk and Safdar Jang when
they acted virtually independently in provincial matters, on
how willing and able the Lucknow government was to accommodate the aspirations of the *zamindars*. The emergence of
Dondia Khera, Jahangirabad, Katesar and Tiloi as important
ta'alluqadaris in the eighteenth century is to be seen in this light.
It was perhaps possible to contain the turbulent *zamindars*

[57] *Akhbarat* FS, 5th R. Y., II, p. 172.

[58] See for instance ibid., 2nd R. Y., II, p. 99; 3rd R. Y., I, p. 149.

[59] Ibid., 4th R. Y., I, p. 155; 3rd R. Y., II, p. 143 for the revolts of the so-called Raja
Mardan Singh of Dondia Khera; also see Shivdas, ff. 72b, 73a.

According to Dr Noman Ahmad Siddiqi, a distinction has to be maintained between
a *mal-wajib* paying *zamindar* and the *peshkashi zamindar*. The former paid revenue on the
basis of actual measurement of land under cultivation or on the basis of previous
records of yields while the latter was not subject to the detailed assessment of land
actually under cultivation. Cf. *Land Revenue Administration*, pp. 22–3.

[60] For some such evidence see Chapter IV, see also M. Alam, 'Aspects of Agrarian
uprisings in North India in the Early Eighteenth Century', in Romila Thapar and
S. Bhattacharya (eds.) *Situating Indian History*, Delhi, 1986, Oxford University Press.

within the existing framework of provincial administration. But the steadily increasing estrangement between the governor and the *diwan*, the two principal officials in the province added to the enormity of the problem. The central government, engaged in its own factional politics, gave little serious attention to local problems. These were generally left to the local officials who were unable to meet the situation with the resources at hand, and in order to protect their own interests, not infrequently, had to ally with powerful *zamindars*. Chin Qilich Khan had to leave the province within six months of his appointment. Muhammad Amin Khan never came to Awadh and Sarbuland Khan, when assessed on the basis of his work in Gujarat and Allahabad, was a man of ordinary achievements. By obtaining the office of the *diwan* for his own associate, Chhabele Ram did muster sufficient resources to deal with the problems effectively. Besides, being more or less a local person he was familiar with the geography of the province as well as with the social roots of the uprisings. He failed because he had to constantly face opposition from the *wazir*. His nephew Girdhar Bahadur, who was free from such hostility from Delhi, made some headway. The imperial forces in one of his campaigns against the *zamindars* are reported to have been reinforced by a large contingent of the local *zamindars*. He was, however, very soon removed to Malwa where his services were thought to be more urgently needed.

Moreover, an unfortunate rivalry among the governors themselves was also responsible for the stalemate. The succeeding governor instead of carrying out the unfinished tasks of his predecessor was more concerned with a show of independent strength and power. For instance, immediately after the removal of Sarbuland Khan, Girdhar Bahadur, the new governor's nephew, carried a successful campaign against the Gaurs of *sarkar* Khairabad. But he paid no attention to the neighbouring fortress of Noner which was held by the rebel *zamindar* and marched towards Katesar. The fortress had been reduced after a 28 day long seige by Sarbuland Khan. The reason for this indifference is given by Chhabele Ram in his letter to the court as 'in this case [in the case of the reconquest of Noner] the people would remark [rather sarcastically] that he [Girdhar]

beat what had already been beaten by Sarbuland Khan.[61]
Thus as the agrarian uprisings caused and accelerated the
imperial decline, they too in turn were accentuated by the
process of decay.

Position of the madad-i ma'ash holders

The strength of the regional elements in relation to the imperial
centre is also illustrated in the defiance of imperial regulations
by the *madad-i ma'ash* holders, who had been the ideologues and
traditional supporters of the Mughal state and had occupied
some local offices. A notable factor of the disturbances in
Awadh was the conflict between the *madad-i ma'ash* grantees,
also known as *suyurghal* holders and *a'immadars*, on the one hand
and the *zamindars* and the Mughal officials on the other. This
accrued possibly from the position and the privileges that the
madad-i ma'ash holders had lately acquired in the province. In
principle, persons belonging to four categories were eligible for
the grant of the *madad-i ma'ash* : (*i*) scholars, who were 'seekers
after truth and renounced the world', (*ii*) persons who
'eschewed the urge for greater gain and chose a life of seclusion
and self-abnegation', (*iii*) the destitute and the poor 'who were
incapacitated to earn their livelihood', and (*iv*) 'persons of noble
lineage,who ignorantly deemed it below their dignity to take to
any employment'.[62]

However, the institution of *madad-i ma'ash* did not represent
simply an act of charity. In Awadh where the *madad-i ma'ash*
holders consituted a considerably strong social force, there were
large number of instances of appreciable alienation of the *jama*
in *suyurghal*. In 9 out of 128 *mahals* the proportion of the revenue
claimed by the grantees crossed the limit of ten per cent. An
analysis of the *siyurghal* statistics in the *Ain* shows that considerable parts of the two blocks of high *siyurghal* figures of modern
Uttar Pradesh were concentrated in the Mughal province of
Awadh.[63] A number of *madad-i ma'ash* holdings in land extended
over more than two to three hundred *bighas* while the influence

[61] *Ajaib*, f. 36a.

[62] *Ain*, I, pp. 140–1; see also Irfan Habib, *Agrarian System*, p. 307; N. A. Siddiqi, *Land
Revenue Administration*, pp. 123–4.

[63] Cf. Shirin Moosvi, 'Siyurghal Statistics in the *Ain-i Akhbari*: An Analysis', *Indian
Historical Review*, Vol. II, No. 2, January 1976, pp. 282–9.

and power of the grantees in certain cases entirely encompassed two or three *parganas*.[64] Our records show that those who held large *madad-i ma'ash* grants acquired enough wealth and power to purchase *zamindaris*. This is borne out by the acquisition of a number of villages in the *parganas* of *Haveli* Bahraich and Husampur in his *zamindari* and *milkiyat* by Mir Saiyid Muhammad Arif, an eminent revenue grantee of *sarkar* Bahraich.[65] In another case, the *qazi* of Mallanwan is reported to have purchased a mango orchard from the *chaudhuris* of the *pargana*.[66]

Large *madad-i ma'ash* holdings were not uncommon in Mughal India.[67] But, with the exception of some families who combined a number of posts in the imperial service with those which were normally renumerated in revenue-grants, the acquisition of *zamindaris* by *madad-i ma'ash* holders seems to be a late-seventeenth century development. By the beginning of the eighteenth century the process seems to have been intensified. The family of the *qazi* of the *pargana* of Bilgram in the time of Muhammad Shah, can be said to illustrate the point. The family is known to have been involved in 'this worldliness' to such an extent that, to quote an eighteenth-century biographer, the 'virtues that had long distinguished them vanished owing to the wealth they obtained in the time of Bahadur Shah'.[68] The

[64] See for example Allahabad, 196, 924 and 1300 for Saiyid Mohammad and Mir Saiyid Muhammad Arif of *sarkar* Bahraich and Bibi Saliha of *pargana* Sadrpur in *sarkar* Khairabad. Saiyid Muhammad held over 645 *bighas* as his *madad-i ma'ash* in *pargana* Husampur, while Mir Saiyid Muhammad 'Arif's holding extended over 999 *bighas*. Bibi Saliha had 200 *bighas* as her *madad-i ma'ash* in *pargana* Sadrpur.

[65] On 22 November 1677, Mir Saiyid Muhammad Arif acquired from one Maha Singh, son of Lal Sahi, a Khatri by caste, the latter's share in the *zamindari* and *milkiyat* of Unchhapur, *tappa* Chaurasi, *pargana* Husampur. On 13 November 1681, he obtained from one Tara Chand, the latter's share in the *zamindari* and *milkiyat* of Debidaspur in the same *tappa*. On 22 May 1687 Daya Ram, Kaidhi and their mother, Brahmans by caste, are reported to have sold to him their *milkiyat* and *zamindari* over half of the village of Baidauri. In 1099/1687–88, Narain and Puran Brahmans sold to him 1/10th of the village of Pasnajat. On 8 January 1694, he purchased 1/45th of the village from Nawazi, son of Kashi, the Brahman (*zamaradar*). Banyanhari, a village in *tappa* Mubarakpur, *pargana* *Haveli* Bahraich is also recorded to have been in the *milkiyat* and *zamindari* of Mir Saiyid Muhammad Arif. Cf. Allahabad, 1284, 1295, 1298, 1300 and 1309.

[66] Ibid., 136.

[67] Shaikh Abd-ur-Rashid, 'Suyurghal Lands under the Mughals', H. R. Gupta (ed.), *Essays Presented to Sir Jadunath Sarkar*, pp. 313–22.

[68] *Sharaif*, p. 70.

temptation to get money to purchase lands encouraged and increased corruption and malpractice in the courts of the *qazis*.[69] Some *madad-i ma'ash* holders appear to have acquired quite a strong position in the land and monetary transactions in the locality and began to act as revenue-farmers and money-lenders as well. In 1677, one Mir Saiyid Ahmad of Bahraich held a number of villages on *ijara*, while in another instance, the *zamindars* of Gondai in *pargana* Husampur are reported to have pawned their village to one Saiyid Habibullah. In another case, Saiyid Muhammad Panah of Bilgram combined *madad-i ma'ash* with *muqaddami* (headmanship) of village Ikhtiarpur in 1723.[70]

As the absence of any other means of income was invariably the sole justification for holding grants, with the acquisition of *zamindaris* and *ijaras* and a capacity to lend money to the *zamindars*, the revenue grantees should have theoretically forfeited their claim to retain *madad-i ma'ash* land.[71] In actual practice, however, they still maintained the grants. In 1678 the *qanungo* of *pargana Haveli* Bahraich realized the *qanungoi* from Mir Saiyid Ahmad and some other grantees of the *pargana*. However, in response to their petition an order (*dastak*) from the *diwan* of the province soon arrived, directing the *qanungo* to return the collected amount of the 'illegal cess' to the grantees.[72] A document dated 1108 *fasli* records *tappa* Mubarakpur in Bahraich as the *ta'alluqa* of both the *madad-i ma'ash* and the *milkiyat-o-zamindari* of Mir Saiyid Muhammad Arif.[73]

---

[69] See for instance *Akhbarat* BS, 5th R. Y., p. 74.

[70] Allahabad, 1224, 1285 and 1317. Significantly the document No. 124 mentions Mir Arif as the '*malik* and *ta'alluqadar*'. For the case of Muhammad Panah, see, *Bilgram Documents*, Nos. 60 and 67. Deptt. of History, Aligarh. I owe this reference to S. Z. H. Jafari.

[71] The grant was liable to forfeiture in cases when the grantee had any other source of income. Compare *Ain* I, p. 287 and an order of Shahjahan cited in Irfan Habib, *Agrarian System*, p. 307n.

[72] Ibid., 1291. We do not have any evidence for the background of, or for the motive that operated behind, this incident. We can presume that the *qanungo*, having legal expertise regarding land possessions and revenue, acted quite expectedly on the proclaimed policy of the Mughals, for he might have thought that the Saiyid after acquiring the *zamindaris*, etc., had forsaken his claim to any exemptions.

[73] Ibid., 1309.

The strength of the revenue grantees is further illustrated from the gradual subordination to their narrow interests of the requirements of an efficient and stable administration. Cases relating to the appointments of the local *qazi* and the *mutawalli* (trustee of *madad-i ma'ash* lands) may specially be noted in this connection. The local departments of the *sadr* and the *mutawalli* looked after the revenue grants and the problems of the grantees. These departments were under the direct control of the imperial centre. In the appointments, promotions and dismissals of even the *pargana mutawallis* an imperial order seems to have been essential. However, in Awadh, in our period the appointment and security of the job of the *mutawalli* of *pargana* seems to have depended more on the goodwill of the *a'immadars*.[74] This development may be noted against the background of the prime responsibility of the *mutawalli* to keep a watchful check on the grants and the grantees.[75]

It would appear that by the beginning of the eighteenth century almost all the offices related to the departments of the *sadr* and *qazi* had become hereditary. The imperial orders conferring these offices usually followed the actual acquisition of the offices. The role of such orders was thus reduced to the status of mere confirmatory directives. In 1718, after the death of the *qazi* of *pargana* Bilgram, his son, who was barely fifteen years old was proclaimed by 'the people of the town of Bilgram' as the successor of the deceased. As he was considered incapable of dealing with the responsibilities of office independently, they also appointed his deputy to assist him. It was two years later in 1721, that the imperial order was issued in favour of the son of the deceased, appointing him the *qazi* of the *pargana*.[76] The Abbasi Shaikhs of Kakori in *sarkar* Lucknow also acquired

---

[74] The appointment and the service of one Shaikh Karim Ali, the keeper of the records (*sarrishtadar*) of the revenue grants of *pargana* Barudanja (?) in *sarkar* Khairabad, is ascribed to his capacity to keep the local grantees appeased. In contrast to this, the appointment of his grandfather and father to the same office is explicitly mentioned to have followed the imperial *farmans*. Allahabad, 1192.

[75] Irfan Habib, *Agrarian System*, p. 299n.

[76] *Sharaif*, p. 166; Qazi Sharif-ul-Hasan, *Tanqih-ul-Kalam Fi-Tarikh-i Bilgram* (An Urdu local history of Bilgram based primarily on eighteenth century MSS, *Sharaif-i Usmani* and *Musajjalat Fi Tarikh-al-Quzat* of Qazi Ahmadullah, son of Qazi Muhammad Ihsan) pp. 193–4.

a hereditary claim to the office of the *qazi* of the *pargana*. Muhammad Hafiz Abbasi who was a contemporary of Burhan-ul-Mulk and Safdar Jang succeeded his father as the *qazi* of *pargana* Kakori. After his death, his son, Muhammad Wa'iz who was in close contact with Safdar Jang is reported to have taken over the office.[77]

The practice of hereditary succession does not seem to have remained confined only to those *parganas* where the office of the *qazi* was held by relatively powerful families. This is illustrated by an incident of the seventeenth century which also reveals the circumstances in which the practice began to evolve. One Wali Muhammad, the *qazi* of *pargana* Husampur, who had been dimissed due to his reported clash with the local *zamindars*, refused to give up his claim to the land revenue which he had obtained against his office.[78] Hereditary control over the office brought to them (obviously at the expense of the imperial government) rich dividends both in terms of land possessions and strong social ties.

The *madad-i ma'ash* grantees in Awadh thus enjoyed an un-usual position which assumes greater significance in the context of their relations with the political authorities since the begin-ning of Mughal rule.

The *madad-i ma'ash* holders occupied a distinct place in medieval Indian society. The *zawabit* (state laws) and secular considerations regulated the policies and the functions of the state in medieval India, but the *sharia* remained the point of reference in daily civil and penal matters and the *ulama* almost exclusively staffed the legal departments. The *ulama* could not be set aside as mere parasites. It was not easy for the medieval rulers to be perpetually in conflict with this class. When Akbar issued a *mahzar* in an attempt to contain their influence, he still needed the support of some members of this class to make it a legitimate proclamation. It was only later that he could fully free himself from the *ulama*. But the strength of this class is reflected in Jahangir's rationalization of *madad-i ma'ash* in terms of a return for the services (prayers) rendered by its holder.

However, the size of the *madad-i ma'ash* grants or the revenues

---

[77] Muhammad Hasan Abbasi, *Abbasiyan-i Kakori*, Lucknow, 1945, p. 9.
[78] Allahabad 882, 935 and 1280 of the 19th R. Y., of Aurangzeb/1676–77.

alienated for them was not very significant, ranging between 1.8
and 5.4 per cent of the total revenues. The holding of the grant
was characterized as *ariyat* (held on loan from the state), and
was required to be renewed and reconfirmed periodically.[79] In
Babur's time, at least, the grantee was also required to pay
one-tenth of the realization (*ushr*) from his *madad-i ma'ash* to the
state. According to the *sharia* the king could impose *ushr* on the
lands in *milkiyat* (proprietary possession) of the Muslims. But
the levying of *ushr* on *madad-i ma'ash* in Babur's time did not
imply change from *ariyat* to *milkiyat* in the character of the grant.
The *madad-i ma'ash* holder resented the characterization of his
holding as *ariyat*. Shaikh Abd-ul-Quddus Gangohi, a contemporary of Babur, advocated the discontinuation of the *ushr* on
the produce of, 'at least, the self cultivated (*khudkasht*) lands' of
the grantees, but there is no evidence to suggest that he made a
plea to convert the grant into *milkiyat*. However, in the late-
sixteenth century, his disciple, Jalal-ud-Din Thanesari pleaded
a case for all the land grants held by the Muslims to be treated
as their *milk*. Thanesari did not object to the grantee's being
asked to pay *ushr* according to the *sharia*, provided the land held
by him was converted from *ariyat* into *milkiyat*.[80]

The plea was in sharp contravention of the principles governing the nature of the grant. The *madad-i ma'ash* was a part of the
revenues alienated by the emperor or a noble from his *jagir* for
the maintenance of its grantee. It simply conferred on the
recipient a right to collect the revenue and keep it, and like the
emperor's and the noble's rights over the surplus produce of the
peasants, it did not interfere with the latter's occupancy and
proprietary rights over land. The plea thus passed unnoticed.
But the *ulama* as representatives of the *madad-i ma'ash* holders
grew in strength in the seventeenth century. It would perhaps
be unfair to say that a section of them under the leadership of
Shaikh Ahmad Sirhindi, the noted Naqshbandi saint, influenced

---

[79] For the extent and the nature of the *madad-i ma'ash* in Mughal times see Irfan
Habib, *Agrarian System*, pp. 298–307 and 313–15. For some information about the
earlier period see Tapan Raychaudhuri and Irfan Habib, (eds.), *The Cambridge Economic
History of India*, I. pp. 75–6.

[80] Compare I. A. Khan, 'Shaikh Abd-ul-Quddus Gangohi's Relations with Political
Authorities: A Reappraisal', *Medieval India: A Miscellany*, Vol. IV, Bombay, 1977,
pp. 73–90.

the course of state politics.[81] However, it is significant that since
Jahangir's time some of them (*mir adls* and *qazis*) were exempted
from prostrating/bowing before the emperor seated on the
throne (*sajda-i tazimi*). It may also be noted that Shaikh Ahmad
Sirhindi had claimed a status spiritually on a par with the First
Caliph of Islam. The Shaikh's 'preposterous' claim had agitated
the Sunni orthodoxy who brought it to the notice of Jahangir.
The Shaikh's imprisonment showed their strength and appeased the Muslim traditionalists who had resented the Shaikh's
claim in no uncertain terms.[82] It may also be noted that the
Mughal endeavour to reform the *suyurghal* administration in the
seventeenth century was never carried out. Shahjahan is reported to have ordered an investigation into the affairs of the
madad-i ma'ash holders. But he could not carry it through and
had to replace the order by a new one in 1644 to the obvious
benefit of the grantees.[83] Aurangzeb's concessions to the orthodox elements, the conditions attending the reimposition of
jiziya in 1679[84] and the royal order of 1690 which made the
madad-i ma'ash completely hereditary,[85] all showed the increasing pressure on the state by the *ulama*, representing the cause of

[81] For such view see K. A. Nizami, 'Naqshbandi Influence on Mughal Rulers and
Politics', *Islamic Culture*, XXXIX, 1965, pp. 41–52. See also Mohammad Yasin, *A Social
History of Islamic India, 1605–1748*, Lucknow, 1958, pp. 148–58. For an opposite opinion,
see Irfan Habib, 'The Political Role of Shaikh Ahmad Sirhindi and Shah Waliullah'
Enquiry 5, December 1961, pp. 36–55; see also S. Nurul Hasan, 'Shaikh Ahmad Sirhindi
and Mughal Politics, *PIHC*, 8th Session, Annamalainagar, 1945, pp. 248–54, and
Yohnan Friedmann, *Shaykh Ahmad Sirhinidi: an Outline of His Thought and a Study of His
Image with Posterity*, Montreal, 1971, pp. 77–86.

[82] Shaikh Abd-ul-Haq Muhaddis Dehlavi and Shaikh Abd-ul-Jalil Siddiqi resented
Sirhindi's 'extravagance', excessive self-esteem and his religious views. Cf. Y.
Friedmann, *Shaykh Ahmad Sirhindi*, pp. 88–92. For Sirhindi's imprisonment and release,
see *Tuzuk-i Jahangiri*, edited by Syud Ahmud (Saiyid Ahmad Khan), Ally Gurh
(Aligarh), 1864, pp. 272–3, 308 and 370. For *mir addl* and *qazi*'s exemption from *sajda*
before the emperor, see *Tuzuk-i Jahangiri*, p. 99.

[83] For details see Shaikh Abd-ur-Rashid, 'Suyurghal Land under the Mughals'.

[84] Cf. Satish Chandra, 'Jizya and the State in India During the 17th Century', *Journal
of the Economic and Social History of the Orient*, Vol. XII, part III, 1969.

[85] Cf. Irfan Habib, *Agrarian System*, p. 306. Among the concessions of Aurangzeb to
the Sunni Muslim orthodoxy may be noted, in particular, his order regarding the
resumption of the grants by the non-Muslims, transforming them into revenue-payers,
even though at a concessional rate. Compare, B. N. Goswamy and J. S. Grewal (eds.)
The Mughals and the Jogis of Jakhbr: Some Madad-i Ma'ash and Other Documents, Simla, 1967,
Document IX.

the *a'imma* holders. The *a'imma* holders' plea found a most arrogant expression in the view of Qazi Muhammad 'Ala, an eighteenth-century jurist, who propounded the theoretical proposition for the earmarking of all land in India for the maintenance of the *a'imma*.[86] This vulgar plea, probably a logical extension of Aurangzeb's compromise with orthodoxy, was obviously impracticable.

The privileges of the *madad-i ma'ash* holders in the late-seventeenth and the early-eighteenth centuries can be seen also in the perspective of the *zamindar* uprisings. The Mughals allowed the *madad-i ma'ash* holders to strengthen their position and even overlooked the cases of violation of existing norms with a view to arresting the growth and expansion of the rural disturbances.[87] The grantees exploited it to full advantage. They increased their fortunes by purchasing *zamindaris* and accumulating enough wealth and influence for money-lending and *ijara*. At the same time they managed to retain their earlier facilities and revenue-free possessions. This obviously violated the established rule and did not accord with their theoretical position. Hence, the local officials' attempt to impose regular cesses on certain *madad-i ma'ash* holdings in Bahraich. These efforts have a bearing on their resentment over the revenue grantees' recently acquired position. It is interesting to note that the orders (*parwanas*) of the *diwan* of Awadh which reprimanded the *qanungo* and the *jagirdar* of Husampur for levying cesses from the grantees show no concern for the difficulties of the local officials. This suggests a basic difference between the approach of those who were actually involved in local problems and of those who ruled the country from a safe distance.

Conflict between the madad-i ma'ash holders and the zamindars

The *madad-i ma'ash* holders could not effect any radical change in the legal status of their holdings, even though they controlled

---

[86] Cf. Zafarul Islam, 'Nature of Landed Property in Mughal India: Views of an Eighteenth Century Jurist', *PIHC*, 36th Session, Aligarh, 1975, pp. 301–9.

[87] The policy seems to have been pursued even later by the autonomous rulers of Awadh. Asaf-ud-Daulah is reported to have visited the Sufi Shrine at Salon and

some offices on account of heredity. The nature of their land-
holdings was still characterized as *ariyat*. However, their aspirations and privileges which often encroached on the rights of the
ancient landholders exacerbated the conflict between them and
the *zamindars*.

It becomes meaningful, in this context, to see that towards
the end of the seventeenth century, in a number of cases the
zamindars' hostility began to be directed against the local
Muslim gentry, the Saiyids and the religious divines (*shurafa-o-
sadat* and *mashaikh*). A military expedition against Lal Sahi, the
zamindar of Manohargarh in Baiswara had to be undertaken on
the petition of *jagirdar*'s agent and the *shurafa*. The *shurafa* of
village Ganjora or Ganjpura in *pargana* Saipur suffered seriously
at the hands of the Chauhan *zamindars*. A list of the excesses
committed by Rajsahi and Jethi, the *zamindars* of *pargana* Harha,
includes serious offences against the Saiyids (capture and
harassment). According to one report, the *zamindar* of Ghaf-
farnagar devastated the Saiyid settlements in the territory of his
zamindari.[88] According to yet another report, seven *zamindars* of
Kothi and some other villages in *pargana* Sidhaur in *sarkar*
Lucknow lost their *zamindaris* to one Mirza Muhammad Tahir,
since they had begun to make illegal exactions from the Saiyids.
Their *zamindaris* were restored to them only after they had given
a bond not to impose levies any longer upon the holdings of the
Saiyids.[89]

The letters of Rad Andaz Khan, the *faujdar* of Baiswara, in
the last years of Aurangzeb's reign strongly suggest that the
zamindars' clashes with revenue grantees were a major source of
disturbance in the villages. Again in June 1713, over five
hundred Rajputs of a neighbouring village invaded the village
of Ahrora, a *madad-i ma'ash* of the Saiyids in *pargana* Husampur.
A number of the resident Saiyids of the village were killed, and
their houses, libraries and other properties were set on fire. Five
of their women were burnt alive, and the surviving women and

granted to it 12 villages by expelling the Kanhpuria Rajputs for their disloyalty. Cf.
H. R. Nevill, *District Gazetteers of the United Provinces of Agra and Oudh*, Vol. 39, pp. 101–3.
For a brief account of the establishment of the shrine at Salon (in the erstwhile
Manikpur *sarkar* of *suba* Allahabad) see S. Z. H. Jafari, 'Two *Madad-i-Ma'ash farmans* of
Aurangzeb from Awadh', *PIHC*, 1979, pp. 302–14.
[88] *Roshan Kalam*, pp. 3–4, 6, 14 and 27.   [89] Allahabad, 1565.

children of their community were driven out barefooted. Simultaneously, the villages of Badholia, Kamalpur, Kanhatta and Malbari which were in the *milkiyat* and *zamindari* of the Saiyids were completely devastated, and the graveyards of their ancestors, the mosques and the *madrasas* were levelled to ground.[90]

In the regions where the rebellious *zamindars* held sway, the *madad-i ma'ash* holders could hardly afford to stay. As a result of the domination of the Gaur *zamindars*, the Muslim gentry including the Saiyids of Khairabad, along with the students of their *madrasas* had to migrate from their home town to the territory of the Bangash Afghans across the Ganga in Farrukhabad. For about ten to twelve years they wandered homeless. At the beginning of Safdar Jang's governorship, when an arrangement with the Gaurs of Khairabad was finally made, Muhammad Khan Bangash recommended to the governor the restoration, to them, of their houses and other properties in Khairabad.[91]

These incidents cut across religious affiliations. The *zamindars* of *pargana* Sidhaur who were punished for their offences against the Saiyids included three Afghans, namely, Nasir Khan, Rustam Khan and Haisham Khan.[92] Further, there is evidence for a Muslim *zamindar*'s clash with Muslim grantees. On April 9 1691, Mulla Qutb-ud-Din of Sahali, father of the better-known Mulla Nizam-ud-Din, founder of the famous *madrasa* at Firangi Mahal in Lucknow, was killed by the Muslim *zamindars* of the *parganas* of Sahali and Fatehpur in *sarkar* Lucknow.[93] Again, the case of the *madad-i ma'ash* grantees of Jais in *sarkar* Manikpur of *suba* Allahabad which also offers an exception to the general trend of their conflict with the

---

[90] Ibid., 1315.

[91] *Khujasta*, pp. 165–6. Also see Shivdas (ff. 736–74a) for Singha Gaur, the *zamindar* of Katesar's atrocities on the revenue grantees of Laharpur and Kheri in *sarkar* Khairabad and *Ajaib*, (ff. 66) and some *Akhbarat* of Farrukh Siyar's reign for conflicts between the *zamindars* and the *madad-i ma'ash* grantees in Daryabad.

[92] Allahabad, 1565.

[93] Mulla Qutb-ud-Din was a *madad-i ma'ash* grantee and ran a well-established *madrasa* in Sahali in the *sarkar* of Lucknow. Two of his students, Shaikh Ghulam Muhammad, a maternal grandson of the celebrated Shaikh Nizam-ud-Din of Amethi, and Shaikh Izzatullah of Sandila were also killed by the assailants. His son, Muham-

zamindars, shows that these clashes were concerned little with religious beliefs and practices. The *madad-i ma'ash* holders of Jais are said to have fought with Balbhadra Singh, the *zamindar* of Tiloi against the *zamindar* of Pratapgarh in *pargana* Arol of *sarkar* Manikpur. It is also said that Mohan Singh, a recalcitrant *zamindar* of the early-eighteenth century used to say with pride that his *zamindari* had the backing of the blessings of Shah Ata Ashraf, a descendant of the celebrated saint of Sultanate period, Shah Jahangir Ashraf. Ata Ashraf is also reported to have been the first to apply the *tika* on Mohan's forehead.[94] There are also instances of support offered by Rajput *zamindars* to Muslim *madad-i ma'ash* holders in the latter's struggles against the bigger grantee-cum-*zamindar*. The *qazi* of the *pargana* of Husampur, for instance, who seems to have been sacked due to his allegedly improper behaviour with Mir Saiyid Ahmad and Mir Saiyid Muhammad Arif, the revenue grantees-cum-*zamindars* of *sarkar* Bahraich, is recorded to have made encroachments upon the village of Katora in the *zamindari* of the Mirs. For this he was instigated and supported by Ram Singh, the *zamindar* of Dasmandi who also plundered and usurped the revenue of Sumanpur, another village in the *zamindari* and *milkiyat* of the Mirs.[95]

---

mad Sa'id, the *qazi* of the *pargana* of Sahali and a number of the Mulla's pupils received serious wounds. The women of the Mulla's family and his other relations in the town were humiliated. The library of the *madrasa* which comprised about 900 books, including the copies of the Holy Qur'an and the *hadis* were set on fire. The atrocities inflicted on the family and the *madrasa* of the Mulla are said to have been due to his intimate relations with the empeor. Cf. Mufti Muhammad Raza Ansari Firangi Mahali, *Bani-e Dars-i Nizami, Mulla Nizam-ud-Din Firangi Mahali*, Aligarh, 1973, pp. 25–30. Ansari reproduces the *mahzar* of Qazi Muhammad Sa'id with its photostat copy and quotes from contemporary and near-contemporary unpublished biographies and family histories.

[94] *Tarikh-i Jais* (a local history of Jais compiled possibly in the late-eighteenth century) MS Dr Abdul Ali Collection, Nadwat-ul Ulama, Lucknow, ff. 27. The story of friendship between the Saiyids of Jais and the *zamindar* of Tiloi is obscure and shrouded in mystery.

It is to be noted that Mohan Singh, out of resentment arising from his father's proposition to nominate his other son, Newal, to succeed to the *zamindari* after his death, had killed the former and usurped the *zamindari* without seeking a formal sanction from the Mughal *diwan*. Cf. W. C. Benett., *Chief Clans of the Roy Bareilly District*, pp. 41–2. In his enterprise, Mohan seems to have been backed by the Saiyids and the Shaikhs which neutralized the loss of the desertion of his own clansmen.

[95] Allahabad 934. An old feud seems to have existed between the *qazi* and the Mirs.

The conflict between the *zamindars*, 'the local despots' and the *madad-i ma'ash* grantees, the symbols and virtually the agents of the central government, originated in their divergent economic and political interests which must have also generated tension in the villages. But the latter's newly acquired position accentuated it and often led to the eruption of violence. The *madad-i ma'ash* holders were held in contempt even by the loyalists among the local magnates.[96]

It is not possible to say whether these developments affected, to the same extent, the towns where, as it has been suggested, the *madad-i ma'ash* holders population was concentrated. However, the opinion that the majority of the *madad-i ma'ash* holders in Mughal India lived in towns[97] needs reconsideration. A fairly large number of these, as our sources conclusively show, were village based. They had their *madrasas*, libraries and mosques in the villages. They also seem to have had close links with the *zamindars* of the neighbourhood. It may also be noted here that none of these instances of conflict indicated any process of basic change in the existing pattern of social relations. Their divergent interests, notwithstanding, the *zamindars* and the *madad-i ma'ash* holders formed two sections of the same class that thrived and flourished on the expropriation of agrarian surplus. There appears also to be little difference in the character of the property of a *jagirdar* and a *madad-i ma'ash* holder.[98]

We can, however, verify certain changes in the caste compo-

Even during the tenure of his office, the *qazi* had seized over a thousand *bighas* in the *pargana* of Fatehpur, *sarkar* Bahraich, where he held 250 *bighas* as his *mashrut madad-i ma'ash*. The land misappropriated was in the *zamindari* of the Mirs. Also, one Jafar, a relative of the *qazi*, is reported to have usurped their *zamindari* and *milkiyat* in the villages of Sahya, Karmallahpur and Kantaur in *parganas* Selak and Husampur Ibid., No. 1280.

[96] *Akhbarat* BS, 2nd R.Y., p. 139, for the offences of the *chaudhuris* of Bilgram against the Saiyids of a village in the *pargana*. See also Allahabad 1316, for one Natha, a *zamindar-cum-thanadar*'s excesses on the *madad-i ma'ash* of one Mian Shaikh Bhavan in the village of Madhopur of *pargana* Sadrpur in *sarkar* Khairabad. Natha raided the village along with his kinsmen (*biradari*).

[97] Satish Chandra, *Parties and Politics*. Introduction, p. xxvi with qualification; Shirin Moosvi, 'Siyurghal Statistics in the *Ain-i-Akbari*: An Analysis'.

[98] For a different interpretation of this kind of conflict see Iqtidar Alam Khan, 'Middle Classes in the Mughal Empire', Presidential Address to the Medieval Indian Section, 36th Session of IHC, Aligarh, 1975. Khan suggests placing the urban intelligentsia including town-based revenue grantees and traders in Mughal times in one

sition of the *zamindars*. According to the *Ain*, Rajputs and
Kunbis were the dominant *zamindar* castes in Sahali and
Fatehpur respectively. By the late-seventeenth century, however, Muslims also seem to have acquired some dominance
among the *zamindars* of these *parganas*. How money contributed
in corroding the caste bastions of old *zamindars* and introduced
new elements in Mughal times is evident from the rise of the
zamindaris by purchase in *Haveli* Bahraich, Husampur and Mallanwan. In the late-sixteenth century, Rajputs, Raikwars and
Bisens and Bais had respectively been the dominant *zamindar*
castes in *Haveli* Bahraich, Husampur and Mallanwan.[99]
However, there is also a possibility that these purchases of
zamindaris were a result of a well-intended Mughal policy of
installing and strengthening reliable *zamindars*.

II

The imperial government did not fail to make a bid to maintain
and restore stability in the province. It adopted, and also
encouraged and promoted some of the earlier administrative
measures with a view to containing the turbulence. The policy
related to the strengthening of loyalists and the creation of new
zamindars in the midst of hostile *zamindaris*, and also effecting
some changes in *jagir* administration. But the measures had
little success.

Consolidation and creation of loyal zamindars

The policy of strengthening the loyalist *zamindars* and the
appointment of the new ones to replace the rebellious ones was
an old device. Aurangzeb, much more than anyone of his
predecessors, had vainly tried it. The objective behind this
policy was to open the gate to outsiders into regions which had
been, or had lately been developing into, strongholds of the
established *zamindar* castes. In *pargana* Unao, for instance,

----

category as against a category of *zamindars* and *jagirdars* who subsisted on the appropria-
tion of 'feudal' surplus.
[99]*Ain*, II (Jarrett), pp. 187, 189–90.

where the Bais had been dominant since the seventeenth century, efforts were made to promote the Saiyid *zamindaris*. The choice of the Saiyids was determined by the fact that they had once enjoyed eminence and had powerful kinsfolk (*ulus*) in the *pargana*. When Rad Andaz Khan proposed that Saiyid Ghulam Muhi-ud-Din be appointed the *zamindar* of *pargana* Unao, he gave the Saiyid's possession of *ulus* and a familiarity with the region as special reasons for his recommendation.[100] Since the Bais were a dominant caste in and around the *pargana* and were always in a position to exploit the peasants' problems to the fullest advantage, the new *zamindars'* strength had to be specially considered. The objective of award of *zamindari*, in some cases, was also to strengthen local officials through an infusion with additional loyal sources of influence and power.[101]

The appointment of *zamindars* was primarily an administrative necessity. Aurangzeb's orthodoxy did not influence it very much. The Gehlots and the Chandels of *pargana* Harha, a Bais stronghold in *sarkar* Lucknow acquired their *zamindaris* from Aurangzeb.[102] In one case, Aurangzeb cancelled the appointment of a Muslim *zamindar* in Baiswara due to the *faujdar*'s resistance.[103] The policy was continued in the early-eighteenth century, even though it had produced no tangible results in Aurangzeb's reign.[104]

Again, we have a number of cases to show how some intermediaries, supported by the state, tried to acquire primary *zamindari* rights in and around the regions disturbed by *zamindar* uprisings. In the early years of the eighteenth century the *chaudhuris* of *pargana* Sandila appear to have strengthened their position by purchasing a number of *zamindaris* in the *pargana*.[105] In May 1714, one Saroman Das, son of Alam Chand, apparently a *qanungo*, was favoured with an *inam* of 30,000 *dams* in *pargana* Sandi, *sarkar* Khairabad, for the plantation of some

[100] *Roshan Kalam*, pp. 7 and 36.

[101] Ibid., pp. 3–4, for the case of one Saiyid Muzaffar who was recommended by the *faujdar*, Rad Andaz Khan, for a *mansab* and the *zamindari* in *pargana* Saipur following the rising of the Chauhan *zamindars* in the *pargana*.

[102] C. A. Elliot, *Chronicles of Oonao*, pp. 53–4. Elliot claims to have seen several of Aurangzeb's *farmans* to the Gehlots.

[103] *Roshan Kalam*, p. 18.

[104] *Akhbarat BS*, 3rd R. Y., p. 222 and 4th R. Y., p. 146.

[105] Allahabad 516, 522–3 and 611.

orchards around the town of Sandi. Again on 31 May 1716,
Kankhat, a village, was granted to him as *inam* for raising a *sarai*
and a *garhi*. The village was subsequently known as the *qasba* of
Saroman Nagar *alias* Kankhat, a centre of military and economic importance. Saroman Das's acquisition of lands and purchase of *zamindaris* in *sarkar* Khairabad went on unabated even
under Burhan ul-Mulk.[106]

The policy of promoting outsiders as intermediaries in the
strongholds of the turbulent clans was of little help when the
government was riven by the internal strife amongst its functionaries. Further, when such intermediaries were encouraged
to build their primary *zamindaris* and *milkiyat* at the expense of
the old landholders, the caste peasants had reasons, greater
than their social ties with the rebel *zamindars*, to be up in arms
with them against the Mughals.

Changes in jagir administration

The *zamindar* uprisings, as well as the developments in the wake
of the newly acquired position of the *madad-i ma'ash* holders,
resulted, in particular, in the dislocation of *jagir* administration
in the province. In the greater part of the province the *jagirdar*
could not manage to collect his due from the peasantry. In the
traditional structure of the *jagir* system there was hardly anything to sustain him against these new difficulties. Two new
features—*jagir-i mahal-i watan* and *jagir* for long tenure—thus
developed in the early-eighteenth century, apparently to adjust
the *jagir* system to the new circumstances.

The *jagir* was normally assigned to the *jagirdar* in a district
with which he had no connection. This was in order to maintain
the unity and cohesion of the empire and to prevent the *jagirdar*
from developing permanent links with his *jagir mahal*. With the
same object in view the *jagir* was subject to frequent transfers.
The *watan jagir* and the *altamgha* were exceptions to this rule.
The *watan jagirs* originated in settlements with the local chiefs
and *zamindars* who obtained *mansabs* against the *jama* of their
ancestral dominions. It was a device to absorb the *zamindars* in,
and make them a part of, the Mughal 'bureaucracy'. It also

---

[106] Ibid., 7 and 11 for *inam*; 2 for reference to Kankhat as *qasba* Saroman Nagar; 2,
4–5, 12 and 14 for purchase of *zamindaris* in Sandi and Sirah.

satisfied the *zamindars* as they had an opportunity to go up, through their association with the Mughal empire, above the level of the other members of their communities. As a rule the emperor did not interfere in the *watan jagir*. This privilege was not available to non-*zamindars*. But as a concession to these *mansabdars*, Jahangir instituted *altamgha*, the *jagir* awarded on a permanent basis, which also served to reinforce the imperial system at lower levels.[107]

It, however, appears that by the eighteenth century the *jagir-i watan* was no longer an exclusive preserve of the chiefs, implying an allocation of *jagirs* in the territories under their *zamindaris*. In a number of cases, in Awadh at least, the holders of *jagir-i watan* or, to follow more accurately the contemporary Persian phrase, *jagir-i mahal-i watan* were not the *zamindars* of the entire area in the *jagirs*. The term apparently began to signify perhaps a new development in *jagir* administration. The *jagir* that lay contiguous to the homeland of the *jagirdar* or of which his native place formed a part was called his *jagir-i mahal-i watan*. The *jagirs* of Sanjar Khan, Shamsher Khan, Shaikh Sanaullah and Khalil Khan Bazid Khail which they received at the beginning of Farrukh Siyar's reign are characterized as *jagirs* of *mahal-i watan*, since these *jagirdars*, as we shall see below, came from *sarkar* Lucknow and their *jagirs* lay within the territory of the same *sarkar*. Mahona and Kakori which were adjacent to their existing *mahals* were also assigned to Sanjar Khan and Shamsher Khan.[108] Similarly, the *jagirs* that Aziz Khan Chaghta of *pargana* Shahabad of *sarkar* Khairabad obtained in 1721 in *parganas* Pali, Sarah and Bawan of the same *sarkar* have also been mentioned in the same terms. What is of greater interest is that Chaghta's *jagir* in *pargana* Harha and Sandila in *sarkar* Lucknow too have been characterized as *jagirs* of *mahal-i watan*,[109] the term *watan* in this case indicating the entire province of Awadh. In an another case, *pargana* Gopamau was given to one Anwar-ud-Din Khan of the same *pargana* as a *jagir-i-mahal-i watan*. Anwar-ud-Din Khan also held the *faujdari* of the *pargana*. Both the *jagir* and the *faujdari* were confirmed to

---

[107] Compare Athar Ali, *Mughal Nobility*, pp. 78–80; Irfan Habib, *Agrarian System*, p. 260.

[108] Shivdas, ff. 3b, 11b, 27b; Mubarak, ff. 78a and 105a.

[109] Ibid., f. 58a.

him by Muhammad Shah in 1721.[110]

The evidence suggests that the *jagirdar* wanted his *jagir* in or around the place of his origin. In the existing situation of widespread *zamindar* revolts and a growing realization of the emperor's inability to assist local officials adequately in administering the territories under their jurisdiction, the *jagirdar* felt that he had to meet the threat to his *jagir* on the score of his own strength. This was evidently the success over the centre by the forces of decentralization, which was nourished steadily by the economic strength of the region. The choice before the imperial authority was either to lose the disturbed territory to the rebels, and in some cases even to the *jagirdars* when they could perhaps ally with the rebels as well, or to keep imperial unity intact by making certain changes in the system. For, whatever the changes in their position the power of the *jagirdars*, unlike that of the *zamindars*, was always regarded as emanating from the emperor's authority. The *jagirdar's* urge was, therefore, conceded to. It was believed that on account of his *biradari* and the social ties in the region the *jagirdar* would be able to muster sufficient strength to overawe the *zamindar*. This probably also explains the policy of simultaneously awarding *mansabs* to certain members of his *biradari*, to bring them also in direct contact with the centre. The *mansab* of Samsher Khan at the accession of Farrukh Siyar has been mentioned by Shivdas as 2500/2000 and 200 *sawar mansabdar-i biradari*.[111] Since the words *biradari* and *barawurdi* when written in Persian styles resemble each other very closely, there is a possibility of mistaking one for the other. But the word *biradari* here could not be mistaken for *barawurdi* and the phrase misinterpreted as indicating merely the nature of the *sawar* rank. For Shivdas who reports this is not very particular about indicating the nature of the *sawar* rank as to whether it was *barawurdi* or *du aspa sih aspa*.[112]

---

[110] *Majmua-i Faramin* (a collection of original Mughal *farmans*, *parwanas* and *hasb-ul-hukms* bound together) Rampur MS. pp. 61–2.

[111] Shivdas, f. 3b.

[112] The Mughal *mansab* (rank) was dual, stated in two numbers, one termed *zat* which represented the status of the rankholder in the hierarchy of the Mughal *mansabdars*, and the other *sawar* which represented the strength of the 'cavalry' under his command. The official formula for stating this, in the case of 2000 *zat* and 1000 *sawar* for example, was *du hazari hazar sawar*. Among the important innovations under Jahangir was *du aspa sih aspa* which was theoretically a part of the *sawar* rank and signified the pay and

In the same passage he gives the *mansab* of Khalil Khan Bazid Khail as simply *du hazari hazar* (2000/1000). Secondly, in the context of Shamsher Khan's promotion, his 200 *sawar mansabdar-i biradari* are clearly distinguished from his usual *sawar* rank.[113]

The *mansabdar-i biradari* were apparently deputed with the chief of the *biradari*. How they were paid and where they were given *jagirs* is not known to us. It can, however, be presumed that they, if not paid in cash, were paid from the revenues of their own regions.

The rise of the Indian Muslims as a power group in the nobility at the Mughal court may also have encouraged these developments in administration. The Mughals promoted the indigenous elements with a view to creating a new group as a counterpoint to ambitions of the *khanazads*. But while the Indian Muslims were encouraged because it was believed they could be easily contained, yet they aspired, in contravention of existing practice, to have their *jagirs* like *zamindaris* in and around their own homelands. Their demands became more insistent as their difficulties in realizing the revenue in the alien districts increased. When the emperor conceded their aspirations, he must have been aware of the fact that the emerging pattern of *jagir* administration was not in the long-term interests of the empire. Absence of interest in the locality together with the frequency of transfers often resulted in the *jagirdar's* indifference to the problems of the development of his *jagir mahal*. At whatever cost, the *jagirdar's* chief concern was to realize his dues from his *jagir*. But so long as the imperial checks through officials like *faujdars*, news-writers, *chaudhuris* and *qanungos* operated effectively, the conduct of the *jagirdar* and his agents was watched over and his immediate benefit could not prevail over the interests of the empire. In the wake of the gradual decline of the imperial checks, control over the *jagirdar's* oppression of the peasantry slackened which in turn added to the strength of the *zamindars*.

The *jagir* for the indigenous noble in his *watan mahal*, together with *mansabs* for his kinsmen, who commanded his contingents

obligations to be twice the number of rank. Is some cases the entire *sawar* rank was *du aspa sih aspa* while in others only a portion of it became so, the rest designated *barawurdi* remaining ordinary. Cf. M. Athar Ali, *Mughal Nobility*, pp. 38–43.

[113] Shivdas, f. 12b.

at various levels, were thus means to enable him to counter effectively the threats to the empire. However, under the prevailing circumstances the *jagir-i mahal-i watan* jeopardized stability instead of being an asset to the mechanics of imperial control in the province. Most of these *jagirdars*, on the strength of their being local men, seem to have obtained services in or around their respective *watans* and then sat idle in their homes, hardly attending to their business. This is what was reported to Farrukh Siyar in 1715, about the big and small *mansabdars* of the *sarkars* of Lucknow and Khairabad.[114] Some of them remained in their *jagirs* and collected revenue even after they were physically disabled and were of no value to Mughal service.[115]

The practice of *jagir-i mahal-i watan* which developed in part in response to the *jagirdar*'s urge to have his *jagir*, like a *zamindari*, in or around his *watan* inevitably encouraged the tendency of holding the *jagir* over a long period. The practice of frequent transfer would at best be enforced within a given region. At any rate the frequent transfer was now of greater detriment to the empire. Assignees of *mahal-i watan* thus held their *jagirs* virtually on a permanent, and sometimes, hereditary basis. Shamsher Khan and Sanjar Khan retained their *jagirs* till 1719.[116] Anwar-ud-Din Khan maintained his *jagir* and *faujdari* in Gopamau for at least nine years. The case of Shaikh Khairullah and the *mansabdars* of Lucknow and Khairabad also bespeak a tendency to defy the principle of transfer of *jagirs*. The following incident further illustrates the circumstances in which the principle and the practice of the transfer had to be given up. 462,280 *dams* from Harharpur and Ranipur and some other villages in *pargana* Fakhrpur, *sarkar* Bahraich, were assigned to Saiyid Jafar Ali. But the Saiyid could not get hold of his *dams*, as Ihtisham Khan, another *jagirdar* in the *pargana* whom he had replaced in these villages, resisted his appointment and appropriated the income for himself. Subsequently, on 14 May 1714, the local *diwan*,

---

[114] *Akhbarat* FS, 4th R. Y., II, p. 78, for a report about a large number of the Awadhi (*mutawattinan-i suba* Awadh) *mansabdars*' obtaining certificates (for *jagirs* and services) from the office of the *bakhshis* on the strength of their residence in the province (*ba ilaqa-i watan*). They then sat idle in their homes and did not perform their duties.

[115] Ibid., 6th R. Y., I, p. 329, dated 5th October 1717, for one Shaikh Khairullah of Panhan town who had for long been blind and had been confined to his house but was still collecting and appropriating the revenue of his erstwhile *jagir* area.

[116] Compare Shivdas, ff. 3b, 11b and 27b; Mubarak, ff. 78a and 105a.

Gobind Das, was directed by the centre to look into the irregularities and help the Saiyid in obtaining his assigned *dams*. The order, however, had little effect. Taking force to be the order of the day, the Saiyid then made a bid to resolve his own difficulties. He made up for the loss he suffered at the hands of the stronger by his excesses on the weaker in the *pargana*. 250 *bighas* in *tappa* Gondai which were held in *madad-i ma'ash* by one Bibi Saira and six others were subsequently misappropriated by him.[117]

The long-term *jagir*, or rather the modification of the principle of frequent transfers of the *jagirs*, came to be accepted even in the cases of ordinary (other than *mahal-i watan*) *jagirs* in the northern provinces. In 1713, eight *parganas* in Bundelkhand, *suba* of Allahabad, were assigned to Muhammad Khan Bangash. In 1720, he received two new *parganas*, Bhojpur and Shahabad, which are referred to as 'in addition to his eight *parganas* in Bundelkhand'. Again, in the late 1720s and the early 1730s in the context of his conflict with the Bundelas, we have references to his *jagirs* in Bundelkhand.[118] In another instance, in the early years of Muhammad Shah's reign Qamar-ud-Din Khan, the *wazir*, was given a *jagir* in *sarkar* Moradabad which he retained till at least 1745, the year of the imperial campaign against the Rohilla chief of Anola. Again, at the beginning of Muhammad Shah's reign, Murtaza Khan is reported to have received the *sarkars* of Benaras, Jaunpur, Ghazipur and Chunar as part of his *jagir*. In 1738, when Burhan ul-Mulk was appointed to the governorship of Allahabad, these *sarkars* were still part of the *jagir* of Murtaza Khan.[119] It is very likely that Murtaza Khan retained his *jagir* in these *sarkars* till his death (1748). Further, sometime in the reign of Farrukh Siyar, the *pargana* of Ghiyaspur, in *suba* Bihar, was assigned to Sher Afgan Khan which he retained till his death in the 14th R. Y. of

[117] Allahabad 962 and 12033.

[118] *Khujasta*, f. 80b; W. Irvine, *Later Moghuls*, II, p. 230.

[119] Compare *Tuhfa*, ff. 3a, 4a and 9b; Kamboh, f. 48a. Murtaza Khan's original name was Hifzullah Khan. He was son of Shukrullah Khan known as Murtaza Khan *Bahadur Shahi* (d. 1712) and was appointed superintendent of the imperial elephant stable under Bahadur Shah (6th R. Y.). In the reign of Jahandar Shah (1713) he rose to the office of the second *bakhshi* and received the title of Wizarat Khan. In the 7th R. Y., of Farrukh Siyar, he was appointed *faujdar* of Saharanpur and in 1719 he got the office of the *qurbegi* (head of armoury) at the court. In the reign of Rafi ud-Daula, he received the

Muhammad Shah (1143/1732–33).[120] It may be noted that none of these cases represents that of a *jagir-i mahal-i watan*. From *watan* as *jagir* perhaps to *jagir* emerging as *watan*? Our sources, however, do not allow us to generalize on these lines for the entire Mughal empire.

If on the one hand the tendency of the *jagirdar* to violate the principle of transfer in *jagir* and to convert it into a permanent holding was a result of the decline of the centre, it also showed, on the other, the strength of the region where such tendency got constant nourishment. This tendency did not have a bearing on the growth of any regional and local affiliations, as it was not confined only to the holders of the *jagir-i mahal-i watan* but also extended to the *jagirdars* from outside. Nonetheless, there is some evidence to suggest that a process of regionalization coincided with eighteenth-century political and administrative decentralization.[120a]

The economic strength of the region followed a long course of growth in the wake of a developing cash nexus in agriculture in the seventeenth and the early-eighteenth centuries. The level of monetization was evident in the fact that in the eighteenth century not only the revenues and the related offices, but also some other government positions which had no direct connection with the revenues, began to be valued in money. Offices like *faujdari* and even *subadari* were held on *ijara*, apparently with the guarantee (*mal-zamini*) of the *mahajans*. In the fact that ordinarily the *jagirdar* preferred to farm out his *jagir* there is some evidence to show the increasing importance of traders, money-changers and the money-lenders. What is more significant is that even the *amils* of the *jagirdars* normally began to be characterized as revenue farming *amils (ummal-i ijaradar)*[121]

The *ijara* was not a new phenomenon in the revenue history of

title of Murtaza Khan and was given the *niyabat* of the *mir atish*. Throughout the reign of Muhammad Shah he appears to have stayed, and held different important offices, at the court. Cf. Kamwar, ff. 306a, 331b, 336a, 358a and 364a.

[120] Cf. Muhammad Ali Khan Ansari, *Tarikh-i Muzaffari*, f. 352a and *Bahr-ul-Mawwaj*, f. 318b, Patna MSS. Sher Afgan Khan, a brother of Khwaja Lutfullah Khan Sadiq of Panipat was *faujdar* of Panipat, Meerut and Sikandrabad in the early years of Bahadur Shah's reign. In his 4th R. Y., he was appointed deputy governor of Malwa, which was in the *subadari* of Prince Jahan Shah. He received the office of *khan saman* and the title of Azz-ud-Daula from Muhammad Shah. Kamwar, ff. 307a, 314b and 377b.

[120a] See Chapter VI.

[121] K.K., I, P. 157.

the Mughals. We have evidence for its widespread practice in the seventeenth century. We also have indirect evidence for the practice of *ijara* among the officials of Aurangzeb. An order of the reign of Aurangzeb lays down that the *amins* and *karoris* of the *khalisa* lands should not farm out villages, in the *pargana* entrusted to them, to any of their relations, to government servants and to the *chaudhuris*.[122] These orders notwithstanding, revenue farming continued to be practised throughout the reign of Aurangzeb. Among government officials, however, it seems to have remained confined mainly to rural and revenue officials. In the time of Farrukh Siyar, people like Ratan Chand, a trader by caste, seem to have appreciated that *ijara* was a sequel to an expanding network of money economy. As *ijara* was then partly officially encouraged and patronized, its practice became extended to non-revenue officials as well. In 1714, the *paibaqi mahals* in *sarkar* Lucknow were farmed out to Saiyid Ahmad Khan, the deputy *faujdar* of Lucknow. In spite of the collection of the full amount from the *mahals*, Ahmad Khan, as was reported to the emperor on 27 April 1715, paid not a single *dam* to the treasury.[123] According to another report dated 27 March 1717, the *sair mahals* in *pargana* Kheri were taken on *ijara* by the *kotwal* of the *pargana*.[124]

In the wake of long-term *jagir* there arose the *ijara* for long-term as well. In the vicinity of Awadh, in the Moradabad-Bareilly region, Ali Mohammad Khan Rohilla held for life the *ijara* of the *jagirs* of the *wazir*, Qamar ud-Din Khan and the others. On similar terms, Murtaza Khan farmed out his *jagir* in the Benares region to Mir Rustam Ali Khan.[125] In the event of the absence of a mechanism of checks either evolved through the mutual consent of the concerned parties or imposed by the political authorities, *ijara* also tended to develop into a hereditary possession.

While the decline of imperial organization at the centre

[122] Compare N. A. Siddiqi, *Land Revenue Administration*, p. 94.

[123] *Akhbarat* FS, 4th R. Y., I, p. 110.   [124] Ibid., 6th R. Y., I, p. 174.

[125] Cf. for the Moradabad-Bareilly region, Muhammad Salih *Tarikh-i Ali*, ff. 94b–95a; *Safarnama* of Anand Ram 'Mukhlis', (ed.) S. Azhar Ali, Rampur, 1946, pp. 2, 3, 27 and 72; see also Muzaffar Alam, 'Zamindar Uprisings and the Emergence of Rohilla Power in *sarkar* Muradabad', *PIHC*, Bhubaneswar, 1977, pp. 221–30. For the Benares region see, *Tuhfa* ff. 3b and 10a–11a, and Kamboh, ff. 6a, 45b–47a and 48b.

created some problems for the provincial government, the dislocation of political relationships in the province led to greater
trouble. The provincial government in Awadh was gravely
disturbed by the agrarian uprisings at a time when factional
politics at the court had assumed serious proportions. These
uprisings extended from the earlier years and reflected a larger
social problem, namely, the conflict between the central government and the regional and local elements in Mughal India,
but they took a serious turn in extent and intensity at a time
when the *zamindars* felt they would be able to dictate terms to
Mughal authority.

These *zamindars* who were the powerful leaders of the dominant clans, took full advantage of economic growth in the region
and on the strength of their links with their kinsfolk among the
peasants resisted the imperial rule which defined their political
position as well as validated their share of the produce. When
the state tried to resist, the *zamindars* mobilized their people,
raised an army, fortified their strongholds and rose up in arms
against the Mughals. They also attacked the *zamindars* and the
peasants who did not belong to their castes and the latter were
compelled to help and seek help from the Mughals.

Whenever they held sway, the *madad-i ma'ash* holders also
became victims of their raids. We may, however, note that the
madad-i ma'ash holders, even though the ideologues and the
symbols of the empire, by themselves were a source of trouble
for the Mughals. Since the beginning of the Mughal rule, the
Muslim theologians and *a'immadars* had had an uneasy relationship with the state. In the course of the seventeenth century,
they steadily gained in strength and acquired a privileged
position, particularly, in Awadh. Even after they had forfeited
their claim to it, they enjoyed 'the revenue free grant', together
with *zamindaris*, sometimes at the expense of the old landholders. The state promoted their interests and also overlooked
these violations particularly in Aurangzeb's time. But the local
officials who encountered the difficulties that these privileges
engendered, did not approve of the concessions that were extended to them by the centre.

The Mughals made certain changes to strengthen the position of the *jagirdars* to enable them to meet the threat from the
region to the centre. But ironically these changes threatened to

further subvert the mechanics of royal absolutism and brought
the government face to face with new problems. These changes
had been in response to a tendency which had lately begun to
gain ground and revealed the strength of the region against the
centre. The principle and practice of frequent transfer which
was intended to reinforce the centralization of all powers in the
hands of the emperor was never convenient to the *jagirdar*. Now
that the inability of the centre, as it was represented in the
position of the *faujdar*, *thanadar* and the other officials in the
region, was increasingly exposed, the *jagirdar* refused to comply
with the emperor's order of his transfer. The *jagirdar* was not
sure if he would be able to take over his new *jagir*. It had now
become clear that unless he had support from the local
magnates, he could not realize the revenues of his *jagir*. And the
jagirdar could think of such a support only when he had *jagir* in
and around his *watan* or else he was allowed to hold it for a
long term and establish local ties. Some *jagirs*, thus, tended to
emerge into virtual *zamindari* holdings, in particular, in areas
where land still promised rich dividends to its possessor.

The condition in the Punjab was worse. While the development at the court alienated the governor from various central
and provincial authorities, the government was here faced with
enormous internal threats.

CHAPTER IV

Mughal Power, the Sikhs and other Local Groups in the Punjab

The problems of local and provincial administration were much more serious in the Punjab. The province continued to be in trouble, notwithstanding the constant efforts and partial success of the governors in restoring a measure of stability for some years. The course of the decay of the imperial authority was largely determined by the nature of the Sikh movement which challenged the very basis of the Mughal power structure and had its own concepts of the ruler and rulership. The developments outside the north-western frontiers also influenced, very crucially, the history of the region in the eighteenth century. While the growth and stability of the empires beyond Kabul and Qandahar enriched the Punjab and the areas around the Indus in the sixteenth-seventeenth centuries, the turmoil and disturbances in Persia and central Asia adversely affected the fortunes of the Punjab and also of different north-western regions of the Mughal empire in the eighteenth century.

A major failure of the Mughals in the region is illustrated in their inability to cope with the Sikh question. Though Banda Bahadur, the formidable Sikh leader of the early-eighteenth century, and along with him over 700 other Sikhs were captured and slain in 1715, Sikh hostility continued to subvert the foundations of Mughal power till the province was in total disarray in the middle of the eighteenth century. The Sikh movement under Banda had a strong social base among the *zamindars*, the peasantry and the lower classes. The movement, however was not free from weaknesses which in part became responsible for its failure in 1715. But the Mughals under Bahadur Shah could not make use of these weaknesses nor did they succeed in mustering their own strength against the Sikhs. Factionalism at the court and some hasty measures to meet the Sikh threat enervated the Mughals, while slackening imperial control over the local administration together with the open or secret support of the hill chiefs to the Sikhs offset the advantages of the local ties that the Mughals had in the province.

Guru Gobind Singh (1666–1708), the tenth and the last Guru of the Sikhs, is said to have transformed the character of the Sikh religion in the late-seventeenth century. He converted it into a militant organization.[1] The *Khalsa*, the name that he gave to his followers, became a symbol of armed resistance to what the Guru considered tyranny. The new doctrine brought the Guru's followers, who comprised largely the Jat peasantry and the *zamindars*,[2] into direct conflict with the hill rajas, and some bigger *zamindars* of the Punjab. The contingents of the hill rajas were a source of substantial strength to the Mughals in suppressing the rebellion of the Sikhs during the last years of Aurangzeb's reign.[3]

Guru Gobind's clash with the chief of Bilaspur signified primarily, the lowly placed Sikhs' inherent conflict with the big *zamindars*. The Guru also had political ambitions of taking over the leadership of the locality.[4] The Sikhs had a serious quarrel with the Mughal state when the state, by supporting the chiefs against the Sikhs, identified Mughal interests with those of the dominant intermediaries. Aurangzeb could not appreciate it, but his successor Bahadur Shah who had governed the Punjab and his *wazir*, Mun'im Khan who had deputized for him in the province, probably recognized the necessity of a new arrange-

---

[1] This does not imply that the elements of *Khalsa* were totally absent in the earlier phases of Sikhism. Elements of struggle against tyranny are discernible in Guru Nanak's denunciation of contemporary rulers and Guru Hargobind's resistance against oppression. The Sikh traditions of catholicity and egalitarianism were unmistakable features of Sikh polity when it matured, even though the Sikh movement under Banda Bahadur was not free from religious overtones. The Sikh rulers patronized personages and institutions of all faiths. Compare, Indù Banga, *Agrarian System of the Sikhs*, Delhi, 1978, pp. 148–67.

[2] Ganesh Das Vadera, *Char Bagh-i Panjab*, edited by Kirpal Singh, Amritsar, 1965, p. 115.

[3] Compare W. Irvine, *Later Moghuls*, I, pp. 84–6; S. M. Latif, *History of the Punjab*, Calcutta (1891), pp. 264–5.

[4] By 1682 when the Sikhs clashed with the chief of Bilaspur the whole setting of Gobind Singh's *darbar* had been that of a regal court and his uncle, Kirpal had begun to invite the chiefs to visit Anandpur Makhowal, the Sikh headquarters. The militarization of the Sikh headquarters alarmed the chief who asserted his authority on the establishment by demanding a tribute from Gobind Singh. S. S. Bal, 'Early Years of the Pontificate of Guru Gobind Singh' in *Proceedings of the Punjab History Conference*, 1966 (Patiala 1968), pp. 63–78.

ment with the *zamindars* in the Punjab. Bahadur Shah invited Guru Gobind Singh to his court, conferred upon him a robe of honour, and asked him to accompany the royal march towards the Deccan.[5] For reasons not known to us, Bahadur Shah could not satisfy the Guru. Our period then saw the resurgence of the Sikh uprisings. The Sikh struggle in our period was directed more vehemently against the Mughal state. To the Sikhs the Mughal state was the source of all tyranny, since the state not only had the largest share in the social surplus but it also legitimized and sustained the existing power-structure in the locality.

The Sikhs, the *zamindars and the* Madad-i ma'ash *holders*

The *zamindars* in the Punjab, like most of their counterparts in the northern provinces of the Mughal empire, had taken full advantage of Aurangzeb's involvement in the Deccan. They had been up in arms against Mughal authority during the last phase of Aurangzeb's reign. Mun'im Khan, the deputy governor of the Punjab, is reported to have raised a strong army to deal with the refractory *zamindars* of *sarkar* Beth Jalandhar and Jammu who had become a menace to merchants and travellers. Also, he had often to cross the Sutlej into the territory of *sarkar* Sirhind in *suba* Delhi along with the imperial artillery (*topkhana*) and wage battles against the rebels.[6]

It appears that Banda Bahadur drew principal strength from the support of the *zamindars*. According to the observation of a contemporary Persian chronicler, Banda appeared first at Kharkauda, about 30 miles north-west of Delhi. The *zamindars* promptly put their trust in Banda and accepted him as their leader. At their instance, hundreds of others collected around Banda and in all directions the Sikhs were apprised of his appearance.[7] Moreover, a large number of the *zamindars* of the *parganas* along both sides of the Beas and the Ravi and the *Shah Nahr* (the canal) sympathized and acted in collusion with the

[5] K. K., II, p. 652; M. A. Macauliffe, *The Sikh Religion, Its Gurus, Sacred Writings and Authors*, reprint, Delhi, 1963, Vol. V, pp. 230 and 235; W. Irvine, *Later Moghuls* I, pp. 89–90; J. N. Sarkar, *History of Aurangzeb*, Calcutta, 1919, Vol. III, p. 361.

[6] *Akhbarat*, BS, 5th R. Y., p. 165.   [7] Warid, p. 282.

Sikhs of Banda.[8] During the entire period of their struggle against the Mughals, the Sikhs of Banda could move almost unchecked in the northern districts of the Bari Doab.[9] The *zamindars* of these districts supplied arms and horses to Banda when he retreated and took shelter in the hills, following the arrival of Bahadur Shah in the Punjab and the deployment against the Sikhs of the entire Mughal army of the northern provinces.[10] The villages of this region remained under Banda's control till as late as the middle of 1714. The *faujdar* of Kangra had to set up special *chaukis* (watch-houses) to deal with the *zamindars* who collected foodgrain and other provisions for the Sikhs.[11]

The fact that the second important region where Banda had a strong following lay on the south-eastern borders of the Punjab in *chakla* Sirhind of *suba* Delhi[12] created additional problems for the Mughal government. It not only threatened to bring the Mughal capital at any moment within the striking reach of the Sikhs, but also to cut off Mughal Punjab from the rest of the empire. We have seen how promptly the *zamindars* of Kharkauda in the cis-Sutlej area put their trust in Banda who launched his campaign from Sirhind.[13] He considered the region secure enough to make it the base for his operations beyond the Yamuna in *sarkar* Saharanpur.[14] Almost the whole region fell to the Sikhs during the first phase of Banda's wars against the Mughals. It is true that soon after, Bahadur Shah's personal command of the campaigns restored imperial authority in the region. But Banda easily recaptured the *parganas* of *chakla* Sirhind and installed his own *thanas* in the wake of the

---

[8] *Akhbarat*, BS, 3rd R. Y., p. 342; 4th R. Y., p. 372; 5th R. Y., pp. 289, 374 and 395.

[9] Ibid., BS, 6th R. Y., p. 16.   [10] Ibid., BS, 5th and 6th R. Ys., II, p. 428.

[11] 'Every night', as it was reported to the Mughal court on 24 Jumada I, 4th R. Y., of Farrukh Siyar, 'about 500 to 600 persons from the villages of *pargana* Batala and the other *parganas* in the neighbourhood carry over one to two thousand *mans* of foodgrains to the accursed Sikhs. Nobody intercepts them on their way to Gurdaspur.' Ibid., FS, 4th R. Y., I, pp. 97, 141–2 and 158.

[12] Ibid., BS, 4th R. Y., pp. 80, 88 and 89; pp. 98, 260 and 282; FS, 1st and 2nd R. Ys., pp. 129 and 137, 3rd R. Y., I, pp. 10, 7, 116, 127–8 and 158.

[13] Ibid., BS, 4th R. Y., pp. 7 and 80; See also W. Irvine, *Later Moghuls* I, p. 72.

[14] Ibid., BS, 4th R. Y., pp. 80, 88, 127–8 and 147 for Banda's invasion of Saharanpur, Buria, Kerana, Kandhla, Jalalabad and Jwalapur.

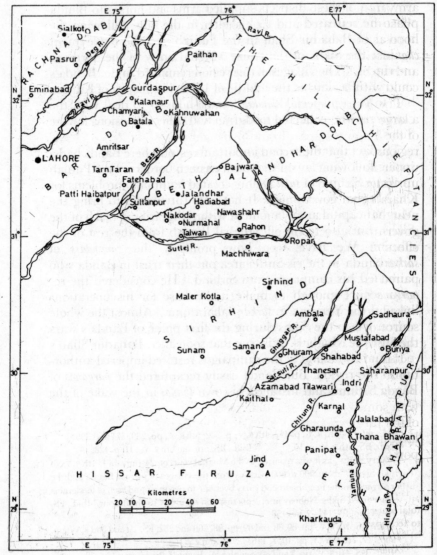

4. *Parganas* affected by Sikh uprisings

disturbances following the death of the emperor in 1712.[15] In moments of extremity when the Sikhs ran off into the hills, Banda could also depend on the supply of provisions for his army from *chakla* Sirhind.[16] It is not unlikely that during the last phase of his struggle, Banda chose Sadhaura and its neighbourhood as the base of his operations due to its proximity with the *chakla* on the one hand, where he had support for his movement, and the Sirmur hills on the other where, as we shall see later, he could withdraw whenever the need arose.

The Mughals were thus confronted with the Sikh menace in a large part of the northern districts of *suba* Delhi on either side of the Yamuna, apart from the danger posed to the two major regions of the Punjab, namely, the *sarkar* of Jalandhar and the upper Bari Doab. Added to this were the *zamindar* and tribal uprisings in the ·other regions of the Punjab. The Bhattis, Kharals and Gujars and some of the *zamindars* of the regions near Multan often posed a serious threat to the provincial government.[17] It appears that in 1714–15, the Mughals had no effective control over, at least, a part of *pargana* Khushab in *sarkar* Singh Sagar Doab.[18] The *zamindars'* resistance had impaired imperial authority even over the *khalisa* villages in *pargana* Bahlolpur in Chanhat Doab.[19] These uprisings were not linked to the movement under Banda. But being in themselves a source of threat to the Mughal government, they emboldened the Sikhs to rise.

It is possible to identify with some qualifications and reservations, the social composition of the *zamindars* who followed Banda. From a brief reference in Khafi Khan, it appears that with some exceptions, Banda led predominantly the uprisings of the Jat *zamindars*.[20] It is also to be noted that the Jats were the largest *zamindar* castes in the *parganas* where Banda had support.[21] Since the ninth century the Jats or the Jatts had

---

[15] The non-Sikh residents of *chakla* Sirhind were so scared of the dangers of Banda's total control over the region that they made an appeal to Jahandar Shah to allow them to accompany the royal retinue to Delhi. Ibid., JS, pp. 98 and 282.

[16] Ibid., FS, 1st and 2nd R. Ys., p. 152.

[17] *Asrar-i Samadi*, edited by M. Shujauddin, Lahore, 1965, p. 9; MM, f. 45a.

[18] *Akhbarat*, FS, 4th R. Y., p. 159.

[19] Ibid., FS, 4th R. Y., p. 149.   [20] K. K., II, p. 651.

[21] Compare *Ain*, II, (Jarrett), pp. 292 and 323–5.

been moving northward from the Sindh region where they had lived as a pastoral community. They were first noticed in Multan area in the eleventh century; sixteenth-century sources refer to their unmistakable presence in the Punjab. From the Punjab they moved across the Sutlej towards the east to settle in the *subas* of Delhi and Agra.[22] By the close of the sixteenth century they had large areas under their *zamindaris* in and around the Punjab, in particular in the Rachna and Bari Doabs and in the west of the Yamuna in the *sarkars* of Sirhind, Hisar Firoza and Delhi of *suba* Delhi.[23] But no exact idea of their concentration as agriculturists in these areas can be had, depending merely on the *Ain*'s column of the *zamindars*. For the *zamindars* listed in the *Ain* perhaps refer only to intermediaries.[24] Their positions as intermediaries in these *parganas* apart, the Jats seem to have been dominant in the villages as *zamindars* and peasant proprietors (*zamindaran-i mauza* and *zamindaran-i dihat*). Besides, in a number of the other *parganas* of Bari Doab, Beth Jalandhar and the cis-Sutlej areas for which the *Ain* records the non-Jat as *zamindars*, the Jats apparently held distinct positions as agriculturists. This, in part, is illustrated from the traditions of the Jats of the southern areas of the Beth Jalandhar. The Jat village settlements in some parts of modern Jullundur district and in Phillaur *tahsil* are traced back to the fifteenth century, even though the *zamindars* of this area, according to the *Ain*, were predominantly Rajputs.[25]

The Jats of the Punjab were thus no longer a moving band of pastoralists. A larger number of them who had acquired wealth

---

[22] Cf. Irfan Habib, 'Presidential Address to the Medieval Section' in the *Proceedings of the Punjab History Conference*, 1971 (Patiala 1972), pp. 49–54; M. K. Kudryavtsev, 'The Role of the Jats in Northern India's Ethnic History' in J. N. Singh Yadav (ed.), *Haryana: Studies in History and Politics*, New Delhi, 1976, pp. 95–103; Iftikhar Ahmad, 'Medieval Jatt Immigration into the Punjab', paper presented to the 43rd Session of IHC, Kurukshetra, 1982 (mimeograph).

[23] Compare *Ain*, II, (Jarrett), pp. 320–36 for the Punjab and Multan, pp. 291–3 for *sarkar* Delhi and pp. 298–301 for Hisar Firoza and Sirhind. See also Iftikhar Ahmad, 'Medieval Jatt Immigation'.

[24] S. Nurul Hasan, 'Zamindars under the Mughals' in R. E. Frykenberg, (ed.), *Land Control and Social Structure in Indian History*, p. 25.

[25] Compare Tom G. Kessinger, *Vilyatpur, 1848–1968, Social and Economic Change in a North Indian Village*, New Delhi, 1979, pp. 28–40 and 44–9. Kessinger analyses the *Ain*'s information together with the nineteenth-century accounts in order to examine continuity and change in pre-British Punjab.

were then looking for social recognition of their status to match their economic position. In the teachings of Sikh religion, whose rise in the region almost synchronized with their settlements in the Punjab, they found an avenue to advance and promote their claims.

The areas of the Jat concentration registered remarkable growth in the seventeenth century. The Jat population concentrated in the Indo-Gangetic plain and the sub-Himalayan zones of the Bari, Rachna and also Chanhat Doabs which together with the Jalandhar Doab, combined regular rainfall, rich soil with extensive areas of the river basins irrigated easily from wells.[26] The high fertility of the soil drew the sturdy Jats to settle and become the chief agricultural community in the region, which in turn was further enriched. We may note the fact that the Jat settlements were also linked to the great route which carried the trade of the country east and south of Delhi with the Punjab and beyond with Central Asia and Persia. The region also had an opening through the Indus to Lahari Bandar, an important seaport of Mughal India.[27]

The countries west of the Punjab were linked with the Indo-Gangetic plain through two important roads, one from Kabul through the Khybar pass and Attock and the other from Qandahar through Fushanj (Pishin) and Pir Kanu (Sakhi Sarwar). The Qandahar route crossed the Indus at points near Dera Ghazi Khan and met at Multan which connected Lahore and the other important towns of the northern Punjab lower down with Bhakkar, Sehwan, the Leti chief's headquarters at Umarkot and Lahari Bandar both by road and the riverine route. A road from Multan across the Sutlej joined the main route *via* Hissar. There was yet another important route which linked Qandahar *via* Sibi and Bhakkar across the Indus with the western regions of the Mughal empire.[28] The commercial traffic through these routes was carried, among others, by the merchants from the region under review. Some entries in

[26] Irfan Habib, *Agrarian System*, pp. 26 and 27 and Tom G. Kessinger, *Vilyatpur*, p. 15.

[27] Cf. H. K. Naqvi, *Urban Centres and Industries in Upper India, 1556–1803*, Bombay, 1968, pp. 44–6.

[28] Cf. Irfan Habib, *Atlas*, Sheets 4B and 5B and Notes, pp. 11–12 and 15–16. Mohan Lal, *Travels in the Punjab, Afghanistan and Turkistan to Balkh, Bokhara, and Herat*, reprint, Patiala, 1971, Chapter VII, pp. 373–462.

Kamwar Khan's account of the early-eighteenth century suggest the presence of traders in Qandahar and different parts of
Iran including Tabriz from Multan and Lahore.[29] Our sources
also mention goods from Persia being sold by the Afghan tribes
of Qandahar in Sindh.[30] Mohan Lal made some interesting
observations in the course of his inquiries regarding the prospects of trade in Multan in the early-nineteenth century.
'The principal marts of Multan', he observed, 'are Amritsar,
Bahawalpur, Khirpur, Dera Ghazi Khan, Dera Ismail Khan,
Laiya, Shujabad, Mitankot, etc., which have a commercial
communication with the merchants of Shikarpur, Qandhar,
Herat, Bokhara, Kabul, Peshawar, Sindh, Hindustan, etc.'[31]
This trade was carried by Lohanis and Shikarpuris largely by
means of pack animals, through 'many roads from the places on
the right bank of the Indus' leading to Qandahar. The
Shikarpuris were the Khatris who had spread themselves in
almost all the regions of Central Asia and Persia.[32] Mohan Lal's
description covered a part of the traditional trade of the region
which appears to have reestablished itself in the times of Ranjit
Singh following several decades of dislocation in the eighteenth
century.[33] The Khatri settlements, like Shikarpur and Gotki in
Sindh, may have come up when the traders of the Punjab
migrated from their ancient habitats in the north.

The Mughal province of the Punjab in the seventeenth
century was among the most prosperous and rich territories of
the Mughal empire.[34] Lahore was regarded 'as the greatest city
of the East, surpassing even Constantinople.'[35] A number of
towns and Sikh settlements, e.g., Jahangirabad, Wazirabad,
Ibrahimabad Sodhra, Rahon, Phillaur, Nur Mahal, Dera Baba
Nanak, Tarn Taran, Amritsar, Hargobindpur, Anandpur,
Kiratpur, Kartarpur and Hoshiarpur emerged and flourished
in the late-sixteenth and the seventeenth century.[36]

---

[29] Kamwar, pp. 53 and 335.

[30] *Bayan-i Waqi*, p. 57.

[31] Mohan Lal, *Travels*, p. 396.   [32] Ibid., pp. 398, 406, 412, 438 and 441.

[33] C. A. Bayly, *Rulers, Townsmen and Bazaars*, pp. 91 and 202–5; H. K. Naqvi, *Urban
Centres and Industries*, pp. 41–9.

[34] Compare Sujan Rai Bhandari, *Khulasat-ut-Tawarikh*, edited by Zafar Hasan, Delhi,
1918, pp. 66, 70–1 and 79; *Asrar-i Samadi*, p. 5.

[35] H. K. Naqvi, Ibid., p. 15 quoting William Finch and Abdul Baqi Nahawandi.

[36] Ganesh Das Vadera, *Char Bagh-i Panjab*, English tr. by J. S. Grewal and Indu

The prosperity of the region is reflected in the increase in the revenues in the seventeenth century. According to our sources, the revenues of the Mughal Punjab since the time of the compilation of the *Ain* rose from, 55,94,58,423 to 1,06,64,19,937 *dams* in Aurangzeb's times with the *hasil* being Rs 2,00,35,791/8¼, 75.15 per cent of the *jama*. What is significant that beside 254 *mahals*, 5 *tappas* and one *mauza* of *mal*, there were 60 *mahals* of *sair*, given as *baldah waghairah* (town, etc.), with Rs 12,77,379/10 of the *hasil* of these *mahals* in *khalisa*.[37] This indicates that the prosperity of the province had a bearing on the growth of trade of and through the region. This is also illustrated from a substantial increase in the number and rearrangement of the *mahals* of Sindh Sagar Doab which linked Kabul and Qandahar to Multan. The entire Doab was included in the Punjab and contained 70 *mahals* as against 42 + 4 of Lahore and Multan *subas* of Akbar's times.[38] The city of Multan with Bhakkar and Sehwan on its south towards Lahari Bandar, as it is evident from their revenues, also rose in importance in the the seventeenth century.[39] It may also be noted that by the time of Aurangzeb, Bhakkar also minted silver rupees.[40] We have further evidence of the increasing importance of the region in the appointment of Prince Muizz-ud-Din to the governorship of Multan in 1696. The Prince held the province till the end of Aurangzeb's reign.[41] He subjugated the country of the powerful turbulent Biloch chiefs on the western borders of Multan and Lahore *subas* and extended the frontiers of Multan further in the west and the north to include almost the entire area of Bilo-

---

Banga as *Panjab in the Early Nineteenth Century*, Amritsar, 1975, for an account of these towns. However, this does not imply a smooth growth in the seventeenth century. The fluctuations in the economy of Sindh may have affected the economy of the Punjab. See Sunita I. Zaidi, 'Problems of the Mughal Administration in Sind during the First-half of the Seventeenth Century', *Islamic Culture*, April, 1983, pp. 153–62.

[37] I. O., 4488.

[38] For Akbar's times, *Ain*, II, (Jarrett), pp. 326–7 and 333; for the 17th–18th century, I. O., 4488.

[39] I. O., 4488.

[40] Irfan Habib, *Atlas*, Sheet 5B.

[41] M. Athar Ali, 'Provincial Governors under Aurangzeb—An Anaslysis', in K. A. Nizami (ed.), *Medieval India—a Miscellany*, I, pp. 117–18. As we have seen earlier in Chapter II, Prince Muizz-ud-Din held Multan in his governorship, also under Bahadur Shah.

chistan under a new *sarkar* (Muizzabad), named after him.[42]

Area	Revenues in *dams* in the Ain	Revenues in *dams* in the 17th century	*Hasil* in the 17th century
Multan city	17,19,168	1,63,87,075	Rs 3,10,816
pargana Bhakkar	74,362	21,05,000	Rs 51,360
pargana Sewistan (Sehwan)	16,69,732	25,64,370	Rs 34,980

With the growth of the areas in and around their settlements, the Jats gained in strength and importance, which, in large measure, was illustrated in their rising positions in the Sikh religion. By the middle of the seventeenth century they had begun to displace the Khatris from the leadership of the Sikh religion[43] while in 1699 the tenth Sikh Guru, as it has been suggested, had to proclaim the features of Jat culture (five Ks) as the essentials of Sikhism.[44] Guru Gobind's proclamation that every male member of the *Khalsa* would thenceforth be a *Singh* also showed the nature of the social status that the Jats, as a rising landed class, sought. Till then only the Rajputs, the community of the rulers and the rural landed magnates and, in some cases, the Khatris, the dominant moneyed class of the merchants and the intermediaries in the Punjab, had this right.

When this relatively lowly placed community struggled for a

---

[42] I. O. 4488. Earlier 3 *mahals* of Dodai land with a *peshkash* of 34,80,000 *dams* under the control of Ghazi Khan Dodai were subject to Multan. A large part of the Dodai country north of Dera Ghazi Khan appears to have been in Qandahar. Abul Fazl mentions the Indus on the east of Qandahar *sarkar*. *Ain*, p. 399. Strangely enough *Dastur-ul-Amal-i Shahjahani* (f. 27) mentions *sarkar* Muizzabad, giving the impression that the *sarkar* was formed in the time of Shahjahan (1626–57). Cf. Irfan Habib, *Atlas*, Notes on Sheet 4A, p. 9. But this reference, I think, needs clarification. It seems that some early eighteenth-century papers have been mixed up with this particular volume.

Sarkar Muizzabad was divided into 26 *zilas* with a *jama* of 5,00,00,000 *dams* and a *hasil* of Rs 6,25,594. For some details of Prince Muizz-ud-Din's expeditions against the Biloch chiefs, see *Akhbarat* (Aurangzeb) 44th R. Y., pp. 235, 245a, 317a, 329b–330a; 45th R. Y., pp. 34, 68, 91, 116a.

[43] *Dabistan-i Mazahib*, Calcutta, 1809, p. 286.

[44] W. H. McLeod, *The Evolution of the Sikh Community*, Delhi, 1975, pp. 1–19.

claim to a higher social position, their first targets in cases of violence and conflict, were not only the rulers but also the beneficiaries of the existing power structure. Those who had traditionally had a higher status in land relations, such as the Rajputs and Rangars and those who were favoured by the Mughals to rise as *zamindars* in the region were identified as enemies of the rising Jats. The Sikh religion reinforced the community bond amongst them, and because of their own egalitarian traditions they were capable of converting their struggle into a battle against the existing social structure. The despising and disdainful adjectives in the Persian records used for Banda's followers are perhaps indicative of the caste, community and social status consciousness of the compilers of these sources rather than of the exact economic position of the Sikhs.

The following of Banda was thus primarily amongst the village-level *zamindars*. The higher *zamindars* as listed in the *Ain* joined them because of their caste and religious affinity, and certainly with a hope to expand their *zamindaris*. Banda's spectacular success and the rapid increase in the strength of his army is to be seen in the light of the spoliations he promised to his Sikhs. Within a period of a year or so the strength of his army increased from four to five thousand cavalry and from seven to eight thousand foot soldiers to thirty to forty thousand. During this period a large part of *sarkar* Sirhind (almost all the *parganas* in the north of the *sarkar*), between the Sutlej and Yamuna came into the possession of the Sikhs. Banda dislodged the old intermediaries there and appointed his own men in their place. By the end of 1708, after he had established his seat at Lohgarh, he was virtually king and called himself *Sachcha Badshah*. He had conquered many territories and issued coins and *hukmnamas* and governed these through his deputies. But it would not be correct to completely identify the Sikhs of Banda with only the Jat *zamindars* and peasants. Apart from the Khatris who had traditionally been the followers of Guru Nanak (*Nanak parasts*), a very large number of the other lowly placed and nondescript communities joined him. 'The scavangers, the leather-dressers and the other low-born had only to leave their homes and join the Sikh leaders when in a short time they would return to their birth place as its rulers'.[45] This

[45] W. Irvine, *Later Moghuls*, I, p. 98.

rulership implied primarily the right to collect the revenue which had hitherto been under the jurisdiction of intermediaries and Mughal *amils*. Even before the conquest of Sirhind, Banda is reported to have appointed his own *amils* and *thanadars* and issued orders to Mughal officials and *jagirdars* to submit and give up their claims to their territories. In 1710 when the Sikhs entered Rahon, they issued threatening orders to the *chaudhuris* and the *qanungos* of Rahon and the adjacent *parganas* calling upon them to submit.[46]

The participation of these communities lower down in the social order highlighted the egalitarian character of the social structure of the Sikh religion. The Sikh movement signified a protest against the beneficiaries of the existing structure of authority. The *madad-i ma'ash* holders therefore also suffered heavily at the hands of the Sikhs. In almost all the towns which fell into their possession, the Muslim *shurafa* and their mosques and the graveyards were the chief targets of Sikh raids.[47] The scholars (*fuzala*) and the gentry (*shurafa*) of Thanesar, for instance, were reported to have been specially affected by the Sikh depredations in the town. 'The ruffians of the town', it was reported, 'in league with the Sikhs, perpetrated atrocities on the Muslims and destroyed their mosques, mansions and mausoleums'[48] On 15 October 1712, the Sikhs killed the *qazi* of Sirhind.[49] The Muslim *madad-i ma'ash* holders therefore lent support to the imperial army in their bid to suppress the Sikhs. The *shurafa* made important contributions to the *faujdar's* victory over the Sikhs when Banda made inroads into the region beyond the Yamuna in *sarkar* Saharanpur.[50] The *thanadar* of Bajwara is said to have been informed by Shaikh Ilah Yar *Durvesh* and the *qazi* about Sikh bases in the *pargana*. Subsequently, the deputy *faujdar* collected his army and along with the *shurafa* marched towards the village of Ajuwal.[51] Haji Yar Beg, Saiyid Inayatullah and Mulla Pir Muhammad Wa'iz were among the important Sunni Muslims who organized the

---

[46] K. K., II, pp. 651 and 658; *Hadiqat*, p. 148; Ganda Singh, *Banda Singh Bahadur*, Amritsar, 1935, pp. 83–4.

[47] W. Irvine, *Later Moghuls* I, pp. 97–8; S. M. Latif, *History of the Panjab*, pp. 275–6.

[48] *Akhbarat*, JS, p. 105.   [49] Ibid., JS, P. 282.

[50] Ibid., BS, 4th R. Y., p. 147.   [51] Ibid., BS, 5th R. Y., p. 346.

defence of Lahore calling it a *jihad* (holy war) against the Sikhs.[52] As the Sikh risings posed a serious threat to the position of the *madad-i ma'ash* holders, a large number of the Muslim divines and the theologians, notwithstanding their old age, joined Abd-us-Samad Khan's campaigns against Banda.[53]

Some aspects of local reaction to Banda Bahadur's struggle

It is true that the Sikh movement posed the greatest threat to Mughal authority in the Punjab. But the fact that it was directed against all the beneficiaries of the state enabled the Mughals to mobilize these interests, as they did in Farrukh Siyar's reign, in their bid to suppress the movement. The movement under Banda also suffered from certain weaknesses. The movement's principal support from the Jat Sikh *zamindars*, gradually alienated it from the non-Sikh, non-Jat *zamindars* and also perhaps the *ri'aya*, as well as from certain urban communities including the Khatris who were otherwise still the followers of Guru Nanak (*Nanak parasts*).

Banda could not coordinate his movement with the other anti-Mughal uprisings in the region. There is nothing in the sources to suggest that Banda ever tried to contact the rebel *zamindars* of Rachna Doab and Sindh Sagar. He also failed to coordinate his movement with the widespread Gujar uprisings in *sarkar* Saharanpur, a serious phase of which was simultaneous with Banda's inroads into the *sarkar*[54] On the contrary, some *zamindars* of Saharanpur supported the Mughals in the latter's bid to drive the Sikhs out of the region.[55]

---

[52] Qasim, ff. 33; W. Irvine, *Later Moghuls* I, p. 103; S. M. Latif, *History of the Panjab*, p. 276.

[53] Ganesh Das Vadera, *Char Bagh*, pp. 119–20.

[54] *Akhbarat*, BS, 5th R. Y., p. 251 for an imperial order to the *faujdar* of Saharanpur to lead an expedition against Lal Kunwar Gujar who had devastated the *khalisa* and *jagir* villages around Saharanpur.

[55] The army of Jalal Khan Rohilla, *faujdar* of the *sarkar* and Saiyid Taj-ud-Din Barha which effected a crushing defeat on the Sikhs in 1710 in Jalalabad comprised a sizeable number of *zamindars* along with the *shurafa* of the region. Later when Jalal Khan joined the emperor near Karnal on their way to the Punjab, his armed contingents included a large number of the *zamindars'* retinues. Ibid., BS, 4th R. Y., pp. 147 and 235.

What lent strength to the Mughals against the Sikhs was that some of the non-Jat *zamindars* and *ri'aya* became victims of the Sikh raids even in the regions where Banda had gained some ground. A report from Jalandhar which the emperor received some time in September 1711, records that 'the Guru (Banda) having left his army behind in Kiratpur has established himself along with some of his followers in the hills of Rampura. His army, according to a report, plundered the villages around Kiratpur, and the *ri'aya* in fear of their excesses, have fled to various places. The town of Ropar [which was also looted by the Sikhs] looks desolate'.[56] It was primarily because of the support of the *zamindars* and the *ri'aya* that Shams Khan, a Qasur Afghan and the *faujdar* of Beth Jalandhar could wage some successful raids against the Sikhs in the Doab.[57]

Indeed, even in the Sikh strongholds, Banda seems to have been opposed by the non-Jat *zamindars*. The Rajput and with some possible exceptions the Afghan *zamindars* consistently supported the Mughal campaigns against Banda. It was in appreciation of his services to the Mughals that Isa Khan, a Mein Rajput *zamindar* of Beth Jalandhar, was appointed deputy *faujdar* of the Doab.[58] According to a chronicler, the *zamindari* of half of the Doab was arbitrarily bestowed upon the Mein Rajputs, the remaining half being awarded to outsiders, namely, the Khweshgi Afghans of Qasur.[59] The Afghans are reported to have fought against the Sikhs of Banda in a number of battles in the Doab as well as in *chakla* Sirhind.[60] They also seem to have served as propagandists of the Mughals and tried to rally the non-Sikh *zamindars* behind the Mughals.[61] The wrath of the Sikhs in some cases was therefore directed particularly against the Afghans.[62]

---

[56] Ibid., BS, 5th R. Y., p. 395, *pargana* Ropar in the sixteenth century was in the Rajput *zamindari*, *Ain*, II (Jarrett), p. 301.

[57] Ibid., BS, 4th R. Y., p. 357, 5th and 6th R. Ys., II, p. 273. The *zamindars* in Beth Jalandhar, according to the *Ain* (Jarrett), pp. 320–1, were predominantly Rajputs.

[58] M. M., ff. 50b–51a; K. K., II, p. 767; Warid, pp. 287–8; *M. U.*, II, pp. 825–8.

[59] *Asrar-i Samadi*. p. 19.   [60] Kamwar, ff. 325.

[61] In November 1711, for example, an Afghan *zamindar* of Beth Jalandhar was deputed to accompany Hoshdar Khan, the *faujdar* of Jalandhar, to the villages to mobilize and bring the *zamindars* for the chastisement of the Sikhs. *Akhbarat*, BS, 5th and 6th R. Ys., II, p. 455.

[62] In 1714, the Sikhs organized themselves under one Jagat Singh and fell upon the

We have also evidence to indicate Gujar conflict with the Sikhs of Banda. In November 1712, in a battle on the banks of the stream at Barsana, Amin Khan defeated the Sikhs. A large number of them, while fleeing, were drowned in the stream and many among the rest who crossed the rivulet were killed by the Gujar *zamindars*.[63]

Of much greater consequence for the Sikh movement under Banda was the gradual alienation from it of the urban communities, especially the Khatris. According to Khafi Khan, the Khatris were one of the two important communities of the Punjab among whom the Sikhs in our period had a following.[64] Khafi Khan's observation is supported from a number of instances in the early phase of Banda's struggle. Khafi Khan himself narrates that at a critical juncture in 1710, when the Mughals were laying seige to the Sikh bases in the hills of Lohgarh, the traders of the imperial army seem to have attempted to maintain a supply of provisions into the fort. 'The beseiged threw off their scarfs from the top of the fortwalls and the traders packed the grains and tied them up and then through the ropes they were drawn up inside'.[65] Again, according to Sikh tradition, one Diwan Hardyal, a prominent figure in the royal camp, helped the Sikhs with provisions as far as he could.[66] In the same battle, one Gulabo Khatri, a tobacco-seller, is reported to have passed himself off as Banda in order to facilitate the Sikh leader's escape. Gulabo's features resembled those of Banda. He therefore volunteered to wear Banda's clothes and appear before the enemy as such.[67] In August 1710, all the Hindus in the imperial service at the court were ordered to shave off their beards, purportedly to distinguish the loyalists from the traitors.[68] A contemporary Persian chronicler explains the order on account of the suspicion that among the large number of Khatri officials at the court there might be followers of Banda.[69]

---

fortress of Umar Ghazi, an Afghan *zamindar* of *Garhi* Pathanan. The *zamindar* and the ri'*aya* of the surrounding villages were forced to take refuge in the *garhi*; the Sikhs carried away a booty worth Rs 60,000 in cash and in kind. Compare B. S. Nijjar, *Punjab under the Later Mughals*, Jullundhar, 1972, pp. 52–3.

[63] *Akhbarat*, BS, 5th and 6th R. Ys., II, p. 440.   [64] K. K., II, p. 651.

[65] Ibid., pp. 672–3.   [66] Cf. Sohan Singh, *Banda, the Brave*, Lahore, 1915, pp. 107.

[67] Kamwar, f. 326a; K. K., II, p. 673.   [68] *Akhbarat*, BS, 4th R. Y., p. 200.

[69] K. K., II, p. 674.

The same period, however, saw the beginning of the Khatri alienation from the *Khalsa*. 'When Guru Gobind Singh gave *pahul* to the Sikhs and made them the *Khalsa*, he asked the Khatris, in the first instance, to wear arms and to fight against the armies of the Muslim rulers to establish their own rule. They submitted, in reply, that they were extremely weak and could not afford to incur the enmity of their rulers. They requested to be left alone.'[70] Abolition of the institution of the *masands* (regional agents of the Guru) which were largely in control of the Khatris might have created disaffection among the Khatri Sikhs especially when the new features of Sikhism, as it has been argued, expressed the dominance of the Jat culture.[71] On the other hand, Banda presumably resented the continued association of the Khatris with the Mughal state service. The meek submission[72] of the Khatris to the imperial order to shave off their beards might have created a breach between them and their associates on the one hand and the Sikhs of Banda on the other. This could have also led to a debate as to whether without the five 'Ks' a Sikh could remain a true Sikh.

A factor which created and widened the gap between the Khatris and the Sikhs of Banda was their altogether divergent political and economic interests. A large number of the Khatris were merchants whose fortunes were very closely linked with political stability which in the prevailing circumstances could be envisaged only through the maintenance of imperial authority. The Sikh uprisings began to cause considerable losses to

---

[70] Ganesh Das Vadera, *Char Bagh*, (English tr. by J. S. Grewal and Indu Banga) p. 124. Vadera's *Char Bagh-i Punjab* is not a contemporary source. But the fact that Vadera was a Khatri and writes on the basis of the reminiscences and records of his own family lends credibility to his observations.

Pahul: generally *Khande ki pahul*, that is water used for initiation according to the ceremony adopted by Guru Gobind Singh.

[71] W. H. McLeod, *The Evolution of the Sikh Community*, pp. 1–19. A section of the Khatris, even after the abolition of *masand*, continued to assert their authority. Compare J. D. Cunningham, *A History of the Sikhs*, reprint, Delhi, 1955, Appendix XXI, p. 348.

[72] Our sources do not record any resistance by the Khatris to the imperial order, while the non-Sikh Hindus appear to have resented it. This is why probably Sarfaraz Khan is reported to have directed the *kotwal* not to extend the order to the non-Sikh Hindus. But a fresh imperial order rejected the modification of Sarfaraz Khan and thereafter all the Hindus with beards were to be denied entry to the court premises. *Akhbarat*, BS, 4th R. Y., p. 203.

the big merchants, the *sahukars* and certain categories of artisans such as weavers. Lahore, Sialkot, Bajwara, Haibatpur
Patti and Batala and Gujarat Shah Dola were among the
important centres of trade and industry in the Punjab. 'In the
abundance of people and merchandise goods and valuables,
Lahore had an edge over the cities of the empire.' Sialkot was
famous for its paper industry, *chikan* work and for manufactur-
ing *jamdhar, katar* and *barchhi* while Bajwara manufactured cot-
ton clothes. Batala is described as a town of the rich Hindus
and Muslims and of lofty buildings. In Gujarat Shah Dola
and Haibatpur Patti, Iraqi horses of high quality were bred.
Some of these horses were priced as high as Rs 1000 and 1500.[73]
As they yielded immense booty in the form of the valuable
goods of the merchants, these towns were the chief targets of the
Sikh raids.[74] 'In the countries of the Punjab and Sirhind, *sahukars* possessed lakhs of rupees; thousands such pursued their
profession. The traders too, each having his own share [in the
wealth of the province] thrived. Those ill-fortuned losers [the
Sikhs) levelled them to ground and left not a single thing to live
with'.[75]

The gap between the Sikhs and the trading community is also
evident from the disturbances on the trade-route passing
through the province. On 8 February 1714, some mercantile
goods worth Rs 11,000 on their way from Lahore to Delhi were
reported to have been plundered by the *zamindars* of the
Jalandhar Doab.[76] On 6 April 1715, they robbed the textile
beoparis near Bajwara.[77] On 30 April, in the same year, it was
reported that the *zamindars* of Jogiara and Ibrahimwal in
Jalandhar often ransacked the travellers and the merchants
passing through the area.[78] On 8 May, the travellers and the

---

[73] *Hadiqat*, pp. 147–9.
[74] Compare K. K., II, pp. 654–5 for Sikh ravages in Sirhind, Jalalabad and some
other towns in Delhi and Lahore *subas*. Also see Ganesh Das Vadera, *Char Bagh*, p. 112.
A new wall was built around the town of Batala in Muhammad Shah's reign, very
likely, to reinforce the defence against the Sikh raids. Cf., J. S. Grewal (ed and tr.) *In the
By-Lanes of History: Some Persian Documents from a Panjab Town*, Simla, 1975, Introduction, p. 18
[75] *Ahwal*, ff. 31.
[76] *Akhbarat*, FS, 3rd R. Y., II, p. 228.
[77] Ibid., FS, 4th R. Y., p. 55.
[78] Ibid., FS, 4th R. Y., p. 115.

merchants were robbed of their valuables again by the *zamindars* of the Jalandhar Doab between Nur Sarai and Nakodar.[79] In Sialkot, (*sarkar* of Rachna Doab) and Bahlolpur (*sarkar* of Chanhat Doab) also, law and order seems to have been broken by the local brigands who were composed of the recalcitrant *zamindars*. On 8 February 1714, a consignment of woollen garments worth Rs 17,000 which was despatched from Kashmir to Lahore was reported to have been looted in the *faujdari* area of Sialkot.[80]

The merchants, especially textile traders and weavers, therefore, extended their support to the Mughals in the latter's bid to suppress the Sikh revolts. The Hindus (apparently the Khatris and the other trading communities) of Lahore financed the voluntary efforts of the Saiyids to fight against the Sikhs. They joined hands with the Muslims in according a welcome to such Mughal forces as could score victories over the Sikhs. Besides, the Muslim textile merchants who were known in the Punjab as *Lakhkhis*, made generous donations for the expenses of the Mughal army.[81] The artisans, who in the main included weavers, formed a detachment of the army of Shams Khan, the *faujdar* of Beth Jalandhar.[82]

There was yet another reason for the breach between the Khatris and the *Khalsa*. The Mughal administration in the Punjab had been weakened by the time Banda took over the leadership of the Sikhs. The *jagirdars* feared not only the *zamindars*, but also, as we shall see later, the consequences of the lower Mughal official's collusion with the rebels. The practice of *ijara* thus gained wide currency. The Khatris seem to have often been the *ijaradars* in the province, since they had money and were in a position to ensure undisturbed realization of the revenue, through their social and professional connections with the villages. As the Mughals were in greater need of money, *ijara* was normally set at a much inflated rate and the *ijaradar* was compelled to be oppressive. For the *ijaradar* had to manage the money he had paid to the *jagirdar*, even if he had to arrogate to himself the customary perquisites of the *zamindars*.[83] The same development, however, as we shall see below, enabled Banda to win over the *banjaras* (roving grain traders) to his side.

---

[79] Ibid., FS, 4th R. Y., p. 140.   [80] Ibid., FS, 3rd R. Y., p. 289.
[81] Qasim, f. 33a.   [82] K. K., II, p. 656.   [83] See also Chapter V.

Banda's attempt to give his struggle against the Mughals the colour of a *dharma yudha* (holy war) to protect the Hindu interests against Muslim tyranny was yet another weakness of the Sikh movement, which, even in the prevailing state of religious consciousness could not give him enough support. Some of his Sikh *sardars* are reported to have invited Raja Jai Singh of Amer to march towards the Punjab and asked him to give a call to the 'Hindus' to join the Sikhs and defend *dharma*.[84] Banda also tried to use the Hindu mendicants, (*bairagis* and *sanyasis*) with whom he had a long association, as a dependable source of information from the imperial camp.[85]

Banda's attempt to make use of the religious susceptibilities of the Hindus may be seen against the background of Aurangzeb's policies. As a shrewd leader, Banda might have calculated on cashing in on the bruised feelings of a section of the Hindus. But it is significant to note that Banda received an indignant rebuff, even from those Hindu nobles who had their own grievances against Aurangzeb.[86] An examination of this aspect of the Sikh movement in the light of the ideological developments in Sikhism under Guru Gobind would perhaps bear better results. Sikhism had hitherto been a kind of heterodox mystic order which rejected both Brahmanical faith and Islam. Its founder Guru Nanak was believed to have possessed the secrets of both Islamic prayers and Brahmanical scriptures.[87] But Guru

[84] Jaipur Records, Sitamau transcripts, pp. 217–18. The Raja, however, did exactly the opposite of what Banda wanted them to do. Subsequently, Jai Singh along with Raja Ajit Singh marched towards Lohgarh, not in response to the Sikhs' invitation but in compliance with the imperial order to chastise the Sikhs. Also when after their arrival at Lohgarh, Banda wrote them a letter threatening them with the consequence of Sikh inroads into their territories, the rajas killed the Sikh messengers and issued orders to kill all the followers and associates of Banda in their camps.

[85] On 28 October 1711, the emperor issued an order that whosoever was found guilty of communicating the news of the imperial camp outside should instantly be put to death and that Hindu mendicants should be debarred from entering the camp. On 18 January 1712, one Balan *Bairagi* of the office of the *wazir* was accused of and imprisoned for spying for the Sikhs. *Akhbarat*, BS, 4th R. Y., p. 23: 5th and 6th R. Ys., p. 429.

[86] For Aurangzeb's relations with the Rajas of Jaipur and Jodhpur, see V. S. Bhatnagar, *Life and Times of Sawai Raja Jai Singh*, pp. 13–28, Delhi, 1974; G. D. Sharma, *Rajput Polity*, Delhi, 1977, pp. 176–94; see also M. Athar Ali, 'Causes of Rathor Rebellion of 1679', *PIHC* 24th Session, Delhi, 1961 pp. 135–41.

[87] Muhammad Qasim Lahori, *Ibrat Maqal* (Bound with *ibratnama*) Patna MS., quoted by S. H. Askari, 'Baba Nanak in Persian Sources', *Journal of the Sikh Studies*, Vol. II, No. 2, August 1975, pp. 112–16.

Gobind's writing bore a clear Hindu impress. The visit of Guru Gobind's 'five disciples' to Benaras to learn ancient Indian thought and philosophy pointed towards his effort to suggest an affinity between Sikhism and the religious susceptibilities of the Hindus.[88]

At any rate, the narrow religious bond among the Sikhs seems to have led to the belief that 'rulership'—the right to collect the revenue—was an exclusive preserve of the *Khalsa*. If Ganesh Das is to be believed, the non-Sikhs in the territories under the Sikh control bore almost the same burden of cesses as they had done under Mughal rule. 'The Sikhs regarded themselves as *Khalisa* and the others as their subjects and servants (*raiyat* and *chakar*), and therefore in the subjugated lands they had their own (Sikh) *amils* to realize tributes and taxes from the non-Sikhs'.[89]

It was not surprising that in some areas the *zamindars*, apparently the Jats, who had supported Banda were unable to accept *pahul*, turned against the Sikhs. Towards the south-east of Sirhind in the plains of Ambala, Thanesar and Karnal, Banda's success was transient. In 1712 only seventeen persons of the entire non-Muslim population of Thanesar could be identified as Sikhs. Fourteen of them were willing to become Muslim to avoid torture and death.[90] Around 1710, the *zamindars* of Ambala, Kharkauda and Karnal had all begun to assist the Mughals in their hunt for the Sikhs.[91] The Jats of

---

[88] Note the contents and imagery of Gobind Singh's compositions, especially, *Chandi Charitar Ukat Bilas* and *Krishna Avtar*. While writing *Krishna Avtar*, the Guru was so impressed by Hindu mythology that he decided to sent five learned Sikhs to Benaras to collect for him the material from ancient philosophy and thought. They stayed in Benaras for seven (according to one report ten) years. They began the 'Nirmal School' of Sikh philosophy. S. S. Bal, 'Early Years of the Pontificate of Guru Gobind Singh; McLeod, *Evolution of the Sikh Community*, p. 13. Kamwar Khan appears to have noted the difference between the early Sikhs (*Nanak parasts*) and the Sikhs of his own time who rose in arms against the Mughals. He captions his account of the Sikh revolts as follows: '*Hazimat yaftan firqa-i zallah, bad mazhaban-i la 'in kih khud ra Nanakparast qarardadah budand wa halankih dar hich mazhab-i qadim na budand*' (Defeat of the misguided, impious and the detested community who considered themselves to have been the followers of Nanak while in actuality they followed no ancient religion at all) Kamwar, p. 108.

[89] Ganesh Das Vadera, *Char Bagh*, p. 17.

[90] *Akhbarat*, JS, p. 105.

[91] Ibid., BS, 4th R. Y., pp. 307–8, 345, 357 and 372; JS, p. 122.

Haryana, as well as of western Uttar Pradesh did not make common cause with the Sikhs. It may be noted that Churaman Jat of Agra *suba* was in the Mughal army.[92]

The Mughals, however, could not utilize the weaknesses of the Sikh movement fully in Bahadur Shah's reign. The advantages of the support from some local groups were outweighed in large part by the hostile attitude of the hill chiefs towards Mughal authority, as well as by the infighting among the nobility and certain impolitic and hasty measures at the court.

The hill chiefs, the Sikhs and Mughal power

There were a number of powerful chiefs in the hills on the periphery of the Mughal province of the Punjab who had close links with the plains, especially the regions affected by Sikh revolts. They had submitted to the Mughals and accepted the latter's suzerainty over their territories. This implied that they would pay the tribute (*peshkash*) without fail and render military services to the Mughals whenever required, at least, in their respective territories.[93] However, the chiefs, like other categories of big *zamindars*, still represented local despotism and their integration into the Mughal empire did not mean the extinction of the conflict between the Mughal state and the locality. It was the insurmountable military might of the Mughals and some prospect of the benefits of political stability which they ensured that had led to the chiefs' acceptance of their authority. Their attitude to the Mughal state therefore vacillated in accordance with the magnitude of threat to it from the region.[94] In the late-seventeenth century, for example, Raja Bhim Chand of Kahlur and certain other chiefs substantially exploited the support of the armed Sikh bands in their (chiefs') bid to resist the payment of the *peshkash* to the Mughals. Soon however, with the expansion of the Sikh Guru's conquests and

[92] Kamwar, f. 326b.

[93] A. R. Khan, *Chieftains in the Mughal Empire*, pp. 209–10.

[94] Compare Muzaffar Alam, 'The Zamindars and Mughal Power in the Deccan, 1686–1712', *IESHR*, March 1974, for the attitude of some Deccan *zamindars* towards the Mughals, in the wake of the Maratha risings.

the extension of his authority, the chiefs' position was threatened. Subsequently the Mughals and the chiefs led joint military operations against the Sikhs of Guru Gobind.[95] When Banda Bahadur exposed the vulnerability of Mughal power, the chiefs again endeavoured to turn the trouble in the Punjab to their benefit. None of these chiefs seems to have supported the imperial forces in the latter's drive against Banda. Whenever Banda and his Sikh comrades were overpowered in the plains, they took shelter in the territories of the hill chiefs. These chiefs either openly defied Mughal authority and supported the Sikhs or turned an indifferent ear to the imperial *farmans* urging them to capture the Sikh leader or drive him out of their domains.

Our sources refer to seventeen chieftaincies in the hills in and around the province of the Punjab.[96] The nature of their relations with Bahadur Shah and their attitude to the Sikh revolts can be analysed from the contents of the imperial *farmans* which are briefly given in the *Akhbarat*, and from their response to these *farmans*. On 26 August 1710, presumably on receiving the intelligence of the Sikh leader's ties with hill chiefs, the emperor sent his envoys, Abu Muhammad Khan and Brij Raj, to the chief (*zamindar*) of Kumaon, an important chieftaincy in the hills on the eastern borders of the Punjab in *suba* Delhi. The chief was ordered to come to the court and join the campaign against the Sikhs. Two days later, *farmans* were sent to Fateh Chand and Bhup Prakash, the rajas of Sirmur and Srinagar Garhwal urging them to properly chastise the Sikhs in their respective territories.[97] We do not know whether the chief of Kumaon ever arrived at court. On 30 May 1711, however, he is reported to have sent 25 severed heads of Sikhs to the emperor.[98] The Sirmur raja's response was in the negative. Suppression of the Sikhs apart, on 26 October, Banda was reported to have visited Nahan, the capital of the Sirmur chieftaincy, and placed

[95] For details see, W. Irvine, *Later Moghuls* I, pp. 84–6; S. M. Latif, *History of the Panjab*, pp. 264–5.

[96] Bilaur, Chamba, Samba, Goler, Hindur, Jammu, Jasrota, Jaswan, Kangra, Kulu, Kumaon, Kahlur (Bilaspur), Nadaun, Nurpur, Rajauri, Sirmur and Srinagar Garhwal.

[97] *Akhbarat*, BS, 4th R. Y., pp. 241 and 246.

[98] Ibid., 5th R. Y., p. 155.

in trust two crores of rupees with the chief.[99] Again on 13 December, following the Mughal failure to capture Banda at Lohgarh, *farmans* were despatched to Fateh Chand and Bhup Prakash directing them to handcuff the Sikh leader and send him to court. These *farmans* also failed to have any impact on the chiefs. Subsequently, Bhup Prakash was brought to the court and ordered to be caged and escorted to Delhi where he was imprisoned in the fort of Salimgarh.[100] Fateh Chand, the Sirmur chief, instead of capturing Banda and sending him to the court, thought it sufficient to send the usual *peshkash* and managed to escape the emperor's wrath.[101] Till the end of Bahadur Shah's reign the Sikhs took shelter in his territory whenever they had to flee from the plains into the hills.[102]

The chiefs of Goler and Bilaur and some other chiefs of the 'snowclad hill' (*zamindaran-i barfi*), though they professed allegiance to the Mughal emperor, were in secret alliance with the Sikh leader. In one instance in 1711, the chief connived at Banda's escape from his territory before the imperial retainers could reach the hill and lay hands upon him. Earlier the emperor had received a report regarding the Sikh hideouts in his territory. The chief was subsequently put in prison in Delhi.[103] In another case, a detachment of the Sikhs was reported to have crossed through the territory of the Goler chief to the territory of the Jammu chief who was then openly hostile to the Mughals.[104] The people of these chieftaincies apparently under the protection of their chiefs often carried horses and arms from the plains to the hills for the Sikhs.[105]

The chiefs of Jammu, Nurpur and Jasrota openly supported the Sikhs and gave them shelter in their territories. In 1711, the chiefs of the Jammu hills helped the Sikhs in establishing a number of military posts (*thanas*) in the *parganas* beyond the Ravi in the north. In June 1711, when the Sikhs, following an encounter, fled to the country of the chief of

[99] Ibid., 4th R. Y.
[100] Ibid., BS, 4th R. Y., p. 412; 5th R. Y., pp. 41 and 81; Kamwar, f. 326b.
[101] Ibid., 5th R. Y., p. 70.
[102] Ibid., p. 374.
[103] Ibid., pp. 344 and 381.
[104] Ibid., p. 346.
[105] Ibid., 5th and 6th R. Ys., II, pp. 427–8.

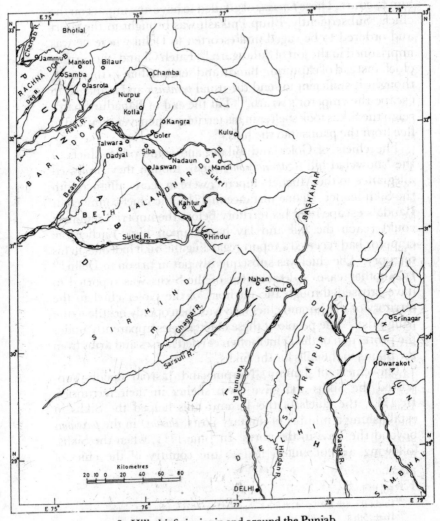

5. Hill chieftaincies in and around the Punjab

Jammu, Rustam Dil Khan, the noble-in-charge of the Sikh campaigns, evidently fearing strong resistance from the chief as well, asked the emperor to depute an additional detachment under his command.[106] Imperial *farmans*, along with *khil'ats* for the chiefs of Jasrota, Nurpur, Bilaur and Samba, directing them to mobilize their retainers for the suppression of the Sikhs, fell on deaf ears.[107] Even when they were forced to come and join the campaign, their sympathy was with the Sikhs. In June 1711, after a severe defeat at the hands of the Mughals, Banda Bahadur entered a pass which led to the interior of the Jammu hills. Saiyid Azmatullah, the chief of Rajauri, and Dhrub Dev, the chief of Jammu, arrived at the northern end of the pass and sealed it. Subsequently, Muhammad Amin Khan, Rustam Dil Khan and Isa Khan, the Mughal generals, joined the chiefs. The *arzdasht* they sent to the emperor records their hope of capturing Banda within a day or two. But ironically the Sikh leader again eluded them and within a month, was reported to be somewhere in the Jammu hills.[108]

The chief (*zamindar*) and the people (*khalaiqs*) of Kahlur are mentioned as friends (*rafiq*) of Banda. On 6 April 1711, some Sikh outposts (*chaukis*) in the Kahlur hills were reported to have been established; immediately after this a Sikh emissary met the Kahlur chief and brought him a letter and some presents from Banda. The chief promised to give refuge to the Sikh leader whenever needed and block the entry of the Mughal army into the hills. The chief is also reported to have raised a big armed contingent for this purpose![109] Within a year, on 23 January, 1712, Banda was reported to have escaped from Kiratpur and plundered an Afghan village on his way to Kahlur. Chasing him, Muhammad Amin Khan occupied and devastated Kiratpur and Kalian which had hitherto been the strongholds of the Sikhs. As the chief of Kahlur gave little assistance to the Mughal general, he could not enter the hills and had to stop at the village of Nimona, about a mile north of Kiratpur.[110] In Kahlur about 200 *sawars* and 5000 *piyadas* joined

[106] Ibid., 5th R. Y., pp. 135 and 231.

[107] Ibid., 5th R. Y., , pp. 27 and 152.

[108] Ibid., p. 175. See also p. 259 for the Nurpur chief's support to the Sikhs.

[109] Ibid., 5th R. Y., pp. 135 and 147–8.

[110] Ibid., 5th and 6th R. Ys., II, pp. 484 and 587.

the Sikhs, a *thana* was set up at Bilaspur and then Banda moved
to Belowal. A number of Sikh generals were deputed by Banda
to encounter Hoshdar Khan, the *faujdar* of Doab Jalandhar,
who was camping at the village of Jhanjun in the territory of
Jaswan about 30 miles north-west of Kahlur.[111]

However, the chief of Kulu and the chiefs (*thakurs*) of Jaswan
and Hindur appear to have been among the few supporters of
the Mughals in the hills. In his campaigns against the Sikhs,
Hoshdar Khan seems to have been considerably assisted by the
chief of Kulu. Since the chief of Kulu was a traditional enemy of
the Sikhs and we have no evidence of any change in his attitude
to them, it can be presumed that he consistently helped the
Mughals against the Sikhs.[112] The *thakur* of Jaswan initially not
only helped Hoshdar Khan in setting up the Mughal military
posts in his territory but also offered his services to guide the
Mughals into the difficult passes of the hills of Kahlur. Hoshdar
Khan recommended that the *thakur* be formally appointed a
guide. But the emperor disapproved of the suggestion, evidently because of his apprehension of the double dealing of the
thakur.[113] This was not unfounded. According to one report even
the *thakurs* of Jaswan and Hindur repented their support to
the Mughals and expressed their desire to come to terms with
the Sikhs.[114]

Apart from one Inayat, the *zamindar* of Talwan, and Sa'adat
Yar, the *zamindar* of Kotla (?), who are recorded as the allies of
the Mughals, we have no evidence regarding the Punjab chieftains' attitude towards the Sikh uprisings in the plains. The
zamindar of Talwan seems to have been a close associate of
Mahabat Khan, son of Mun'im Khan, the *wazir*, and was once
deputed to mobilize and escort the *zamindars* to the court to

---

[111] Ibid., 5th and 6th R. Ys., p. 619.

[112] Guru Gobind is said to have visited Kulu to seek assistance from the chief against
the Mughals. The chief seems to have treated the Guru inhospitably. The local
tradition also records an exchange of the performance of miracles between the Guru
and the chief. The Guru was then imprisoned in an iron cage, but he managed to
miraculously escape to Mandi where he was courteously entertained by Sidh Sen, the
chief of that state. Cf. J. Hutchison and J. Ph. Vogel, *History of the Panjab Hill States*,
Lahore, 1933, II, pp. 464–5.

[113] *Akhbarat*, BS, 5th and 6th R. Ys., II, p. 457.

[114] Jaipur Records (transcripts) Sarkar Collection, XIV, p. 218.

chastise the Sikhs.[115] One Raja Bakhtawar, the *zamindar* of
pargana Dadyal in *sarkar* Beth Jalandhar, however, is reported to
have given shelter to Banda in his territory. Later, the Raja died
in an encounter against the *amil* of the *pargana*.[116]

It was with his tactfulness and statesmanship and the demonstration and use of force that Banda made the hill chiefs his
allies. He also aspired to capitalize upon the discontent of Jai
Singh and Ajit Singh over their fortunes under Bahadur Shah.
The letter that some Sikh *sardars* namely, Bakht Singh,
Bhagwan Singh, Jai Singh and Gaur Singh wrote to Raja Jai
Singh allegedly in reply to the latter's note to them shows how
the Sikh leader endeavoured to mobilize the Rajput chiefs to his
support.

But Banda's individual manoeuvrings do not alone explain
the chiefs' role. With the Sikh movement the hill chiefs, who by
themselves were unable to unite and evolve into a unified
political power, saw the possibility of the emergence of an
another political centre in the region. Even earlier at the time of
their integration into the Mughal empire in Akbar's reign, the
chiefs had divided loyalties so long as there was more than one
centre of political power.[117] In this connection the difference in
the attitude of the hill and the plain chiefs is to be particularly
noted. The *thakur* of Jaswan and the *zamindars* of Talwan could
not afford to make use of the Sikh movement as much as the hill
chiefs could, since they did not have the advantage of the
latter's geographical position nor the benefits of an informal
and loose integration of their territories into the imperial
system. This is further illustrated from the fate of Raja Bakhtawar of *pargana* Dadyal on the fringe of the hills who died
fighting against the retainers of a mere *amil* of the *pargana*.

The Sikhs had not yet, however, emerged as the destroyers of
Mughal power. Hence, evident vacillations in the attitudes of
even some of the hill chiefs. They always tried to keep a door
open to the Mughals. Some of them sent severed heads of dead
Sikhs,[118] apparently collected from battle-fields where the Mug-

---

[115] Ibid., 5th and 6th R. Ys., II, p. 455.

[116] Ibid., 5th R. Y., p. 374 (28 September 1711).

[117] Cf. A. R. Khan, *Cheiftains in the Mughal Empire*, chapters on *subas* Lahore and
Gujarat.

[118] Kamwar, f. 327b.

hals had fought against the Sikhs. Not a single living Sikh is
reported to have ever been captured and sent to the court by
any one of these chiefs, despite repeated imperial *farmans* to this
effect. Some others despatched *peshkash*[119] in order to reduce the
impact of their constant failings in their obligation to the Mughal state, namely, military assistance in their respective territories. This was why they could still expect help from some
eminent nobles, together with their open or secret support for
the Sikhs. In November 1711, for instance, some officials of the
Sirmur chieftancy approached Raja Jai Singh and Raja Ajit
Singh to secure their recommendation for the release of their
chief. The chief of Bilaur is also recorded to have written to
them explaining his position and the Sikh 'excesses' in his
territory. The rajas, however refused to intercede on their behalf, for, as they asserted, 'without the connivance of the
zamindars (of the hills) who could have entered the hills?'[120]

It may be noted that it was not only the chiefs but also the
people (*khalaiq*) of some of the chieftaincies who extended their
help to the Sikhs. Again, some of these chiefs and people seem to
have acted in unison with the roving grain traders (*banjaras*)
who took and sold foodgrains from the plains to the hills. In
1710, in the wake of Banda's flight to the hills, the imperialists
under Rustam Dil Khan and Firoz Khan Mewati had to encounter stiff resistance from the *banjaras* who had led the Sikhs
through the difficult routes of the jungles. Later it was reported
that the *banjaras* ravaged a number of the villages around.[121] On
4 July 1715, the *banjaras* of Kangra carried weapons along with
grain to the Sikh hideouts in the hills.[122] Our sources do not give
any explicit reason for the resistance of the hill peoples and the

[119] *Akhbarat*, BS, 5th R. Y., p. 70.

[120] Ibid., BS, 5th and 6th R. Ys., pp. 481–2. It was in recognition of the supremacy of
Jai Singh and Ajit Singh as well as of their enviable position at the Mughal court that
the hill chiefs approached them to intervene on their behalf. The hill chiefs, however,
must have been familiar with the rajas' discontent over their existing position and it is
not unlikely that by writing to them in confidence, they sought the possibility of
exploiting the Kachhwaha and Rathor Rajas' existing unhappiness to their advantage.
For details of the relations between Bahadur Shah and Jai Singh and Ajit Singh see,
Parties and Politics, pp. 29–39; G. D. Sharma, *Rajput Polity*, pp. 195–218.

[121] *Tarikh-i Shah Alam I*, National Archives, New Delhi transcript, p. 46; *Akhbarat*, BS,
4th R. Y., p. 403.

[122] *Akhbarat*, FS, 4th R. y., p. 263.

banjaras against the Mughals. There is a possibility that some people in the hills of Kahlur who have been mentioned in our sources as friends of the Sikhs and the roving bands of the grain traders were Jats. We may also presume that the inflated rates of *ijara* leading to the exorbitant rise in the prices of foodgrains hit both the *banjaras* and the peoples in the hills.

The question of the support for Sikhs in the hills perhaps required more than a political answer. However, Bahadur Shah tried to tackle it at a politico-administrative level. He took certain measures with a view to integrating the chiefs' territories into the imperial administration more fully. On 21 November 1711 all the *parganas* on the edges of the Jammu and Kumaon hills held by the *zamindars* as their *jagirs* or *in'ams* were ordered to be converted into *khalisa* while *pargana* Kashipur and four other adjacent *mahals* which had hitherto been an *in'am* of the Kumaon chief were given in *jagir* to Mahabat Khan. Within a few weeks, on 30 December, Inayatullah Khan was made the *darogha* of the *mansabs*, the *jagirs* and the *in'ams* of the hill chiefs of the area extending from Jammu to Kumaon. Subsequently, the local officials' suggestions either for an increase or decrease in the *jagir* or *in'am* of a hill chief were to be examined first by Inayatullah Khan. It was only after his investigation into the formal approval of these suggestions that the relevant papers were to be presented before the emperor.[123]

These measures were meant to curtail and restrict the power of the chiefs, but they did not affect their concord with the Sikhs. The emperor therefore decided to march in person to the hills and on 26 January 1712, the officers who provided the details of the geography of the imperial highways (*khushmanzils*) were ordered to measure and report the distance and the stations between Lahore and Kangra.[124] Simultaneously, Ghazanfar Khan, the *qiladar*-designate of Kangra, on the recommendation of Zulfiqar Khan who was in favour of a compromise with the Sikhs, was replaced by Fauj Ali Khan.[125] The journey was, however, delayed and then it could not be taken due to the

---

[123] Ibid., BS, 5th and 6th R. Ys., II, pp. 469 and 482.

[124] Kamwar, f. 330a.

[125] *Akhbarat*, BS, 5th and 6th R. Ys., p. 549; Kamwar, f. 331a. Fauj Ali Khan's appointment also formed part of the centre's attempt at curtailing the power of the governor of the Punjab, Asad Khan. See Chapter II, Section 2.

emperor's illness and death in February 1712.

We cannot speculate as to what would have resulted with the emperor's expedition to the hills. It may be noted that certain political steps tilted the balance in favour of the Mughals in Farrukh Siyar's reign. But before we examine them, we shall try to describe some of the factors which contributed to the Mughal failure against the Sikhs.

The Sikhs and Mughal court politics

At Lohgarh when the emperor and the *wazir* were 'frantically striving to capture Banda and liquidate the seat of Sikh power, Zulfiqar Khan', according to Kamwar Khan who was an eyewitness to the event, 'set out at a leisurely pace and constantly tried to impress upon the emperor the advisability of marching slowly.' This negligence and dilatoriness was in part due to Zulfiqar Khan's dislike for and his quarrel with the *wazir*.[126] In an another instance, Rustam Dil Khan had to retire from the Sikh campaigns in disgust because of the non-co-operation of the fiscal officers. Rustam Dil Khan was one of the leading Mughal generals who had scored victories over Banda and earned the titles of Ghazi Khan Rustam Jang from Bahadur Shah for his services in the Sikh campaigns. By 1711, however, he seems to have been disgusted with the existing situation and on 21 August 1711, retired from the Sikh expedition. The prime reason for his withdrawal was the *diwans'* reluctance to pay arrears (amounting to Rs 12,000) to him. Rustam Dil Khan's protest was apparently justified, since the amount had formally been sanctioned. But the emperor showed no concern for his difficulty. He believed in the version given by Rustam Dil's opponents, took his withdrawal from the expedition as an act of defiance and instead of commissioning an investigation into his grievances, issued orders for his imprisonment in the fort of Lahore.[127] The consequence of such hasty steps is perhaps better illustrated in a letter to the emperor from Muhammad Amin Khan, another important general. The letter which was recieved at the court within a few days of Rustam

---

[126] Kamwar, f. 325b.
[127] Ibid., ff. 329b; *Akhbarat*, BS, 5th R. Y., p. 305.

Dil Khan's imprisonment included the details of Amin Khan's failure in securing money from the local treasury for the payment to his soldiers.[128]

These incidents show the crippled control of the centre over the various departments of finance and local administration. This is further illustrated from a number of other similar instances which we shall see later in Chapter V. Banda had a considerable number of followers and sympathizers among the lower Mughal officials and among the associates and retainers of the nobles.[129] This might have had an impact on the process. But the Sikh movement cannot be taken as the single most important factor leading to the decay in the local administration. As we have seen earlier, and shall also see later in the context of clashes amongst the big and small Mughal officials, the decay in administration continued perhaps with greater intensity after 1715. Bahadur Shah's failure, despite his sincere efforts, in completely freeing the state from Aurangzeb's discriminatory policies is perhaps a matter of considerable consequence in the examination of the sources of strength or weakness of both the Mughals and the Sikhs. Support for Banda's cause was undoubtedly strong among the Jats, and some Hindu employees at the Mughal camp also sympathized with the Sikh movement. Nonetheless, it seems to have cut across caste and creed distinctions.[130] This highlighted an alignment of certain interests in support of the Sikhs. But the imperial order to shave their beards discriminated against the Hindus alone. The order smacked of the emperor's suspicion regarding the loyalty of the Hindus to the state. The Hindus appear to have received it with some resentment and anguish. Some nobles, like Sarfraz Khan, realized the implications of the order and tried to restrict its implementation to the Sikhs (*Nanak parasts*) only. But a fresh

[128] *Akhbarat*, BS, 5th R. Y., p. 321 (27 August 1711).

[129] One Dayanat Rai, for instance, who worked in the *sarkar* of Musawi Khan as his *peshdast* was handcuffed by the *kotwal* for his alleged adherence to the Sikh faith. At Dayanat Rai's instance some hill chief connived at Banda's escape from his territory. Cf. *Akhbarat*, BS, 5th R. Y., p. 344; K. K., II, p. 674.

[130] The Sikh leader seems to have had a following even among some Muslims. On 15 February 1711, one Pir Muhammad Bhatti possibly a member of the rebel Bhattis of Jalandhar Doab, is said to have shouted '*Wah Guru*' '*Wah Guru*' at the court. *Akhbarat*, BS, 5th R. Y., p. 50.

imperial order rejected the modification of Sarfaraz Khan and thereafter all Hindus with beards were denied entry to the court.[131] Again, Aurangzeb's policy of encouraging the conversion of the *zamindars* and thereafter taking it for granted that they were sincere supporters of the imperial policy also seems to have been continued. On 31 August 1711, Mehr Chand and six other *zamindars* of the suburbs of Batala, a town in the stronghold of the Sikhs, accepted Islam after which each of them received *khil'at* and *in'am* from the emperor.[132]

These incidents explain, in a measure, the Mughal failure against the Sikhs. They show how Bahadur Shah under pressure of circumstances, had to abandon or rather reverse, the process of his departure from the policy of Aurangzeb. Towards the end of his reign, however, he had fully realized the consequences of these measures and had decided to finally dissociate the Mughal state from orthodoxy. The *khutba* episode at Lahore, which we have noticed in Chapter I, probably marked the beginning of the new policy. And the death of the emperor, too, could not disrupt its implementation. Again, it is not unlikely that Bahadur Shah had also realized, as is illustrated from the delay in the emperor's plan to personally lead an expedition against the hill chiefs, the necessity of winning over the hill chiefs through the kind of gesture which he had shown the Kachhwahas and the Rathors in 1711.

The Mughal rulers, the hill chiefs and the Sikhs: 1712–1714

A change in the general tenor of imperial policy is discernible immediately after the death of Bahadur Shah. The new Emperor, Jahandar Shah had governed Multan and thus had direct experience of the region. He had raised Isa Khan Mein, a *zamindar* of Jalandhar Doab, to a high position which indicated how much he valued the support of the local magnates, especially in the existing circumstances. His *wazir* Zulfiqar Khan, who was the real ruler in Jahandar Shah's time also believed in, as it was reflected in his attitude towards the Marathas and the

---

[131] Ibid., 4th R. Y., pp. 200 and 203: K. K., II, p. 674. For Sarfaraz Khan, see *T. Muhammadi*, p. 93.

[132] Ibid., 5th R. Y., p. 303.

Sikhs, a policy of all possible adjustment with the local and regional potentates. Towards the hill chiefs therefore a kinder and more benign policy began to be pursued. Bhup Prakash, the chief of Sirmur, was released on bail and *khil'ats* were despatched to the chiefs of Kumaon who professed friendship with the Mughals but had given them little support against the Sikhs.[133] This benevolent attitude together with some concrete administrative measures was maintained under Farrukh Siyar. The revenues of the territories of the hill chiefs seem to have been reassigned to the chiefs themselves or else they were resumed into *khalisa*.[134]

The policy had a perceptible bearing on the relations between the chiefs and the Sikhs. According to a newsletter of 2 October 1712, the Sikhs clashed with the retainers of Bhup Prakash in the Sirmur hills. The chief informed the Mughal general of the whereabouts of the Sikhs and guided him in his hunt for the Sikhs in the Kulu hills. He is also reported to have requested help from the Mughals for the Kulu chief against Sikh attacks. With the Sirmur chief won over by the Mughals, Banda began to lose his base in the Sirhind region from where the Sikhs could threaten inroads even into the Mughal capital. On 16 March 1713, therefore, the Sikhs invaded the country of Bhup Prakash with a huge army and the chief had to run away. But the Mughals at this stage were making special efforts to restore their full control over the region. They forced the Sikhs to retreat down to Dabar where again the Sikhs lost heavily at the hands of the imperial forces.[135]

The change in policy towards the chiefs had an important strategic dimension. The Mughals wanted to prevent the Sikhs from having any base in the hills east of the Shivalik. The chiefs' support in these hills gave Banda an opportunity to strike at the Mughals over a very wide area, extending from the Jalandhar Doab in the Punjab to Bareilly in *suba* Delhi. In 1716, in the wake of celebrating a victory over Banda, a *khil'at* was specially conferred on the Sirmur chief. Also for the same reason, favours were extended to the chief of Kumaon, the more so, because the Srinagar-Garhwal chief in his neighbourhood was still a strong sup-

---

[133] *Akhbarat*, JS, pp. 133 and 162.

[134] The chiefs of Kangra and Nurpur, for instance, are described in our sources as *zamindars* of the *khalisa mahals*. Ibid., FS, 4th R. Y., I, p. 263.

[135] Ibid., FS, 1st and 2nd R. Ys., I, pp, 129, 152 and 259.

porter of the Sikhs and the other rebels.[136] As a result, the Kumaon chief rendered valuable service to the Mughals in arresting the Sikh advance into this region. On 13 July 1715, a detachment of the retainers of the Kumaon chief was reported to have intercepted, and clashed with, a joint army of Banda and the Srinagar-Garhwal chief on the latter's way to Moradabad and Bareilly.[137]

The Kumaon chief was encouraged to keep on containing and chastising the Srinagar-Garhwal chief, till the latter submitted unconditionally to the Mughals. Twice in the second year of Farrukh Siyar's reign (between 25 July and 19 December 1713) the Kumaon chief sent him booty obtained in the battles against the combined forces of the Srinagar-Garhwal chief and his Jat and Gujar allies to whom he had given shelter in his territory.[138] Early in 1715, the Kumaon chief, now honoured with the title of Raja Bahadur, again fell upon Srinagar, finally disolodged the chief and took the town into his possession.[139] The incident which was described in Mughal records as a victory of the Mughal Emperor, forced the vanquished chief to make entreaties to the Mughal court. In a letter to Raja Jai Singh giving details of his eviction from, and devastation in, his *zamindari* by the Kumaon chief, the Srinagar-Garhwal chief requested the raja's intercession for his reinstatement. In the meanwhile, the Srinagar-Garhwal chief also assisted Saiyid Najm-ud-Din Ali Khan Barha against the rebel Gujars.[140]

[136] With the help of the Srinagar-Garhwal chief and the *banjaras*, the Sikhs marched and aspired to invade as far as the territory of *sarkar* Moradabad and *chakla* Bareilly in' *suba* Delhi. *Akhbarat*, FS, 1st and 2nd R. Ys., I, pp. 259 and 327.

[137] Ibid., 3rd R. Y., II, p. 23.

[138] Ibid., 2nd R. Y., II, pp. 24 and 213; Kamwar, f. 344a. A Gujar uprising is first noticed in the *Akhbarat* of 23 Jumada II, 1123/28 July 1711, when a Gujar, Lal Kunwar by name, was reported to have ravaged the *khalisa* and the *jagir* villages in *sarkar* Saharanpur. Jalal Khan, the *faujdar* of the *sarkar* who had been directed to chastise Lal Kunwar seems to have been unable to contain the rebel Gujar. Cf. *Akhbarat* BS, 5th R. Y., p. 231.

[139] Ibid., 4th R. Y., I, p. 137.

[140] Saiyid Najm-ud-Din Ali Khan Barha with a large army hot on the chase of the rebel Gujars was then camping in the Doon valley in the territory of the Srinagar-Garhwal chief, where the rebels had taken shelter. The chief, as he stated in his letter to the raja, sent a detachment under his *diwan* and *bakhshi* to the valley. The Gujars could not hold out against the joint army of the chief and Najm-ud-Din Ali Khan and had to run away from the valley. On the suggestion of Najm-ud-Din Ali Khan, the emperor and the *wazir* each sent a *khil'at* and a horse for the chief. His fort was, however, still in

By the end of 1714, the Sikhs seem to have been almost totally isolated from the hill chiefs. During the last phase of his struggle, Banda Bahadur was cornered, his resistance of the Mughals was confined to Gurdaspur and its neighbourhood in Bari Doab. Even in this area, the chiefs of Kangra and Nurpur and some others had turned their back against the Sikhs. In the beginning of 1715 the Nurpur chief invaded the Sikh fort. In June 1715 imperial *farmans* to the chiefs of Kangra and Nurpur and to some other hill chiefs were considered sufficient for the blockage of the *banjaras* in the hill passages.[141] The Mughals could now also deal with some of their persistent foes in the hills with uncompromising sternness.[142]

The chiefs with a few exceptions were reconciled through leniency and generosity and also through, whenever it was necessary, tough and ruthless measures. The army of Abd us-Samad Khan which eventually stifled the Sikh power in 1715, consisted of the chieftains and thousands of their retainers.[143]

Position of the Khatris in Mughal service after 1712

A significant feature of the change in the general tenor of the policy of the Mughals after the death of Bahadur Shah was their

the control of the Kumaon chief. Therefore he approached Raja Jai Singh to intercede and recommend that the fort and the plundered wealth of Srinagar-Garhwal be returned to him by the Kumaon chief. Compare *Akhbarat*, Miscellaneous, III, pp. 154–6. Letter of the Garhwal chief to Jai Singh.

Saiyid Najm-ud-Din Ali Khan Barha was one of the brothers of Saiyid Abdullah Khan and Husain Ali Khan. He was given a *mansab* of 4000/2000 in the beginning of Farrukh Siyar's reign. In 1719 he was made the *darogha* of the *diwan-i khas*. In the same year he was appointed the governor of Delhi. He was imprisoned after the fall of the Saiyids. In 1726 he was released and appointed the governor of Ajmer on the recommendation of Sarbuland Khan. Later, he was made *faujdar* of Gwalior where he died in 1728. *M. U.*, II, pp. 508–10; *T. Muhammadi*, p. 67; Kamwar, ff. 323b. 344a, 456a, 347b, 351b, 360a, 360b, 361b, 362a, 263b, 365b, 366a, 371b, 374b, 375b and 376a.

[141] *Akhbarat* FS, 4th R. Y., I, p. 263 and II, p. 181.

[142] In July 1714 when about 10,000 Sikhs had taken refuge in the territory of Goler, and the *zamindar* along with these Sikhs was reported to have made incursions into, and plundered, the imperial territory, Ilah Yar Beg, the deputy *faujdar* of Jammu, invaded the territory of the Goler chief along with the retainers of the other chiefs and dispossessed him of his fort at Goler. Ibid., FS, 4th R. Y., I, p. 142.

[143] Ganesh Das Vadera, *Char Bagh*, p. 122.

conscious attempt at making use of the gradual alienation of the Khatris from Banda's movement. The Khatris obtained high positions under Jahandar Shah and Farrukh Siyar. Sabha Chand, a mere *munshi* of Zulfiqar Khan, for example, obtained the title of raja from Jahandar Shah and rose to the office of the *diwan-i khalisa*.[144] Sabha Chand was a close associate of Zulfiqar Khan and the treatment that Zulfiqar Khan's friends and associates received from Farrukh Siyar need not be repeated here.[145] Sabha Chand, was handed over to Mir Jumla (24 June 1713) and within a week the tongue of the ill-fated *diwan* was cut off on the grounds of his using false languge. Saiyid Abdullah Khan, however, seems to have realized the implications of any drastic punishment against Sabha Chand and therefore either under the influence and pressure of his *diwan*, Raja Ratan Chand, or owing to his own enlightened policy, pleaded and eventually secured his release. The fact that Sabha Chand's release came after a year and coincided with Abd-us-Samad Khan's departure for the chastisement of the Sikhs is not without significance.[146] Although Sabha Chand was not reinstated to his earlier position, his son Kunwar Har Sevak who died in April 1735, is mentioned by a contemporary historian as one of the 'notables of the time'.[147]

Ratan Chand, who came from a trading community and Muhkam Singh Khatri both began their careers as *munshi* and *diwan* in the *sarkars* of Saiyid Abdullah Khan and Saiyid Husain Ali Khan respectively. Ratan Chand acquired the reputation of being the 'key of wisdom' (*kalid-i aql*) of the Saiyid brothers while Muhkam Singh who was simply a *mutasaddi* in *chakla* Bareilly received the title of raja and was promoted to 3000/2000 under Farrukh Siyar. Later, in the beginning of the reign of Muhammad Shah, he rose to the rank of 7000 *zat*.[148]

On 20 November 1711, during the reign of Bahadur Shah, Bakht Mal, an associate, and a *diwan* in the *sarkar* of Muhammad Yar Khan[149] was imprisoned and handed over to Ihtimam

---

[144] Satish Chandra, *Parties and Politics*, p. 68.
[145] Cf. W. Irvine, *Later Moghuls*, I, pp. 253 and 275–81; see also, Chapter I, Section 2.
[146] Kamwar, f. 345b.   [147] Ibid., f. 345b.
[148] Ibid., ff. 319b; 347a and 373b; *M. U.*, p. 331. According to Kamwar, f. 373b, the *mansab* of Muhkam Singh in the beginning of Muhammad Shah's reign was 6000/4000.
[149] Muhammad Yar Khan son of Bahman Yar Khan and a grandson of Yamin-ud-

Khan for his alleged sympathy and support for the Sikhs. We know nothing about him till the end of the seventh year of Farrukh Siyar's reign (February 1717 to February 1718), when on the recommendation of Saiyid Abdullah Khan he rose to 2000/200 and replaced Inayatullah Khan as the *diwan-i tan*.[150] A substantial number of Khatris, as the following table shows, acquired such an eminent position in Mughal service or otherwise that they have been mentioned by a contemporary chronicler among the nobles (*umara*) and notables (*a'yan*).

Besides, a number of Khatris in the category of *peshkars* in the office of *diwan-i tan-o-khalisa* and as minor officials are mentioned in our sources. Kamwar mentions Kirpa Ram, Dina Nath and Jagat Ram as *peshkars* of the *tan* in the reign of Muhammad Shah; Rai Phul Chand, Jaswant Rai and Bishwa Nath are described as *peshkars* of the *khalisa*, and *mustaufi* (auditor) respectively while Qabil Ram was in charge of records relating to the dignities and honours of the nobles (*maratib nawis*).[151] Anand Ram 'Mukhlis' describes a number of his relations, e.g., Kirpa Ram, Fateh Singh and Basant Ram as being associated with various departments of the office of the *diwan*.[152]

	Name	Position	Year of death	Source
1	Pandi Mal Gandhi	*diwan* of Abd-us-Samad Khan	1722	*T. Muhammadi*, p. 46.
2	*Rai Rayan* Muhkam Singh	a notable	1725	*T. Muhammadi*, p. 55.

(contd.)

Daulah Asaf Khan, began his career with a *mansab* of 400 *zat* in the 12th R.Y., of Aurangzeb. In the 40th R.Y., he was appointed the governor of the *suba* of Delhi. He retained the governorship of Delhi (deputy governorship) along with the *qiladari* of the fort under Bahadur Shah. In the reign of Farrukh Siyar, he was promoted to 5000/2000 and was given the charge of imperial household (*khan-i saman*) in addition to his office of the *qiladari* of the Delhi fort. He retained the office of *khan-i saman* till 1718 when he was replaced by Inayatullah Khan Kashmiri. Though he did not hold any office after the reign of Farrukh Siyar, he retained his *mansab* and *jagir* till his death in January 1726. *M. U.*, III, pp. 706–11; Kamwar, ff. 312b, 314a, 330a, 320a, 327a, 339a, 339b, 342a, 351b, 356a, 360b and 376b; *T. Muhammadi*, p. 61.

[150] Kamwar, ff. 320a and 360a.   [151] Kamwar, f. 338 (Paris MS.).

[152] *Safarnama*, pp. 4, 8, 10, 12, 17–18, 25–6, 36, 39, 57, 60, 62, 92, 100 and 108; *Badai*, p. 40 (Rampur MS.).

(*contd.*)

	Name	Position	Year of death	Source
3	Raja Hirday Ram	*vakil* of Amin Khan, Sarbuland Khan and the other nobles, 2000/500	1724	*T. Muhammadi*, p. 57; *Safarnama*, p. 9.
4	Raja Daya Ram	*vakil* of Qamar-ud-Din Khan	1726	*T. Muhammadi*, p. 60; Kamwar, f. 373b.
5	Har Sahai	*vakil* of Amin-ud-Daulah and Saiyid Hasan Khan	1726	*T. Muhammadi*, p. 60.
6	Ikhlas Khan (an oil merchant and convert)	a noble	1727	*T. Muhammadi*, p. 65; *Majma-un-Nafais*, f. 499a; *Fathiya Asafiya*, f. 89a.
7	Raja Raghunath	*amin* and *faujdar* of *chakla* Sirhind, 2000/500	1729	*T. Muhammadi*, p. 70.
8	Raja Mansukh Ram	*amin* and *faujdar* of *chakla* Bareilly	1731	*T. Muhammadi*, p. 80.
9	*Rai Rayan* Majlis Rai	*amin* and *faujdar* of Batala	1733	*T. Muhammadi*, p. 85; *Safarnama*, p. 92.
10	Rai Sahib Singh	a notable	1733	*T. Muhammadi*, p. 87; *Badai*, f. 58b.
11	Raja Jaswant Singh Khatri	a notable	1733	*T. Muhammadi*, p. 87.
12	Raja Lachhi Ram	a noble, 2000/500	1734	*T. Muhammadi*, p. 88; Kamwar, p. 376b.
13	Raja Muhkam Singh	a noble, 7000 *zat*	1734	*T. Muhammadi*, p. 89; *M. U.*, II, pp. 330–2; Kamwar, ff. 342b, 347a and 373b.
14	Kuwar Har Sewak	a notable	1735	*T. Muhammadi*, p. 92.
15	Shaikh Sa'adatmand	*vakil* of Nizam-ul-Mulk	1735	*T. Muhammadi*, p. 94; Kamwar, f. 381a.
16	Balkishan	*vakil* of the governor of Bengal	1736	*T. Muhammadi*, p. 96.
17	Mehta Sadanand	*faujdar* of Etawah	1735	*T. Muhammadi*, p. 94.

	Name	Position	Year of death	Source
18	Raja Bakht Mal	a noble, *diwan-i khalisa*	1738	*T. Muhammadi*, p. 100; *T. Muzaffari*, f. 83a.
19	Raja Sambhu Ram	a notable	1739	*T. Muhammadi*, p. 106.
20	Rao Kashi Ram	a notable	1739	*T. Muhammadi*, p. 106.
21	Rai Naunidh	a notable	1739	*T. Muhammadi*, p. 112; Kamwar, f. 376a.
22	Rao Babu Rai	a notable	1739	*T. Muhammadi*, p. 113.
23	Rao Harnand	deputy *faujdar* of Moradabad	1741	*T. Muhammadi*, p. 117; *T. Muzaffari*, f. 101b; *M. U.*, II, p. 841; *Safarnama*, p. 55.
24	Shaikh Sa'dullah Khatri	a noble, *diwan-i tan*	1744	*T. Muhammadi*, p. 122; Kamwar, p. 337; *Safarnama*, p. 57.
25	Raja Dhirendar	a notable, *diwan* of Amir Khan	1747	*T. Muhammadi*, p. 137.
26	Bhupat Rai	*faujdar* of Panipat		Kamwar, f. 376a.

These Khatris, though we have no evidence for all of them, appear to have originally belonged to the province of the Punjab, for the Punjab is mentioned as the homeland of those Khatris about whom we can gather some biographical details. Ikhlas Khan hailed from Kalanaur and Hirday Ram, Daya Ram, Har Sahai and Majlis Rai belonged to Sodhra, a *pargana* town in Rachna Doab.[153] Again some of the other Khatris whom we have not listed here, e.g., Atma Ram, the *diwan* of Awadh and his sons, also came from the Punjab. Though most of them were not very highly placed in the traditional hierarchy of Mughal officials, they acquired eminence mainly due to their close relations with big merchants and *sahukars* and have been characterized in our sources among the *a'yan*. Notwithstanding

[153] *Safarnama* (Introduction of the editor), p. 7; Bindraban Das 'Khushgo', *Safina-i Khushgo*, ed. Ata-ur-Rahman Kakwi, Patna, 1959, p. 331.

their official position, they seem to have retained their ancestral professions and were thus in command of considerable wealth and prestige.[154] It was through the efforts of Gajpat Rai that Khwaja Muhammad Qasim (Samsam-ud-Daulah's father) could obtain a high *mansab* and honour. Again, it was Gajpat Rai who managed his marriage to the daughter of Ruhullah Khan. Raja Hirday Ram is reported to have secured for Samsam-ud-Daulah the governorship of Gujarat and an amount of Rs 50,000 from the court. In 1720 after the death of Saiyid Husain Ali Khan, Emperor Muhammad Shah handed his personal ring to Raja Daya Ram and deputed him to go to Ratan Chand and persuade the latter to submit to the court.[155] Again, the aristocratic establishments of these Khatris, in spite of the fact that they were apparently mere agents and clerks of the Mughal nobles, speak of their wealth and rich possessions. They seem to have maintained, for instance, one or two elephants and camels, a number of horses of different breeds, *karkhanas* and servants to look after their establishments.[156] This probably partly explains the emergence of the Khatris as *vakils* of the nobles in Mughal India, for the prime responsibility of the *vakil* was to keep the economic position of their clients on secure footing. The working of the institution of the *vakil* and the nobles' trust in, and their sole dependence upon the Khatris also show the nature of the relationship between these two important social groups of Mughal times.

The increase in strength of the Khatris, an important trading community of northern India, in imperial service may probably be viewed against the background of the fact that the fortunes of the merchants in Mughal India were closely tied with the prosperity of the nobles.[157] The financial difficulties of the no-

[154] In this respect, the following comment of Anand Ram 'Mukhlis' which reflects the attitude of even those Khatris who were a part of the Mughal administration is interesting: 'Trade is many times better than nobility: Nobility makes one subject while in (the profession of) trade one leads the life of a ruler. The wealth accumulated by a noble is a misfortune whereas the money earned in trade is lawfully enjoyable'. *Safarnama*, (Introduction of the editor), p. 22.

[155] *Badai*, pp. 30 and 31.

[156] Cf. S. A. Ali's article in Urdu on Anand Ram 'Mukhlis' in the *Oriental College Magazine* (Urdu), Lahore, November 1941, pp. 92, 112, 124. Ali quotes extensively from the works of 'Mukhlis'.

[157] Cf. Irfan Habib, 'Potentialities of Change in the Economy of Mughal India'. *The Socialist Digest*, No. 6, September 1972, p. 121.

bles must have affected the prospects of trade as well.[158] Subsequently, the merchants began to seek some new avenues to build their fortunes which might also have led to their increased political participation. Again, they had to defend the existing political framework in the face of the agrarian uprisings. Their donations to the imperial treasury to finance the campaigns against the Sikhs may also be considered in this light.

With the ascendancy to power of Zulfiqar Khan and, following him, the Saiyid brothers, the Mughal state's association with orthodoxy came to a final end. The Sikh menace under the leadership of Banda continued till 1715, but the discriminatory measures to meet the challenge such as the shaving-off of beards by the Hindus alone were not repeated after the commencement of Jahandar Shah's reign. Further, the Mughals tried to widen, and make full use of, the differences among the various sects of the Sikhs. According to Macauliffe, the Sikhs had already been divided into two groups, *Jat Khalsa* (real Sikhs) and *Bandai Khalsa* (followers of Banda). When Banda assumed royal ensignia and claimed to be the Guru, the *Jat Khalsa* refused to recognize him as the true *Singh* and accused him of having disregarded and violated the Guru's commandments. Farrukh Siyar took advantage of the rift and utilized the influence of Gobind Singh's widow to isolate Banda from the Sikhs.[159] On 16 August 1715, Guru Gobind's son was honoured with a *khil'at-i matami* on the pretext of the death of the Guru.[160] It cannot be ruled out that the *khil'at-i matami* bestowed on the son of the Guru about five years after the death of the Guru signified the extension of official patronage to those who could possibly be pitted against Banda.

The changes in Mughal policy coupled with some weaknesses in the Sikh movement itself gave it a serious jolt. Banda along with 700 followers was captured and put to death in Delhi in 1715.

[158] In this connection see also M. Athar Ali, 'The Passing of Empire: The Mughal Case', *Modern Asian Studies*, Vol. 9, No. 3, 1975, pp. 387–9.

[159] M. A. Macauliffe, *The Sikh Religion*, p. 250.

[160] *Akhbarat*, FS, 2nd R. Y., II, p. 88.

CHAPTER V

The Punjab after 1715, the *Zamindars* and the Problems facing the Provincial Government

Political and administrative developments in Awadh and the Punjab until the beginning of the 1720s were, in a large measure, similar. The governors of both these provinces struggled for additional powers which they obtained eventually, to enable them to meet the threat from local conditions. Rural disturbances together with conflicts in the province at various levels and the steady erosion of the classical pattern of the relationship between the emperor and the nobility with its consequent stormy politics at the court, influenced the course of change in the position of the governors. With the beginning of the third phase of the period of our study, however, when the process of provincial independence from the imperial centre set in, these provinces took different directions. This difference had a bearing principally on the development, as in Awadh, or the lack of development, as in the Punjab, of what have been called 'successor states'.

The period from 1715 until the formation of the *misls* in the mid-eighteenth century is perhaps the least known and most confused chapter in the history of the Sikhs in the eighteenth century. 'The few remaining Sikhs', as a late-eighteenth century observer puts it, 'fled to the mountains after the execution of Banda in Delhi where they concealed themselves; and the zamindars and riots of the country who had joined them during their insurrection, partly to secure themselves, and partly for the sake of plunder, now cut off their beards and hair, and returned to their original occupations'.[1] This statement needs qualification, for we have instances of the same kind of plunder and banditry as before by the Sikhs or their supporters, even though Abd-us-Samad Khan tried to reconcile a section of the

[1] Ganda Singh (ed.), *Early European Accounts of the Sikh*, Calcutta, 1962, p. 31.

Sikhs (*Tatva Khalsa*). On 24 September 1717, goods and valuables of traders and travellers were reported to have been plundered in the suburbs of Lahore. As the *amil* had a very small armed contingent, he could not provide protection to them.[2] The entire trade-route which passed through the province of the Punjab, seems to have been disturbed. About two months after, in another case, six merchants were killed and their belongings were looted at the village of Aurangpur on their way from Lahore to Delhi.[3] Our sources ascribe these incidents to the *mufsids* and *maqahir* (the seditious and the vanquished ones), a generic term to denote 'the disturbers', 'seditious elements', namely, rebels in Mughal times. But a close scrutiny of the nature of these 'disturbances' which had a striking resemblance with the earlier Sikh and *zamindar* attacks on the trade caravans lead us to identify the *mufsids* with the Sikhs. Besides, the term *maqahir* in our sources has generally been used for the Sikhs.

Following the death of Banda the Sikhs reorganized themselves and concentrated on increasing their strength and maintaining unity in their ranks.[4] This seems to have been accomplished around the early 1720s. With better organization and enhanced striking power, they then began to attack contingents of Mughal officials. In 1721, they made a successful night-assault on a Mughal detachment under Ruh-ul-Amin Khan in *pargana* Pasrur.[5] In 1726, they plundered an imperial caravan and killed some Mughal officials somewhere between Lahore and Sirhind.[6] The Sikhs and their supporters continued to pose dangers to the government of Zakariya Khan (1726–45) in the late 1720s and the 1730s.[7]

In 1733, Zakariya Khan reportedly extended concessions to some Sikh leaders. Kapur Singh, for instance was given *jagirs* and the title of nawab. The Sikh leaders, now settled in Amritsar, used this opportunity to organize their community,

---

[2] *Akhbarat*, FS, 6th R. Y., I, p. 287.   [3] Ibid., 6th R. Y., II, p. 50.
[4] For details of the Sikh sects and their differences see George Foster, *A Journey from Bengal to England*, London 1798, I, p. 310, Macauliffe, *The Sikh Religion*, II, pp. 115–16.
[5] *Tabsira*, f. 61b.   [6] Ibid., f. 82a.
[7] Sohanlal Suri, *Umdat-ut-Tawarikh*, Vol. I, p. 108; J. S. Grewal, *From Guru Nanak to Ranjit Singh*, pp. 97–8; Gurtej Singh, 'Bhai Mani Singh in Historical Perspective', *Proceedings of the Panjab History Conference*, Patiala, 1968, pp. 120–7.

as the tradition goes, under *Budha Dal* (old party) and *Tarun Dal* (young party), each divided into five units (*deras*). But even before the invasion of Nadir Shah, the *jagirs* of the Sikh *Sardars* were confiscated and a large number of the Sikhs were forced to take shelter in the hills and the Lakhi jungles.[8] For a period of five months in 1739–40 during which Nadir Shah was in India, the Punjab and the areas in its neighbourhood were thrown into great confusion. The Sikhs took advantage of this confused and helpless state. 'They established themselves in the Bari Doab under the leadership of Bhag Singh Ahluwalia. They stopped traffic, plundered and raided a large number of villages and towns and exacted heavy tribute from the neighbouring *zamindars*. Jassa Singh Ahluwalia, the son of Bhag Singh's sister, was his deputy and exercised full authority over matters and things concerning Bhag Singh. The other Sikh chiefs also accepted the leadership of Ahluwalia and willingly worked under him. The administration of the whole Doab thus seemed, at the time, to be passing into the hands of the Sikhs.'[9] In 1743 they killed the official in charge of the escort (*badraqa*) and plundered the treasury on its way from Emanabad to Lahore. Azimullah Khan was sent to chastise the Sikhs and he succeeded, but his success seems to have been shortlived. Zakariya Khan, therefore, deputed Adina Beg to make the Sikhs submit. 'The force he had with him was fully equal to the execution of that service, but Adina Beg, considering that if he should entirely put an end to all disturbances in that district, there would remain no necessity for continuing him in so extensive a command, carried on intrigues with the chiefs of the Sicks [Sikhs], and secretly encouraged them to continue their depredation, at the same time, pretending to be very desirous of subduing them. From this management, the Sicks became daily more powerful and seized upon several places in the distant parts of the *Subah* of Lahore. They also began again to perform public pilgrimage to the Holy Tank at Amritsar, without molestation.'[10]

---

[8] Gian Singh, *Shamsher Khalsa* (Vol. II of his history, *Tawarikh-i Khalsa*) Sialkot, 1893, pp. 45–6 and 120–1. See also H. R. Gupta, *Evolution of the Sikh Confederacies* (Vol. II of his *History of the Sikhs*), second revised ed., Delhi, 1978, pp. 46–50.

[9] Sohan Lal Suri, *Umdat-ut-Tawarikh*, p. 109.

[10] Ganda Singh (ed.), *Early European Accounts*, p. 32.

Towards the end of his life, Zakariya Khan again tried to win over the Sikhs through his *diwans*, Lakhpat Rai and Jaspat Rai. They were encouraged to settle and improve on agriculture. Earlier, the governor took measures to rehabilitate the economy of the province following the Persian invasion. Soon, however, Zakariya Khan died, and the subsequent civil war between his sons again gave the Sikhs an opportunity to organize themselves through successful raids and plunders. 'Bodies of armed men in tens and twenties called *Dharwee* in the dialect of the province, that is highwaymen, infested the routes of communication, attacked villages or plundered towns ....'[11] During these troubles, 'the Sick chiefs Jassa Singh Kalal and Chrisa Singh, and Kirwar Singh, had got together about 5000 horses which army they gave the title of Dul Khalsa Gee, or the Army of the State and with which they made themselves masters of the Doab of Bary. Moin-ul-Mullock [Muin-ul-Mulk, the governor then] again appointed Adina Beg Khan to the Faujdary of that Doab, who marching thither, began as formerly to intrigue with the Sicks and took no effectual means to suppress them.'[12]

The *Dal Khalsa* organization changed the character of the Sikh resistance, enabling them to moblize a multitude of plunderers into some sort of rude cavalry regiments. The organization formed the basis of coming together of the different (according to a tradition 65) groups under eleven leaders in 1748 with Jassa Singh in supreme command. These armed bands of the eleven leaders together with those of the Phulkian states (Patiala, Nabha, Jind, etc.) of the cis-Sutlej region came to be known as the twelve *misls* in the eighteenth century.[13] In the period between 1746 and 1748 the Sikhs also built the fort of Ram Raumi at Amritsar (30 March 1747); this marked the rise of Amritsar as an important centre of political and military activities. Thus, by the end of our period the Sikhs

[11] Henry T. Prinsep, *The Origins of the Sick Power in the Punjab*, Calcutta, 1834, (reprint, 1970), p. 3.

[12] Ganda Singh (ed.), *Early European Accounts*, pp. 33–4.

[13] Of these six belonged to the *Budha Dal*, namely, (1) The *Ahluwalia Misl* under the leadership of Jassa Singh who also held the chief command of the *Dal Khalsa*, (2) The *Dallewal Misl* under Gulab Singh of village Dallewal near Dera Baba Nanak on the Ravi, (3) The *Faizullahpuria or Singhpuria Misl* under Nawab Kapur Singh of village

were again organized, but this time principally as a band of
bandits and plunderers, to wage a joint and effective resistance
against the state. Their unity was strengthened by their gather-
ings (*sarbat Khalsa*) on the occasions of Baisakhi and Diwali at
Amritsar where they passed resolutions (*gurmattas*) to guide
their actions. These resolutions also made them realize that
obedience to their leaders was a religious duty, a command-
ment of the Guru, imposed upon them by the community
(*panth*) in whose body the Guru had merged his personality.

The revival of the Sikh challenge can in part be explained in
terms of administrative failure. According to Henry Prinsep
'the early neglect of the ruling authority enabled the associa-
tions to prosper, and the most successful chiefs purchased
horses with the proceeds of their spoils and mounted and armed
their followers.'[14] One can extend it further by adding that the
death of Zakariya Khan in 1745 and the subsequent civil war
between his sons also enervated the Mughals against the Sikhs.
We have also noted that some Mughal officials like Adina Beg
made secret deals with the Sikhs in order to promote their own
interests.

But the administrative failure also needs to be explained,
particularly when we know that Zakariya Khan was an able
and efficient administrator and that more than once he tried to
reconcile with the Sikh chiefs. It appears as if arrangements
with the leaders was of no use as the rank and file had a great
deal of influence on them and compelled them, after the 1720s
to take certain lines of action.

The change in the nature of the Sikh movement from one of
relatively strong peasantry for raising themselves socially in the
seventeenth and the early-eighteenth century to the one of

Faizullahpur, (4) The *Karorasinghia Misl* under Karora Singh of Panjgarh, (5) The
Nishanwala Misl under Dasaunda Singh, the standard bearer of *Dal Khalsa*, (6) The *Shahidi
Misl* or Dip Singh's unit. The remaining five belonged to the *Tarun Dal*, namely, (1) The
Kanhiya Misl under Jai Singh Kanhiya of village Kanha near Lahore, (2) The *Bhangi
Misl* under Hari Singh, (3) The *Nakai Misl* under Hira Singh of village Baharwal in
Chunian near Lahore, (4) The *Ramgarhiya Misl* or the unit of Nand Singh Sanghania,
(5) The *Sukarchakia Misl* under Nodh Singh of village Sukarchak in Gujranwala. Cf.
H. R. Gupta, *History of the Sikhs*, Vol. IV, *The Rise and Fall of the Sikh Misls*, Delhi, 1980,
pp. 91–2.

[14] Henry T. Prinsep, *Origins of the Sick Power*, p. 3.

impoverished *zamindars* and peasants struggling for survival and maintenance of their existing positions in the eighteenth century can only be appreciated in the light of the history of the economy of the region. While the Punjab registered unprecedented growth in the seventeenth century, its economy seems to have suffered some setbacks since the last years of Aurangzeb's reign. The silting of the Indus affected its riverine trade.[15] This is also reflected, in a measure, in some of the available *jama* figures of the province for the seventeenth century. The increase in the *jama* in the first half of the century was spectacular, rising steadily from 55,94,58,423 *dams* at the time of the compilation of the *Ain* (1595) to 1,08,97,59,776 in 1658. On the contrary, in the second half of the century, the *jama* fell to 89,30,39,039 *dams* in the 41st year of Aurangzeb's reign and after that the increase was very slow and nominal.[16] We should not, however, hasten to characterize the economy of the region as stagnant on the basis of the *jama* figures for only a few years of a century. We may also note that trading centres like Gujarat, Wazirabad, Sialkot, Eminabad, Lahore, Sultanpur, Nakodar and Phillaur, and the richer soil areas of the Punjab concentrated around the great land route linking the Mughal empire with the land of the Safavids and the central Asian Khanates. We can legitimately speculate that the seventeenth century trade on this route made up for the losses accruing from the silting Indus. In the late-seventeenth century Sujan Rai boastfully listed the Punjab among the richest provinces of the Mughal empire.[17] Even as late as the 1720s, a biographer of Abd-us-Samad Khan described the Punjab in glowing terms, giving no indication of a province engulfed by a crisis.[18] In the early-eighteenth century the villages around Batala and Kalanaur were producing enough surplus to feed the armed Sikh bands under Banda.[19]

In the eighteenth century, however, trade of the Punjab and the other parts of Mughal empire with central and west Asian countries received a serious setback. The Ghilzai risings

[15] Cf. Chetan Singh, 'Socio-Economic Conditions of Punjab during the Seventeenth Century'.

[16] For the *jama* figures of some years of the 17th and 18th centuries see, N. A. Siddiqi, *Land Revenue Administration*, Appendix E, p. 167.

[17] Compare Sujan Rai Bhandari, *Khulasat-ut-Tawarikh*, pp. 67, 60–1 and 79.

[18] *Asrar-i Samadi*, p. 5.

[19] *Akhbarat*, FS, 4th R. Y., I, pp. 97, 141–2 and 158.

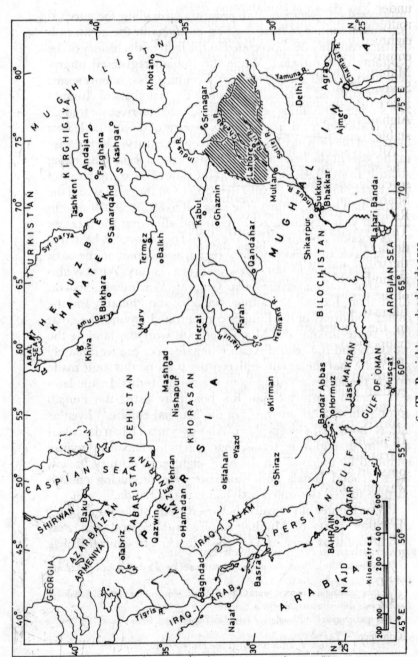

6. The Punjab's overland trade area

under Mir Wais in Qandahar in 1709 disturbed even the land route which connected our region with Persia. The early-eighteenth century also witnessed the rapid decay of the Safavid empire, leading eventually to the capture of Isfahan by Mahmud Ghilzai in 1722. Later, Nadir Afshar, a general of the Safavid Shah, averted the danger of the Safavid Persia falling apart into the hands of the Russians, the Ottomans and the Afghans; but the country north-west of our region was never stable through the end of the period of our study.[20]

All this seems to have dislocated the economy of the Punjab. The *hasil* of the province fell from Rs 2,00,35,791/8¼ in the seventeenth century to Rs 1,25,18,182/9¼ in Muhammad Shah's reign. The decline was the heaviest (from Rs 7,58,957 to Rs 1,98,328/14¼) in the income from the *sair mahals* of *khalisa*. The revenues of *sarkar* Multan including the city of Multan also declined heavily.[21] Such being the condition, a large number of the tribal and the pastoral communities who had settled in and around the rich areas of the Punjab,[21a] may then have felt the brunt of the decline, and of these the poor peasants and half-settled tillers would have been the worst sufferers. The Sikh movement in the eighteenth century seems to have lived on these pauperized sections. No arrangement with their individual leaders could have been effective, for even as the leaders organized them for joint and united actions, they had to make evident concessions to the demands of those most affected. All participated in the deliberations to pass the resolutions, the Guru responded not to the leaders but to the entire community. In the face of the steady decline of revenues and the constant threat and finally the invasion from the north-west, it was not possible for Zakariya Khan to resolve the Sikh problem, for it was not rooted in factors or policies under his control.

The merchants and the traders perhaps appreciated the reasons for the malaise. They continued their association with the state, and in the face of the decline of trade, their strength in government service may well have increased. Indeed, the

---

[20] L. Lockhart, *Nadir Shah*, London, 1938, pp. 35–45; Roger Savory, *Iran under the Safavids*, Cambridge, 1980, pp. 226–54.

[21] I.O. 4488.

[21a] Chetan Singh discusses the process in Chapter VII of his 'Socio-Economic Conditions of Panjab during the Seventeenth Century'.

Mughals seem to have ruled the Punjab in our period through eminent Khatris, like Jaspat Rai, Lakhpat Rai and Kauramal. But the gap between them and the Sikhs and the other agrarian communities steadily became unbridgeable. Apart from the trading caravans, the towns still seem to have been the principal targets of the dislocated communities. Possibly as a measure of defence against them, Batala was fortified in Muhammad Shah's reign.[22] A large number of the traders seem to have migrated from their hometowns in northern and western Punjab to the east and to the south of Multan in Sindh.[23]

In this context it becomes meaningful to note that besides the Sikhs almost all the *zamindari* risings in post-1715 Punjab concentrated on and around the great route or its branches. The *zamindars* posed a threat to the imperial power even after the Mughals had demonstrated their might forcefully by executing Banda and his comrades. On 26 July 1716, Qatil, a *zamindar* in *pargana* Gujarat was reported to have built a strong mud fortress near the *qasba* of Jakobar(?). He mobilized the *zamindars* of the entire *pargana* against the Mughals. No *amil* of the *jagirdar* was in a position to enforce imperial regulations and realize revenue from the villages.[24] The Mughal *jagirdar* and *amil* could not realize a single penny from the Awan *zamindars* along the southern fringes of the route in Sindh Sagar Doab.[25] The Salharia *zamindars* were up in arms against the Mughals in a number of *khalisa* and *jagir* villages in and around the *pargana* of Sialkot in Rachna Doab.[26] In an instance from Bari Doab, the *zamindars* of *tappa* Sarhani, Naushahra and *pargana* Haibatpur patti along with 500 *sawars* and *piyadas* were reported to have invaded and devastated a number of villages in *pargana* Fathabad. Many were killed while many others were wounded in their encounter against the invaders. The rest managed to escape in different directions.[27] In an another instance in 1718, the Khokhar

---

[22] J. S. Grewal (ed. and tr.), *In the By-Lanes of History*, Introduction, p. 18.

[23] Cf. C. A. Bayly, *Rulers, Townsmen and Bazaars*, p. 202.

[24] *Akhbarat*, FS, 5th R. Y., II, p. 305.   [25] Ibid., 6th R. Y., I, pp. 165–6.

[26] Some time in 1717, the Salharias seem to have been contained, some of them reportedly having been captured and put into prison by the *amil* of the *pargana*. The Salharias offered to pay Rs 5,000 for their release, but since the Salharias still did not refrain from plundering the other *khalisa mahals*, the *amil* refused to release these prisoners. Ibid., 6th R. Y., II, pp. 201–2.

[27] Ibid., 5th R. Y., II, pp. 29–30. Fathabad was a town next to Govindwal towards the

zamindars invaded the villages of Sadiqabad and Khalilpur, a *ta'alluqa* of one Khwaja Muhammad Sadiq and dislodged the *muqaddams* of the villages.[28] In an another case from Jalandhar Doab, the *amil* of *pargana* Rahon is reported to have died in 1722 in the encounter with the rustic villagers (*ganwars*) of the *pargana*.[29] The road from Lahore to Multan also seems to have been vulnerable against the *zamindar* raids.[30]

In the late 1720s and early 1730s, almost the entire upper northern tract in the Chanhat, Rachna and Bari Doabs seems to have been disturbed by *zamindar* risings. A large part of the area between Hasan Abdal and the Ravi was under the control of Panah, a powerful leader of the Bhattis, while in the region between Lahore and the Sutlej Mir Mar often took to loot and plunder. Two major campaigns against these *zamindars* were led in person by the governor of the Punjab. Moreover, in 1734, the emperor is reported to have ceremoniously sent off the governor to chastise Mian Khan, a rebel *zamindar* of the province.[31]

As the Mughals failed to contain the Sikhs and the *zamindars*, their uprisings succeeded, to a very large extent, in dispelling the fear of the Mughal sword. They demolished 'the impenetrable wall that represented the majestic awe.' In consequence, the whole province became disturbed and the hill chiefs now showed scant regard for the Mughal crown.

---

west after the Beas on the route. Fathabad was made centre of a new *pargana* of the same name in the seventeenth century. The armed strength of the *zamindars* of Haibatpur *Patti*, etc., may not be taken to suggest that the invaders belonged to the higher echelons of *zamindars*. For, 500 *sawars* and *piyadas* under the joint command of a number of *zamindars* was by no means a big army. The incident, may in fact suggest the possibility of a rift even between various categories of village-level petty *zamindars*.

[28] Ibid., 6th–8th R. Ys., p. 131 (29 September 1718). We are unable to identify these villages. But it may be noted that the Khokhars in Bari Doab were mostly in control of the *parganas* on the route connecting Lahore with Kangra. In Rachna Doab they were the dominant *zamindars* in Eminabad while in Chanhat they controlled Hario and Lohar, Cf. *Ain*, II (Jarrett), pp. 320–8.

[29] *Tabsira*, f. 63b.

[30] In 1721, for instance, *zamindars* of all denominations in *pargana* Palibaith collected at a fortress at Narok which had lately been a stronghold of the rebels of the *pargana*. The *faujdar* of the *pargana* led an expedition against the rebels and laid seige to the fortress. But the *zamindars* could not be contained. They managed to flee from the fortress, despite a strong reinforcement under the command of Sher Afgan, the governor designate of Multan. Shivdas, f. 67a.

[31] *M. U.*, II, p. 106; *Badai*, f. 58a.

*Conflict between Mughal officials and the
chiefs, c. 1714–1748*

In 1712–15, the Mughals exploited the differences between the
chiefs and the Sikhs to their advantage and succeeded in suppressing the movement under Banda. This, however, did not
minimize, let alone obliterate, the basic differences the Mughals themselves had with the chiefs. The chiefs seem to have
been aware of the fact that it was largely through their help and
cooperation that the Mughals could meet the Sikh challenge.
They thus tried to buttress their position by using their own
strength and the weakness of the Mughals. Kangra and Kumaon were the only two exceptions to the general trend of
insubordination among them.[32] But there is little evidence to
show if even these two chieftains remained loyal to the Mughals
beyond the first decade of Muhammad Shah's reign.

The chiefs' endeavour to cash in on the weakness of the
Mughals to their full advantage is perhaps best illustrated in
the activities of the chiefs of the Jammu hills. The chief of
Nurpur who had lately helped the Mughals against Banda
Bahadur was reported on 22 September 1717, to have built a
strong *thana* and mobilized the other *zamindars* of the hills
against the *faujdar* of *chakla* Jammu.[33] In an another instance,
Anand Dev, the chief of Jammu, and Dhrub Dev, the chief of
Jasrota, jointly commanded a campaign against the Mughals in
November 1720.[34] This was in spite of some serious differences
between them which the Mughals had recently tried to ex-
ploit.[35] By 1723–4 during a Kashmir expedition of Abd-us-
Samad Khan, the governor of the Punjab, they began to act as
independent rulers and took possession of the *parganas* adjoining the mountain valley. On his return from the expedition,
Abd-us-Samad Khan intended to chastise the chiefs, but he was

---

[32] Compare Kamwar, f. 376b, entry 4 January 1721, for an *arzdasht* of the Kumaon
chief to Muhammad Shah along with 100 *muhrs*, 5 horses, 2 *katars*, 7 swords and a few
hill birds. For the Kangra chief we have no direct evidence. But the fact that Khalilullah
Khan, the *faujdar* and *qiladar* of Kangra, had a peaceful tenure till his death in 1730, (*T.
Muhammadi*, p. 75) presumably suggests the absence of any major disruption of conventionally accepted relations with him.

[33] *Akhbarat*, FS, 6th R. Y., I, pp. 273–4.   [34] *Tabsira*, f. 63b.

[35] On 5 June 1716 Anand Dev, the chief of Jammu who had half of Jammu in his
zamindari was reported to have revolted against the Mughals. Subsequently, on 20 June

prevented, as a contemporary chronicler informs us, from doing so because of the demise of his wife.[36]

In the meanwhile, the chiefs intercepted trading consignments and plundered even the presents that were sent to Abd-us-Samad Khan from the governor of Kashmir. Subsequently in 1726, the Mughals, under the command of Abd-us-Samad Khan and Zakariya Khan, set up some strong garrisons in *pargana* Bhau which had so far been in the *jagirs* of the chiefs. In a battle which lasted for over three days and ended in the victory of the Mughals about 3000 retainers of the chiefs were killed. In the arrangement that followed, the *faujdari* of Jammu was given to Adina Beg Khan and *pargana* Bhau was taken away from the control of the chiefs.[37]

By expressing their allegiance to the Mughals, the chiefs, however, only sought a respite to reinforce themselves. They looked for an opportunity to throw off their obeisance to the Mughal Emperor. In the wake of Nadir Shah's invasion of Hindustan and the subsequent disturbances, they again revolted, this time never to submit.[38]

Under the circumstances, the Mughal governor had either to accede to the chiefs' ambitions or to cow them down with a heavy hand. The chiefs were too strong to be easily subdued for a long period, and though there are instances of individual arrangements with them, we have no evidence for any new arrangement made by the governor with the chiefs or for that matter with any other category of *zamindar* in the Punjab. Indeed, an arrangement with the Punjab chiefs within the imperial framework had become exceedingly difficult. *Mansab* could not gratify them even in cases when they had administrative assignments in their territories. The Ghakkar chief of

---

1716, in an encounter with Ikhlas Khan, Anand Dev was defeated and dispossessed of his *zamindari* which was then awarded to Dhrub Dev, the chief of *pargana* Jasrota, on the condition of the annual payment of Rs 86,000. Within a few years, however, the arrangement with Dhrub Dev got disrupted. In the meanwhile, Anand Dev had patched up his differences with Dhrub Dev and staged a joint resistance against the Mughals. Ibid., 5th R. Y., II, pp. 186 and 215.

[36] *Asrar-i Samadi*, pp. 45, 48 and 53; Warid, pp. 289–90.

[37] *Mirat-ul-Haqaiq.*, f. 432b; Miscellaneous Administrative Series, V (Sitamau Collection), pp. 75–6. Later, in the time of Ranjit Dev, however, on the recommendation of Raja Jai Singh Sawai, the *pargana* seems to have been restored to the chief of Jammu.

[38] Compare *Tazkira Mukhlis*, p. 270.

pargana Bahlolpur who had a *mansab* of 2000/200 and the *faujdari* of the *pargana* in the name of his minor son, paid no heed to the petitions of the local officials, even though he was repeatedly directed by Delhi to chastise one Kamal, apparently another Ghakkar *zamindar* of the *pargana*, who had ravaged the *jagir mahals* and dispossessed several *gumashtas* of the *jagirdar* in the *pargana*. And perhaps, the Ghakkar chief's defiance of Mughal authority came into the open when on 16 March 1716, he was reported to have arbitrarily appointed Kamal as the deputy *faujdar*.[39] In another case, on 14 October, some relatives of the chief of *pargana* Dadyal who had shares in the revenue of the *khalisa* lands in the *pargana* and also in other adjoining *parganas*, were reported to have put the *parganas* to ransom.[40] In yet another case the settlement with the chief of Jasrota broke down within a period of over four years.[41]

The personal position of the governor seems to have had a bearing on the relationship with the local potentates. There emerged in Awadh a kind of stability in the provincial government's relations with the *zamindars*, since Burhan-ul-Mulk and Safdar Jang, the governors of Awadh in the last two phases of the period of our study, effected a change in the existing arrangement with them. On the contrary, Abd-us-Samad Khan and Zakariya Khan, the governors of the Punjab, pursued a policy of total supression of the rebels. The difference in their approaches may partially be explained in terms of their different political equations. In the following chapter, it will become clear that Burhan-ul-Mulk and Safdar Jang took virtually independent decisions relating to provincial matters, while Abd-us-Samad Khan and Zakariya Khan could not dissociate fully from court politics, notwithstanding their power in the province. Abd-us-Samad Khan and Zakariya Khan were associates and close relatives of Qamar-ud-Din Khan, the *wazir*, who favoured an all-out war against the insubordinate local elements. This equation also added to the breach between the governors of the Punjab and Samsam-ud-Daulah who, as we have noticed earlier, advocated a policy of readjustments with the *zamindars*.[42]

---

[39] *Akhbarat*, FS, 5th R. Y., I, p. 31.   [40] Ibid., 5th R. Y., p. 127.
[41] See footnote 35 above.   [42] See Chapter II, Section II.

But the individual governors' position and policies alone did not determine the course of political formations in these provinces. Awadh did not encounter the problems which constantly shattered the economy of the Punjab in the eighteenth century. A large part of Awadh and the areas in its neighbourhood registered growth through the seventeenth and eighteenth centuries, enriching the different privileged local sections. There was a uniformity of purpose in the movements and disturbances which involved them; the *zamindars*, the revenue grantees and the *jagirdars* all struggled to augment their share in the surplus, and establish their own domains in the region. The governors used their weaknesses to their advantage, established their hegemony and simultaneously attempted to integrate their interests with those of the local and the regional groups by acting independently of the centre. On the contrary, the decay in the Punjab, beyond the control of the governors, steadily engulfed the province. With the possible exception of the instances of the rebellion of the chiefs, there seems to be chaos and the cases of revolts, disturbances and violation of the imperial regulations which involved the local elements as well as the local Mughal officials appear to have been directionless, desperate bids to survive. The problems of administration indicated the economic malaise which afflicted the province.

Imperial control over the Jagir and local administration

The Sikh and the *zamindar* revolts and the consequent confusion disturbed almost the whole administration in the province. The military campaigns against them drew heavily on provincial finance and created an atmosphere of uncertainty among the local officials. This exacerbated the political crisis at the court and was in turn affected by the estrangement between the governor on the one hand and the *wazir, mir bakshi* and the provincial *diwan* on the other.

Jagir administration was probably the worst hit by the Sikh and *zamindar* disturbances. As early as 1711, some local officials began to create difficulties for the *jagirdars*.[43] The tendency

---

[43] On 17 November 1711, for example the entire revenue of the *jagir* of Umar Khan Khweshgi was reported to have been acquired by the *faujdar* of the *mahal*. *Akhbarat*, BS, 5th R. Y., II, p. 440.

seems to have been fairly widespread. The big nobles too had to contend with this problem.[44]

To be sure, the centre did try to maintain its control over the working of the *jagir* system in the Punjab during the reign of Bahadur Shah. The centre still had control over the offices intended to maintain efficiency in the *jagir* administration.[45] An attempt was made to enforce the rule in the disturbed *mahals*.[46] Some specific measures like the *faujdari* of the *jagir mahals* also seem to have been adopted to ensure the payment of revenue from the *jagir mahals*.[47] Encouragement was also given to assign the areas under the jurisdiction of the refractory *zamindars* to powerful nobles.[48] In one or two cases *jagirs* for long terms also seem to have been given in the *parganas* in and around the province which were affected by the Sikh uprisings. In the wake of the emperor's expedition against the Sikhs—Thanesar, Azamabad Talawri, Sadhaura, Shahabad and Mustafabad were assigned possibly on a permanent basis to Mun'im Khan and a few others who built fortresses and established *thanas* in these *parganas* to consolidate their position to counteract the Sikhs more effectively.[49]

But the extent of success in such efforts is a matter of conjecture. On the contrary, a number of other instances suggest a definite decline in the centre's control over the local administration. In one case the merchants of Lahore who supplied grain and other commodities to the imperial army are reported to have been subjected to pay the *rahdari*, an illegal cess, twice in 1711. The officials of both the city and the camp markets levied

[44] Ibid., 5th R. Y., I, p. 4 (11 January 1711) reports misappropriation of the revenue of the *jagirs* of Qilich Muhammad Khan by the *amils*.

[45] On 9 November 1708, for example, some Ram Chand was appointed the *mushrif* of the *dagh-o-tashiha* while in an another instance on 4 March 1709 one Abu Sa'id Khan was made the *darogha* of *dagh-a-tashiha* of the province of Lahore.

[46] Qurban Beg Khan *gurzbardar*, for instance, was sent towards Lahore to make the *bandobast* of *jagirs*. Ibid., 5th R. Y., p. 225.

[47] Thus in November 1708, Mahabat Khan, who had held *pargana* Phillaur in Beth Jalandhar in his *jagir* was appointed the *faujdar* of the *pargana* as well. Ibid., 3rd R. Y., p. 212.

[48] Ibid., p. 212 (10 November 1708) reports the revenue of the territory of the *zamindar* of Kangra as having been given in *jagir* to Mun'im Khan and his sons.

[49] *T. Shah Alam*, p. 46. Mun'im Khan raised a strong fortress and established *thanas* near the tank of Krukhet (Kurukshetra) in *pargana* Thanesar. Subsequently, the Mug-

cesses upon them which seemingly resulted in the subsequent slack supply of the provisions to the camp. The imperial order following the merchants' complaints at the court seems to have had little effect on the officials.[50] Another case bears on the sluggish maintenance of the army and the provisions in the forts of the province. According to a report of 27 October 1711, the forts of Taragarh, Kangra, Kotla and Attock did not contain even half the usual armed retainers, and the little provisions these forts had were misappropriated by the fort managers.[51]

The impaired imperial control over the province could be reviewed in the light of the developments at the court as well. The civil war in 1712 and later in the reign of Farrukh Siyar the *wazir*'s endeavour to have his own man as *diwan* in the province aggravated the problems of the *jagirdars*. Admittedly the *wazir*'s endeavour was in keeping with the established Mughal convention, as a number of those *jagirdars* who were associated with the central administration or were employed in other provinces and had no connections whatsoever with the Punjab, had their *jagirs* in the Punjab. Saiyid Husain Ali Khan, Mir Jumla, Saiyid Salabat Khan, Nasir Khan, and Sarbuland Khan, for instance, are mentioned among such nobles.[52] Since it was the *wazir*'s responsibility to ensure payment to them from their *jagirs*, he insisted on his full control over provincial finance. In the existing situation when the governor was an obvious associate of one of his enemies at the court, the *wazir*'s attempts in this direction were strongly resisted in the province. We have seen in Chapter II the disastrous consequences of the conflict between the governor and the *diwan* for provincial administration. The following cases further illustrate the process. In 1714, the deputy *faujdar* of *chakla* Jammu misappropriated over Rs 33,000 of the revenue of the *jagir* of Rai Ghasi Ram and some other *mansabdars*. Reacting to an emissary (*sawar-o-piyada*) of the *diwan* imploring him to hand over the amount, the deputy *faujdar* further arrogated the revenue of all the *parganas* in the *chakla*.

---

hal authority, as the author of the *Tarikh-i-Shah Alam* states, was restored in Thanesar and the adjoining *parganas* up to the bank of the Sutlej.

[50] *Akhbarat* BS, 5th R. Y., p. 284.

[51] Ibid., 5th and 6th R. Ys., II, p. 427.

[52] Cf. Shivdas, f. 3a, Mubarak, f. 77a; M. M., ff. 105b and 113b–114a; Qasim, f. 76a; *Akhbarat* BS, 6th R. Y., p. 582.

Subsequently, Rs 3,000 of the *jagir* of only Rai Ghasi Ram who had approached the emperor through Mir Jumla was ordered to be restored to him. No prompt action seems to have been taken regarding the rest of the amount.[53] In another case the *amin* of *paibaqi* in Sialkot who was also a financial assistant (*peshkar* and *diwan*) of Ghazi-ud-Din Khan Ghalib Jang misappropriated the revenue of the *jagirs* of the *walashahis*.[54]

In the context of these two cases it may be noted that in 1714 the *faujdari* of Jammu was held by Zakariya Khan and that Mir Jumla on whose intervention Rai Ghasi Ram could regain his money was a close associate of the governor. The *walashahis*, on the other hand, were associated with Samsam-ud-Daula who made a bid to dislodge Abd-us-Samad Khan from the Punjab.[55]

The difficulties of the *jagirdars* sometimes arose out of the conflict between the *jagirdars'* agents on the one hand and the imperial officials associated with the *pargana* administration on the other. In 1716, for example, the *amils* of the *jagirdars* of *parganas* Bahlolpur lodged a complaint against the office of the *amin* of *paibaqi* stating that even after they had submitted Rs 240—at the rate of Rs 10 for each *lakh* of *dams* of the *jagir*—the clerk in-charge (*mutasaddi*) of the office did not release the *mahals* assigned to the *jagirdars*. As the *faujdar* of the *pargana* expressed his inability to take any action in this regard, the matter was referred to the court.[56]

---

[53] *Akhbarat* FS, 3rd R. Y., I, p. 166 (14 June 1714).

[54] Ibid., 3rd R. Y., II, pp. 40–1 (9 September 1714). Ghazi ud-Din Ahmad Beg Ghalib Jang, a foster-brother of Jahandar Shah, was in charge of the *sarkar* of the prince. When Jahandar replaced him by one of his other foster-brothers, Ali Murad (Khan Jahan Kokaltash), Ahmad Beg resented it and joined the service of Azim-ush-Shan. Azim-ush-Shan deputed him with Farrukh Siyar in Bengal. In the reign of Farrukh Siyar he was promoted to 7000/6000 and was made the third *bakhshi*. He was one of the chief supporters of Farrukh Siyar throughout his reign. But he managed to reconcile with the Saiyids after the deposition of Farrukh Siyar. In 1720 when Saiyid Abdullah Khan heard the news of the death of his brother, Husain Ali Khan and raised Prince Muhammad Ibrahim to the throne, Ahmad Beg was appointed the *mir bakhshi* with the title of the *Amir-ul-Umara*. In the court of Muhammad Shah also he retained his *mansab* and the title of Ghazi-ud-Din Khan Ghalib Jang. He died in 1726, *M. U.*, II, pp. 879–82; Kamwar, pp. 183, 198–9, 205, 211, 243, 250, 260, 276, 285–6, 294, 309, 328, 340 and 357; *T. Muhammadi*, p. 62; also see W. Irvine, *Later Moghuls*, I, pp. 266–7; Satish Chandra, *Parties and Politics*, pp. 91, 93, 95, 144 and 162.

[55] See Chapter I.

[56] *Akhbarat* FS, 5th R. Y., I, p. 39. The incident throws interesting light on the details of

Sometimes the *jagirdars* also caused the local officials' difficulties. The *jagirdars* do not seem to have appreciated the
nature of the local problems and often resented military moves
against the local 'disturbers'. Such moves, seldom being successful, were feared to cause further dislocation, depriving them
even of the little they managed to collect from their *jagirs*. This is
illustrated from an incident of 1715. As the trading caravans
were the principal targets of the Sikhs, and the other turbulent
peasants and *zamindars* and the settlements on and around the
roads were seriously affected, a number of *thanas* were established on the imperial highway (*shahrah*) in 1715 with a view 'to
ensuring and facilitating the collection of revenues.' The *faujdars* of the adjoining *parganas* and the *chakla* were ordered to
assist the *thanadars* whenever needed. But when one such
thanadar approached a *faujdar* for assistance, the *faujdar* refused
to help and asked for a fresh and unequivocal order from the
centre, as 'in the case of his assisting (the *thanadar*)', the *faujdar*
stated, 'the *jagirdar* may lodge complaints with the court'.[57]

In this connection we quote extensively, an observation of a
contemporary chronicler on the state of the working of the *jagir*
system in the Punjab. The chronicler, Mirza Muhammad, was
very closely associated with the Mughal administration and his
observation provides an insight into the nature of the problems
of the *jagir* administration. The passage clearly brings out the
political context in which the local officials and the *zamindars*
defied the imperial regulations. Mirza Muhammad, an *amil* of
khalisa had come into conflict with the *amin* of *paibaqi* and Mir
Muhammad Husain, an Iranian, who had secured the support
of the local magnates against Sabha Chand, apparently a local
man. The office that implied control over *jagir* or *khalisa* was still
sought after and was evidently profitable, but only for those
who could muster up sufficient strength to collect the revenue.

In the middle of Zi Hijja 1130 [end of October, 1718], the *chubdar*
(mace-bearer) of Nawab Inayatullah Khan came to me and said, 'You have
been given the service in Dardak *alias* Rahon *mahal*; go to Rai Bhog
Chand'. The next morning, therefore, I rode to the Rai's who was the

---

the working of *jagir* administration as well. It seems that the *jagirdar* as a rule had to pay
a certain amount to the office of the *amin* of *paibaqi* to enable his *amils* to take charge of
the assigned *mahals*.

[57] *Akhbarat* FS, 5th R. Y., p. 160.

peshkar of the *khalisa*. It became known that I had been appointed the *amin faujdar* of [the villages yielding] 4,200,000 *dams* which were earmarked for the *khurak-i dawab* from the *jagir* of Nasir Khan and the other nobles[58] in *pargana* Dardak *alias* Rahon in Bist Jallandhar and which had been ruined due to the excess of the displaced *amil*. In addition, [the villages yielding] 10,00,000 *dams* from the same *mahal* and 8,00,000 from *pargana* Chandandurg in Rachnao Doab were added to these. I thus received a *sanad* for 60,00,000 *dams* in all in the first ten days of Muharram [13–22 November].[59]

[Subsequently, Mirza Muhammad left for Dardak] On my way, Desraj *chaudhuri*, Nawal Rai *qanungo* of *pargana* Dardak and Nanhe Khan and some other *jama'adars* (petty commanders of troops) came and met me. On Monday I left Machhiwara and then crossed the river Sutlej by boat. All along the way, the *zamindars* came to welcome me. At a distance of about 4 miles from Rahon, Fath Chand son of Nigahi Jatt who is a big *zamindar* (*zamindar-i-umda*) and notorious for his recalcitrance came along with hundred *sawars* and met me.

I set to work and unfortunately came into clash, over 27,00,000 *dams* of *khurak-i dawab* from the *jagir* of Nasir Khan, with Mir Muhammad Ali, the *amin* of *paibaqi* in the Doab who had come to seize in escheat the *mahals* of Nasir Khan [following his death in November, 1718]. The clash lasted for about twenty days and the ill-fated *zamindars*, having seen the confusion because of the two conflicting orders [from the court] took to defiance. I [then] enlisted an army and thought of restoring order. The above-mentioned Mir therefore could not do any damage to the [village of these] *dams*, carried out the other work relating to the *dams* of the late Nasir Khan and left for his residence in Hoshiarpur in the beginning of Rabi I [second week of January, 1719].

Subsequently I dismissed the additional retainers and began the assessment and collection in the *mahals* of [*khurak-i dawab*] without altercation. But since it was learnt from a note from the court that the *mahals* of Nasir Khan had been assigned to Sarbuland Khan, the governor designate of Kabul, and that he was exempted from the *khurak-i dawab*, [my] heart was

[58] This was in accordance with the reform instituted in *jagir* administration during the reign of Bahadur Shah. It was decided that after a *mansabdar* had been allotted a *jagir*, the charges for feeding the animals (*khurak-i dawab*) should be deducted from his total emoluments and the balance paid to him as *tankhwah*. Thus the *khurak-i dawab* became a central responsibility. K. K. II, p. 603. Earlier *khurak-i dawab* was deducted from the *tankhwah*. Cf. M. Athar Ali, *Mughal Nobility*, pp. 50–1.

[59] This is interesting to note that the same person was appointed the *amin faujdar* of the villages in two different *sarkars*, namely, Beth Jalandhar and the Rachna Doab, which were separated by the Bari Doab. Cf. *Ain*, II (Jarrett), pp. 315–16 for the geography of the *sarkars* in the Punjab.

heavily dejected.[60] Owing to this, the *zamindars* of the *mahal* also did not submit.

I then had no concern in *pargana* Dardak, save 25,00,000 *dams* and this trivial work suited the other [as well]. Still I had to encounter great trouble [lit. much headache] and was extremely anxious due to the termination of the crop season, untimely assessment and collection and the diabolical act of the *zamindars*. Then the letter of the *vakil* and dear brother that had been despatched on 24 Safar [5 January 1719], reached on Thursday. It stated that in lieu of the transfer of the *dams* of the [*khurak-i dawab*] of the late Nasir Khan which were assigned to Sarbuland Khan, Nawab Inayatullah Khan had appointed me the *amin*, *darogha* and *faujdar* of Bajwara and Hoshiarpur along with the remaining 25,00,000 *dams* of the [*khurak-i dawab*] [of Dardak], and that the [appointment order] *sanad* would follow.

[My] heart was thus greatly relieved, but it was learnt from the following letters that before the appointment paper reached the *diwan-i a'la* for his signature, Inayatullah Khan had been transferred from the office of *khalisa-o-tan* and appointed *khan-i saman*.[61] After his transfer Rai Bhog Chand took the related paper to the *diwan-i a'la*. But since the preparation of the *sanad* and its submission for the signature [*baiz*: a mark on public writings by a principal officer] and seal of Nawab Qutb-ul-Mulk, Raja Ratan Chand had withheld it and was asking for *ta'ahhud* [guarantee] and Rai Bhog Chand was trying to get it through.

Till the end of the month [Rabi I/beginning of the second week of February] each letter that came [from Delhi] contained the same. I was therefore greatly dejected, for whatever Ratan Chand does not want is impossible to carry through, and my temperament did not allow me to [simply] remain the *amil* of 25,00,000 *dams*. Further, due to the transfer of Nawab Inayatullah Khan, even there was no hope that this would be confirmed.

. . .In the middle ten days of Rabi I, a strange incident took place in Rahon. Summary of that [incident] is as follows. When I left Shahjahana-bad for Rahon, an Iranian person, Mir Muhammad Husain by name, also left for that direction in connection with the office of the *amil* of 4,00,00,000 in *pargana* Dardak, the *jagir* of the emperor's brother-in-law, Saiyid Salabat Khan. We were together for two *manzils* [stations]. Since he was in a hurry, he then parted from me and reached Rahon two days in advance of me. Inciden-tally, the same day, it was learnt that he had been replaced by someone else in the *pargana*. The aforesaid Mir could not take the charge.

[60] Exemption from the *khurak-i dawab* was an additional favour to Sarbuland Khan which the *wazir*, who needed the support of as many nobles as he could, obtained for him. For the circumstances of Sarbuland Khan's appointment see Satish Chandra, *Parties and Politics*, pp. 132–6.

[61] His transfer was manipulated by Saiyid Abdullah Khan who wanted to keep the revenue matters under his own control.

A few days later, the deputy of the *amil* and following him, the *amil* himself whose name was Sabha Chand, arrived. Since the day of his dismissal, the Mir had repeatedly written to Salabat Khan [promising] an increase in [the amount of] the *ta'ahhud* and told the people that the *sanad* confirming his appointment would reach soon. Sabha Chand, therefore, considered the Mir a source of disturbance for his own authority and asked him to leave the town. But the Mir paid no heed to his entreaties. Sabha Chand got annoyed over this and sent his army against the Mir. The Mir's retainers who were all new, retired aside and the army of Sabha Chand captured the Mir and carried him to their chief. The Mir was greatly humiliated and some of his goods were plundered.

[When] Shaikh Abd-ur-Rahman, the *qazi* of the town learnt about it, he rushed to Sabha Chand's house, condemned him for what he had done, released the Mir and took him to his own house. The Mir prepared a *mahzar* under the seals of the *qazi* and the local notables about his humiliation and plunder of his effects. Sabha Chand also realized the sordidness of his act and came to the Mir to apologize. His apology, however, was not accepted.

At last, a week later, the *sanad* under the seal of Salabat Khan replacing Sabha Chand by the Mir arrived. The Mir mustered up his army and decided to take revenge while Sabha Chand asserted that 'I am [still] in office and that the *sanad* of the Mir is fake.' [Sabha Chand] therefore did not remove his army nor did he withdraw his hand from the work and both sides were prepared for a fight. No offence was, however, committed by either side till the news of the revolution [deposition of Farrukh Siyar] came on 10 Rabi I and both [Sabha Chand and the Mir] became dispossessed.'[62]

Mirza Muhammad's observations and the incidents noted above typify the apathy and non-cooperation among the local officials and further illustrate how the conflict among the high nobles percolated down to the province and the locality. The deputy *faujdar* of *pargana* Wazirabad in one instance offered strong resistance to an attempt by the provincial *diwan* to assess and collect the details of the existing revenue situation (*tumar-i jama*) of the *pargana*.[63] In another case, the *sazawal* (steward) who had gone to *pargana* Kathua in *chakla* Jammu to enforce the imperial regulations in the *mahals* of the *khurak-i dawab* encountered similar resistance from the *faujdar*. For over a fortnight, the *sazawal* looked in vain for a meeting with the *faujdar* and eventually when he protested he heard improper words from the *peshkar* and was driven out of the office of the

[62] M. M., ff. 109a and 113a–114a.

[63] *Akhbarat* FS, 5th R. Y., II, p. 270, (9 July 1716).

faujdar. 'Such was the plight of the slaves of the emperor.'[64]
Within a few days, a petty commander of the retainers
jama'adar) of the *faujdar* is reported to have taken away over
1200 animals from the villages of the *jagir* of Iwaz Khan. The
faujdar distributed them among his own soldiers.[65] In yet another
incident in *chakla* Jammu, the *bakhshi waqai'nigar* of the *chakla*,
due to the non-cooperation of the *sawanihnigar* (news-reporter)
and the *faujdar*, was reported to be in trouble in discharging the
duties of his office. Neither was the question relating to the
waqai' and *dak*, as the *arzdasht* of the *bakshi waqai'nigar* of 30
Shaban 1128/8 August 1716 records, referred to him nor did the
commanders of the retainers and the other *mansabdars* deputed
with the *sawanihnigar* come to his office. The despatches of the
sawanihnigar, as he alleged, contained false details about the
working of his office. Subsequently, the *sawanihnigar* was dismissed, but Zakariya Khan, the *faujdar* remained unpunished.[66]

There are also cases of violence and armed clashes amongst
the local officials to the obvious dislocation of the system of
'checks and balances'. In an instance the *gurzbardars* (mace-
bearers) who had come from Delhi to collect from the *diwan* the
papers relating to the *khalisa mahals* came to blows with the
diwan. They even threatened to get the *diwan* dismissed.[67] In
another instance, an Afghan commander of *pargana* Sialkot,
along with his 35 supporters, was killed in an encounter with
the *amil* of the *pargana*. The *amil* in this specific case seems to
have been supported by the *kotwal*, for the severed heads of the
Afghans were put on display in the office of the *kotwal* (*chabutra-i
kotwali*). The *faujdar* of the *pargana* seems to have shown the least
concern. On the contrary, in July 1716 he had himself misappropriated Rs 2,50,000 out of Rs 6,00,000 of the *rabi* collections
from the *pargana*.[68]

The *faujdar*'s indifference to the problems of other local officials and even the transgression of certain regulations by him
was a logical reaction to what he received from the provincial
diwan. His own resources were insufficient to meet the expenses

---

[64] Ibid., 5th R. Y., p. 325 (2 August 1716).

[65] Ibid., 5th R. Y., p. 335 (6 August 1716).

[66] Ibid., 5th R. Y., p. 67.   [67] Ibid., 5th R. Y., p. 293.

[68] Ibid.

of his armed retinue and the demand for an additional amount was hardly entertained by the *diwan*. In May 1715, for instance, the deputy *faujdar* of Jammu had to give away the elephant, the horses and other items of his personal establishment to his soldiers against their pay-claim which had accumulated to a total of Rs 30,000.[69] The growth of a tendency among the local officials to make their fortunes at whatever cost is to be also seen in this perspective. The problem, however, did not begin or end with a change in the attitude of the *diwan*. Even the mace-bearers from Delhi could threaten to get him dislodged. We have seen earlier how in 1717 the *diwan* of the province lost his job in the province in an attempt to solve the difficulties of local administration.

The local officials' total disregard for imperial regulations is perhaps best illustrated in the breakdown of the time-honoured rule of transfers, a device through which the Mughals had maintained the centralization of their administrative set-up. The local officials, in some cases, flagrantly defied the order of their transfers while in some other instances, the transferred or dismissed officials became a major source of trouble for the new appointee.[70]

The breakdown of the institution of communication (*waqai* and *sawanih*) which we have seen above had a strong bearing on the problems of derelictions at local level. Sometimes the centre's ignorance of the local problems was appalling. If there were any imperial orders following the cases of offence by the local officials, their associates and supporters both at the court and at the local level tried to prevent the news from reaching Delhi or at least they twisted it to suit the interest of the

[69] Ibid., 4th R. Y., I, p. 160.

[70] Ibid., 4th R. Y., I, p. 125 (3 May 1715) which records the refusal of Abd-ul-Jabbar Beg, the dismissed *bakshi waqai'nigar* of the *parganas* of Batala, Sialkot, Aurangabad and Pasrur to give way to Muhsin uz-Zaman, the new *bakshi waqai 'nigar* of these *parganas*. This seems to be a part of the conflict between the governor and the Saiyid Brothers. For Abd-ul-Jabbar Beg was a Mughal and the appointing letter (*dastak*) of Muhsin uz-Zaman, apparently an Indian Muslim, bore the seal of Saiyid Husain Ali Khan, the *Amir ul-Umara*. See also Ibid., 4th R. .Y., pp. 58 and 81 for Khwaja Rahmatullah the dismissed *amil* of *pargana* Bhira who became a major source of difficulty for the *faujdar* of *chakla* Gujarat. Khwaja Rahmatullah could defy law and order on account of the support of the *mansabdars* who were associated with him and were still in service in the Salt Range at this time. These *mansabdars* were, therefore, ordered to be transferred to other places.

offender. Orders for transfer of the existing official and the appointment of an associate could be secured on the strength of misinformation.[71] In some cases, the imperial orders following complaints against the local officials seem to have never reached the relevant local authorities.[72]

It was under these circumstances that the *jagirdars* in the Punjab began to farm out their *jagirs* to the *mahajans*. The widespread practice of *ijara* indicated an atmosphere of uncertainty and apprehension that compelled the *jagirdar* to give up his cherished right of collecting the revenue from his *jagir mahals* directly through his agents. And since the *mahajans* were local men, it also created a local interest in the maintenance of *jagirs*. With the *mahajan ijaradars*, however, there emerged some new problems. The *mahajans* had some inherent conflicts with the different categories of landed elements which seem to have sharpened when the *mahajans*, as *ijaradars*, exploited the *zamindars* and peasants (*ri'aya*). In 1717 two *mahajan ijaradars* who had taken the *jagirs* of three *jagirdars* in *pargana* Wan on *ijara* were reported to have arrogated the customary perquisites of the *zamindars* and *qanungos*, ravaged the village and carried off the goods and animals of the *ri'aya*.[73] The *ijaradar* had to be oppressive because *ijara* in the prevailing circumstances, in the province was normally fixed at a much inflated rate. On 11 March 1716, an *ijaradar* of the *khalisa mahal* in the town of Wazirabad was reported to have unlawfully levied half a rupee as *rahdari* on each of the two hundred horses of the revenue of

---

[71] This happened in the case of one Abd-ul-Malik, a neo-Muslim, who was the hereditary *qanungo* of *pargana* Srinagar (?) in *chakla* Gujarat and functioned in complete accord with the established Mughal rule. None of the people concerned, e.g., the *zamindars*, the *riaya* and the *gumashtas* of the *jagirdars*, had ever lodged any complaints against him. And yet one Har Narayan, apparently on the strength of misinformation to the centre managed to displace him and obtained the *qanungoi* of the *pargana* for himself. The *riaya*, etc., then protested over the appointment of the new *qanungo* and led a delegation to the *diwan's kachahri* at Wazirabad. Cf. Ibid., 5th R. Y., I, pp. 3–4.

[72] On 17 December 1717, the *darogha* of the Lahore mint was, for example, reported to have begun minting sub-standard coins. Subsequently, the *darogha* of the *dak* was ordered, but to no avail, to look into the matter. Over a month later, it was reported that the *darogha* of the mint had begun to demand, from the people, additional discount for minting coins and that on protest from the people he had locked the mint. *Akhbarat* FS, 6th R. Y., II, pp. 57 and 171–2.

[73] *Akhbarat* FS, 6th R. Y., I, p. 147.

suba Kabul which were being taken by the traders to Delhi. In reply to the protest of the traders over the levying of the prohibited cesses and other excesses on the *ri'aya*, the *ijaradar* said that 'he had paid Rs 70,000 to the imperial coffers and that there was nowhere any check on the excess'.[74] In an another instance the *faujdar* of *pargana* Attock farmed out the *sair mahal* in the *pargana* for Rs 50,000 a year while the collection (*mahsul*) from the *sair* did not exceed Rs 20,000 a year.[75]

It appears that in some cases, if not often, the *ijaradar* expressed his resentment against over-assessment, since it implied a greater gap between the stipulated sum and the paying capacity of *ijara mahal* and also added to his difficulties in collecting the revenue. The *ijaradar* of Wazirabad probably referred to this gap between the stipulated *ijara* amount and actual paying capacity when he stated that there was no check on the excess. Again, if the *mahajans*, as town-based money-lenders and traders, had differences with the *zamindars* and the peasantry, a substantial number of them being Khatris must have had caste ties with most of the *qanungos* who had, in turn, their own stake in keeping the rural tax payers satisfied.

The administrative difficulties in the Punjab, in contrast to those of Awadh, continued to increase even after the first two phases of the period of our study. The Sikhs and the *zamindars*, of course, constituted the major source of problems in the province. Zulfiqar Khan did utilize the differences between the Sikhs and the big *zamindars* as well as the latter's internal differences to the advantage of the Mughal state. However, the Mughal victory over the Sikhs was not due to any change in the administrative and social structure of the empire. The reconciliation with the chiefs and some other categories of *zamindars* solved the problem only temporarily. It appears that the Mughals began to accommodate a larger number of Khatris into imperial and provincial administration, but the favour thus shown to the Khatris had only a marginal bearing on the Sikh movement. Since the time of Guru Gobind, a fundamental change seems to have occurred in the composition of the Sikh community. The Sikh uprisings had largely assumed the

[74] Ibid., 5th R. Y., I, p. 12.
[75] Ibid., 6th R. Y., I, pp. 385–6.

character of an agrarian movement that encouraged and further aggravated the conflict between the agrarian communities on the one hand and the Mughal ruling class, the merchants and the other urban communities on the other. The ruthless execution of Banda in 1715 could not contain the movement. Since then the Sikh movement became essentially a movement of the dispossessed and impoverished *zamindars* and peasants.

The revolts by the *zamindars* of almost all categories in the Punjab clearly suggest that the problem was of a bigger and certainly a different magnitude as compared to such uprisings in Awadh. It seems that an arrangement with the landed magnates was difficult to work out, even if the provincial government favoured a policy of maximum integration of the local elements, with the administration. The silting of Sindh, the disturbances and instability beyond the western borders of the Punjab and devastations of the province by Nadir Shah and Abdali told heavily on the economy of the region. The revenues declined by over 37 per cent; the fall in the income from trade and the urban centres was very substantial. We may also estimate the extent of the decline of the urban centres from the cases of *ijara* from Attock, the gateway to the Punjab from the north-west, and Wazirabad, the town which developed in the seventeenth century on the Chenab and was known for its boat-building.[75a]

But our evidence is limited and the question needs further investigation. We may still note the changes in the caste composition of the *zamindars* and speculate what direction Punjab political history could have taken were it free from social and economic flux. Isa Khan gained prominence only in the late seventeenth century. The *Ain* refers to the Mein as the dominant *zamindar* caste only in three *parganas*, namely, Talwan, Muhammadpur and Nakodar in *sarkar* Beth Jalandhar whereas the major part of the *sarkar* seems to have been in the control of Isa Khan in the early-eighteenth century. It was in recognition of his *de facto* position in the *sarkar* that Jahandar Shah conferred on him a high *mansab* and appointed him *faujdar* of the *sarkar* and Lakhi jungle. In the reign of Farrukh Siyar he was considered

---

[75a] Compare Irfan Habib, *Atlas*, Sheet 4B and Notes p. 13; Chetan Singh, 'Socio-Economic Conditions of Punjab during the Seventeenth Century', Chapter V.

by Samsam-ud-Daulah for the deputy governorship of the province. The Bhattis are recorded as the *zamindars* of Qasur in the *Ain* while Husain Khan, a Khweshgi Afghan, was the most prominent *zamindar* of the *pargana* in our period. In *pargana* Dadrak where Khori Wahas, according to the *Ain*, were the dominant *zamindars*, one Fateh Chand Jatt is mentioned as a *zamindar-i umda* in our period. The Jats, the Ghamans and the Chimahs shared the *zamindaris* in *pargana* Sialkot in the late-sixteenth-century, but the Salharias are noted as a major *zamindar* caste in our period. It is also significant that our sources mention a Ghakkar as the *faujdar* and *zamindar* of *pargana* Bahlolpur whereas the Jats had constituted the only dominant *zamindar* caste in the *pargana* in 1595.[76] Again, it is not without significance that a Bhatti *zamindar* was in control of the *parganas* in the region stretching from Hasan Abdal to the bank of the Ravi during the governorship of Zakariya Khan.

The *zamindars* who find a prominent place in the records of our period may have displaced the dominant *zamindars* of the time of the compilation of the *Ain*. It is also not unlikely that they acquired wealth and power, together with the erstwhile dominant castes in the course of the growth in seventeenth century. They may thus have strived for recognition and legitimate intermediary position in their respective areas. There was a possibility of their responding favourably to the offers extended to them by the Mughals, who still commanded an exalted position in the existing power structure. The cases of Isa Khan and Husain Khan Khweshgi who so readily responded to the 'instigations' of Samsam-ud-Daulah and the Saiyids, for instance, substantiate this point. We may presume that in a different economic context with a different policy and in a different political equation of the governor with the court, these *zamindars* could have grown into a substantial social base of a new *subadari*.

The presence of substantial and effective outside elements as *jagirdars* or their agents in the province may also be considered when we examine the factors restricting the prospects of the

---

[76] *Ain*, II (Jarrett), pp. 320 for Khori Waha in Dardak; pp. 320 and 321 for the Mein in Talwan, Muhammadpur and Nakodar; p. 322 for the Bhatti in Qasur; p. 324 for the Jat, the Ghaman and the Chimah in Sialkot; p. 325 for the Jat in Bahlolpur.

growth of the new *subadari* into a virtually independent *nawabi* rule in the Punjab. The erstwhile structure of the *jagir* system under the formal jurisdiction of the centre was retained both in Awadh and the Punjab in our period. But in Awadh, as we shall see in the following chapter, the governor brought the system virtually under his control by dispensing with the agents of the *jagirdars* and also by reducing to the minimum the number of the large sized *jagirs* of the big nobles. By the 1740s the entire province of Awadh was divided into small *jagirs* assigned to over 500 insignificant officials and military men, quite a considerable number of whom were in the service of the governor himself. On the other hand, the *jagirs* in the Punjab till the end of our period were very large in size, assigned to powerful nobles, in addition to the revenues earmarked for the imperial hospitals and kitchens and for the imperial armies posted in Kabul and on the western borders of the Punjab.[77] This implied constant outside interference in the province, even when the centre as such was weak and the governor had virtual control over the office of the provincial *diwan*.

We are not in a position to make any broad generalizations on the evidence of the merchants' cooperation with the Mughals in the latter's campaigns against the Sikhs and the rise of some Khatris to high position. The Mughals tried to consolidate their power in the Punjab through the trading community. The Mughals may not have recognized the economic advantages of the absorption of the Khatris into the imperial service; they appear to have appreciated its political implications. As the crisis enveloped the region and the threat to the Mughal power increased from the peasants, its dependence grew on the Khatris and the other trading communities. But the decline in trade and the consequent slump in agriculture resulting in the fury of the *zamindars* and the peasants havng been directed against the towns weakened the merchants. Even earlier the Sikhs under Banda Bahadur raided the caravans and the trading centres. Thus, the new policy, if we are historically permitted to call it so, only marginally and temporarily reduced the magnitude of the political and administrative malais in the province.

[77] I. O. 4506, Parts I and II for a list of the *jagirdars*, with details of the areas and the revenues assigned to them, in Punjab and Awadh respectively.

CHAPTER VI

Growth of *Nawabi*
Rule in Awadh and its Relation
with Local Social Groups

In contrast to the Punjab, the new *subadari* in Awadh was established on substantially stable ground. Despite the unmistakable signs of the decline of imperial control over the province, growth in a large part of Awadh and the regions close to its borders on the west, south and east continued from the seventeenth to the eighteenth century. The new *subadar* was strong and could effect changes in administration, make an arrangement with the local magnates, namely, the *zamindars*, the *madad-i ma'ash* holders and some other urban elements. By 1722 when Burhan-ul-Mulk took charge of Awadh, the province was barely out of its difficulties. The *zamindars* still resisted the imperial regulations successfully which in many cases also implied difficulties for those in the disturbed areas who did not have caste links with the rebels. They also had to bear the oppression of local officials—the *jagirdars* or the *ijaradars* who seem to have hardly been accountable to any superior authority. Under Burhan-ul-Mulk and later in the time of the *subadari* of Safdar Jang, a number of changes were introduced in the administrative structure of the province. These changes related to *jagir* administration, the position of the *faujdars* and *ijara* and had strong bearings on the provincial government's relations with local social groups.

The jagir *administration*

The *jagirdars* and their agents seem to have posed a number of problems for the governor. Some of these accrued from the irregularities committed by the *amils* and other local officials, while the control of the powerful *jagirdar* over his *jagir mahals* imposed certain checks on the political ambition of the governor. The *amils*, in principle, belonged to the personal staff of the *jagirdars* while in a number of cases the big *jagirdars* had *faujdari* rights over their *jagir mahals*. In certain cases, the *jagirdars* sub-assigned parts of their *jagirs* to their troopers and officials in their service.[1] All this implied obvious outside interference in the provincial administration. It can therefore be presumed that immediately after a turn in his relations with the centre,[2] Burhan-ul-Mulk gave full attention to fiscal and financial questions, as well as to the problems of *jagir* administration in Awadh.

It appears that he began his drive to rectify the finances of the province by sending his men to the *parganas* to assess the yield anew. But he soon realized that landed magnates apart, some local officials even would not welcome his effort to change the existing situation. The *amils* and the *gumashtas* (agents) of the powerful *jagirdars*, for instance, tried to obstruct the implementation of the proposed scheme.[3] No exact assessment of the prevailing levels of production nor of the actual revenue realized was possible till the working of the *jagirdari* system was modified to effect a change in the position of the *amils*.

The *amil* occupied an important place in the maintenance and administration of the *jagir*. In some cases, the *amil* seems to have been a local man with considerable power and prestige and some of the *amils* managed to stick to their office in the same *mahal*, notwithstanding the changes and transfers of the *jagirdars*.[4] The *amil* in a number of cases thus practically became

---

[1] Allahabad 789; C. A. Elliot, *Chronicles of Oonao*, pp. 106–7.

[2] See Chapter VII, Section I.

[3] For example, Shaikh Farid-ud-Din Bukhari who was deputed to assess the revenue of the *parganas* of Mahona and Bangarmau, the *jagir mahals* of Muhammad Khan Bangash, apparently enhanced the *jama* of the *mahals*. Moreover, the amount collected by the *amil* of the Bangash chief was resumed by his men. It was promised to be reimbursed later after a re-examination of the existing situation. This brought them into conflict with the *amil*. The *amil* with his troops came to the office of the assessors and demanded, at least, the reimbursement of the arrogated amount without any delay. The matter could not be settled till Shaikh Farid himself intervened and forced the *amil* and his troops to retreat. *Maktubat*, p. 209.

[4] The case of one Mir Saiyid Bhika of Bilgram illustrates the power of the *amil* in the *jagir* administration. Mir Saiyid Bhika is reported to have been in charge of the *mahals* of Sisandi and some adjacent *parganas* in the *sarkar* of Lucknow as the *amil* of the *jagirdars* for over thirty years. He managed to remain in the same position chiefly because of the influence and contacts he had in these *mahals*. *Ma'asir-ul-Kiram*, II, p. 360.

a revenue contractor who assured the *jagirdar* his due amount
and kept a part of the revenue himself. This he did on the
strength of his influence and by offering a lucrative amount in
advance (*qabz*) to the *jagirdar*.[5] The revision of the revenue
administration by Burhan-ul-Mulk implied a denial to the *amils*
of their existing shares of the revenues.

The *amils* therefore viewed and presented to the *jagirdars* the
whole procedure as an attempt by the governor to misappropriate their *jagirs*.[6] The governor was alarmed, since he feared
that the *amils'* representation of his scheme would antagonize
the nobles who had *jagirs* in Awadh and thus add to his difficulties in the province. The governor also recognized the
futility of making efforts at reorganizing the existing pattern of
revenue administration without an attempt to isolate the
jagirdars from their *amils* in the province. Subsequently, the
governor seems to have brought the *amils* under his own control
and he imposed a discount on the *jagir* amount of the *jagirdars*,
for the *amils'* services in looking after the management of the
jagirs. The arrangement was welcome to most of the *mansabdars*,
since it was to the benefit of most of them who were hardly
capable of managing their *jagirs* against the dangers of the
turbulent *zamindars*. Moreover, for a number of them it was no
less difficult to keep a check on the irregularities committed by
their own *amils*.

The arrangement is characterized by the author of the *Imad-
us-Sa'adat* as *ijara*.[7] The nature of this *ijara* was, however,
apparently different from the more familiar *ijara* of the eighteenth century. It was an administrative device to secure a

---

[5] Earlier in the seventeenth century, as it is known, it was a common practice with the
jagirdars to displace an *amil* by another who offered bigger *qabz*. Cf. Bhim Sen, *Nuskha-i
Dilkusha*, f. 138. This possibly partly explains the concentration of the office of the *amils*
in the hands of the local people in our period. The local people offered greater *qabz*,
since they were in a better position to realize the full amount of the revenue, and also
due to their influence and social ties with the *mahals* could embezzle a greater sum.

[6] According to a report of the *amil* of the *jagir* of Raja Girdhar Bahadur, the governor's
move was aimed towards the resumption of the *jagirs* of the imperial *mansabdars* in
Awadh. In reply to a letter from the raja, Burhan-ul-Mulk, therefore, had to explain to
him the situation and assured him that the scheme was not intended to take possession
of the *jagirs* (of the nobles posted outside Awadh) and that his *jagir* was still in the
control of the existing *amil*. *Ajaib*, f. 71b.

[7] Compare *Imad*, p. 8.

uniform pattern in the management of the *jagirs* in the province. The arrangement, while ensuring the payment of their dues to the *jagirdars*, brought stability and regularity in provincial ad-ministration. The *jagirdars* no longer had to send their *amils* and *gumashtas* to their *jagirs*. The *amils* and the *amins* were henceforth appointed by the governor. It was the governor to whom they were now accountable for their acts. The local officials and the *chaudhuris*, the *qanungos* and the *muqaddams* were to approach the *amils* of the governor for matters relating to the revenue and their own customary perquisites. In other words, the administrative right that the *jagirdars* had over their *jagir*, namely, collection of land revenue and other authorized cesses, was taken over by the governor.

The *amil* on the governor's instructions was to measure and separate from the *paibaqi* the revenue assigned to the *jagirdar* and then after having collected the *peshkash* from him to release the lands in his name. The additional revenue (*taufir*) was to be retained with the office of the *amil* and the *jagirdar* was to be helped in the matters referred to the *amil*.[8]

For any trouble in his *jagir*, the *jagirdar* was now required to write to the governor and the latter was accordingly to direct the *amil* concerned. Samsam-ud-Daulah had his *jagir* in Bilgram and Bhutgam (Bhogaon?). On the pretext of disturbance by the *zamindars*, the *amil* who managed the *jagir* on behalf of the governor, evaded the despatch of revenue to Samsam-ud-Daulah. On the latter's petition, the *amil* was reprimanded by Safdar Jang, the deputy governor. The *amil* was also directed to write the details of the *jama* and the *hasil* of the *mahals*, the strength of the recalcitrant *zamindars* and whatever army was required to chastise them. 'For there is no difference between us and the Nawab (Samsam-ud-Daulah) and in case it is not possible to make up for the Nawab's loss, let us be informed in details.'[9] This was how the governor tried to allay the apprehensions of the nobles posted in Delhi and other places outside Awadh. In another case, Badan Singh, the Jat chief who had his

[8] Compare *Maktubat*, p. 174 for Safdar Jang's letter to the *amil* of *sarkar* Gorakhpur to help one Muhammad Khudadad who was assigned 99990 *dams* from *pargana Haveli* Gorakhpur.

[9] Ibid., pp. 171–2.

jagir in Awadh is reported to have complained to the deputy
governor against the *amil* of the *pargana* where his *jagir* lay. The
amil had withheld the revenue. He was accordingly directed to
release the amount to Badan Singh and inform the governor if
there was any difficulty over it.[10]

The arrangement seems to have, in general, been welcomed
by the small *jagirdars*, since earlier even they, in most cases,
were unable to collect the revenue from their *jagirs* through their
own agents. They farmed out their territories to the local
ijaradars.[11] But the big *jagirdars*, however, strongly condemned
Burhan-ul-Mulk's action and demanded an immediate restoration of earlier regulations. Besides the fact that the arrangements implied a restriction of their patronage, they resented the
peshkash and discount that the governor began to levy from the
jagir. In one of his letters to the *mir bakshi*, Girdhar Bahadur, the
governor of Malwa, urged him to restore his *jagir* in Awadh in
accordance with the previous rule and characterized the governor's measure as unprincipled interference.[12] The same problem probably provoked Muzaffar Khan's quarrel with Burhan
ul-Mulk in 1726–7.[13]

These complaints were not groundless. Burhan-ul-Mulk did
exercise greater control over the *jagirs* of those *jagirdars* whom he
feared would develop local ties through their long-term *jagirs*
and thereby prove to be a potential threat to his ambition. We
do not know what happened to Muzaffar Khan's *jagirs*;
Girdhar's *jagirs* were, however, transferred to Malwa which he
held in his governorship.[14] Later when Muhammad Khan Bangash was appointed governor of Malwa, Burhan-ul-Mulk managed to secure an order from the centre for the transfer of
Muhammad Khan's *jagir* from Shahabad and Nurpura in
Awadh to Sironj and Bhilsa in Malwa. But owing to the re-

[10] Ibid., p. 191.

[11] Compare National Archives of India 1754, 37th R. Y. of Aurangzeb; see also
Donald Butter, *Outlines of the Topography and Statistics of the Sourthern Districts of Oudh and of
the Cantonment Sultanpur-Oudh*, Calcutta, 1839, p. 99.

[12] *Ajaib*, ff. 80b and 82a.

[13] Muzaffar Khan accused Burhan-ul-Mulk of having taken possession of his *jagir*
and the *jagirs* of some other *mansabdars* in Awadh. Cf. Satish Chandra, *Parties and Politics*,
p. 185.

[14] *Ajaib*, f. 82.

peated protests of Muhammad Khan, the order could not be implemented.[15]

Burhan-ul-Mulk tried to reduce to the minimum, the number of the *jagirs* of the *mansabdars*, especially the powerful ones, who were posted outside the province of Awadh. For in the case of any difficulty in the management of their *jagirs* and break or delay in payment the *mansabdars* would inevitably interfere. The case of the *jagir* of Raja Jai Singh illustrates this point. The *vakil* of Jai Singh at the court, had certain grievances about the raja's *jagir* in Ibrahimabad in *sarkar* Lucknow. Initially he sought the permission of the governor to send, and then without the latter's prior notice actually sent, his representative to supervise the settlement. The governor who had directly written to Jai Singh about it violently resented the nomination of the representative.[16]

Burhan-ul-Mulk, however, could not succeed in bringing the *jagir* administration fully under his control. A *jagirdar*, for instance, realized the revenue unlawfully from a *madad-i ma'ash* village in *pargana* Kakori for over three years. It was on the repeated, firm orders of the governor that the local *amil* could manage to restore the village to the *a'immadars*.[17] Subsequent to such developments, Burhan-ul-Mulk might have thought of completely abolishing the *jagir* system in Awadh. But since it clashed with the interests of so many, he was not able to do it. His successor, Safdar Jang, seems to have achieved a little success in this direction. In 1745 when Awadh was in the grip of severe famine, Safdar Jang requested the emperor to resume the *tankhwah jagirs* of the imperial *mansabdars* in Awadh. Some big nobles like Qamar-ud-Din Khan and Amïr Khan, however, continued to hold their *jagirs* in the province.[18] Towards the end of our period only the nawab and his family members and close associates had big *jagirs* in Awadh. A *jagir* roll of the time of Muhammad Shah (1720–48) shows that Awadh was assigned to over 500 small *jagirdars*; of them a large number were officials and military commanders mentioned as the companions (*hamrahiyan*) of Safdar Jang.[19] This expression obviously indicated that they had been or were in the service of the nawab.

Initially, Burhan-ul-Mulk tried to reassess the *jama* of the

[15] *Khujasta*, 124.   [16] *Maktubat*. p. 158.   [17] Ibid., p. 176.
[18] Mubarak, f. 164b.   [19] I. O. 4506, Part II and 4508.

jagir mahals, but when he realized the strength of the *amils* in foiling his plan, he brought them under his control and thus endeavoured to check the irregularities committed by the *jagirdars'* agents. He imposed a levy on the *jagir* in lieu of the responsibility he undertook for the regular payment of the revenue to the *jagirdar*. These steps enabled him, in some measure, to build up his power and personal treasury in the province. His ambition for greater independence from the centre probably led him to aspire to totally liquidate the imperial *jagir* system. He was unable to achieve this, but his successor, Safdar Jang succeeded a great deal in eliminating from Awadh the big *jagirdars* from elsewhere.

The faujdari *administration*

In Awadh in the early-eighteenth century, there were eight *faujdaris*; five of these corresponded to the five *sarkars* of the province, namely, Lucknow, Awadh, Khairabad, Bahraich and Gorakhpur, while Baiswara, Bilgram and Sultanpur Bilehri to which we have occasional reference in our sources were in size small *faujdaris*.[20] By 1722 all the *faujdaris* in the province as we have seen earlier, had come under the jurisdiction of the governor. Selection, appointment and security of the office of the *faujdar* who was now, for all practical purposes, a representative and deputy of the *subadar* in the *sarkar* and *chakla* came under the discretion of the governor.[21] The *faujdar's* appointment was made without any reference to the centre.[22]

Since the *faujdar* represented the governor in a district of the

----

[20] Compare for instance *Akhbarat* BS, 1st R. Y., pp. 25, 53, 214, 259, 302, 311 and 389, 2nd R. Y., p. 14, 4th R. Y., pp. 103, 146, 165, 301, 441, 5th R. Y., pp. 41 and 421; *Akhbarat* FS, 1st R. Y., pp. 103, 3rd R. Y., I, p. 240; 4th R. Y., II, p. 97, 6th R. Y., I, pp. 174, II, p. 80; Kamwar, ff. 307a, 346a and 357b.

[21] One Sharif Khan, for instance, who had held, and been dismissed from the *faujdari* of *sarkar* Jaunpur secured his reappointment to the same from Burhan-ul-Mulk some time early in 1730 when the *sarkar* along with three other *sarkars*—Benaras, Chunar and Ghazipur—was practically attached to the *suba* of Awadh. Yar Muhammad Khan Qalandar, *Dastur-ul-Insha*, Patna MS., ff. 210–11.

[22] *Siyar*, III, p. 850 for the case of Saiyid Hidayat Ali Khan who was appointed by Safdar Jang to the *nizamat* and *faujdari* of *chakla* Khairabad in 1743.

province, he seems to have had control over the finance of his
faujdari area as well. This is evident from a number of disputes
which related to the *diwani* and revenue matters and were
referred to the office (*kachahri*) of the *faujdar*.[23] On some occasions, the *faujdar's* assertion of authority seems to have brought
him into direct clash with the *qazi*, whose judgement had conventionally been sought in disputes over *diwani* matters. The
conflict between the *faujdar* and the *qazi* of the *pargana* of
Bilgram which we shall discuss later, is a case in point.

The *faujdar* with new powers, especially when he had a wide
area under his jurisdiction, also seems to have now been
mentioned sometimes as *nazim* and *naib* or deputy (of the governor).[24] It is also significant that in a few cases a *chaudhuri* or a
qanungo held *faujdari* rights or for that matter *niyabat* (deputy-
ship) and *nizamat* (governorship of the district) as well. The
faujdars of *pargana* Bilgram and the *naib faujdar* of *pargana* Selak
at the time 'of Safdar Jang, for instance, had *chaudhurai* and
qanungoi rights over their respective *parganas* as well.[25] Since it
implied rights of *diwani* and thereby some monetary benefits,
the new *faujdari* could also be farmed out. Some time in the reign
of Muhammad Shah, the *faujdari* of Jaunpur is reported to have
been taken on *ijara* by one Mir Abd-ur-Rahim of Qanauj.[26]
Though the case does not relate strictly to Awadh, it highlights

[23] In 1735, one Diler Khan, for example, came into conflict with two persons, Aziz
and Izzatullah over an orchard in Sandila which was then in the possession of the latter.
The case was referred to the *faujdar* of the *pargana*. The *faujdar's* verdict after his
examination of the relevant papers was accepted by both the parties. In another case, in
1737, Mir Muhammad Raza and Mir Fath Ali, *a'immadars* in the town of Bahraich,
quarrelled over the effects of some of their relatives. Subsequently, the deputy *faujdar* of
the *pargana Haveli* Bahraich appointed several notable persons of the town to look into
the matter and give their judgement. Allahabad 1002 and 1203. Some cases in our
sources indicate that the *faujdar's* authority began to extend over *diwani* matters as early
as 1705–6. Following the death of a revenue grantee in the 49th R. Y. of Aurangzeb, the
faujdar was directed to see to it that the successors of the deceased could bring the
holding into their possession without any hindrance. *Firangi Mahal Documents* (transcripts) No. 50, Edited with English translations by Iqbal Husain, Deptt. of History,
Aligarh University.

[24] Compare *Maktubat*, pp. 172 and 178 for the *naib* and *nazim's* claim to the *faujdari*
abwab.

[25] *Tabsira*, f. 106b and Allahabad 505.

[26] *M. U.*, III, pp. 609–10.

the development of a trend in the region of our study.

Our impression is that the institution of *faujdari* which symbolized imperial authority at the *sarkar* level was gradually decaying, even though our sources for the early 1740s occasionally refer to one or two *faujdars* and their deputies in central Awadh;[27] and it was being mixed up with the new institution of *nizamat* and *niyabat*, representing the new *subadar* in the *sarkar* and *parganas*.

The zamindars *and the provincial government*

No significant Baiswara *zamindar*, according to our sources, rose to serious armed revolt during the period after 1722. For this sudden change in their actions and relations with the state there is no explicit explanation in the existing documentary evidence. On the basis of some contemporary ballads, however, it can be presumed that Burhan-ul-Mulk, immediately after his arrival in Awadh, tried to make some arrangement with the *zamindars* of Baiswara. A personal tour through Baiswara and examination into the state of things seem to have convinced him of a wide gap between the revenue fixed on each peasant in the last assessment and the actual amount paid by the peasants to the *zamindar*. In recent years, the actual production in agriculture seems to have appreciably increased, but the benefits of improvement in land were enjoyed by the *zamindars* alone. Nothing reached the imperial coffers. Subsequently, on the basis of the details he obtained from the *qanungos*, Burhan-ul-Mulk seems to have substantially increased the assessment of Baiswara.[28]

The military superiority of the Mughal governor seems to have been a factor in making them accept the new arrangement. The consistent drive of the imperial campaigns for about forty

[27] *Akhbarat*, Muhammad Shah, 25th R.Y. Supplement Persian 313; Bibliotheque Nationale, Paris for the *faujdars* of Khairabad and the *mahals* of the *Shahrah*. The words *faujdar* and *faujdari*, e.g., *tahsil-i faujdari*, *Kharat*(?) *faujdari*, *faujdari-o-amaldari*, *akham-i faujdari-o-diwani*, appear in different contexts in some documents of the late-eighteenth and the early-nineteenth centuries, but these terms did not indicate the same power and position as under the Mughals in the seventeenth centur. Cf. *Firangi Mahal Documents*, Iqbal Husain's edition. Nos. 97–101; see also *Khairabad Documents*, transcripts, Deptt. of History, Aligarh No. 100.

[28] Our inferences are based on a ballad which extols the valour and bravery of Chait

years seems to have broken the strength of the rebels in
Baiswara.[29] Apart from their encounters with the Mughals, they
had to defend their *zamindaris* against the encroachments of the
neighbouring *zamindars* as well.[30]

Besides, the arrangement was not without some gains for the
zamindars. Mardan Singh, the *zamindar* of Dondia Khera, a
prominent leader of the erstwhile rebel Bais, was received into
high favour by Burhan-ul-Mulk. Mardan Singh was accountable to the governor not only for the realization of the revenue in

Rai, the *zamindar* of *pargana* Morawan, and states that when Sa'adat Khan (Burhan-ul-
Mulk) took charge of Awadh, he found the revenue administration of the *suba* in great
disorder. Sa'adat Khan resolved to repair this by a personal tour through the country
and enquiry into the state of things. When he reached Morawan, he summoned all the
qanungos of Baiswara and asked them to produce the *daul* (rent roll) of their respective
parganas. They said 'what *daul* will you have?' and on being asked the meaning of their
answer, they explained that there were two *dauls* which a *qanungo* could give, the 'coward's
daul' and the 'man's *daul*'. In the 'coward's *daul*', against every landowner's name
was written only the sum which had been fixed on him at the last assessment, but in the
'man's *daul*' everyone's rent was indicated on the basis of what it should have been taking
into account the improvement that had taken place in land. Sa'adat Khan called for the
'man's *daul*' and on that basis, doubled the assessment of Baiswara. Then, having
summoned the representatives of all the *zamindars*, he placed before them on one side a
heap of *pan* leaves, on the other a heap of bullets, and bade them, if their masters
accepted the terms to take up *pan*; if not, the bullets. One after one they came forward
and everyone took up the *pan* leaves. Cf. C. A. Elliot, *Chronicles of Oonao*, p. 73.

The story is interesting and, apart from showing the *qanungos'* loyalty to Mughal
authority, throws considerable light on the nature of the relationship between the big
zamindars and the peasants. The Ujjainiya intermediaries of Bihar are also reported to
have enjoyed, over a fairly long period, the benefits of the gap between the actual
revenue collected by them (*tahsil*) which went on increasing and the assessed revenue
(*jama-i dami*) which remained constant. Compare S. Nurul Hasan, *Thoughts on Agrarian
Relations*, p. 35.

[29] After the successful expedition of Chhabele Ram in 1715, Amar Singh, a leader of
the Bais, is said to have never recovered his position, and it was not till some twenty
years later that his grandson, Pher Shah was admitted to engage for the four villages of
Khajurgaon, Sareli, Bajpaipur and Hajipur. W. C. Benett, *Chief Clans of the Roy Bareilly
District*, p. 36. See also Chapter III.

[30] According to family records, Mohan Singh, the *zamindar* of Tiloi, made encroachments upon the *zamindaris* of neighbouring Shaikhs, the Bais and the Bhale Sultans. He
led expeditions towards Hardoi, Baiswara and against the Naihasthas of Bachhara-
wan. Thus by the time Burhan-ul-Mulk came to Awadh, fourteen *parganas*, namely,
Jais, Nasirabad, Salon, Rai Bareli, Manakpur, Hardoi, Inhona, Subeha, Takia,
Baswarhi, Rudauli, Daryabad, Saidanpur and Bilwan were under him. Ibid., pp. 42–3.

Baiswara but also seems to have had the same jurisdiction which formerly belonged to the Mughal *faujdar*. Later, his son, Achal Singh also enjoyed the same position under Safdar Jang,[31] while Udat Singh, another son of Mardan Singh, who took a hostile attitude towards the Mughals, was crushed by the forces of the Bais *zamindars* themselves.[32] The Mehrors who enjoyed hereditary protection of the Bais, improved their position in the *parganas* of Harha and Purwa. They acquired two *tappas* in Harha and eighteen villages in Purwa.[33]

Privileges were extended to the *zamindars* in proportion to their strength and the benefits that were expected from their support. Chait Rai, a *zamindar* of Baiswara was asked to pay only half the sum that had been fixed on his *zamindari* when he demonstrated his strength by offering a sham fight to Burhan-ul-Mulk.[34] The Bisen *zamindar* of Gonda is reported to have been won over by Burhan-ul-Mulk on the condition that his territory would be independent of the jurisdiction of the *nazim* of Gorakhpur and Bahraich and subject only to the payment of a tribute to the governor.[35]

The policy of wooing powerful *zamindars* and with their support strengthening and broadening the social base for the Mughal governorship, was extended by Burhan-ul-Mulk and his successor, Safdar Jang, to smaller *zamindars* as well, some of them being given *mansabs*.[36] Ordinarily, however, no *zamindar* was allowed to accumulate so much power that he could aspire

---

[31] C. A. Elliot, *Chronicles of Oonao*, pp. 123–4. The following incident also highlights the nature of relationship between the nawab and the Bais *zamindar*. In 1765, when Shuja-ud-Daulah had been defeated by the East India Company's troops at Buxar, he fled along the banks of the Ganga to Farrukhabad. Achal Singh gave him both men and supplies, and as he was travelling too lightly to carry a large treasury with him, sent a quarter's revenue which was due from Baiswara to him at Farrukhabad. Ibid., p. 76.

[32] Ibid., p. 75.

[33] Ibid., p. 62. The Sengars who occupied a relatively inferior position in the social heirarchy also were in the service of the *zamindar* of Dondia Khera and thus supporters of the governor. Ibid., p. 48.

[34] Ibid., p. 73. W. C. Benett (*Chief Clans of Roy Bareilly District*, p. 35) has a different version.

[35] Compare, R. Mitra, 'The Bisen Talukdars of Northern Oudh' *Calcutta Review*, LXXIV, 1882, pp. 367–70.

[36] At the time of Burhan-ul-Mulk, Samrota was held by Mandhata Singh. He was left in possession of his ancestral *zamindari* in lieu of a *mansab*, with additional distinctions

to a basic change in the character of his holding. The intermediary *zamindar* did not become an autonomous raja, even if he
now had some additional privileges. An illustration of this is the
case of the *zamindar* of Harha who was murdered by his eldest
son, Kesari, in the wake of a dispute over the fragmentation and
distribution of his *zamindari* among his eight sons. The incident
was probably a logical follow-up of the wealth and strength the
zamindar had recently acquired. It is not unlikely that Kesari
wanted to institute the practice of primogeniture in the family.
This was an open violation of the existing rule. As a punishment, therefore, Kesari was deprived of his share in the
zamindari.[37]

The new *subadar* also tried to consolidate his strength against
the big rebellious *zamindars* by providing opportunities for the
extension of power and influence of apparently non-Rajput
elements over land. A number of cases of the purchase of
zamindaris by *chaudhuris* and *qanungos*, especially in *sarkar*
Khairabad and parts of Lucknow where the Rajputs still posed
a serious threat probably bear this out.[38] We have noticed
earlier how Saroman Das of Sandi continued to acquire lands
and riches under Burhan-ul-Mulk. In another instance, the
Rajput *zamindars* of *mauza* Matun in *pargana* Sandila lost their
entire *zamindaris* to *chaudhuri* Banwari Lal, because they failed to
pay in the stipulated period the amount they owed to the
chaudhuri.[39] It is to be noted that in all cases the lands were sold

---

and a drum. In another case, one Jaswant Singh, a *zamindar*, seems to have been
harassed by Jai Singh, probably a neighbouring *zamindar*. The former approached the
governor, Safdar Jang. Subsequently, the governor is reported to have sent a *parwana* to
Jai Singh with strict instructions to abstain from his misdeeds along with a consolatory
letter to Jaswant promising him his full support. Compare, W. C. Benett, *Chief Clans of
Roy Bareilly*, p. 47 and *Maktubat*, p. 183.

[37] This followed a long unsuccessful seige of the fortress at Harha and the governor's
failure to kill Kesari or capture him alive. Mardan Singh who was in the army of the
governor then offered to mediate. On his intercession probably, the governor agreed to
a mild punishment for Kesari. Kesari was exiled for 40 years from his *zamindari*. In the
meanwhile, his *zamindari* was granted to Mardan Singh's son Achal Singh. Cf. C. A.
Elliot, *Chronicles of Oonao*, p. 65.

[38] Compare Allahabad, 516 and 626 for *chaudhuris*, Muhammad Masum of Sandila
and Ruh-ul-Amin, 127 for Mohan Lal, the *qanungo* of *pargana* Mallanwan.

[39] Ibid., 536. The village was later known as Banwaripur *alias* Matun.

by the Rajput *zamindars* and the transactions were executed in accordance with Mughal regulations.

Again, we have some instances to show the governor's special efforts to create and encourage certain *zamindaris* in these areas. For instance, Burhan-ul-Mulk obtained from the emperor the grant of a large estate for Mutahhir Ali Khan in Rasulabad. By 1740 Rasulabad was made a *pargana* wherein almost all the offices were held by the members of Mutahhir Ali's family. Similarly, the Panwars of Safipur, an off-shoot of the Panwars of Etonja (in Lucknow district) obtained about 12 villages through the favour of Nawal Rai in 1740.[40]

Burhan-ul-Mulk's policy of the extension of the power of the non-Rajputs was specially concentrated in and around *sarkar* Khairabad where the Rajputs, in particular, of Katesar and Nabigarh, unlike those in Baiswara, were still in a defiant mood.[41] The policy, however, seems to have further intensified the caste *zamindars'* resistance against the Mughals, even in the areas outside *sarkar* Khairabad.[42]

The policy of creating and encouraging the non-Rajput *zamindaris* did not pay much dividends, as the Rajputs as such

[40] C. A. Elliot, *Chronicles of Oonao*, pp. 56 and 101.

[41] Compare *Maktubat*, pp. 6–7 for the Gaur Rajputs and *Akhbarat*, Muhammad Shah, 5th–9th R. Ys., pp. 19–20 for the *zamindars* of Gujarati and Kharkale in *sarkar* Khairabad. It is interesting to note that after the governor's victory over the *zamindars* of Gujarati and Kharkale, the *garhi* of the rebels was handed over to the Saiyids of the neighbouring village, Mankapur, with a grant of Rs 1,000 for its repair and maintenance.

Dr A. L. Srivastava, basing his account on the family tradition, states that Nawal Singh Gaur of Katesar and Nabigarh was a descendant of one Raja Chandra Sen, a Rajput of the Brahma-Gaur who had migrated with Sa'adat Khan (Burhan-ul-Mulk) to Awadh and settled at Katesar. *First Two Nawabs*, p. 92. This opinion which does not quote any evidence in its support, is untenable. Even before Burhan-ul-Mulk, the Gaur Rajputs of *parganas* Sadrpur, Laharpura and Kheri (Katesar was situated in *pargana* Laharpur) had taken to armed resistance. Two important expeditions against them are recorded to have been undertaken by Chhabele Ram and Girdhar Bahadur. In 1721, Girdhar Bahadur seems to have destroyed almost all their fortresses, except Katesar where they had ultimately taken shelter. Katesar as it is recorded in our document, was promised to be reduced soon. See *Ajaib*, f. 36a and Shivdas, f. 73a.

[42] On 12 June 1723, the Rajput *zamindars* of *mauza* Khora, *pargana* Unao, *sarkar* Lucknow, for example, were reported to have made encroachments upon the lands of some Saiyid Phool and Saiyid Gaddan. The lands in dispute were earlier purchased by the Saiyids from the ancestors of the Rajput invaders. Allahabad 2743.

were very powerful in Awadh. It was thus the policy of extending favours and privileges to the powerful *zamindars* that proved
of greater help and enabled Burhan-ul-Mulk to build a base in
Awadh. Burhan-ul-Mulk, however could not resolve the problems of the other disturbed *zamindaris* or curtail the ambitions of
the other big *zamindars*. All of them like the Bais were strong in
their areas. Safdar Jang, therefore, extended the terms and
conditions of his predecessor's agreement with Mardan Singh
and later his son, Achal Singh of Baiswara to the *zamindar* of
Tiloi as well. As a result, Balbhadra Singh who succeeded
Mohan Singh's son Pem Singh as *zamindar* of Tiloi, though
initially resisting the governor, is seen in his service in the
latter's campaigns against Bharatpur and the Marathas. A
zamindar whose ancestors had been referred to in the Mughal
official records as a mere *malguzar* was then to pay a fixed
amount of 2½ lakh rupees as revenue. In addition, the
zamindar's army was to be maintained at the expense of
Lucknow.[43] The obvious explanation for this is that the *zamindar*
under the new agreement held some administrative and military duties under the provincial government.

The re-establishment of the old powerful *zamindars* with certain new privileges was a new arrangement. In some cases, the
arrangement was termed as *ta'ahhud* according to which the
zamindar had to pay a fixed amount for the contracted territory.[44] Sometimes, a provincial official also contracted a

---

[43] W.C. Benett, *Chief Clans of Roy Bareilly District*, pp. 44–5. Benett quotes a *wajib-ul-
arz* of Balbhadra Singh to Safdar Jang which runs as follows: 'I am an old *zamindar* of 14
parganas inherited from Mohan Singh, namely, Jais, Nasirabad, Salon, Roy Bareilly
(Rai Bareli), Manakpur, Hardoi, Inhona, Subeha, Takia, Basarhi, Rudauli, Daryabad,
Saidanpur and Bilwan. This *zamindari* has been reduced. Let me again hold it on the
payment of Rs 2½ lacs revenue.' 'Let me deduct the expenses of my army from the
revenue, or have them paid in fully by Government.' Safdar Jang's order was, 'Deduct
from the revenue.' Balbhadra Singh apparently did not engage for the entire area of
these *parganas*, for we have evidence to show the existence of another *ta'alluqdar* for
pargana Daryabad. Again, according to the *Ain*, the *jama* figures of only Manakpur, Rai
Bareli and Jais, for instance, exceeded Rs 2,50,000. Cf. *Ain*, II (Jarrett), p. 176.

[44] See *Maktubat*, p. 220 for one Dharam Singh, a *zamindar* of *pargana* Daryabad who is
reported to have presented himself to Safdar Jang and agreed to become a *muta'ahhid* for
his *ta'alluqa* and pay a fixed amount of Rs 24,000 per annum against the state revenue
demand. See also Allahabad 1322 of the year 1155/1742–3 which records one Shah
Hidayat, a local *zamindar*, as a *muta'ahhid* of *pargana* Haveli Bahraich.

ta'ahhud.[45] In the case of the *zamindars* the arrangement was virtually an *ijara* contract which in some cases also involved some administrative and military responsibilities.[46] In this we can presumably trace the origins of the formation of some of the *ta'alluqas* of the eighteenth century.[47]

It is also to be noted that in our period in Awadh it was not merely greedy speculators who became *ijaradars*. The *ijaradars* included government officials and *zamindars* as well. Indeed, with the office of *diwan* and the *jagirs* under his control, the governor became a party to all the *ijara* contracts in the province.[48] We can presume that the province of Awadh as part of the Mughal empire was practically held in *ijara* by its governor who further farmed out parts of it to other provincial government officials, the *zamindars* and to some others. So long as the governor paid the stipulated sum and showed due deference to the centre, he was free to act as independently in provincial matters as he could. This arrangement which implied money contracts at various levels of government obviously showed a very high degree of monetization.[49]

[45] Ismail Khan, a *risaladar* in the army of Safdar Jang, took the *pargana* of Jahangirabad, for instance, on *ta'ahhud* at an annual payment of Rs 50,000. Subsequently Isa Beg Khan, the *naib* and *chakladar* of Khairabad and the *mahals* of Selak was directed by the governor to hand over the *thanas* and the hostages of the *pargana* to the agent of Ismail Khan. *Matkubat*, pp. 190–1. For Ismail Khan see Allahabad 1322 and C. A. Elliot, *Chronicles of Oonao*, p. 98.

[46] In such cases the *zamindar* appears to have had the *faujdari* rights over the territory under his *ta'ahhud*, while the government would insist on having its representative who was called *naib*, *naib faujdar* or *nazim*. For reference to such *naibs* see *Akhbarat*, Muhammad Shah, 25th R. Y., Bibliotheque Nationale, Paris.

[47] Compare also N. A. Siddiqi, *Land Revenue Administration*, p. 27. Dr Siddiqi refers to the British Revenue Records which give an idea of how the *ta'alluqadars* later took advantage of their superior position to convert the *ta'alluqadari* tenure into real *zamindari* rights, p. 27. Indeed, a number of the *ta'alluqadars*, benefiting very likely from the position which they later obtained in the new circumstances, became a major threat to the Lucknow government.

[48] The following instances also illustrate the point. A sum of Rs 30 from the *sair* of Jaunpur formed a part of the emoluments of one Ali Naqi. The *gumashta* of the *mustajir* of the *sair*, Bhikam Rai refused to pay the amount to him and demanded a new *parwana* from the governor. On Ali Naqi's petition, therefore, the governor wrote to the *gumashta* confirming his earlier order. The *faujdar* of *pargana* Bilgram, Mir Baqar Chaudhuri, is also recorded as the *ijaradar* of the *pargana*. *Maktubat*, p. 175 and *Sharaif*.

[49] It is probably in this perspective that we can explain why the centre did not object to the gross violation of a Mughal convention when Mir Mu'in-ul-Mulk farmed out the *subadari* of Ajmer to Raja Jai Singh. See Chapter I, Section III.

Some *ijaradars* might have been merchants and money-lenders (*mahajans*). Our sources, however, do not contain any positive evidence in this regard. Similarly, we know little of the details of the modalities, such as the period and the items of the *ijara*. From the cases of the neighbouring *sarkars* of Jaunpur, Ghazipur, Chunar and Benaras which were administratively a part of the province of Allahabad it can safely be presumed that the *ijara* contract by the *zamindars* and the government officials was for a relatively longer period. Renewal in such cases meant a revision and readjustment of the rate of *ijara* in accordance with prevailing prices and the actual revenue yield which in the four *sarkars* of Allahabad mentioned above showed an upward trend. At the beginning of Muhammad Shah's reign, these *sarkars* were taken by the *ijaradar* on an annual payment of Rs 5,00,000. In the beginning of 1730s, the same *ijaradar* was required to pay Rs 8,00,000; in the late 1730s, the governor began to demand a bigger sum from the *ijaradar* which ended with the latter's replacement by another *ijaradar* and eventually by the end of our period the amount was raised to Rs 16,00,000. Again, the greater part of the reigion of Moradabad and Bareilly was held on *ijara* by Ali Muhammad Khan Rohilla, the Afghan chief, for about the whole of the second quarter of the eighteenth century. It is interesting to note that these *ijaras* in our sources are characterized as *hukumat* and *nizamat* which denoted some kind of accountability and an administrative authority for the *ijaradar*.[50]

The madad-i ma'ash *holders and the* provincial government

The *madad-i ma'ash* holders, as we have noticed earlier, had acquired a formidable position in Awadh and been responsible for a number of problems of the provincial government. Ini-

---

[50] Compare *Tuhfa* ff. 4a, 10a–11a, 14a–16a; Kamboh, ff. 5a, 6a, 16b–17a, 21b–24a, 54b–57a and 65b; Saiyid Mazhar Husain Korwi, *Tarikh-i Benaras*, I, Benaras, 1916, pp. 88–91, 111–14, 124–5. See also *Tazkira Mukhlis*, pp. 324–5 for *sarkar* Moradabad of Delhi province.

It must be added here that unless we know the prices of foodgrains and the actual state of agricultural production, we are not in a position to explain the rise in the rate of *ijara* in the *sarkars* of Jaunpur, Ghazipur, Chunar and Benaras.

tially Burhan-ul-Mulk therefore seems to have been very strict with the *madad-i ma'ash* grantees. He seems to have begun with the resumption of the *a'immas* in the province and with a policy of subjecting the grants to assessment.[51] This brought him in conflict with some powerful *madad-i ma'ash* grantees. The *faujdar* and the *diwan* of the *pargana* of Bilgram for instance faced stiff resistance from the *a'imma* holders of the *pargana*. Under the leadership of the *qazi*, they fought several times against the army of the *faujdar*. While the others seem to have accepted the *fait accompli*, the *qazi* could not be subdued for seven years. The *qazi* then visited Delhi and presented his case to the emperor.[52] The emperor ordered the *diwan-i khalisa* to look into the matter. Burhan-ul-Mulk appreciated the weight that a noble's or a group of nobles' support to the *qazi*'s case carried and also realized the consequences of such an eventuality for his plans of consolidating the new *subadari* in the province. The *vakil* of Burhan-ul-Mulk at the court, therefore, hurried to bring the *qazi* to terms. As an exceptional favour to the *qazi* his *madad-i ma'ash* villages were released to him.[53]

For about eight years, 1722–30, as we know from the evidence

---

[51] *Ma'asir-ul-Kiram*, I, p. 222. The *madad-i ma'ash* villages of Qazi Muhammad Ihsan, for instance, were assessed for Rs 2,200. Cf. *Sharaif*, p. 175. As the authors of the *Ma'asir-ul-Kiram* and the *Sharaif-i Usmani* were closely related to those who were severely hit by Burhan-ul-Mulk's new regulations, their statements in this regard should be accepted with certain qualifications. Burhan-ul-Mulk's measures seem to have been directed against those grantees who held the land in excess of their require-ments or those who combined *zamindari* holdings with large revenue grants and had become a source of disturbance in the villages. For, we have evidence of unbroken revenue grants for some families in Awadh. The *madad-i ma'ash* of the family of Mulla Nizam-ud-Din of Sahali is one example. Compare *Firangi Mahal Documents*. Mulla Nizam-ud-Din maintained a *madrasa* at Firangi Mahal, Lucknow and served as the official *mufti* to the government of Safdar Jang. Cf. M. Raza Ansari, *Bani-e Dars-i Nizami*, pp. 64–86.

[52] Initially, the *qazi* approached Muhammad Khan, the governor of Allahabad. Since Muhammad Khan hailed from the region and aspired to have a strong base in Allahabad *suba* and also, if possible, in Awadh, he considered it to be a good opportu-nity to weaken Burhan-ul-Mulk. More so because Burhan-ul-Mulk's machinations had put him in great difficulty. Muhammad Khan promised the *qazi* to recommend his case to the emperor and took him to Delhi. Muhammad Khan, however, could not help him in Delhi. He lost even his own governorship of Allahabad and was transferred to Malwa. See Chapter VII, Section II.

[53] But since the policy of assessing the *madad-i ma'ash* grants was still operative in the remaining parts of the province, the new *amil* who took the charge of the *pargana* of

of the *Ma'asir-ul-Kiram* and the *Sharaif-i Usmani*, Burhan-ul-Mulk seems to have struggled to maintain his policy of subjecting the large revenue grants to assessment. The new regulations might also have contributed to the reported increase in the revenue of Awadh immediately after Burhan-ul-Mulk's assumption of the charge of the province.[54] Soon, however, the conditions that came up due to the new regulations became unmanageable.

The *madad-i ma'ash* grantees did not form an exclusive social category. A number of them, as we have seen earlier, were *zamindars* as well. To resist the new regulations, they did not hesitate to mobilize whatever force they had in the villages. In the case of the *qazi* of Bilgram, cited above, the *ri'aya* seem to have supported him in his struggle against the governor. One of the measures that Burhan-ul-Mulk took was to round up the *ri'aya* of villages of the *qazi*.[55] Again, the *madad-i ma'ash* grantees had close links with the Shaikhzadas who were in the imperial service,[56] while a number of these grantees were related by marriage to the Shaikh *zamindars* of the province.[57] These Shaikhzadas, as we will see later, constituted a substantial local force. It was also not easy for Burhan-ul-Mulk to disregard the support of some eminent nobles for their cases. Sarbuland Khan who had long been associated with Burhan-ul-Mulk as the latter's employer, made a special plea for the *qazi* of Bilgram

---

Bilgram, again confiscated the *madad-i ma'ash* of the *qazi*. See Allahabad 117 for the local officials' attitude towards the revenue-grantees in and around the *qasbas* of Daryabad and *Sarai* Shah Alam. For the details relating to the *qazi* see *Sharaif*, pp. 167–78; Qazi Sharif-ul-Hasan, *Tarikh-i Bilgram*, pp. 192–5.

[54] See Chapter III.   [55] *Sharaif*, p. 175.

[56] The *qazi* of Bilgram, for example, was related to Ruh-ul-Amin Khan and the other Shaikhzadas from Awadh who were in the imperial service while Shaikh Jarullah, an Abbasi Shaikh of Kakori, who held a rank of 7000 *zat* under Aurangzeb belonged to the family of the *qazis* of the town. Cf. *Qazi* Ahmadullah Bilgrami, *Al Musajjalat Fi Tarikh-al-Quzat*, f. 32b; *Mashahir-i Kakori*, p. 95. See also *Firangi Mahal Documents* No. 68 for the *jagir* of Muhammad As'ad of Firangi Mahal in Amethi Dongar. Muhammad As'ad was brother of the founder of the famous *madrasa* of Firangi Mahal.

[57] Compare *Sharaif*, pp. 126–8, for an account of the matrimonial relations of a family of the *qazis* of Bilgram in and around 1100/1688–89. Qazi Kamal was, for example, married to the daughter of Qazi Maruf, the *qazi* of Kachhandu. Maruf was a nephew of Akhi Jamshed, a Qidwai Shaikh of Rajgir. The father of Maruf was a *zamindar* and was a nephew of the *qazi* of Araha. A daughter of Maruf was married in Sandila . . . and so on and so forth.

in 1730.[58] Zakariya Khan, the governor of the Punjab recommended the case of one Saiyid Muhammad Ghaus,[59] while Muhammad Khan Bangash strongly disapproved of the policy and warned Burhan-ul-Mulk against the danger of 'following the example of the *zamindars*' and thus landing the Saiyids and the *Shurafa* in any more trouble.[60]

The new regulations were introduced to increase the revenue of the state so that the governor could organize a sufficiently big army to enforce his rule in the province. By 1730 almost all the powerful *zamindars*, barring the Gaurs and Kanhpurias of *sarkar* Khairabad, either by persuasion and diplomacy or through the demonstration of force were reconciled. The revenue must have gone up subsequently. The necessity to maintain strictness regarding the grants was now not so urgent, particularly when it tended to lead to opposition to the governor by the Shaikhazadas and a number of nobles. There is no evidence of any attempt by the administration to enforce these regulations again for the remaining years of the period under review. Instead, there are instances of directives from the governor to the local officials for the renewal and confirmation of the grants and for probes into daily allowances and disputes over the *madad-i ma'ash* land. Most of the documents bearing these directives, that we have examined, relate to the period after the 10th R. Y. of Muhammad Shah (1729).[61]

---

[58] Ibid., p. 177.   [59] *Maktubat*, p. 79.

[60] *Khujasta*, p. 165. Muhammad Khan had given shelter to the revenue grantees of *sarkar* Khairabad who had earlier been displaced by the insubordinate *zamindars*. Muhammad Khan also made a strong recommendation for the rehabilitation of these grantees.

[61] See for instance Allahabad 96–7 and 923; *Maktubat*, pp. 173–4 and 180–1. In an instance from *pargana* Fatehpur, one Fatima had received a *madad-i ma'ash* grant as early as in 1722. But the necessary follow-up in the local office was taken up only in the 12th R. Y./1730–31 when she was asked to produce *tashiha* (verification) and signatures of reliable local persons confirming her claim to the grant. Allahabad 920. But a previous grant to the sons of Muhammad Sa'id, son of Shaikh Qutb-ud-Din of Sahali, was confirmed from the centre during the 5th–6th R. Ys. of Muhammad Shah. *Firangi Mahal Documents* Nos. 53–4.

Some local officials, however, seem to have maintained the earlier regulations even after the proclamation of the general order of their repeal. The *naib* of the *mahals* of *sarkar* Lucknow wanted a special new *parwana* from the deputy governor for the restoration of a *madad-i ma'ash* village, Basoli, in *pargana Haveli* Lucknow to its claimant. In an another instance the local official in charge of *pargana* Mohan seems to have kept 450 *bighas* of the

Yet there was no unconditional restoration of the pre-1722 position of the revenue grants. Intensive investigations into the claims to grants seem to have been carried out even after 1730.[62] Revenue-free lands continued to be assessed, though very lightly. In the documents of the eighteenth century, the *madad-i ma'ash* grant seems to be no longer treated as something held on loan (*'ariyat*). The *madad-i ma'ash* began to be bracketed with the *zamindari* and the *milkiyat* in such a way as to suggest their being identical in character. On occasions they seem to have been used interchangeably. A *parwana* of Safdar Jang dated 15 Ramzan 1153/23 November 1740, confirming the grant of an old pond in Kakori to the *qazi* of the *pargana* characterizes the latter's possession of the pond as proprietary (*malikana*).[63] A *madad-i ma'ash* land dispute document of 9 Muharam 1158/31 January 1745, which bears the seals of the *qazi*, the *mufti*, the *qanungo* and the *faujdar* of Sandila describes the *madad-i ma'ash* and the *milkiyat* interchangeably.[64] In a *mahzar* document from the *pargana* of Laharpur, *sarkar* Khairabad, the revenue grant is mentioned as *madad-i ma'ash* and *zamindari*. The Laharpur document is undated, but from the reference to the context the date can be worked out as some time in the late 1760s. The land in dispute belonged to the *qanungo* of the *pargana* who was a descendant of Shaikh Dost Muhammad, the original recipient of the grant from Aurangzeb. The land had earlier been in possession of Gulab Rai Khatri and after being resumed in *khalisa* it was granted to Shaikh Dost Muhammad. In the document under review one of the descendants of Gulab Rai is stated to have been instigated by the local *amil* to forcibly seize the land.[65] The incident also points to the circumstances in which the *madad-i ma'ash* holders began to be finally recognized as a category of *zamindars*.

---

madad-i ma'ash land in confiscation for some years after the general order of revocation. He handed them over to the rightful grantees only after he received a specific directive from Safdar Jang, who held the charge of the *suba* in the absence of Burhan-ul-Mulk. *Maktubat*, pp. 173 and 182.

[62] *Maktubat*, p. 173.

[63] Muhammad Hasan Abbasi, *Abbasiyan-i Kakori*, p. 12 which records the *parwana*.

[64] Allahabad 505; *Jais Documents* transcripts, Dept. of History, Aligarh, No. 84.

[65] Cf. *Kaghazat-i Pargana Laharpur, Sarkar Khairabad*. This is to be noted that in all the extant relevant papers of Aurangzeb's reign, the land in question has been referred to as

The practice of assessment, though light, might have appeased the *zamindars* who, as we have noticed earlier had resented the privileges enjoyed by the grantees. On the other hand, the grantees accepted it, for it was its assessment that gradually lent the *madad-i ma'ash* the strength of a *zamindari* holding. From an unrelenting sternness to a compromise, Burhan-ul-Mulk thus tackled the problem of the *madad-i ma'ash* holders in Awadh. In a measure, eventually he conceded to the aspirations of the *madad-i ma'ash* holders who, in turn, constituted one of the chief props of the new *subadari* in Awadh.

Awadhi communities in imperial service and their gradual absorption in provincial government

Awadh was probably one of those Mughal *subas* which supplied the rank and file of the Mughal imperial army. Lucknow, **Bilgram, Gopamau, Rudauli, Kakori, Malihabad, Daryabad,** Shahabad and Amethi were among the important towns of Mughal Awadh. A number of Indian Muslims in the Mughal imperial service hailed from one or other of these towns.[66] For Muhammad Faiz Baksh, the author of the *Tarikh-i Farh Baksh*, 'tales of the glory of Delhi related by the noble persons of advanced years of Kakori who had been in their prime employed in Delhi', constituted an important source of his history.[67]

Although our sources do not contain detailed references to the noble persons from Kakori, Muhammad Faiz Baksh's statement is amply supported by a survey of the careers of some of the Awadhi elements in the Mughal service in the late-seventeenth and early-eighteenth centuries. For instance, Shaikh Ilahyar of Bilgram better known as Rustam Zaman Khan joined the Mughal state service through Prince Muhammad Azim-ush-Shan some time during the last years of Aurangzeb's

---

madad-i ma'ash. It may be noted here that the *madad-i ma'ash* began to be generally treated as virtually a *zamindari* holding only in the eighteenth century, and that the possibility of a few cases of sale and purchase of the *mu'afi* land together with the *kharaji* one cannot be ruled out. I am indebted to S. Z. H. Jafari for references to two such cases for 1661 and 1697 in Allahabad 733–F and National Archives of India, 144.

[66] Compare for instance *Sharaif*, pp. 68, 137 and 246–7; Muhammad Ali Hyder Alavi, *Tazkira-i Mashahir-i Kakori*, (Urdu) Lucknow, 1927, p. 96.

[67] Author's preface in William Hoey's translation as *Memoirs of Delhi and Faizabad*, Allahabad, 1889.

reign. He was attached to Mirza Muhammad Rafi[68] (later Sarbuland Khan) at the *sarkar* of the prince, to look after the latter's *jagir* in Sahenda, in Bundelkhand. Later, in the reign of Farrukh Siyar, during the tenure of Sarbuland Khan's governorship of Allahabad, Ilahyar is reported to have held the *faujdari* of *sarkar* Arail and Harhar. In 1715 when the province of Bihar was assigned to Sarbuland Khan with a direction to chastise the turbulent Ujjainiyas, he was ably assisted by Ilahyar. Ilahyar seems to have been generously rewarded for his services in the campaigns. He got a promotion of 3500 *zat* raising his *zat* rank to 6000 with the titles of Mubariz-ud-Daulah, Ashja-ul-Mulk, Hind Pehelwan, Rustam Zaman Khan, Shaikh Ilahyar Bahadur Nahtaman Jang.[69]

Shaikh Murtaza Husain, son of Shaikh Ilahyar, entered into the service of Sarbuland Khan during the latter's second term of governorship of Allahabad in the early 1730s. After his dismissal, Murtaza Husain accompanied him to Delhi where he was honoured with a rank of 2500 *zat* and the title of Khan. Murtaza Husain served under him till the latter's death. Then he joined the service of Safdar Jang in response to the latter's *parwana*, with a contingent of 200 *sawars* and *piyadas*.[70]

The process can be further illustrated by a detailed reference to the careers of Ruh-ul-Amin Khan and Shaikh Pir Muhammad. Ruh-ul-Amin Khan, another Shaikhzada from Bilgram joined the Mughal service through Mun'im Khan, the *wazir* of Bahadur Shah. He entered into the service of Mun'im Khan along with sixty *sawars* and *piyadas* from Bilgram. Soon he rose to a rank of 6000/2000. After Mun'im Khan's death in 1710, Ruh-ul-Amin associated himself with Sipahdar Khan, the governor of Allahabad and acted as his deputy in Allahabad. After Sipahdar Khan's transfer from Allahabad, Ruh-ul-Amin, very likely on the persuasion of Shaikh Ilahyar, joined Sarbuland Khan who then held the *faujdari* of Kara. Shortly afterwards, Sarbuland Khan sent him to the Punjab to administer his *jagirs* in the *parganas* of Sialkot and Jalandhar. Sometime in the reign

---

[68] Mirza Muhammad Rafi (Sarbuland Khan) was closely connected with Prince Azim-ush-Shan by marriage. One of the daughters of Ruh··llah Khan was married to Sarbuland Khan while the other was a wife of the prince. Compare *M. U.*, III, p. 801.

[69] For the biographical notices see *Sharaif*, pp. 255–7 and 269 and *Hadiqat*, p. 131.

[70] *Sharaif*, p. 269.

of Farrukh Siyar, he joined the service of Muzaffar Khan, brother of Samsam-ud-Daulah. In the time of the governorship of Saiyid Muzaffar Ali Khan in Awadh, Ruh-ul-Amin acted as his deputy in the province.[71]

He was among the eminent Shaikhzadas of Awadh who resisted Burhan-ul-Mulk's new regulations. After a few years of service under the *faujdar* and *ijaradar* in Moradabad and Sambhal he left for Delhi around 1725 and made all possible but vain efforts to regain his earlier position by allying himself with the opponents of Burhan-ul-Mulk at the court. Again, with a hope of rehabilitating himself in Awadh he joined Qaim Khan, son of Muhammad Khan Bangash and fought with him against the Bundelas.[72] Later Muhammad Khan Bangash took him to Delhi to recommend his case to the emperor. In Delhi, however, on the question of the dues of the *fawazil* (excess amounts) he came into conflict with the Bangash Nawab. Tired and dejected, he finally decided to lead a quiet life in his hometown. At this juncture, on the recommendation of Sarbuland Khan, Burhan-ul-Mulk invited him to join his service in Awadh. He responded to the invitation and joined the nawab with a contingent of 2000 *sawars* and *piyadas*.[73]

Shaikh Pir Muhammad, again a Shaikhzada from Bilgram, was initially in the service of Saiyid Husain Ali Khan sometime in the reign of Farrukh Siyar. He, along with Mir Musharraf, an Afghan from Malihabad, Lucknow, was promoted to the rank of 6000 *zat*.[74] Shaikh Abd-us-Samad, yet another Shaikhzada from Bilgram, is mentioned as an associate of the Barha Saiyids. He held a rank of 2500 *zat* and is reported to have been killed fighting with his nephew, Alam Ali Khan against Nizam-ul-Mulk.[75] After his death, his son, Shaikh Ahmadullah was given the same *mansab* and *jagir* along with an additional *jagir* in the suburbs of Delhi.[76]

Apart from these, who rose to eminence, a number of other

---

[71] Ibid., p. 232.

[72] For Burhan-ul-Mulk and the court politics and Burhan-ul-Mulk's relations with the Bangash chief see Chapter VII.

[73] *Sharaif*, pp. 235–6.   [74] Ibid., p. 283.

[75] For details of the battle and its antecendents see W. Irvine, *The Later Moghuls* II, pp. 15–48; Satish Chandra, *Parties and Politics*, pp. 154–66.

[76] *Sharaif*, p. 282.

Shaikhzadas from Awadh are reported to have been in the service of one or other prince or noble.[77] The Saiyids and the Shaikhzadas of Awadh were among those few who remained with Saiyid Abdullah and lost their lives in the battle of Hasanpur in 1721.[78]

The Afghans comprised the second important group of Awadhis in Mughal service. Ma'ali Khan and his son, Alavi Khan and a number of other Afghans from Lucknow are mentioned among those who sided with Prince Azim-ush-Shan in the Civil War at Lahore in 1712.[79] Jalal Khan Bazid Khail of Malihabad was among the chief associates of Saiyid Husain Ali Khan. He was seriously wounded in the encounter between Farrukh Siyar and Jahandar Shah. Later, he was suitably rewarded with a rank of 2000/1000 and a *jagir* in Awadh.[80] A large number of Afghans joined Mir Jumla at Kora, Kara, Allahabad, Benaras and Sahsaram on the latter's way to Patna.[81] One Tarin Khan of Damla was among those who died fighting with Sarbuland Khan in Gujarat.[82]

Mir Musharraf and his brother Mir Ashraf, Samsher Khan and Sanjar Khan were among those Afghans who gained prominence in our period. Mir Musharraf, who according to Shivdas ultimately rose to a rank of 7000/7000, is mentioned among those Afghans who joined the contingents of Saiyid Husain Ali Khan in 1712 during the latter's march against Jahandar Shah. Mir Musharraf and Mir Ashraf came to the camp of Farrukh Siyar at the head of three or four thousand horsemen of their clan (*biradari*).[83] Immediately after ascending the throne, Farrukh Siyar appointed him governor of Allahabad with a *mansab* of 4000/4000.[84] In 1715 he accompanied Husain Ali Khan to the Deccan and fought with him in the latter's encounter against Daud Khan Panni in Burhanpur.[85] He was also involved in the Saiyid Brothers' intrigue against Chhabele

[77] Compare *Sharaif*, pp. 205, 227, 250–1, 261, 272 and 275; Qasim, f. 45a; Alavi, *Mashahir-i Kakori*, p. 37.

[78] *T. Hindi*, ff. 248. For the battle of Hasanpur and the issues involved, see W. Irvine, *Later Moghuls*, II, pp. 68–95.

[79] Qasim, f. 41a.   [80] Mubarak, f. 78a.   [81] Shivdas, f. 5b.

[82] *Sharaif*, p. 231.   [83] *Ijad*, f. 65b; Qasim, f. 52b.

[84] Qasim, f. 57a; Kamwar, f. 342b.

[85] W. Hoey, *Memoirs of Delhi and Faizabad*, I, p. 226.

Ram, the governor of Awadh in 1714–15.[86] He remained a close associate of the Saiyids till the final eclipse of their power. In the confusion that followed the death of Saiyid Husain Ali Khan in 1720, Mir Musharraf received minor injuries. At this juncture, he held a *mansab* of 5000/5000. Later in the wake of reconciliation and compromise, Muhammad Shah not only retained his existing rank and the *jagir*, but further honoured him with a promotion to 7000/7000.[87] What happened to him after that is not known.

Samsher Khan and Sanjar Khan, who hailed from Malihabad, were associated with Samsam-ud-Daulah. Samsher Khan, whose real name was Dilawar Khan, is said to have proclaimed the rule of Farrukh Siyar in Awadh while the latter was still on his way to Agra.[88] He arrived at the court of Farrukh Siyar in 1712 with a sufficiently large contingent (*jami'at-i shaista*). He was presented to the emperor by Samsam-ud-Daulah. Subsequently a rank of 2500/2200 with the title of Samsher Khan was conferred upon him.[89]

Sanjar Khan is first mentioned in the context of those eminent Afghan leaders of Awadh who joined Mir Jumla in 1715 on the latter's way to Patna. He along with his two sons, Abd-un-Nabi and Diler Khan, came to the camp of Mir Jumla with a contingent (*jami'at*) of over 4000 *sawars* and *piyadas*.[90] Mir Jumla, as we know, could not handle the problems of the *subadari* in Bihar and returned to Delhi. In 1716, he was reproved for his sudden arrival at Delhi and was ordered to withdraw to Sirhind. Sanjar Khan, however, managed to escape the punishment. Eventually, through the mediation of Samsam-ud-Daulah, he presented himself before the emperor and received a rank of 3000/2000, together with appropriate *mansabs* for a large number of his attendant clansfolk.[91] Both Samsher Khan and Sanjar Khan were among the important commanders of the *walashahi* troopers. In April 1716, they were involved in a clash between the contingents of Samsam-ud-Daulah and Muhammad Amin Khan.[92] Later when Jai Singh

[86] *T. Hindi*, f. 244b.   [87] Shivdas, ff. 48a–49a.
[88] Mubarak, f. 78a.   [89] Ibid., f. 78a.   [90] Shivdas, f. 6a.
[91] Ibid., f. 10a.   [92] Ibid., f. 11b.

was deputed to lead the campaigns to subdue Churaman Jat,
Samsher Khan and Sanjar Khan along with 1200 *mansabdars* of
their clansmen were directed to guard the road at Palwal.[93] The
last reference to them is found in the context of the Agra tumult
of 1719 under the leadership of Neku Siyar and Mitr Sen
Brahman. They were sent with Saiyid Ghairat Khan to quell
the disturbance and were directed to reach Agra before the
reported arrival of Nizam-ul-Mulk.[94]

It may be noted that the Awadhi elements in imperial
service—big and small—associated themselves with either the
Saiyid Brothers or Sarbuland Khan or Samsam-ud-Daulah.
The Afghans with the sole exception of Mir Musharraf formed
an important part of the contingent of Samsam-ud-Daulah
while the Shaikhzadas with the possible exception of one or two
seem to have been allied either with the Saiyids or were in the
employ of Sarbuland Khan. The elegy that Mir Abd-ul-Jalil of
Bilgram[95] composed on the assassination of Saiyid Husain Ali
Khan in 1720 shows how far the Awadh Shaikhzadas, and for
that matter the Indian Shaikhzadas, were allied with the Saiyid
Brothers. The death of Husain Ali Khan reminded the poet of
the great martyrdom of Karbala when the world of the descendants of the Prophet of Islam was overclouded with agony
and distress. Husain Ali Khan was identified by the poet with
the great martyr, Husain, the Prophet's grandson while his
assassins, according to him, represented the ingratitude, incle-
mency and faithlessness of Yazid, Ziyad and Shimr, the enemies
of Husain.[96]

After 1722 when Burhan-ul-Mulk took charge of the *suba* of
Awadh, not a single eminent Shaikhzada or Afghan of Awadh is

[93] Ibid., f. 12b.

[94] Ibid., f. 27b. For Agra disturbance see Irvine, *Later Moghuls*, I, pp. 408–16 and
422–8.

[95] Mir Abd-ul-Jalil Wasiti Bilgrami (1071–1138/1660–1–1725–6) was an eminent
scholar and poet of the late-seventeenth and early-eighteenth centuries. In 1111/1699–
1700 he was appointed *bakhshi waqai'nigar* of Gujarat Shah Dola in the Punjab. In
1116/1704–5 he was transferred to Bhakkar and Sewistan in Sindh where he remained
till 1126/1714 when he was dismissed from his office at the instance of Mir Jumla.
Later, however, he approached Saiyid Husain Ali Khan and on his recommendation
was reinstated to his office. See *Ma'asir-ul-Kiram*, II, pp. 253–86 for his biography and
some details of his association with Saiyid Husain Ali Khan.

[96] *T. Hindi*, f. 245a.

found associated with Samsam-ud-Daulah or with any other
noble in Delhi who was or could be considered as a possible
enemy of Burhan-ul-Mulk. Samsam-ud-Daulah made a vain
effort to keep Murtaza Husain Khan with himself.[97] Ruh-ul-
Amin Khan could not get ahead with Muzaffar Khan after
1725. His relations with the Bangash chief whom he had served
against the Bundelas were marred with suspicion which, but for
the timely intervention of some nobles, might have erupted into
an open fight. Sarbuland Khan seems to be the sole person who
enjoyed the confidence, and benefited from the support, of the
Awadh Shaikhzadas in this period. Murtaza Husain remained
with him till his death in 1742. We know that after 1730
Sarbuland Khan, apart from certain occasional administrative
assignments, was no longer in active service.[98] What did they
then get from their association with him in this period? An
analysis of the relations between Sarbuland Khan and Burhan-
ul-Mulk and the initial difficulties that the latter faced while
settling Awadh affairs would possibly explain this and other
relevant developments at the Mughal centre.

Before we go into the period of Burhan-ul-Mulk and Safdar
Jang, the following points may also be taken into account. First,
those nobles with whom the Awadhis were associated proved
an effective check on the governor of Awadh. During the reign
of Jahandar Shah, Qilich Muhammad Khan held the *subadari* of
Awadh. Apparently he had accepted the legitimacy of the claim
of the emperor. But he could not prevent Shamsher Khan and
Sanjar Khan and the others from proclaiming the rule of Farrukh Siyar in Awadh while the latter was still far from occupy-
ing the throne.[99] Secondly, if the governor was unable to form an
alliance with the nobles, it would have been extremely difficult
for him to administer the province successfully. The Saiyid
Brothers could manage to remove Chhabele Ram from Awadh
also because they had the support of Mir Musharraf, a powerful
local Afghan. Thirdly, in view of the imperial delay leading to

---

[97] The day when Murtaza Husain was given the rank of 2500 *zat* and the title of
Khan, Samsam-ud-Daulah reportedly invited him to join his 'party'. Murtaza Husain,
however, refused to desert Sarbuland Khan. *Sharaif* p. 269.

[98] Cf. W. Irvine, *Later Moghuls*, II, pp. 214–15.

[99] Compare *Ijad*, f. 65b; *Ahwal*, f. 53b; Shivdas, f. 11a; Qasim, ff. 52b and 57a;
Mubarak, f. 78a.

the decline in employment opportunities at the centre and the gradual shrinkage of better prospects outside Awadh, the Awadhis could aspire for the highest possible office only in the province itself. Mir Musharraf obviously aspired for the *subadari* while Ruh-ul-Amin Khan contented himself with no less than the deputy governorship. Ruh-ul-Amin's opposition to Burhan-ul-Mulk, as we shall see, owed largely to his failure in securing at least the same position under the new governor in 1722. Fourthly, since the Awadhis had close family ties with the local *zamindars* and the revenue grantees, the latter's resistance to any political or administrative measures that affected the fortunes of the local potentates thus acquired added strength. Again, a number of Awadhis seem to have held their *jagirs* in Awadh which involved obvious difficulties for the internal administration.

From the last years of the seventeenth century, the *subadar* and the *faujdar* had begun to appreciate the fact that without an adequate participation of local elements, administration in the province would be unwieldy. The complaints made by Rad Andaz Khan, the *faujdar* of Baiswara, against the Shaikhzadas suggest the magnitude of the problems that their alienation from administration resulted in. His recommendation for the incorporation of some local people in the administration may be considered against this background. Muzaffar Ali Khan had the wisdom of selecting a local man, Ruh-ul-Amin Khan, as his *naib*. And probably it was in recognition of these difficulties that Aziz Khan Chaghta, an Afghan from Shahabad, was chosen in 1716 as the *subadar* of Awadh. The involvement of one or two individuals, however, represented a partial remedy. Moreover they had relations with the growing Afghan powers—the Rohillas and the Bangash—in the neighbourhood as well which further complicated the problem.

Burhan-ul-Mulk's rise to 7000/7000 and the *subadari* of Awadh owed much to the help he had given to Muhammad Amin Khan and the emperor in their bid to dislodge the Saiyids from power. He had been associated with the opponents of the Saiyids. The Shaikhzadas of Lucknow[100] who had mostly sup-

---

[100] Cf. A. L. Srivastava, *First Two Nawabs*, pp. 32–3, for the early history of the Shaikhzadas and their resistance to Burhan-ul-Mulk.

ported, and been encouraged by, the Saiyids thus logically resisted his *subadari* in Awadh. Besides, he was still an ally of the enemies of their patrons and was of course, an outsider. Burhan-ul-Mulk had probably anticipated this challenge. He was also aware of the fact that the strength of the Lucknow Shaikhzadas lay more in their relations in the *qasbas* around Lucknow than in their links within the town of Lucknow. To meet the threat of the Shaikhzadas of Lucknow, he is reported to have sought the support of the Shaikhzadas of Kakori and thus tried to alienate them from their relations in the country around.[101]

Significantly the petition of the *qazi* of Bilgram who represented the interests of the *madad-i ma'ash* holders and the manoeuvrings of Ruh-ul-Amin who embodied the ambition of the Shaikhzadas coincided at the imperial court. Muhammad Khan Bangash who was never seen by Burhan-ul-Mulk as a friend was approached by both parties to recommend their case to the emperor. Again, there was every likelihood that Burhan-ul-Mulk's rivals at the centre would exploit the local potentates to their own advantage. Under the circumstances, he could not afford to alienate them. An effort to conciliate these elements and encourage them to join the provincial service thus marked the beginning of a new pattern of administration in Awadh.

The provincial army was subsequently reinforced by a number of contingents composed of the local people under the command of the Shaikhzadas.[102] Our sources also record a number of local Shaikhzadas holding different administrative

---

[101] According to Qazi Khadim Hasan Alavi, the author of the *Tarikh-i Kakori* the Shaikhzadas of Lucknow and the Afghans of the twelve villages posed a serious threat to Burhan-ul-Mulk. Accordingly to meet their challenge, he camped first at Kakori, summoned the elders of the town and earnestly sought their help for his plan to subdue the disturbers. Thus was founded the government of the Nawabs of Awadh in which the '*shurafa* of Kakori were far ahead of the others' in so far as the titles, honours and offices were concerned, p. 8.

[102] In 1730 Burhan-ul-Mulk sent Mir Muhammad Salah Khan, along with one Saiyid Munawwar Ali Tirmizi of Bilgram to see if he could get any recruits for his army. Subsequently over 200 *sawars* and 1000 *piyadas* joined the provincial armed forces under the leadership of one Mir Saiyid Muhammad Roshan. Mir Nur-ul-Hasan Khan and Mir Azim-ud-Din Khan followed them with a large contingent of their kinsmen (*biradari*). In 1732 a large number of the Shaikhzadas from the contingent of Sarbuland Khan joined the army of Burhan-ul-Mulk. After that Burhan-ul-Mulk's reliance on the

assignments in the province.[103] Burhan-ul-Mulk's effort also expressed itself sometimes through the personal friendship bet-ween the Shaikhzadas and the family of the governor.[104]

It was in the context of the absorption of the Shaikhzadas in provincial government that an armed resistance by a Shaikh *zamindar* in Amethi, in the wake of the disturbances that fol-lowed the invasion of Nadir Shah, was characterized by a chronicler as a disgraceful act of ingratitude.[105] To the chroni-cler, the Shaikh *zamindar*'s insubordination especially in the circumstances when the other *zamindars* took to revolt did not augur well for the changed atmosphere of mutual trust and friendship between the Shaikhzadas and Burhan-ul-Mulk.

Burhan-ul-Mulk's successor, Safdar Jang keenly followed and further advanced these measures during his regime. In-deed, under Burhan-ul-Mulk, the policy of compromise and conciliation with the local people seems to have been taken largely under Safdar Jang's initiative. The restoration of the *madad-i ma'ash* and the task of inviting and persuading the Shaikhzadas to join the army and the administration of the province were undertaken by Safdar Jang.[106] Safdar Jang also

---

Shaikhzadas of Bilgram and for that matter on all the Shaikhzadas of Awadh seems to have grown stronger. Compare Saiyid Ibn Hasan Bilgrami, *Burhan-i Awadh*, MS, Maluna Azad Library, Aligarh, p. 36; Qudratullah, *Jam-i Jahan Nama*. II, Rampur MS, p. 61; *Sharaif*, pp. 263–4, 268 and 274.

[103] A document dated 7 Zi Hijja, 1150/17 November 1733, mentions Shaikh Muham-mad Jamal as the deputy *faujdar* and in charge-in-full (*mukhtar-i kar*) of *pargana Haveli* Bahraich. Mir Haider, presumably an inhabitant of Sandila, held the *faujdari* of the *pargana* of Sandila in the 18th R. Y. of Muhammad Shah/1736–7. Shaikh Muhammad Akabir, an Abbasi Shaikh of Kakori who had earlier served under Daya Bahadur is said to have been ordered by Burhan-ul-Mulk to accompany Mir Rustam Ali Khan, the *nazim* of the *sarkars* of Jaunpur, Chunar, Ghazipur and Benaras. Later, he secured the *faujdari* of Ghazipur from the nawab. Compare Allahabad 1002, 1009 and 1203; Alavi, *Mashahir-i Kakori*, p. 341.

Daya Bahadur was a son of Raja Chhabele Ram and held the office of the *subadari* of Malwa in the reign of Muhammad Shah. For details see W. Irvine, *Later Moghuls*, II, pp. 247–8; Raghubir Sinh, *Malwa in Transition*, Bombay, 1936, pp. 153, 157, 163–4, 189, 194, 200, 202, 204–5 and 206.

[104] Shaikh Ghulam Mina of Kakori for example who died prematurely is said to have been a close friend of Sher Jang, the nephew of Burhan-ul-Mulk. Alavi, *Mashahir-i Kakori*, p. 308.

[105] *Ausaf*, f. 29b.   [106] *Sharaif*, p. 274.

used to regularly visit different *qasbas* to meet the important Shaikhzada families of the province.[107]

The fortunes of an important section of the local magnates were thus gradually tied up with the new *subadari* in Awadh. A large number of the local people formed a substantial part of the army of Burhan-ul-Mulk in 1739. Over a hundred persons from Bilgram alone died fighting for him in the battle of Karnal.[108] In 1751 when Bangash Afghans occupied Lucknow, Shaikh Mu'izz-ud-Din organized the Shaikhzadas and forced the Afghans to vacate the town.[109] Around Lucknow in the *qasbas* also the Shaikhzadas reportedly defended the *nawabi* rule against the Afghan invaders.[110] According to Ghulam Ali Azad Bilgrami, in this historic defence of Awadh against the Afghan inroads 'scores of the noble-born (*shurafa-o-nujaba*) of the province specially the Saiyids and the Shaikhs of Bilgram laid their lives'.[111] After their victory over the Bangash, the Shaikhzadas sent a letter (*arzdasht*) to Safdar Jang expressing their loyalty and dedication to the nawab. The nawab's letter in reply to their *arzdasht* significantly reveals how they had been accommodated in the new provincial administration. Safdar Jang expected much more than this from the Shaikhzadas, for he, as

---

[107] Hakim Abdullah of Kakori who had accompanied Burhan-ul-Mulk to Awadh is reported to have been frequently visited by Safdar Jang. Safdar Jang was in close contact with Qazi Muhammad Wa'iz, the hereditary *qazi* of Kakori. All the three sons of the *qazi* are said to have been in the service of the nawab. One of his sons, Abul-Barakat Khan held the office of *mir bakshi* in the *sarkar* of Safdar Jang. Zain Khan, a local Afghan, is stated to have once served as the deputy of Safdar Jang. Compare Alavi, *Mashahir-i-Kakori*, p. 263; M. H. Abbasi, *Abbasiyan-i Kakori*, pp. 9 and 15; Allahabad 1323.

[108] *Sharaif*, p. 242.

[109] *Siyar*, III, p. 880; *Imad*, pp. 50–1; Qasim Ali Hamdani, *Tarikh-i Shahiya Nishapuriya*, Rampur MS., pp. 34–5; also see *Sharaif*, pp. 250 and 254. Muhammad Imam Khan and Hidayatullah Khan, respectively the *ta'alluqadars* of Balehra were among those Shaikhzadas in the neighbourhood of Lucknow who cooperated gallantly with Shaikh Mu'iz ud-Din. Darogha Hafiz Abbas Ali Khan, *Ta'alluqadaran-i Awadh*, pp. 9–10 and 17. According to the author of *Yadgar-i Bahaduri*, the Shaikhzadas chasing the Afghans came up to Phaphamau. Bahadur Singh Bhatnagar, *Yadgar-i Bahaduri*, U. P. State Archives, Allahabad MS., f. 475.

[110] Compare Alavi, *Mashahir-i Kakori*, p. 95 for Shaikh Sanaullah's effort to defend, and keep the order in, Kakori on receiving the news of the death of Raja Nawal Rai.

[111] *Khizana-i Amira*, p. 80. See also *Jam-i Jahan Numa*, II, p. 60.

he wrote back, always considered them much more than his 'mere servants and *raiyat*'.[112]

The Awadh people took maximum advantage of the stable imperial political order as long as there remained the possibility of making a bigger fortune outside the home territory. With the weakening of central authority, the chances of moving up in the imperial services gradually diminished. Some of them, notwithstanding their existing imperial services, accepted the provincial services with alacrity while some others preferred to remain jobless despite offers outside the province. Still others expressly sought to obtain offices or at least to regain their hereditary family position in their hometowns.[113] In this context is to be seen the fact that in 1732 a large number of the Shaikhzadas from the contingent of Sarbuland Khan joined the army of Burhan-ul-Mulk.[114] This obviously indicates a trend.

The resentment and the resistance that the Shaikhzadas showed over the occupation of Lucknow by the Bangash Afghans in 1751 and the tendency among the local people to refrain from taking service outside Awadh, along with a desire to obtain office within the province can be safely construed as stages of the development of a definite attitude towards the new regime in the province. This attitude found much more ruthless expression in their continued support and battle for the reestablishment of the rule of Safdar Jang in Awadh even after the emperor in Delhi had ordered the confiscation of his properties (*khana-o-amwal*) following the nawab's defeat at the hands of the Afghans.[115] This implied a blatant defiance of the imperial

---

[112] *Tarikh-i Shahiya Nishapuriya*, pp. 34–5.

[113] Shaikh Muhammad Salih who is reported to have been proposed by Muhammad Shah for the office of the *sadr* of the *subas* of Bengal and Orissa refused to accept it. Distance and a desire to regain the hereditary family administrative office within his hometown are given as the reasons for his refusal. In 1730 Khubullah of Kakori was offered a number of offices in the empire, e.g., the office of the *qazi* of Patna, the *amin* of Moradabad, the *sadr* of Bareilly and the *faujdari* of Sirhind. Khubullah, however, preferred to stay in Lucknow without any office. Around 1748, one Maulana Hamid-ud-Din of Kakori who had fought with Safdar Jang against Abdali is said to have been offered a job in Ambala in the Punjab. The Maulana declined to accept it and wanted to go back to his hometown. Alavi, *Mashahir-i Kakori*, pp. 139, 153–4 and 352. A few of them, however, went to the Deccan towards the mid-eighteenth century due to their personal association with Nizam-ul-Mulk. Compare *Sharaif*, pp. 232, 244, 248 and 270.

[114] *Sharaif*, pp. 263–4.

[115] Compare *Yadgar-i Bahaduri*, f. 475b. For some details and the background of the

directive by a powerful section of the ruling class in the *suba*. It also showed their active appreciation of the prevalent social and political conditions which had resulted in the new *subadari* in Awadh.

In the prevailing political circumstances, they had no other alternative. The Marathas had exposed the vulnerability of the Mughal might. They had inundated almost all the major provinces of the empire. The threat to the Shaikhzadas which the Maratha occupation of Awadh posed can be conjectured from the following passage of the *Khizana-i Amira* where Azad Bilgrami assessed the consequences of the Maratha dominance in the Deccan:

> During this short period of ten years when the Marathas had their government over the land between the two seas so much distress befell the Muslims of that area that even if the water of the Ganga and the Yamuna is used as the ink it cannot exhaust the details. The *madad-i ma'ash* lands and the villages of the Saiyids, the Shaikhs and the *ulama* which had been granted to them by the Kings of Islam and upon which sustained their economy were in a moment all confiscated. They were reduced to beggary. Even that was not available to them, for to give alms to the Muslim beggars is a sinful act in the religion of the Brahmans. On account of starvation in which to eat the dead body is permissible, if any one of them wants to take to employment to fill up his stomach, that too is difficult under the regime of the Brahmans. For, besides the people of their own stock the Brahmans do not employ anyone else. The Muslims are particularly discriminated against. If supposedly they are employed they are kept as mere soldiers and in wretched condition. That they would invest the Muslims with any authority, is impossible.[116]

Azad's observation is exaggerated, prejudiced and obviously subjective. This much is, however, beyond any controversy that the statement represented at least the fear of a particular section of the Mughal ruling class in north India. Burhan-ul-Mulk saved Awadh from the Marathas. His diplomatic manoeuvring and even occasional display of force kept the Marathas away from the province. This was not all, Burhan-ul-Mulk's achievements in restoring political stability and order were by no

---

Bangash's clash with Safdar Jang and the subsequent imperial order for the confiscation of Safdar Jang's properties, see, A. L. Srivastava, *First Two Nawabs*, Chapters XIII-XV, pp. 137–87.

[116] *Khizana-i Amira*, p. 96.

means meagre. He chastised and contained the turbulent *zamindars*; effected new arrangements with them and converted a number of them into pillars of the new provincial administration. All this implied for the Shaikhzadas the security of their honour and property.

We do not have any evidence for the presence of Awadhi Hindus in the Mughal imperial service in the early years of the eighteenth century. Small or moderate *mansabs* for one or two local Hindu chiefs cannot be ruled out. Apart from these few, the Shaikhzadas and the Afghans seem to have been the only Awadhis in the employment of the empire. A number of Hindus, however, were in the army and the administration of Burhan-ul-Mulk. Most of them must have been local people and the incorporation of these Hindus in the provincial administration must have been actuated by the same motives that governed the inclusion of other local elements. Unfortunately on the basis of the evidence at our disposal we cannot ascertain, with the sole exceptions of Saroman Das and Tika Ram, the family or the house of the Hindu officials.

Rai Saroman Das, probably a *qanungo*, had begun to rise since the time of Farrukh Siyar. We have seen how he had gradually increased his landholdings. Sandi, a *qasba* in the *sarkar* of Khairabad is mentioned as his hometown. By the time Burhan-ul-Mulk assumed the charge of Awadh, Saroman Das had risen to considerable power and eminence. What exact office he held under Burhan-ul-Mulk is not known. But two documents dated 17 Shawwal 1141/5 May 1729 and 22 Shawwal 1144/7 April 1732, from the Allahabad Archives record one Mir Muhammad Taqi, a *mansabdar*, as his agent. The documents show the Mir as acting on behalf of Saroman Das in two cases of purchase of land.[117] That a *mansabdar* was accredited by Saroman to deputize for him indicates his status in the hierarchy of Mughal service. For, in the normal circumstances no other than a Mughal noble could have directed a *mansabdar* to act, even temporarily, as his deputy. Again the way in which Saroman is mentioned in the documents speaks of his status in the Mughal official heirarchy.

Tika Ram was initially a *qanungo*. A sale document dated 4

---

[117] Allahabad 4 and 5.

Safar 1144/23 July 1731, relating to Sandila contains his signature and seal as Tika Ram Qanungo. A *mahzar* document which bears the names of twenty respectable persons of Sandila, of whom ten were *chaudhuris* and ten *qanungos*, also includes Tika Ram among the latter.[118] His name occurs in the context of a dispute over a *madad-i ma'ash* orchard in Sandila.[119] Two more names of Hindu officials—Diwan Nawal Singh as the *faujdar* of Malihabad and Lala Parsottam Rai—are also mentioned in this document. The case of Tika Ram is probably an example to indicate the class from which Hindu officials largely originated.

We can obtain an idea of the position and the nature of the powers Hindu officials exercised in Awadh in the period from the context in which their names occur in our sources. It is not known if they were local Hindus. This may however be noted that a Hindu official, even if he was not strictly a local man, had some link with local Hindu *zamindars* and *qanungos*.

Name	Context	Source
Ballabh Ram	Led an expedition against the *zamindars* of *sarkar* Khairabad in July 1723. Was directed to resolve a dispute between the *qazi* and the *muhtasib* over the claims to road-toll (*chungi*) on 29 July, 1731.	*Akhbarat-i Muhammad Shah*, pp. 19–20; Allahabad 1321.
Mehta Ram Singh	A land-dispute case in *pargana* Sidhora was referred to him.	Allahabad 1562.
Gulab Rai	Mentioned in a *parwana* of Burhan-ul-Mulk with complimentary addresses (*izzat-o-ikhlas dargah*). Was directed to release to Shaikh Muhammad Sa'id, a revenue grantee, the village Shyampur Nandona in *sarkar* Bahraich.	Muhammad Raza Ansari *Bani-e Dars-i Nizami*, p. 178.
Rai Fateh Chand	Friend of Safdar Jang. Deputed to explain to Sarbuland Khan, the governor of Allahabad, in 1732 the conditions of the *khalisa mahals* in *sarkar* Jaunpur which had been handed over to the charge of the governor of Awadh.	*Maktubat*, p. 69.

[118] Ibid., 488 and 1018.   [119] Ibid., 505.

Name	Context	Source
Hari Chand Rai	His name occurs in the context of the *jagir* of Isma'il Khan, the *naib* of Bahraich. Probably held the office of the *diwan* in Bahraich.	Allahabad 1322.
Pratap Rai	Took three letters to the Maharana of Gahadwala from Safdar Jang giving details of the expedition to Patna and about the Marathas.	
Raghunath Singh	Directed to release the *madad-i ma'ash* village in *tappa* Kedar to one Shaikh Ruh-ul-Amin.	Ibid., pp. 182–3.
Bhaiya Madan Mohan	Mentioned as *faujdar* of Bahraich under Burhan-ul-Mulk.	Ibid., p. 216.

We do not know whether these names included or were in addition to those Khatris and Kayasthas who enjoyed benefits from the patronage of Diwan Atma Ram and Maharaja Nawal Rai. Atma Ram was a Punjabi Khatri and had been associated with Burhan-ul-Mulk since the days of his governorship of Agra. He was eventually made the *diwan* of Awadh. He had three sons, Har Narain, Ram Narain and Pratap Narain. All three of them held important offices. Har Narain was Burhan-ul-Mulk's *vakil* at the court of Delhi. According to the author of the *Tarikh-i Farh Bakhsh,* Atma Ram's sons laid out a long bazaar with rows of shops outside the enclosure in the town of Faizabad which Burhan-ul-Mulk had laid out and Safdar Jang had expanded.[120] Lachhmi Narain, Shiv Narain and Jagat Narain, the three sons of Har Narain also held important posts under Burhan-ul-Mulk and Safdar Jang. Lachhmi Narain was their *vakil* at Delhi. The family of Atma Ram retained an eminent position throughout the eighteenth century.[121]

Nawal Rai's story is well known. In the 1740s it was he who virtually ruled Awadh. How many of his family members and associates gained eminence under Safdar Jang is not known. He is, however, accredited by a Kayastha chronicler of the early-

[120] Compare W. Hoey, *Memories of Delhi and Faizabad,* II, p. 3.

[121] A. L. Srivastava, *First Two Nawabs,* pp. 79–80, 89, 98, 101, 169, 224 and 232. From the account of the *Sharaif* Atma Ram appears to have hailed from Allahabad. He was initially encouraged and patronized by Ruh-ul-Amin Khan when the latter was in service of Sipahdar Khan in Allahabad. Cf. *Sharaif,* p. 233.

nineteenth century as 'the promoter and supporter of his community (*biradari*) and friends ... who elevated his associates to high position'.[122]

Although Burhan ul-Mulk and Safdar Jang, the new *subadars* of Awadh, retained almost the entire machinery of Mughal administration, the institution of the *faujdari* and the working of the *jagir* system seem to have, however, undergone certain modifications. Burhan-ul-Mulk took over to himself the duty of the agents of the *jagirdars*. Owing to the mounting pressure of *jagirs*, Burhan-ul-Mulk could not, as did Murshid Quli Khan in Bengal, cut the size of the *jagir* lands, but Safdar Jang succeeded in reducing to the minimum the outside interference in the provincial administration by allowing only his relations and close associates to have big *jagirs* in Awadh. Thus, they managed to introduce certain changes in the working of the *jagir* system in the province which established their fuller control over the *jagir* administration and also enabled them to extend their patronage to the local people. The office of the *faujdar* continued till about the end of our period. The stature of the *faujdar* was, however, steadily diminishing and the size of a *faujdari* area was almost invariably limited to a *pargana* while the *faujdars* of *sarkars*, *chaklas* or a group of *parganas* began to give place to *naibs* or *nazims* whose power included executive, military and fiscal matters. The decay of the institution of *faujdari* may possibly be partly explained in terms of the development of *ijara* with some *zamindars* and government officials. In this *ijara* arrangement which has also been termed as *hukumat* and *nizamat* in our sources, the *ijaradar* had some administrative authority over the territory of his contract. With the spread of such *ijaras* among other *zamindars* and government officials, the importance of *faujdari* correspondingly decayed.

In the context of Burhan-ul-Mulk and Safdar Jang's relations with the *zamindars* it may be noted that it was not a policy of creating and encouraging new *zamindaris* in the clan strongholds of the old *zamindars* that paid richer dividends but favours and privileges to the latter. This had a precedent in the history of the Great Mughals. The Mughals had tried to reduce their conflict with some powerful *zamindars* through a show of

---

[122] *Yadgar-i Bahaduri*, f. 475a.

favours and the policy of absorbing them in the state service
while some others were cowed down through a forceful demonstration of military might. They insisted on their suzerain
authority over all kinds of local potentates and saw to it that the
latter paid the revenue regularly in the form of either *peshkash* or
mal collected from the lower categories of *zamindars* and the
ri'aya. In a measure, however, the new *subadars'* arrangement
with the *zamindars* was different. Some powerful intermediaries
seem to have been engaged to pay a fixed annual revenue for the
territories under their jurisdiction, and their *ta'ahhud* vested
them with some kind of military and administrative power as
well. The rise of some of the rich *ta'alluqadaris* in the eighteenth
century can possibly be explained against this background.

Burhan-ul-Mulk's initial attempt to tackle the problems of
the *madad-i ma'ash* with a heavy hand had a rationale. As we
have seen in Chapter III, many *madad-i ma'ash* holders had
theoretically forfeited their claims to revenue-free grants. Soon,
however, he realized the strength of the *madad-i ma'ash* holders
in Awadh. The *madad-i ma'ash* grantees together with the town-
based Shaikhzadas, quite a large number of whom were socially
associated with them, formed a considerable local force in the
province. Burhan-ul-Mulk's experience with the Shaikhzadas
of Lucknow immediately after his arrival in Awadh must have
convinced him of the strength or weakness their support or
opposition to the provincial government implied. He, therefore,
had to modify his earlier measure, and simultaneously initiated
a policy of encouraging the absorption of the local elements in
the provincial administration.

Towards the middle of the eighteenth century, Awadh witnessed the rise and growth of the new *subadari* or a 'successor
state' on firm grounds largely owing to the nature of the problems of administration. The problems in Awadh emanated from
the movements and uprisings of the regional and *quasi*-regional
magnates to have at least a share in political power. Burhan-ul-
Mulk seems to have understood this; he planned to take over
the leadership of these movements by making use of their
weaknesses. At the beginning of his governorship, he seems to
have appreciated the prospects of a stable and virtually independent regional rule in the province, provided he could coordinate his ambitions with the interests of those who were resisting

the imperial authority. It is not without significance that he rushed back to Awadh from Delhi in 1726 in face of a standing imperial order of his posting in Malwa.[123]

The developments outside Awadh all over the empire in the eighteenth century also helped Burhan-ul-Mulk and Safdar Jang to establish their own rule in the province. Decline of job prospects in the empire forced the local communities in imperial service to look for their fortunes in and around their hometowns. They joined the nawab's army and administration as they calculated that by doing so they would also strengthen their defence against internal and external threats. The Shaikh-zadas, the Afghans and certain sections of the Hindus can be said to have formed a very loosely organized regional ruling group in Awadh. But we must not lose sight of the fact that Burhan-ul-Mulk and Safdar Jang were outsiders and that Qazilbash formed a substantial part of the Awadh army in the middle of the eighteenth century.[124]

[123] See Chapter VII.

[124] While regional and local magnates unmistakably struggled for political power, it is difficult to suggest a positive sense of regional solidarity or regional consciousness having existed amongst these Shaikhzadas and Afghans who seem to have manned the lower and middle ranks of the Awadh army and administration. Whether the formation of 'regionally oriented ruling groups' in 'the successor states' was a cause or an effect of the decline of the Mughal empire is open to debate. For some discussion see, Philip C. Calkins, 'Formation of a Regionally-Oriented Ruling Group in Bengal', *Journal of Asian Studies*. XXIX, pp. 799; M. Athar Ali, 'The Passing of Empire: the Mughal Case', *Modern Asian Studies*, Vol. 9, No. 3, 1975, pp. 392–3.

CHAPTER VII

The Imperial Court, the New *Subadars* and the Region

In the earlier chapters we have tried to discuss the decline of imperial authority and the beginnings of changes in the nature of imperial control over the provinces of Awadh and the Punjab, as well as the political, administrative and social circumstances within the provinces which influenced such changes. Developments in the first quarter of the eighteenth century immensely strengthened the position of the governor and gradually led to a total breakdown of the conventional pattern of his relations with the centre as well as with the emerging powers in the region. Whatever the governor did in this period was motivated by a desire to entrench himself further in the province. His relations with the neighbouring powers as well as his attitude towards the Mughal court were both oriented towards the independence which he wanted in matters relating to his province. For, the *suba* was now the *suba-i mulki* (home province) and the *subadari* much more than a mere administrative assignment conferred by the emperor. The governorship was practically self-earned and permanent (*bil-istiqlal*), tending to become hereditary, even though the governor was theoretically still a Mughal *subadar*.

I AWADH

Burhan-ul-Mulk and politics at the court

Initially Burhan-ul-Mulk, like his predecessors, maintained the existing pattern of relations between the Mughal court and the province. He visited Delhi three times,[1] was associated with a faction and tried to obtain an important office at the court during the first five years of his *subadari*. At the beginning of this phase he was associated with the 'Mughal group' (the

---

[1] Cf. Kamwar, f. 380b, *Mirat-ul-Haqaiq*, ff. 248b, 357a and 413b.

Turanis), as his rise to power derived from his assistance to
Muhammad Amin Khan in the latter's bid to remove the
Saiyids.[2] But after the death of Muhammad Amin Khan, when
his cousin, Nizam-ul-Mulk, the new *wazir*, tried to enforce his
(Nizam-ul-Mulk's) reforms, Burhan-ul-Mulk broke away from
the 'Mughal group'. Nizam-ul-Mulk's scheme of reforms, as we
know, included the reduction of the *jagirs* of the 'new nobles'
and the reinstatement of the *khanazads* and the old and 'deserv-
ing' *mansabdars*. Burhan-ul-Mulk, a non-*khanazad*, therefore,
tried to retain and enhance his position at the court by developing close connections with the 'new nobles', like Roshan-ud-
Daulah, Mu'izz-ud-Daulah, Haidar Quli Khan and their associates.[3]

Soon Burhan-ul-Mulk's success against the *zamindars* in
Awadh gave him a distinct position among the other members
of his faction which he tried to ensure by acquiring the leadership of his group at the court. He tried to influence appointments in other provinces[4] as well as at the centre[5] and en-

---

[2] For details see W. Irvine, *Later Moghuls*, II, pp. 52–62; Satish Chandra, *Parties and Politics*, p. 161; also see Kamwar, ff. 373b, 374a and 374b.

[3] *Mirat-ul-Haqaiq*, ff. 248b and 350b; *Bahar-i Khayal*, Rampur MS., pp. 46–7; Kamwar, f. 381a.

[4] This is illustrated from the case of Sarbuland Khan, the governor of Gujarat. Sarbuland Khan's deputy, Shuja'at Khan, a protege of Haidar Quli Khan, had utterly failed against Nizam-ul-Mulk's man, Hamid Khan and the Marathas in Gujarat. By the beginning of 1725 Qamar-ud-Din Khan who represented the interests of Nizam-ul-Mulk and the 'Mughal group' at the court began to persuade and pressurize the emperor to remove Sarbuland Khan from Gujarat, and appoint instead his own son-in-law, Ghazi-ud-Din Khan, son of Nizam-ul-Mulk. Subsequently, Sarbuland Khan was divested of his *mansab*. This was alarming for Roshan-ud-Daulah and Haidar Quli, for Nizam-ul-Mulk's control over Gujarat meant consolidation of his power as an indepen-dent governor in the Deccan. Burhan-ul-Mulk who had earned much acclaim from the emperor as the governor of Awadh was thus invited to plead the case of Sarbuland Khan. On 15 September 1725, Burhan-ul-Mulk along with Roshan-ud-Daulah and Haidar Quli approached the emperor and requested him to reinstate Sarbuland Khan to his earlier *mansab* so that he might leave for Gujarat to personally lead the campaign against Hamid Khan and the Marathas. Qamar-ud-Din Khan, being the *wazir*, re-sented Burhan-ul-Mulk's intercession. On 13 October 1725, a verbal dispute took place between him and Qamar-ud-Din Khan. Haidar Quli's sudden death and Burhan-ul-Mulk's absence from the court, however, gave the *wazir* an opportunity to secure Gujarat for Ghazi-ud-Din Khan in July 1727. Burhan-ul-Mulk then rushed to the help of his friend and, very soon, on 14 August 1727, this appointment was can-celled in favour of Sarbuland Khan. *Mirat-ul-Haqaiq*, ff. 357b 361a and 441b.

[5] The case of Kazim Beg Khan, son of Haidar Quli Khan following the death of the

deavoured to obtain an important office at the centre.

Burhan-ul-Mulk aspired to secure the office of the *darogha-i topkhana*.[6] By doing so Burhan-ul-Mulk obviously endeavoured to retain his control over developments at the court. This caused an estrangement between him on the one hand and Samsam-ud-Daulah and his brother, Muzaffar Khan, who held the office at the time on the other. Tension between him and Muzaffar Khan continued mounting until it erupted in an open dispute between the two. The dispute which had its roots in court politics was related to Burhan-ul-Mulk's reorganization of *jagir* administration in Awadh. Ultimately at the suggestion of Mir Jumla, it was agreed that Muzaffar Khan would resign from his existing office and take over as *subadar* of Awadh and Burhan-ul-Mulk would replace Girdhar Bahadur as governor of Malwa. Burhan-ul-Mulk apparently accepted the decision and giving an impression of leaving for his new assignment in Malwa, proceeded towards Agra. At Agra, however, he suddenly crossed the Yamuna and set out for Awadh.[7]

Burhan-ul-Mulk's act was one of open defiance of the imperial court. But in the circumstances there was no other course open to him. The emperor's order, especially to the powerful governors, no longer carried weight. Burhan-ul-Mulk had seen how imperial authority had been eroded in the Deccan and Gujarat. Following the defeat and death of Mubariz Khan at Shakar Khera, the emperor had to confirm Nizam-ul-Mulk as the viceroy of the Deccan. Yet Nizam-ul-Mulk showed little deference to the emperor's arrangements in Gujarat. He instigated his cousin, Hamid Khan, to refuse to comply with the imperial order of his dismissal from the governorship of

---

latter in April 1727, is an example. Burhan-ul-Mulk initially wanted Kazim Beg Khan to inherit the office of the *mir atish* which his father had held. On the other hand, Samsam-ud-Daulah wanted the office for his brother, Muzaffar Khan. Since Burhan-ul-Mulk's suggestion was also opposed by the *wazir* and the *diwan-i khalisa*, Muzaffar Khan succeeded in obtaining the office. Muzaffar Khan also occupied Haidar Quli's mansion, dispossessing the deceased's relations. Compare *Mirat-ul-Haqaiq*, f. 413b; *Bahar-i Khayal*, pp. 46–7; *T. Muhammadi*, p. 62.

[6] *Ausaf*, ff. 41b–42a.

[7] Muzaffar Khan then got the *subadari* of Ajmer and the *faujdari* of Narnaul and Sambhar while Khwaja Sa'd-ud-Din Khan who had replaced him as the *mir atish* was retained in his existing office. *T. Hindi*, ff. 257b–258a.

Gujarat.[8] It was thus very difficult for Burhan-ul-Mulk to pass through Malwa. The governor of the province would not have assured him a safe passage.

Again, the governorship of Malwa in 1727 was not free from hazards. It was very difficult to contain the *zamindars* and the inordinately ambitious Afghans of the province. More than this was the challenge of the Marathas. Though they were officially put forward only in 1717, the claims to the *chauths* of Malwa had been advanced as early as the time of Shivaji. The Maratha raids into Malwa are recorded since 1699 while after 1720 it became a regular feature of the policy of the Peshwa to send an annual detachment to the province. In 1724 the Peshwa himself crossed the Narbada. Further, Nizam-ul-Mulk's involvement in Malwa politics was not a secret to anyone. Within a year after the appointment of Girdhar Bahadur, Nizam-ul-Mulk managed to remove him in favour of his cousin, Azimullah Khan. Though Girdhar Bahadur was reappointed to Malwa in June 1725, Nizam-ul-Mulk was suspected to be secretly encouraging the Maratha raids in Malwa.

It is very likely that Samsam-ud-Daulah by sending Burhan-ul-Mulk to Malwa wanted to bring him into direct conflict with Nizam-ul-Mulk. In such a situation, it was not possible for Burhan-ul-Mulk to accept the Malwa assignment, all the more because he had begun to build his base in Awadh.

Burhan-ul-Mulk had so far attempted to build a strong base at the centre. For about five years the group with which he had allied himself dominated the court. Haidar Quli's death came as a severe blow to his strength. Roshan-ud-Daulah could not cope with the machinations of Samsam-ud-Daulah, the *mir bakshi*. Burhan-ul-Mulk himself was completely out-manoeuvred by the *mir bakshi*. The way he flouted the emperor's order of his transfer to Malwa sealed the prospect of his obtaining any higher office at the centre. He now attempted to firmly and permanently establish himself in Awadh and to convert the province into a personal domain. It will, however, be seen that he could not afford to ignore the claims of the imperial court.

[8] For details see W. Irvine, *Later Moghuls*, II, pp. 144–54, 169–96 and 242.

The new subadar *and the regions around Awadh*

Growth in the regions around Awadh, like developments within the province, also lent strength to the process of the new *subadari*. Eighteenth-century regional powers under the Rohillas (in the Moradabad-Bareilly region), the Bangash (in Farrukhabad) and the local *zamindar* (in the Benaras region) on the north-west, south-west and the south-eastern borders of Awadh indicated the economic stability of the areas in the neighbourhood of the *suba*. Evidence of the availability of considerable sums of money with the *zamindars* and in the villages is significant. In 1714, Madar Singh, a *zamindar* of the Moradabad-Bareilly region paid over Rs 52,000 to his Afghan soldiers out of the cash and valuables he had plundered from the villages in *pargana* Anola in Moradabad.[9] In 1712 when Farrukh Siyar (1712–19) needed money, on his way from Patna to Agra, to avenge the death of his father and contest the throne against Jahandar Shah, he was able to appropriate Rs 100,000 from a Benaras *zamindar* in addition to what he obtained from a *sahukar* in the city.[10]

One indication of the prosperity of these regions was their brisk trade. A very large number of *banjaras* carried items of trade between Bihar and Awadh in the 1730s.[11] Valuables and merchandise of the *banjaras* worth Rs 400,000 were reported to have been among the goods plundered by the *zamindar* of *pargana* Rajpur in Moradabad in 1715.[12] Developments in the Benaras raj region which included a large part of the four eastern *sarkars*, namely, Jaunpur, Ghazipur, Chunar and Benaras of *suba* Allahabad in the late-seventeenth and early-eighteenth centuries are to be particularly noted in this connection. At least three large market centres for local products, namely Azamgarh, Bhadohi and Mirzapur, came into existence and occupied an important place in the region during this period.[13]

[9] *Akhbarat* FS, 3rd R. Y., II, p. 78.

[10] Saiyid Mazhar Husain Korwi, *Tarikh-i Benaras*, p. 56.

[11] Karam Ali, *Muzaffarnama*, Patna MS., ff. 11b and 25b–26a.

[12] *Akhbarat*, FS, 4th R. Y., I, p. 24.

[13] Information about Azamgarh in the following four paragraphs is based on the manuscript copies of a local history of the family of the Rajas of Azamgarh. This history was originally written by one Girdhari, a member of the local Kayastha *qanungo* family, in 1801. Girdhari claims to have drawn on the *qanungo* papers of his ancestors for his

The area under the modern district of Azamgarh which formed part of the Mughal *pargana* of Nizamabad seems to have witnessed a considerable increase in cultivation from the time of Jahangir (1605–26). Jahangir is reported to have awarded *zamindaris* to the Gautam Rajputs of the region. He encouraged them to settle in the area and build habitats and villages for the cultivators. Subsequently a number of Gautam Rajput villages and *zamindari* settlements came up. By the beginning of Aurangzeb's reign (1657–1707), the Gautams of *pargana* Nizamabad were strong enough to command armed contingents, artillery and a large number of elephants and horses. Some time during the last years of the seventeenth century, the chief of the Gautams, Bikramajit Singh, had to become a Muslim to avoid execution at Aurangzeb's order for a conspiracy the chief had hatched to kill his brother, Rudra Singh. Aurangzeb's order followed an appeal from the widow of the deceased. On conversion to Islam, Bikramajit Singh married, as the tradition goes, a Mughal woman in Delhi who bore him two sons, Muhammad Azam Khan and Muhammad Azmat Khan. Subsequently when after the death of Bikramajit, Azam Khan succeeded him as the chief of the Gautams, he founded the town of Azamgarh after his own name while his brother, Azmat Khan founded another town, Azmatgarh.[14]

By 1720, Azamgarh had grown into an important adminis-

---

work. The title of his work is *Intizam-al-Raj* or *Intizam-i Raj-i Azamgarh*, as the cataloguer puts it. But there is little on *intizam* (administration) in the book. It is a straight political and genealogical history in a very involved and highly ornate Persian. The prose is interrupted by poetic interpolations, sometimes from the classical Persian poets and often Girdhari's own compositions. A manuscript copy of the work (No. 238) is preserved in the University Library, Edinburgh.

Later in the second half of the nineteenth century, two other histories of Azamgarh (actually based on Girdhari's work) were compiled. These are in simple, direct Persian prose style. A copy of one of these titled *Sarguzasht-i Rajaha-i Azamgarh* by Saiyid Amir Ali Rizwi is preserved in the Edinburgh University Library (No. 237) while the other titled *Tarikh-i Azamgarh* is in the India Office Library, London (I.O.4038). The author of the I.O. manuscript, is not known. Individual references are from the I.O. manuscript, as the other two MSS of Edinburgh are not foliated. Much of the information contained in these manuscripts is available in the District Gazetteers of Azamgarh. Mr Najmul Raza Rizwi of Allahabad University has also based his brief narrative of the Azamgarh royal family on these manuscripts. Compare *PIHC* 41st Session, Bombay, 1980, pp. 239–44.

[14] *Tarikh-i Azamgarh*, I.O.4038, ff. 14b–17a.

trative centre (*chakla*), next only to Jaunpur in the area. Azam Khan is also reported to have cut out a canal connecting the river Tons with the Kol.[15] In the early decades of the eighteenth century, a number of bazaars and *ganjs* were founded by the successors of Azam Khan and Azmat Khan. At almost the same time when Mahabat Khan, a son of Azmat Khan, revolted against the Mughals, Azmat Khan's other son, Babu Iradat Khan, built a bazaar in Kopaganj. In addition, 'in a number of places Iradat Khan founded a *ganj* after his own name'. All of these *ganjs* survived till the middle of the nineteenth century.[16] Subsequently at least five more *ganjs* and a *zamindari* centre with a fortress were built by the members of these neo-Muslim Rajput *zamindars*. Iradat Khan's son, Jahan Khan built Mehrajganj, Jahanaganj and Shahgarh while his cousins, Babu Sufi Bahadur, Babu Husain Khan and Babu Jahangir Khan founded Sufiganj, Husainganj and Jahangirganj named after themselves.[17]

The growth of Azamgarh into a *chakla* headquarters together with the founding of these *ganjs* or grain markets must have followed a substantial increase in commercialized agriculture and the prosperity of the *zamindars*.

Bhadohi was another important town in the Benaras region which came into prominence in the early-eighteenth century. Around Bhadohi too, successive village settlements began to grow from the time of Jahangir. We have found references to no less than twelve villages having come up in the immediate vicinity of the town from a quick survey of an early-nineteenth century local history. This history, it may be noted, was purportedly written to highlight, and establish the claims to, the powers and properties of just one family of the town.[18] A number of *mohallas* are mentioned as having been settled and inhabited by the immigrants from outside during the seventeenth century. Some members of a *qanungo* of Kara for example, who had earlier migrated to Jaunpur came and settled in Bhadohi in Shahjahan's time. The same years saw the rise of a *mohalla* inhabited by the Faruqi Shaikhs of Mandiaon. Towards the end of Aurangzeb's reign, the Malik family of Rampur came in and

---

[15] Ibid., ff. 15a and 26b.   [16] Ibid., f. 26b.   [1] Ibid., ff. 27.
[18] Qazi Muhammad Sharif of Bhadohin, *Tarikh-i Bhadohin*, I.O., 437.

founded *mohalla Malikana*.[19] At least four important bazaars of the town, namely bazaar Salabat Khan, bazaar Rustam Khan, bazaar Ahmadganj and *Katra* Rusukhiat Khan, were founded during the twenty-five years between 1712 and 1737.[20]

The growth of Mirzapur in the late-seventeenth century with its central position, second only to the city of Benaras, in the economy of the region during the eighteenth and early-nineteenth centuries further shows the wealth of the region. We know very little of the antecedents of the founding of the town. But the little available information does suggest that the hinterland of Mirzapur responded to the demands of regional and perhaps also of long-distance trade. According to the *Tarikh-i-Bhadohin*, one Mirza Abd ul-Baqi Beg was sent to the area some time in the last years of Aurangzeb (when the emperor was in the Deccan) to deal with the refractory *zamindars* of *pargana* Kantit. The Mirza was welcomed by the Omars, a local merchant community and they appear to have assisted him in his campaigns against the *zamindars*. Subsequently, following the emperor's order, the chief of the Omar community, Nand Lal Omar, founded a town on the bank of the Ganga and named it after the Mirza. Soon after, Mirzapur was linked to the trade between the region and beyond through *Mandvi* Phulpur and Benaras. By the time of Muhammad Shah, Mirzapur had grown into a major town with a large *katra* in its centre and at least three *ganjs*, Muzaffarganj, Lalganj and Munnuganj in its vicinity to connect it with its rural hinterland. The town, like the other big towns of the Mughal empire, had a full-fledged *shahna/kotwal* in Muhammad Shah's time.[21] It is very likely that the trade of Mirzapur provided a major incentive for the subsequent clearance of jungles and extension of agriculture around Latifpur and Ahraura under Balwant Singh and Chait Singh, the Rajas of Benaras.[22]

---

[19] Ibid., ff. 9, 11, 14b, 15a, 16b, 17b and 19a.   [20] Ibid., ff. 21b, 26 and 30b.

[21] Ibid., ff. 37b–38. For Lalganj and Munnuganj see Ghulam Ali Khan, *Shah Alam Nama*, edited by Al-Mamun Suhruwardi and Aqa Muhammad Kazim Shirazi, Bib. Ind., Calcutta, 1874, p. 87.

[22] Ghulam Husain Khan, *Zikr-us-Siyar*, ff. 22a, 26b–27a and 31–7. For a comprehensive study of the growth of the towns, grain markets and their links to the agricultural production in the Benaras region in the later half of the eighteenth century see C. A. Bayly, *Rulers, Townsmen and Bazaars* Chs. 2–5. See also K. P. Mishra, *Banaras in Transition, 1738–1795*, New Delhi, 1975, pp. 93–167.

Some general references to the prosperity of the city of Benaras, even though scattered and irritatingly brief, are significant. In 1740, the city of Benaras, according to an eye-witness account, had large numbers of the community of *mahajans*. Two of them, Gopaldas and Gowaldas controlled the bulk of the monetary transactions of the city. Gowaldas was very rich and since he had financed Mir Rustam Ali Khan whom Mansa Ram, the founder of the Benaras raj, had replaced as the chief *mustajir* of the region, he lost his position under Balwant Singh to Gopaldas. Subsequently, he allegedly involved himself in a plot to assasinate the raja, was captured and released only when he agreed to pay to the raja a sum of Rs 5,00,000. Initially Balwant Singh demanded Rs 10,00,000 and it was on Gopaldas's intercession that the amount was reduced to Rs 5,00,000 which Gowaldas paid within a week's time. Gopaldas is mentioned as the sole financer of the Benaras raj. At his accession to the raj, Balwant paid at least Rs 24,00,000 annually to the Nawab of Awadh while towards the end of his time the revenues of Benaras had certainly gone up to over Rs 50,00,000. By the middle of the eighteenth century (1752–3), Benaras city was noted in particular for its wealth and money (*anqusht numa ba farawani-e zar*).[23]

The prosperity of the city of Benaras certainly owed a great deal to its leading position as an entrepot for the medium level and long-distance trade. The geographical location of Benaras in the intra- and inter-region trade also encouraged local industries which in turn further enriched the city. The extent of the percolation of city wealth to the countryside in our period is a matter of conjecture, but we have ample evidence of this for the later period.[24] It is, however, interesting to note that in a period of ten years in the middle of Muhammad Shah's reign, 1731–41, the revenues from the *khalisa* from *pargana Haveli* Benaras rose from Rs 42,248/7½ in 1731 and Rs 49,246/7½ in 1737 to Rs 75,000 in 1741. What is significant is the fact that in

---

[23] *Zikr-us-Siyar*, ff. 65b, 70b and 71a. The descendants of Gopaldas and Gowaldas survived to continue as leading *mahajans* of Benaras in the late-eighteenth century. C. A. Bayly, 'Indian Merchants in Traditional Setting, 1780–1830', in Clive Dewey and A. G. Hopkins, *The Imperial Impact : Studies in the Economic History of Africa and India*, London, 1978, pp. 171–93; K. P. Mishra, *Banaras in Transition*, pp. 172–4.

[24] C. A. Bayly, *Rulers, Townsmen and Bazaars*, Chapter 2.

nine out of these ten years the actual collections were 100 per
cent of the *jama* and that the reasons for shortfall in 1740 were
purely administrative.[25] The rise in state demand indicated an
upward trend in production. It also had a bearing on the
prosperity of the intermediaries, specially when we have evidence to show that the amount paid to the treasury during this
period was sometimes much less than what they actually collected from the assessees. According to Ghulam Husain
Kamboh, in the late 1720s and early 1730s, Mansa Ram, as an
ijaradar of the *parganas* which later formed the core of the
Benaras raj, paid only Rs 5,00,000 while his actual collection
was no less than Rs 20,00,000.[26] This gap probably explains
how within a decade, Mansa Ram so easily built up enough
power to displace his Mughal patron. When the region came
under the control of Burhan-ul-Mulk, he demanded and obtained Rs 13,00,000 for the same *parganas* while his successor,
Safdar Jang insisted on a still higher sum from Mansa Ram's
son, Raja Balwant Singh.[27] Far from being an index of the actual
state of production the rise and fall in the revenues in a number
of cases probably simply showed the strength or weakness of the
collector. With the change of the collector or the terms dictating
his position, there was sometimes a very substantial rise in the
revenues.[28]

Agriculture in the regions around Awadh registered a
marked development in the course of the seventeenth and early
eighteenth centuries. This is illustrated from a comparison of
the available revenue figures of the early and mid-eighteenth
century with those of the late sixteenth century as recorded by
Abul Fazl in the *Ain*. The rise in *jama* since the time of the *Ain*
(1695) was spectacular. While in Awadh, as we have noted
earlier in Chapter III, the *jama* rose by over 85 per cent, in the
Benaras region it rose by over 107 per cent and in *sarkar* Kora on
the southern borders of Awadh the rise was by over 134 per
cent. In the Rohilla country in the Moradabad-Bareilly region

[25] I.O., 4491   [26] Kamboh, f. 45a.

[27] *Tuhfa*, ff. 10a–11b; Kamboh, f. 65b.

[28] I.O., 4491 for increase from 49,246/7½ in 1146 *Fasli* to Rs 75,000 in 1147 with a
change from the *amili* of one Abd-ur-Rahim to the *ta'ahhud* of one Mir Abdullah. It may
be noted that Abd-ur-Rahim collected (or submitted from his collections) only Rs
17,000 in 1146 *Fasli*.

the rise according to our figures was almost incredible, over 247 per cent.[29]

Region	Jama in dams in the Ain	Jama in dams in the early and mid-18th century	
Awadh	20,17,58,172	37,46,74,559 (rose by 17,29,16,387)	c. 1755
Benaras	8,45,05,384	17,51,27,980 (rose by 9,06,22,596)	
Sarkar Kora	1,73,97,567	4,07,92,385 (rose by 2,33,94,818)	c. 1720
Moradabad-Bareilly	10,17,58,494	35,35,07,068 (rose by 25,17,48,574)	c. 1750

The rise in *jama* had a bearing on the increase in agricultural production. The *hasil* figures, whether taken as representing actual yields or as the revenues collected by the state officials, also show that the *jama* figures bore a relationship to the actual production and the paying capacity of the assessees. The *hasil* in Awadh was 63 per cent of the *jama*; while in Benaras, *sarkar* Kora and Moradabad-Bareilly the *hasil* figures ranged between 84 per cent to 87 per cent of the assessed revenues. Over a number of years in Aurangzeb's reign, even in Awadh in most of the *mahals*, the *hasil* approximated the *jama* figures, while in

[29] For *Ain's* figures see Ibid., Vol. II (Jarrett), pp. 173–6, 184 and 293–6. For eighteenth-century figures compare I.O., 4485, 4487 and 4489. The break up of the figures for the Moradabad-Bareilly and Benaras regions in our sources are as follows:

Region	Jama in dams in the Ain	Jama in dams in the early and mid-18th century
Sarkar Sambhal	6,69,41,431	21,16,82,068
„ Badaon	3,48,17,063	14,18,25,000
„ Jaunpur	5,63,94,107	9,27,02,303
„ Ghazipur	1,34,31,308	3,42,30,204
„ Chunar	58,10,654	2,88,36,578
” Benaras	88,69,315	1,93,38,895

some *parganas* the former also exceeded the latter.[30]

In this connection some early European observations on the soil conditions of these regions are worth noting. Northern Rohilkhand, the central districts of Awadh around Lucknow and Faizabad and the alluvial tracts along the river Ganga between Chunar and Benaras down towards Buxar were noted by the Europeans in the eighteenth century as among the most fertile and populated parts of the whole subcontinent. The Benaras region was exceptionally rich and had much in common with contemporary Bengal. Cultivation in central and southern Awadh could be resumed without much capital, as the soil was moderately light and fertile and the water table was not so low as to make the cost of irrigation prohibitive. In the Benaras region good natural irrigation was also available for watering the *rabi* crops while parts of the Moradabad-Bareilly region profited splendidly from the spring torrents 'which rushed down into the plains from the foothills of the Himalayas'.[31] It is also significant to note that the European merchants rushed to these regions following the East India Company's victory over the Nawab of Awadh in 1764 at Buxar. The growth of exports from these regions to Bengal was 'spectacular' in response to the 'great expansion' of Calcutta's seaborne trade in the late-eighteenth century.[32]

Thus, among the important steps Burhan-ul-Mulk and his successor, Safdar Jang, took to consolidate their power in Awadh was their policy towards the powerful chieftains and the nobles in control of these regions. These areas were growing

---

[30] I.O., 4489 and 4485. However, the fact that the *hasil* figures in most of the cases included not only the collections of the current year but also the arrears of the past and the repayment of the loans (*taqawi*) should not be overlooked while considering the relationship these figures bore to the assessed revenues.

[31] Compare C. A. Bayly, *Rulers, Townsmen and Bazaars*, Chapter 2.

[32] Compare P. J. Marshall, 'Economic and Political Expansion: The Case of Oudh' *Modern Asian Studies*, 9, 4 (1975), pp. 465–82; Tom G. Kessinger in his article on the northern Indian Economy (1757–1857) also notes expansion of production and trade in the region in response to the stimulus which came from the demand for export goods. Cf. Dharma Kumar and Meghnad Desai (ed.), *The Cambridge Economic History of India*, Vol. 2: *c. 1757–c. 1970*, pp. 242–70. Almost the whole northern Indian region, east of Delhi seems to have responded positively to this stimulus. For some evidence about Aligarh and Etah regions, see S. Nurul Hasan's comments on 'Du Jardin Papers' *The Indian Historical Review*, V, 1–2, July 1978–January 1979.

rich with a higher rate of increase and were in themselves important for the new *subadars* who endeavoured to build a base for themselves in the region independent of the imperial centre. The areas also had close social and economic connections with Awadh, particularly its border districts.

Burhan-ul-Mulk and the governorship of Allahabad

As early as 1715 when the new *subadari* was yet to take shape it was appreciated that to rule Awadh effectively the governor should have some amount of control over the province of Allahabad. This had now become all the more necessary as the new *subadar*, Burhan-ul-Mulk expected little assistance from the centre to govern the province. The fact that Muhammad Khan Bangash held the province of Allahabad[33] was yet another reason for Burhan-ul-Mulk to try to combine the governorship of Awadh and Allahabad. Since Muhammad Khan's homeland lay on the borders of Allahabad province (he hailed from Farrukhabad) and he had a large long-term *jagir* in the area,[34] Burhan-ul-Mulk was apprehensive of his efforts at building a base in Allahabad. Muhammad Khan's links with Awadh through the Afghans of Shahabad also posed a threat to Burhan-ul-Mulk's position.[35] Again, the disaffected elements of Awadh were often encouraged by him to foment trouble against Burhan-ul-Mulk.[36]

Burhan-ul-Mulk thus not only had to remove him from the governorship of Allahabad; he also wanted to weaken him to prevent him from ever challenging his authority in the region. With this in view, Burhan-ul-Mulk did not even hesitate to help the Bundelas who often plundered Muhammad Khan's *jagirs*

---

[33] He held the governorship of Allahabad since November 1720, Cf. Kamwar, f. 376b; Shivdas, f. 58a; *T. Muzaffari*, f. 123b.

[34] Since the reign of Farrukh Siyar, he held eight *parganas* in Bundelkhand in his *jagir*. Cf. Ijad, f. 80b.

[35] Not infrequently Muhammad Khan and Aziz Khan Chaghta of Shahabad visited the court together. Cf. Kamwar, f. 347b; Aziz Khan Chaghta whom we have noticed in Chapter II as governor of Awadh was the son of Bahadur Khan, son of Darya Khan Rohilla and held a rank of 7000/7000 when he died in 1723. *T. Muhammadi*, p. 49.

[36] See Chapter VI, section on the *madad-i ma'ash* holders.

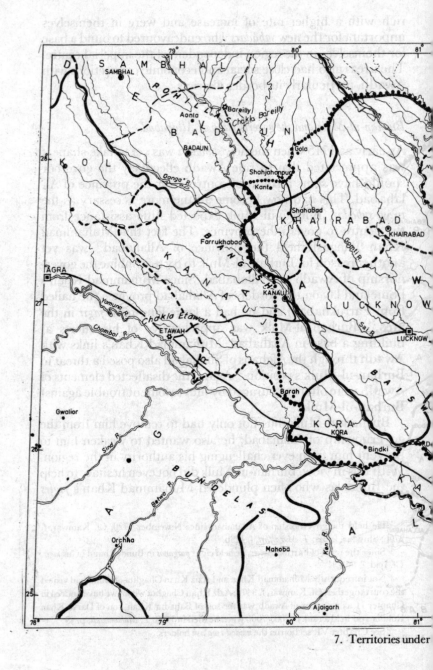

7. Territories under

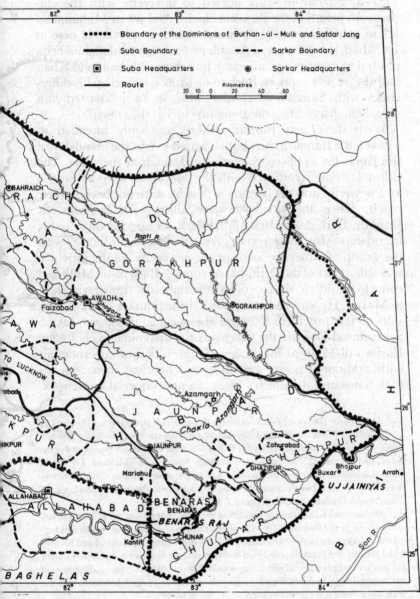

Boundary of the Dominions of Burhan-ul-Mulk and Safdar Jang

Symbol	Description	Symbol	Description
••••••	Boundary of the Dominions of Burhan-ul-Mulk and Safdar Jang		
——	Suba Boundary	– – –	Sarkar Boundary
▣	Suba Headquarters	◉	Sarkar Headquarters
——	Route		

Kilometres
20 10 0   20   40   60

-Mulk and Safdar Jang

and constantly threatened his authority in **Allahabad**.[37] In 1727–8, Burhan-ul-Mulk offered to intercede with the emperor on behalf of the Bundela chief.[38] And when Muhammad Khan sent his son, Qaim Khan to him to plead his case at Faizabad, the governor of Awadh instead of extending him help, plotted to capture and imprison him. Since Muhammad Khan had the *wazir*'s support, Burhan-ul-Mulk patched up his differences with Samsam-ud-Daulah who, in turn, assisted him greatly in discrediting the Bangash chief at the court.[39]

With these acts Burhan-ul-Mulk not only intended to weaken the Bangash chief but also tried to win the friendship of the Bundelas as also of Samsam-ud-Daulah at the court. The Bundelas now in alliance with the Marathas were ambitious and powerful and the borders of Awadh were not beyond their reach. Since the Bundelas were allied with Samsam-ud-Daulah, Burhan-ul-Mulk appreciated the special value of his friendship. Also, the governor of Awadh had to ally himself with the group of either the *wazir* or the *mir bakshi*, as the province was still a part of the Delhi-based empire. Burhan-ul-Mulk had come to Awadh in the face of an imperial order transferring him to Malwa. He thus had to establish the legitimacy of his possession of the province. Between the *wazir* and the *mir bakshi*, Samsam-ud-Daulah, the latter was the unavoidable choice for Burhan-ul-Mulk at this stage. His ambition of governorship with additional power and independence was in agreement with Samsam-ud-Daulah's ideas of a new imperial framework.

[37] As the entire land of the Bundelas except the *sarkar* of Kalpi lay within the territory of Allahabad, Muhammad Khan had to contain Satarsal, the recalcitrant Bundela chief. All the eight *parganas* of his *jagir* in Bundelkhand were under the control of the rebel. In 1724 and 1727 he led two series of expeditions in Bundelkhand. The first of these was inconclusive while the second which would otherwise have ended in victory was foiled by the Maratha support to the Bundelas and also by the hostile acts of Samsam-ud-Daulah. Compare *Khujasta*, f. 18b.

[38] Muhammad Khan wrote to his *vakil* at the court that he was not in favour of any concessions to the Bundelas. For the sake of Burhan-ul-Mulk, however, he was prepared to accept the latter's recommendation for them 'provided Satarsal and his sons Udai Narain and Jagat Raj presented themselves to the emperor and sincerely sought his pardon and gave in writing that they would no more obstruct to the establishment of the imperial *thanas* in their territory ... they should also be content', he added, 'with the *mahals* bestowed upon them by the emperor.' *Khujasta*, 208.

[39] W. Irvine, *Later Moghuls*, II, p. 240.

Further, their common hatred for Muhammad Khan Bangash, though for different reasons, also played its part in bringing them together.[40]

It also seems that Samsam-ud-Daulah had lately begun to exercise considerable influence on provincial matters. It is well known that he had full control over the affairs of Kabul and that the governor of Bengal was his friend. In 1730 under his influence the emperor replaced Sarbuland Khan by Abhai Singh in Gujarat. On the other hand, Samsam-ud-Daulah also had his own axe to grind in his reconciliation with Burhan-ul-Mulk. Samsam-ud-Daulah had a *jagir* in Awadh,[41] and perhaps feared that the governor of Awadh, on the plea of making reforms in *jagir* administration, could withhold the revenues of the *jagir*.

Thus, it was his interest in the province which governed the new *subadar*'s political alignments with the emerging power groups in the region as well as with the central authorities. Subsequently sometime towards the beginning of 1730 or the end of 1729[42] Burhan-ul-Mulk's fourth visit to Delhi marked his re-entry into the arena of court politics.

Soon after, Sarbuland Khan, a friend of Burhan-ul-Mulk, became the governor of Allahabad while Safdar Jang was appointed *faujdar* of four important eastern *sarkars* of the province, namely, Jaunpur, Ghazipur, Chunar and Benaras.[43] Since Muhammad Khan also had interests in the region, he still tried

---

[40] Samsam-ud-Daulah reportedly promised a reward to Satarsal, if he brought the head of the Bangash chief to the emperor. On the other hand the *wazir* was not only a strong supporter of Muhammad Khan, but there was also no love lost between him and Burhan-ul-Mulk's friends. This is illustrated from the stand the *wazir* and Roshan-ud-Daulah took on the occasion of the shoe-sellers riot. Cf. W. Irvine, *Later Moghuls*, II, 257–62.

[41] See Chapter VI, section on *jagir* administration.

[42] We do not know the exact date of Burhan-ul-Mulk's fourth visit to the court. It is, however, certain that he was present at the court in 1730. Early in 1730, the Persian envoy, Ali Mardan Khan Shamuli was received and then introduced at the court by Burhan-ul-Mulk. (Ashub, p. 24). As he was engaged in the encounters against the *zamindar* of Chachendi in the middle of 1729, the beginning of 1730 or the end of 1729 can be safely said to have been the date of Burhan-ul-Mulk's fourth visit to Delhi.

[43] *Tabsira*, f. 89a and *Sharaif*, p. 264. According to Dr A. L. Srivastava these *sarkars* came under Burhan-ul-Mulk around 1728. But unfortunately he cites no evidence for this. Cf. A. L. Srivastava, *First Two Nawabs*, p. 42.

to regain the province. Eventually he obtained the *faujdari* of Kora which was close and to the east of his hometown, Farrukhabad and also provided a base for his operations to defend his *jagirs* towards the south in Bundelkhand. He managed to secure this important western *sarkar* of Allahabad under the pretext of chastising, and securing the revenues of the *jagir* of the *wazir* from, Bhagwant Udaru,[44] a powerful 'recalcitrant' *zamindar*. But the rebel could not be subdued until Burhan-ul-Mulk was given the charge of the *sarkar*.[45]

To promote and strengthen his position as governor of Awadh, Burhan-ul-Mulk extended his authority to a large chunk of Allahabad in a manner which amounted to a virtual seizure of these *sarkars*.[46] A demonstration of military power he believed would be an effective device in preventing his possession or part of it from falling into the hands of others. Later in 1736, Burhan-ul-Mulk on presenting a *peshkash* of Rs 15,00,000 obtained the governorship of Allahabad.[47]

[44] *Sarkar* Kora was in the *jagir* of Qamar-ud-Din Khan. Earlier Jan Nisar Khan whose sister was married to him and had held the *faujdari* of the *sarkar* had been killed in an encounter against Bhagwant. The *wazir*, therefore, had sent his nephew, Azimullah Khan, with a strong army to chastise the rebel. Azimullah had also been made *faujdar* of the *sarkar*. Outnumbered, the frightened Bhagwant had run away and hid himself in the jungle. But Azimullah's success had proved short-lived. For immediately after his return to Delhi, his deputy, Khwajim Beg Khan had been put to death by the rebel. It was at this juncture that Sarbuland Khan was replaced by Muhammad Khan Bangash who had accompanied the *wazir* in the latter's march against Bhagwant. The fortress of the rebel was occupied and preparations were then being made to pursue him into the territory of the Bundelas where he had taken refuge. Before the expedition was undertaken, the *wazir* had to rush back to Delhi to foil a combination against him between Samsam-ud-Daulah, his arch-enemy and Burhan-ul-Mulk. Muhammad Khan was left to settle the matter. For the details of Bhagwant Singh's revolt and the subsequent expeditions see *Siyar*, II, pp. 467–8; *Shakir*, ff. 27; *Ma'dan-us-Sa'adat*, f. 79a; *Ausaf*, f. 20a; A. L. Srivastava, *First Two Nawabs*, pp. 44–6; W. Irvine, *Later Moghuls*, II, p. 277.

[45] *Khujasta*, 283–84; *Aziz-ul-Qulub*, f. 96b; *Siyar*, II, p. 967; *Shakir*, f. 27b; A. L. Srivastava, *First Two Nawabs*, p. 47. It is interesting to note that the deputy of Burhan-ul-Mulk collected 25 to 30 lakhs of rupees from the *sarkar* of Kora. Cf. *Hadiqat*, p. 679. The amount was more than six or seven times higher than the assessed revenue of the *sarkar* in the late-sixteenth century. Compare *Ain*, II (Jarrett), p. 178.

[46] Compare *Khizana-i Amira*, p. 74; *Jam-i Jahan Numa*, II, p. 22. *Tabsira*, ff. 93b–94a. According to *Jam-i Jahan Numa*, Burhan-ul-Mulk conquered these *sarkars*.

[47] *Khujasta*, ff. 18. Earlier in November 1735, Muhammad Khan managed to get the

A crucial factor which led to the control by the governor of Awadh of these *sarkars* and eventually the entire province of Allahabad was the fairly widespread disturbance in the region. The road from Bengal to Delhi which passed through Benaras, Allahabad, Kora Jahanabad, Bindki and Etawah, and was used to carry the Bengal treasury to the capital, for example, had long been disturbed. According to a mid-eighteenth century chronicler of Allahabad, the *zamindars* of the eastern *sarkars* of the province, namely, Jaunpur, Ghazipur, Chunar and Benaras had refused to pay the revenue and taken to plunder and highway robbery. 'Some of the *zamindars*, e.g. Rajputs of *pargana* Keswar in Benaras', he added, 'had acquired so much power and influence that they dislodged the imperial officials in Benaras and had the audacity to think in terms of building up their own independent territory (*wilayat*) in the region'.[48] The chronicler's statement is amply illustrated from a large number of *akhbarat* bearing on the *zamindar* revolts in the region.[49] In the intervening period there were some attempts to make an arrangement with recalcitrant *zamindars*,[50] but to no avail. On the contrary, the disaffected officials who suffered due to the arrangement became a source of trouble to the imperial administration.[51]

Early in Muhammad Shah's reign, a large part of the region comprising of the *sarkars* of Jaunpur, Ghazipur, Chunar and Benaras, was taken over in *ijara* by Mir Rustan Ali Khan. Mir Rustam engaged Mansa Ram to collect the revenue. Later, Mansa Ram founded the Benaras raj.[52]

The antecedents of the revolt of Bhagwant Udaru in *sarkar* Kora can be conjectured. Beyond Kora, the road partly lay in the province of Agra where the Jats successfully challenged Mughal power. As early as 1714, the *waqai'nawis* of *chakla*

---

governorship of Allahabad, but within a few months, on 5 May 1736 Sarbuland Khan was reinstated. Burhan-ul-Mulk replaced Sarbuland Khan.

[48] *Tuhfa* f. 3a.

[49] Compare, for example, *Akhbarat*, BS, 2nd R. Y., p. 77; 3rd R. Y., p. 213; 4th R. Y., p. 120; FS, 3rd R. Y., I, p. 192; II, pp. 4, 22, 23 and 157; 4th R. Y., II, pp. 87, 134, 143, 205 and 227.

[50] *Akhbarat*, FS, 3rd R. Y., II, p. 268.

[51] Ibid., FS, 4th R. Y., II, pp. 91–2, 120 and 130.

[52] *Tuhfa* ff. 4a, 10a–11a, 14a–16a; Kamboh, ff. 5a, 6a, 16b–17a, 215–24a, 54b–57a.

Etawah reported no less than five incidents of *zamindar* revolts in and around the *chakla*. The *ri'aya* of *pargana* Shikohabad were reported to have abandoned cultivation and fled away, while Debi, a refractory *zamindar* would have occupied the fort of Shahabad but for the timely intervention of Raja Gaj Singh. Babar Afghan, a resident of Rashidabad *alias* Sioli who had been given a *sanad* for *khidmat* in the *parganas* of Siohar, Karauli and Patiali was reported to have turned defiant.[53]

Moreover, the road was within striking distance of the Bundelas. Since the early 1730s it was suggested that the route of the Bengal treasury, therefore, should be diverted to the road that passed through Benaras, Chunar and Jaunpur to the territory of Awadh, and thence to Bareilly and Delhi. It was also suggested that the deputy governor should provide sufficient armed contingents to escort the treasury. As this meant greater importance for Awadh and more power and privileges for its governor, Safdar Jang welcomed the suggestion and himself conducted the treasury through the province of Awadh.[54] From that time Mir Rustam Ali Khan, the *ijaradar* of the four *sarkars* of Allahabad, would customarily go to Sahsaram (Bihar) to escort the treasury to Benaras from where Safdar Jang took charge and conducted it to the north-west borders of Awadh.[55] It was also possibly in appreciation of this assistance that initially some *sarkars* and later the whole of Allahabad province was allowed by the centre to pass into the charge of Burhan-ul-Mulk.

Burhan-ul-Mulk and Chandela chief

The area adjacent to the southern borders of Awadh in *sarkar*

[53] *Akhbarat*, FS, 2nd R. Y., II, pp. 61–2.

[54] Murid Khan, the noble in charge of conducting the treasury, is reported to have written to Burhan-ul-Mulk's deputy, Safdar Jang 'due to its uncertainty and insecurity it is better and safer to abandon the imperial highway (*shahrah*) in favour of the road of *suba* Awadh.' *Maktubat*, pp. 15 and 26.

[55] Compare *Maktubat*, p. 8 Safdar Jang's *arzdasht* to the emperor in response to a *farman* and a *hasb-ul-hukm* from the *wazir*, p. 98. Safdar Jang's letter to the governor of Bihar apprising him of the authority that a *hasb-ul-hukm* from Samsam-ud-Daulah had invested him in this regard to send his own man to Bihar to escort the treasury. In one case, however, the treasury was carried *via* Jaunpur to Qanauj where the deputy of Raja of Bhadawar waited to escort it further to Agra, *Maktubat*, pp. 44 and 60–1, Safdar Jang's letters to the *wazir* and Burhan-ul-Mulk.

Qanauj of Agra province was in the *zamindari* of the Chandelas who under the leadership of Hindu Singh were a constant source of danger to the governor of Awadh. In November 1722, Burhan-ul-Mulk led an expedition against him and though the *zamindars* were temporarily contained, Burhan-ul-Mulk suffered a serious loss and the *bakshi* of his army was killed in the battle.[56]

Burhan-ul-Mulk wanted this area to be under his own control or at least in the hands of a friend in order to watch the movements of the Afghans in Farrukhabad. In 1729, with the collaboration of his ally, Gopal Singh Bhadauria, therefore, he again led a campaign against the Chandelas and besieged the fortress of Chachendi where they had taken shelter. Eventually with the help of what is alleged to have been a deceitful act on the part of the Bhadauria Raja, the fortress and the *zamindari* of the Chandela chief came into the possession of Burhan-ul-Mulk. Hindu Singh fled to the territory of the Bundelas. After his death, the *zamindari* and the fortress were restored to his son, Antrit Singh, on the mediation of the Bundela chief.[57]

Safdar Jang and the Bangash Afghans of Farrukhabad

Since Allahabad province and for that matter any other province or group of *sarkars* of the region were no longer under Muhammad Khan, the prospects of his rising to a position at par with that of the governor of Awadh had ended. Safdar Jang,

---

[56] *T. Muhammadi*, p. 49.

[57] No progress could be made in the operations till the Bhadauria Raja was sent to Hindu Singh to persuade him to make a compromise. Gopal Singh impressed upon the Chandela chief the inexpediency of coming into conflict with the Mughal nobles. He advised him to vacate the fortress for three days for the sake of Burhan-ul-Mulk's prestige and promised him to strike a compromise after the passage of three days when he could reoccupy it. As Gopal Singh pledged his word on a solemn oath, Hindu Singh accepted his advice and left the fortress with his family and belongings. In violation of his word, Gopal Singh at the instance of Burhan-ul-Mulk took possession of the *zamindari* and fortress of the Chandela chief. *T. Hindi*, ff. 258–59a.

A. L. Srivastava writes that the area constituted a debatable frontier of the three provinces of Agra, Allahabad and Awadh and that the estate of Hindu Singh passed into the hands of Burhan-ul-Mulk (*First Two Nawabs*, p. 44). But unfortunately these statements are not supported by any contemporary evidence.

however, had to reckon with the Afghans in Farrukhabad, in particular when the Rohillas of the Moradabad-Bareilly region on the north-western borders of Awadh had openly turned hostile to him.[58] These Afghans when unified could give the governor of Awadh a great deal of trouble. Friendly postures towards the Bangash Afghans of Farrukhabad signifying a modification in Burhan-ul-Mulk's policy, were thus thought to be more pragmatic.

On the other hand, the old and ageing Bangash chief had also accepted reality. He diplomatically rejected Safdar Jang's overtures by assuring him of his cooperation in the latter's bid to suppress the disturbances in and around the province of Awadh.[59] In 1743 when Safdar Jang left for Delhi, the Bangash chief wrote to him inviting him to pass through Bangash territory and make a brief stopover at Farrukhabad.[60] Again, during the imperial campaigns against the Rohillas of Moradabad, Qaim Khan remained allied with Safdar Jang, even though Qamar-ud-Din Khan, the *wazir*, made every possible effort, as we shall see below, to alienate him from the governor of Awadh.

Yet, Safdar Jang was not unmindful of the threat the Bangash Afghans were capable of posing to his authority in Awadh. Since control over Qanauj was thought to be necessary to watch and check the movements of the Afghans of Farrukhabad,

---

[58] See below the section 'Safdar Jang and the Rohillas of the Moradabad-Bareilly Region'.

[59] In one of his letters to Safdar Jang, Muhammad Khan Bangash writes,—'With the grace of God our pure love and conciliation of hearts is so strong that even a fraction of it is beyond description. It is our bounden duty to further the foundation of our unity. For the sake of these stages [of friendship] we should assist each other when needed. That is to say that God forbid if there arises any commotion in the districts under your officers, consolidation of the bases of our mutual affection will take place by despatching the troops from this side. And in case the dust of storm raises its head in this district, you shall gracefully depute your officials to help us. Earlier there were certain doubts and suspicions between me and the late Nawab Burhan-ul-Mulk. Now the hearts have been so much conciliated that there remained no difference between us. From this side you should be completely comforted and assured.' *Aziz-ul-Qulub*, ff. 57b–58a.

[60] Compare *Aziz-ul-Qulub*, f. 55b. Safdar Jang accepted the invitation but since he had to rush to the court, he abandoned his plan to march through Farrukhabad. Muhammad Khan then sent his *chelas*, Samsher Khan and Afzal Khan to communicate the message of his good-will to Safdar Jang. Yet, when he heard that Safdar Jang had crossed the Ganga, Muhammad Khan wanted to proceed in person and meet the Nawab. Owing to his illness and old-age, however, he could not move out of Farrukhabad. Saiyid Ataullah was subsequently sent to the camp of Safdar Jang.

Safdar Jang secured a *jagir* in *pargana* Bara in *sarkar* Qanauj.[61] He also obtained on *ijara* the *jagirs* of a number of the other nobles in the *sarkar*.[62] It is very likely that his *jagir* and *ijara* implied *faujdari* powers as well. A fairly big area in *sarkar* Qanauj was thus virtually under his control.

Besides, there appears to be a change in Safdar Jang's attitude towards the Bangash Afghans after the death of Muhammad Khan when the *wazir* tried constantly to incite the young Bangash chief, Qaim Khan, against the governor of Awadh. When Ali Muhammad Khan, the rebel Rohilla chief of *sarkar* Moradabad died in 1748 Safdar Jang persuaded the emperor to appoint Qaim Khan to the *faujdari* of the *sarkar* and call upon him to recover it from the possession of the Rohillas. This was obviously a device to keep the Bangash chief engaged with the Rohillas. Qaim Khan would thus be unable to rise to a position whereby he could endanger the stability in Awadh. Safdar Jang got much more than he had hoped for. Qaim Khan perished with most of his *sardars* in his encounter against the Rohillas.[63]

With the death of Qaim Khan came the best opportunity for Sardar Jang to finally dismantle the Bangash power in Farrukhabad. As the *wazir* of the empire, he pressed on the emperor to confiscate the *jagirs* and the properties of the Bangash chief. In view of the decaying finance of the empire, Ahmad Shah readily agreed to the proposal.[64] As Safdar Jang

William Irvine however does not take notice of the evidence of the *Aziz-ul-Qulub* and suggests that relations between Lucknow and Farrukhabad remained strained even under Safdar Jang. According to him, in 1743 Safdar Jang's march to Delhi was intercepted at Bilhaur by Samsher Khan, who was in charge of Muhammad Khan's *jagirs* there. Safdar Jang's protest against Muhammad Khan over Samsher Khan's act brought an equally strongly worded and hostile response from the Bangash chief. Safdar Jang then ordered an encounter which was averted after great persuasion by his friends. They suggested that 'if you win the battle it will hardly bring credit to you, for Shamsher Khan is an ordinary *amil* and if you lose the odium will ever remain with you.' Cf. William Irvine, 'The Bangash Nawabs of Farrukhabad' in *Journal of Asiatic Society of Bengal*, 47, No. 1, 1878, pp. 259–383.

[61] *Siyar*, III, p. 875.

[62] *Maktubat*, pp. 108 and 124. Safdar Jang's letters to Abd-ul-Majid Khan and Jawahar Khan regarding the payment of the revenues of their *jagirs* in *sarkar* Qanauj.

[63] *Siyar*, III, 874; Shakir, ff. 60b–61a; *Tabsira*, f. 254b; *Hadiqat*, p. 141 and *Imad*, pp. 44–5; *Jam-i Jahan Numa*, II, pp. 48–9.

[64] For a decade, escheat, which though in principle a part of the Mughal *mansabdari*

feared stiff resistance from the Afghans, he marched along with
the emperor and a huge army. Though he failed in his bid and
the Afghans even captured several districts of his province, the
set-back was only temporary. Very soon he invited the
Marathas to his assistance and then gave a crushing blow to the
Afghans. The Afghans had to part with one-half of their country
to the Maratha allies of Safdar Jang in order to purchase peace
from the governor of Awadh.[65]

Safdar Jang and the Rohillas of the Moradabad-Bareilly region

Towards the second quarter of the eighteenth century, the
Rohillas under the leadership of Ali Muhammad Khan had
emerged as a power to reckon with in the Moradabad-Bareilly
region.[66] Since this region lay on the north-west frontiers of
Awadh, the governor was alarmed. As the deputy governor of
the province Safdar Jang had always been aware of the implications of the developments in Moradabad. Owing to the absence
of effective natural barriers between the *sarkar* of Moradabad
and the province of Awadh, the disaffected *zamindars* of
Khairabad when chased often fled to this region. Again, because of the diversion of the route taken for the Bengal treasury
Safdar Jang visited Bareilly regularly, and he seems to have
taken an interest even in the internal administration of the
sarkar.[67] The relationship between Safdar Jang and Ali Muham-

---

system had rarely been applied, had been suggested as a possible cure for the financial
ills of the empire. The suggestion however, came from the nobles in relation to the
property of their rivals and reflected the infighting among the nobility more than any
desire, on their part, to effect financial reforms. In 1739–40 Amir Khan advised the
emperor to confiscate the *jagir* and properties of Badr ud-Din Khan, son of Qamar-ud-
Din Khan, which could not be carried out due to resistance by the *wazir* and Nizam-ul-
Mulk. Cf. Shakir, f. 77a.

[65] For details see W. Irvine, 'Bangash Nawabs of Farrukhabad'.

[66] For some details of the circumstances leading to the rise of the Rohilla power in
Moradabad see Muzaffar Alam, 'Zamindar Uprisings and the Emergence of the
Rohilla Power in *Sarkar* Moradabad', *PIHC*, 38th Session, 1977, pp. 221–31.

[67] The *zamindar* of Takiapur, *pargana Haveli* Moradabad was, for example, an associate (*mutawassil*) of Safdar Jang. In one of his letters to the *amil* of Moradabad, Safdar
Jang recommended the case of the *zamindar* who was then being harassed by the other
zamindars of the *pargana*. *Maktubat*, p. 180.

mad Khan also appears to have been amicable.[68] They remained friendly, even during the periods when the Rohilla chief came into conflict with some of the nobles who had *jagirs* in Moradabad.[69]

Ali Muhammad Khan was, however, ambitious and tried to capitalize on the factional politics of the court. Coming gradually into close contact with the *wazir*,[70] he became the principal *ijaradar* in the region and then began to violate the stipulated terms of contract even in the case of the *jagirs* of the big nobles. Again, in 1742 Ali Muhammad invaded the territory of the Kumaon chief and annexed Kashipur, Rudrapur and two other *parganas* from the latter's *zamindari* to his own territory. This was alarming for Safdar Jang since the Kumaon chief was his old ally. Soon after Ali Muhammad Khan intercepted certain employees of the Awadh government who were carrying logs of wood from the Kumaon teritory to Lucknow.[71]

Safdar Jang thus decided to cut him to size. He was amply assisted in this by Amir Khan, his greatest ally at this juncture. Amir Khan had a *jagir* in Moradabad and had also faced troubles from the Rohilla chief.[72] In 1745 when Safdar Jang and Amir Khan dominated the political scenario at the court and the emperor seems to have been entirely under their spell, they

---

[68] Ali Muhammad Khan had met Safdar Jang at Bareilly during one of his visits to the town. Since then Ali Muhammad Khan seems to have consistently intimated the governor of Awadh about his own affairs. He had also taken utmost care in preventing the exiles of Awadh from entering his dominion. Ibid., pp. 148–9.

[69] In one of his letters Safdar Jang replied to Ali Muhammad's *arzi* wherein the latter told him about recent developments in Moradabad. The governor of Awadh advised him to settle the dispute amicably. Ibid., p. 149. Ali Muhammad Khan had built a fairly big *zamindari* and almost all the *jagirdars* in and around Moradabad had farmed out their *jagirs* to him. But apart from the *wazir*, a few of his associates and some big nobles the other *jagirdars* received little from him regularly. Ali Muhammad's association with the *wazir* emboldened him to misappropriate the revenues of the *jagirs* of his (*wazir*'s) rivals as well. This brought him into conflict with Amir Khan in 1727. But, in the wake of Nadir Shah's invasion, he refused to pay the revenue to the *wazir* too. For details see M. Alam, 'Zamindar uprisings and the Emergence of the Rohilla Power in *sarkar* Moradabad'.

[70] *Hadiqat*, p. 139; *Badi'*, 193; *Siyar*, III, 854, for the *wazir*'s recommendation in 1738 for a *mansab* of 5000/5000 for Ali Muhammad Khan.

[71] Shakir, f. 77b; A. L. Srivastava, *First Two Nawabs*, pp. 105–6.

[72] In 1727, Amir Khan's *amil* in *pargana* Mu'azzam Nagar *alias* Manuna was killed in an encounter with Ali Muhammad. *Hadiqat*, p. 139; *Jam-i Jahan Numa*, II, p. 29.

convinced him that he should personally lead a military campaign against the Rohilla chief.[73] Safdar Jang promised to meet the major part of the war expenditure.[74] The expedition was to be under the personal command of the emperor. The emperor left Delhi in February 1745 with Safdar Jang, Amir Khan and other nobles and a huge army of about 1,00,000.[75]

However, the *wazir* pressed for a compromise and amicable adjustment with Ali Muhammad Khan, when he realized the real purpose of the expedition.[76] But he could not dictate the terms of the compromise.[77] The Rohilla chief was asked to present himself before the emperor with a *peshkash* of Rs 1,00,00,000, surrender his arsenal (*topkhana*) and all claims over *sarkar* Moradabad.[78] Ali Muhammad Khan, however,

[73] For the details of the campaign see A. L. Srivastava, *First Two Nawabs*, pp. 103–9. J. N. Sarkar, *Fall of the Mughal Empire* I, pp. 36–41. Neither of them, however, discusses some of the crucial developments which took place during the campaign.

[74] *Hadiqat*, p. 140. W. Irvine, *Army of the Indian Moghuls*, pp. 291–4 quoting from Khush-hal Chand.

[75] *Safarnama*, pp. 2–3 and 72.

[76] Initially the real objective of the march was kept secret from the *wazir* and his dependants. See Ibid., p. 2. The author who was in the service of the *wazir* describes the aim of the outing as 'a pleasure hunt outing in the wake of which the emperor had thought of reprimanding Ali Muhammad Khan who had acquired some strength and an air of insubordination'. See also W. Irvine, *Army of the Indian Moghuls*, pp. 291–4. Safdar Jang, however, did not fail to appreciate the implications of the *wazir*'s open opposition to his move. He kept up his efforts to secure his agreement to his plan. On 5 March, when the emperor was staying near Loni, Safdar Jang is reported to have gone to the *wazir* and apologized for whatever had happened in the past. The *wazir*'s visit to Safdar Jang and a luncheon in his honour at the latter's residence followed a few days after. On 26 March 1745, the *wazir*'s son, Intizam-ud-Daulah, who had arrived from Jaipur was received near Garh Muktesar by Amir Khan. On 8 April, near Shah-bazpur, when the Qazilbash units of Safdar Jang's army plundered the adjoining villages, the *wazir* lodged a strong protest and wanted to depute an armed contingent to protect the fields and villages against such outrages. Safdar Jang, the *mir atish*, did accordingly. The Qazilbash offenders were severely punished and two of them were whipped to death. Shahbazpur and the adjoining villages were in the *jagir* of Sani Quli Khan, the foster-brother of the *wazir*. *Safarnama*, pp. 5, 27 and 34.

[77] The *wazir* had hoped that being an Afghan and a rival of Safdar Jang in the region, Qaim Khan Bangash would effectively present the case of the Rohillas to the emperor. On 22 April 1745 when Qaim Khan arrived at the court he was enthusiastically welcomed by the *wazir* and the other Mughal nobles. Qaim Khan was, however, won over by Amir Khan. Safdar Jang thus took over the negotiations with the Rohilla chief, so far handled by the *wazir*, himself. The terms and conditions of the compromise were first discussed between Amir Khan and Qaim Khan and then only were they put before the *wazir*. Ibid., pp. 51–2.   [78] Ibid, pp. 55–6

refused to accept these conditions and the encounter became inevitable which ended, on the *wazir*'s intercession, in his formal submission to the emperor. He was then appointed the *faujdar* of *chakla* Sirhind while his office and dominion in Moradabad were divided between Safdar Jang's associates.[79]

The Rohilla chief's exile from Moradabad did not resolve the problem of the governor of Awadh. Although Safdar Jang managed to place his own men in the region, the *faujdari* (*bil-isalat*) remained under the *wazir*. In March 1748 after the *wazir*'s death, his son, Intizam-ud-Daulah inherited the *faujdari*. Ali Muhammad Khan, availing himself fully of the disturbed conditions in Sirhind, had returned and driven away Safdar Jang's men from the region. The possibility of collusion between the Rohilla chief and Intizam-ud-Daulah against their common foe, Safdar Jang, could not be altogether ruled out. In September 1748, however, Ali Muhammad died, and Safdar Jang who was then the *wazir* of the empire was now free to carry out his plan. He managed to appoint Qaim Khan as the *faujdar* of Moradabad and thus created a cleavage of distrust and suspicion between the Bangash chief on the one hand and Intizam-ud-Daulah and the Rohillas on the other.[80]

Ijara was a major source of strength for the Rohilla chief in *sarkar* Moradabad. It was through the *ijara* contract that the Rohillas came into contact with the *wazir* and his associates who held a large part of Moradabad in *jagirs*. When Safdar Jang himself became the *wazir* in 1748, he succeeded in large measure in striking at the base of the strength of the Afghans who were no less broken due to the sudden death of their leader, Ali Muhammad Khan. It was also the question of who held the *jagirs* in Moradabad which perhaps, partly, forced Safdar Jang to finally obtain the office of the *wazir*. For, as the *wazir* he expected to obtain in Moradabad the *jagirs* of the former *wazir*, namely, Qamar-ud-Din Khan and thus tried to prevent the presence of any other powerful noble in a region in the neighbourhood of Awadh.

Both Burhan-ul-Mulk and Safdar Jang regarded the possi-

---

[79] Compare *Imad*, p. 43; *Maktubat*, p. 180.

[80] For the details of these events see A. L. Srivastava, *First Two Nawabs*, pp. 109 and 139; J. N. Sarkar, *Fall of the Mughal Empire* I, pp. 41 and 237.

bility of a powerful chief on the borders of Awadh as a threat to their ambition. They fought, uprooted, allied with and made friendly overtures to all of them primarily to secure their own position, without any reference to the centre. This comes out more vividly from the details of their relations with the Marathas and the Bundelas.

The Maratha question

Initially Burhan-ul-Mulk was more or less indifferent to the Maratha problem, because the Marathas did not threaten his authority in Awadh.[81] In 1728 when the Marathas besieged Muhammad Khan Bangash at Jaipur, he supported the cause of their ally, Satarsal Bundela. But when the Bundela territory began to be used by the Marathas to strike at areas close to the borders of Awadh, Burhan-ul-Mulk desperately entered into correspondence with the *wazir* and Nizam-ul-Mulk. He was ready to check the Maratha advance to the north provided he was given the charge of Agra and Malwa in addition to his existing governorship of Awadh.[82] The *wazir* conceded to Burhan-ul-Mulk's demands, as he (*wazir*) probably planned to weaken Samsam-ud-Daulah, the *mir bakshi* by taking the two provinces out of the control of the latter's friend, Raja Jai Singh. Faced with the Maratha danger to his dominion, Burhan-ul-Mulk thus drew closer to the *wazir*, breaking away from Samsam-ud-Daulah, an erstwhile ally who was in favour of propitiating the peshwa.[83]

In 1736, the Marathas in cooperation with Hiredesa and Jagat Rai invaded the territory of Anirudh Singh, the Raja of Bhadawar. The raja offered stiff resistance, but eventually had to surrender. This was a direct challenge to the governor of

[81] Compare *Siyar*, II, p. 475 which extols Burhan-ul-Mulk's bravery for his later policy of resistance to the Marathas 'nothwithstanding the fact that the *suba* lay even beyond the Ganga towards the north'.

[82] This happened towards the end of 1735 when it was rumoured that Rup Singh, the son of the *zamindar* of Kora, Bhagwant Singh, who had been defeated and killed at the hands of Burhan-ul-Mulk's army at the beginning of the same year had taken refuge in Bundelkhand and was trying to enlist the support of the Marathas to recover the *zamindari* of his deceased father. A. L. Srivastava, *First Two Nawabs*, pp. 51–2; J. N. Sarkar, *Fall of the Mughal Empire*, I, p. 160.

[83] Compare S. Chandra, *Parties and Politics*, pp. 210–17.

Awadh, because the chief of Bhadawar was his political ally.[84] Burhan-ul-Mulk therefore left his province and marched in the direction of Agra. This was exclusively at his own discretion and was done with a view to safeguarding his own interests.[85] At Jalesar, he inflicted a severe defeat upon the Marathas under Malhar Rao Holkar, Pilaji Jadav and Vithoji Bule.[86] In view of the constant defeats of the Mughal army at the hands of the Marathas, the victory was of great significance. Samsam-ud-Daulah was alarmed. The position of the 'hawks' at the court was substantially strengthened and it seemed likely that Burhan-ul-Mulk's plea for the *subadari* of Agra and Malwa would be conceded. But Jai Singh and Samsam-ud-Daulah would have never let anyone else control Agra. On the borders of Jai Singh's ancestral territory lay Agra where the Jats had recently emerged as a potential threat to the raja. Jai Singh and Samsam-ud-Daulah's moves ended in the withdrawal of Burhan-ul-Mulk to his own province.[87] Before his withdrawal, however, he concluded, through his envoy Ram Narain, a treaty with the Marathas on terms that ensured the safety of Awadh.[88]

Burhan-ul-Mulk had marched with a two-fold objective; to

[84] Compare Shakir, f. 38b; *Siyar*, II, 475; *T. Muzaffari*, f. 206a and *T. Hindi*, f. 258b, for Anirudh's father, Gopal Singh's assistance to Burhan-ul-Mulk in the latter's campaigns against the Chandela *zamindars* of Qanauj, on the south-western borders of Awadh.

[85] According to A. L. Srivastava the march was in response to an imperial order which directed Burhan ul-Mulk to cooperate with the *wazir* and the *mir bakshi. First Two Nawabs*, p. 53. It is not possible to accept his opinion. For the Persian sources he quotes to support it do not mention the *farman*. Cf. Shakir, f. 39a, *Siyar*, II, 475. On the other hand some other sources clearly suggest it to have been undertaken without an imperial order. Cf. *Tabsira*, f. 94a; *Khizana-i Amira*, p. 43; *Imad*, p. 16.

[86] *Khizana-i Amira*, p. 44; A. L. Srivastava, *First Two Nawabs*, p. 54; W. Irvine, *Later Moghuls*, II, p. 287.

[87] There is more than one version of Samsam-ud-Daulah's letter to Burhan-ul-Mulk. According to *Imad* (p. 17), for example, Samsam-ud-Daulah reproached Burhan-ul-Mulk for marching against the Marathas and directed him to immediately retreat. According to *Siyar* (II, p. 476) Samsam-ud-Daulah grew jealous of Burhan-ul-Mulk's achievement and wrote to him to wait till he arrived to embark upon a joint expedition against the Marathas.

[88] The three terms that the author of *Imad-us-Sa'adat* (p. 17) cites on the basis of the news that circulated among the people and also among certain nobles were as follows: (1) The Marathas would never lay claims to the *chauth* of Awadh so long as the province remained under the control of Burhan-ul-Mulk or any member of his family. (2)

assist the Raja of Bhadawar and to show his power so that he could acquire the governorship of Agra and Malwa. His victory over Holkar and Jadav had unmistakably demonstrated his armed strength. His plan of proceeding into the Bhadawar country to assist Anirudh Singh was thwarted by court intrigues. And it was not easy to go much beyond the Yamuna where Baji Rao was preparing to avenge the defeat. It was no longer possible for him to obtain both Agra and Malwa or even one of these provinces. Nothing could have indicated the strength of the Marathas more than the recommendation to the emperor by Jai Singh the governor for the appointment of Baji Rao as the deputy governor of Malwa.[89] It is in this light that the terms of the treaty contracted by Burhan-ul-Mulk with the Marathas will have to be viewed. Treaties contracted by governors independently—without the emperor's consent—were not uncommon in this period. Nizam-ul-Mulk, for example, had entered into more than one such agreement with the Marathas.

The treaty seems to have effectively influenced the pattern of relations between the Marathas and the governor of Awadh. There is no evidence of any further direct clash between the Marathas and Burhan-ul-Mulk, even though he was apparently involved in some campaigns of the Mughal nobles against them.[90]

Burhan-ul-Mulk came back to Awadh after signing a treaty of peace with the Marathas and without making a serious bid to obtain Malwa or Agra. The *wazir* perhaps did not appreciate it, since he still pleaded for total confrontation against the Marathas and he had also intended Burhan-ul-Mulk to in-

---

Whenever he needed it and asked for it, the governor of Awadh would be assisted by the Marathas against his enemies. (3) The Marathas would not come to northern India without informing and consulting Burhan-ul-Mulk.

[89] J. N. Sarkar, *Fall of the Mughal Empire*, I, p. 168. Burhan-ul-Mulk was still mindful of Anirudh's difficulties and went out of his way to write to Muhammad Khan to assist him. Cf. *Aziz-ul-Qulub*, f. 126b.

[90] In 1737, for example, he sent Safdar Jang to the relief of Nizam-ul-Mulk at Bhopal. Safdar Jang along with Durjan Sal, the Raja of Kota, was however, intercepted on the way. But it is curious that it was only Durjan Sal who was later punished by Baji Rao for the unfriendly act of providing assistance to Nizam-ul-Mulk. J. N. Sarkar, *Fall of the Mughal Empire*, I, p. 169.

terfere in Agra or Malwa to the disadvantage of his (*wazir*'s)
foes, Samsam-ud-Daulah and Jai Singh. But in his break with
Samsam-ud-Daulah or the revival of his association with the
Mughal group, Burhan-ul-Mulk had little regard for its effect
on various factions at the court.

Safdar Jang and the Marathas

Safdar Jang not only respected the treaty of Burhan-ul-Mulk
with the Marathas, but also refused to comply with the repeated imperial directives to him to help Jai Singh against
them.[91] Subsequently, the emperor through another *farman* directed Safdar Jang to stay in, and look after the affairs of his own
province.[92]

For his refusal to assist Jai Singh, Safdar Jang gave three
reasons, the threat of a Maratha attack on Awadh, the *zamindar*
disturbances in the province, and the 'honour of the faith',
namely, the plea of disgrace for a Muslim *khanazad* to serve and
fight under a Rajput.[93] These reasons are however, not borne
out by facts. If at all there was any possibility of a Maratha
invasion of Awadh it was in 1743.[94] But it did not prevent Safdar
Jang from rushing to the court at Amir Khan's invitation.
Similarly it is difficult to accept Safdar Jang's version of the

[91] This was in March 1741 when Balaji Rao, the Maratha Peshwa reached Gwalior.
Jai Singh wrote to the emperor about the inability of his *sardars* to withstand the
Maratha warfare and sought the assistance of the nobles of the empire from the
emperor. Accordingly, an imperial *farman* was sent to Safdar Jang. No assistance,
however, could be provided to Jai Singh who then sent his envoys to open peace
negotiations with the peshwa and asked him to remain contented with the *chauths* of the
subas of Gujarat and Malwa and not to disturb any other provinces. The peshwa agreed
to do so and eventually on the recommendation of Jai Singh, the deputy governorship of
Malwa was conferred on Balaji Rao. See for details J. N. Sarkar, *Fall of the Mughal
Empire*, I, pp. 172–3.

[92] Safdar Jang received this *farman* at Benaras where he had gone to receive the
Bengal treasury and subsequently escort it *via* Lucknow to Delhi. *Maktubat*, p. 24.

[93] *Maktubat*, pp. 10–12.

[94] In the beginning of 1743 the Maratha Peshwa is reported to have been in Allahabad and Benaras. In compliance with the imperial order to assist Ali Vardi Khan,
Balaji Rao left for Bengal and reached Allahabad on 26 January 1743 and remained
there up to 30 January. On 8 February he reached Mirzapur and on 12 **February** he

magnitude of the threat posed by the insubordinate *zamindars* to his authority in the province. When he left for Delhi in 1743 he could place the province in charge of Nawal Rai without undue anxiety and stay at the court for about a decade. In fact, by the time Safdar Jang became the governor, a number of *zamindars* of Awadh, as we have seen earlier, had been largely subdued and accommodated in the provincial administration. As for the point of the 'honour of the Faith', Safdar Jang clarified it in his letter to Abd-ul-Majid Khan. He asserted that 'in the past the slaves and the servants of this court who were endowed with the honour of being the *khanazads* never served under the command of this crowd (the Rajputs)'.[95] It is needless to say that Safdar Jang's claim was not supported by the military history of the Mughals.

Muhammad Shah's second *farman* to Safdar Jang shows the extent of autonomy of the new *subadar*. It was the emperor and not the governor who acted on the directive of the latter. The emperor wanted Safdar Jang to join Jai Singh's expedition against the Marathas. Safdar Jang refused to comply with the order and then made the emperor issue a *farman* approving what he had done.

Safdar Jang thus made every possible effort not to come into open conflict with the Marathas. But since the *wazir* and Nizam-ul-Mulk were by no means well disposed towards Safdar Jang, the governor of Awadh feared that at their instigation the peshwa could violate the treaty any time it suited him and thus the Marathas could adversely affect his authority in Awadh. He, therefore, seems to have been also prepared to face any Maratha threat to the province. This is illustrated from his letters to Muhammad Khan Bangash and the Maharana of Gahadwala, informing them about his Patna expedition, about the rumours of the peshwa's plan to invade Awadh and the preparation he had made to encounter the Marathas.[96] There is also evidence of Muhammad Khan's reply to Safdar Jang assuring the latter of his assistance in the event of a Maratha

---

encamped at Rampura near Benaras where he halted for two days and then crossed the river Karamnassa and entered the territory of *suba* Bihar. *Satara Rajas and Peshwas Diaries*, II, p. 242, SPD (New Series), I, L. No. 57.

[95] *Maktubat*, p. 104.   [96] Ibid, pp. 154–7.

invasion of Awadh.[97] According to Ghulam Husain Tabatabai, it was only after he had heard of the peshwa's passage through Vindhyachal and Benaras that Safdar Jang rode back from Patna.[98]

Our sources, however, do not mention any conflict between the Marathas and Safdar Jang till the end of our period. On the contrary, in 1743 when the peshwa was in and around Awadh for over a fortnight, he apparently avoided confrontation with the governor of Awadh. Different reasons have been given by our authorities for this. According to Marathi sources, the Brahmans of Benaras were responsible for preventing the peshwa from committing atrocities. Safdar Jang had threatened to kill the Brahmans of Benaras if Balaji entered the town. Under the leadership of one Narayan Dikshit they therefore met the peshwa and urged him immediately to march towards Bihar. Malhar Rao who accompanied the peshwa thought of destroying a mosque, but this was not done on the intercession of the Brahmans.[99]

However, from the account of Ghulam Husain Tabatabai it appears that it was primarily to safeguard the interests of the Maratha traders in Benaras that the peshwa, on the recommendation of Gobind Naik, refrained from doing anything which later might cause them sufferings at the hands of the governor.[100] Whatever the reasons, it can be safely inferred from this evidence that the peshwa had his own interests in maintaining relations which were detached, if not cordial, with the governor of Awadh. This was also compatible with the spirit of the treaty of 1736.[101]

[97] *Aziz-ul-Qulub*, ff. 55b–56a.

[98] *Siyar*, II, 522. According to the *Siyar* Safdar Jang became alarmed at Balaji's movements, for they were hereditary enemies. Burhan-ul-Mulk had severely defeated Balaji's father, Baji Rao and had captured a large number of the Maratha *sardars* who were still in the custody of Safdar Jang.

This statement is erroneous. Burhan-ul-Mulk had never defeated Baji Rao and there is no evidence of there being any Maratha *sardar* in the custody of Safdar Jang in 1743.

[99] Compare V. K. Verma, 'Subah of Allahabad, 1707–65', unpublished Ph.D. thesis submitted to the University of Allahabad, 1969, p. 104n.

[100] *Siyar*, II, p. 523.

[101] In this connection it is interesting to note that even an unsavoury incident in 1744 did not affect the peshwa's relations with Safdar Jang. The peshwa's envoy at the court, Mahadeva Bhat Hingane represented the Jaipur Raj as well. Sometime in February

It was again in accord with this spirit, perhaps, that in the late 1740s Safdar Jang and the Marathas often acted in unison at the court. In 1747 Safdar Jang and Balaji Rao were great friends.[102] The Maratha envoy to the Mughal court helped him in his struggle for the *wizarat* and in late 1748 when intrigues and counter-intrigues marred court politics, the Marathas were his reliable allies.[103] Again, in 1754 it was with the help of the Marathas that Safdar Jang finally crushed the Bangash Af-

1744 in the midst of a discourse with Safdar Jang to adjust certain matters relating to the Jaipur Raj, Mahadeva Bhat abused Safdar Jang. This led to violence between the supporters of the two leaders in which Mahadeva Bhat received fatal wounds. His son too was injured. However, relations between the peshwa and Safdar Jang, instead of deteriorating, soon took a new turn towards friendship. For details of the incident see A. L. Srivastava, *First Two Nawabs*, p. 170.

[102] Compare G. S. Desai, (ed.), *Selections from the Peshwa Daftars*, II, Letters 2, 4, 9 and 13.

[103] Nasir Jang, a son of the late Nizam-ul-Mulk was secretly invited from the Deccan to dislodge Safdar Jang from the office of *wazir*. Realizing Safdar Jang's strength, Nasir Jang, however, tried to humour Safdar Jang and wrote to him expressing his desire to befriend him. He suggested that Safdar Jang should not rely on the peshwa. He also sent letters to his elder brother, Ghazi-ud-Din Firoz Jang and Intizam-ud-Daulah. Bapuji Hingane, the Maratha *vakil* at the Mughal Court who was aware of Nasir Jang's scheme, disclosed the contents of these letters to Safdar Jang. He also warned him to be on his guard against the deep conspiracy which, he believed to be an attempt to isolate Safdar Jang from the peshwa and thus reduce his strength at the court. Safdar Jang then posted his Maratha allies, Malhar Holkar and Jayoti Sindhia in Kota to prevent Nasir Jang from crossing the Chambal and entering Hindustan. Further, he asked Hingane to despatch a letter on his behalf to the peshwa expressing his full confidence in his friendship and instructing him to make adequate arrangements to check Nasir Jang. Subsequently, Safdar Jang's foes at the court were frightened. The emperor visited him along with his mother and Nasir Jang was directed to immediately return to Aurangabad with a *farman* formally appointing him the viceroy of the Deccan. *Siyar*, III, p. 886; *M. U..*, III, p. 850. Lachmi Narayan 'Shafiq', *Ma'asir-i Asafi* MS. Asiatic Society of Bengal, f. 127b; Najm-ul-Ghani in his *Tarikh-i Haidrabad Deccan* (Urdu), Nawalkishore, Lucknow, pp. 180–3 gives translations of some of these letters. *Tarikh-i Ahmad Shah*, f. 36b; *Selections from Peshwa Daftars*, II, letters No. 12 and 13.

There is hardly any support in the authorities that A. L. Srivastava quotes for his opinion that Safdar Jang was disappointed by his Maratha allies and made his own arrangements to meet the threat (*First Two Nawabs*, pp. 130–1). Evidently, besides seeking the support of the Marathas, Safdar Jang made his own preparations as well. His summoning of Nawal Rai and instigation of Sadullah, the deputy governor of Bijapur to revolt against Nasir Jang were elements of these preparations.

ghans of Farrukhabad and also the joint forces of the Rohillas and the Bangash.[104]

Safdar Jang and the Bundela and Bhadauria chiefs

Immediately after his succession to the governorship of Awadh, Safdar Jang received a congratulatory letter from Jagat Raj which also conveyed the Bundela chief's condolence on the death of Burhan-ul-Mulk. Safdar Jang's reply assured him of a continuation and further consolidation of the old friendship between the two houses. He also expressed the hope of meeting him to discuss some matters personally.[105]

Himmat Singh, the *zamindar* of Bhadawar and Safdar Jang exchanged letters regularly informing each other of the progress of their respective plans.[106] In 1740, Himmat Singh was at the court. In one of his letters, Safdar Jang acknowledged the information Himmat Singh had despatched to him about the activities of Nizam-ul-Mulk at the court.[107]

Relations between Safdar Jang and the Bundelas may also be viewed against the background of the latter having entered into an offensive agreement with the Marathas. In 1733 the Bundelas had agreed to join the peshwa's standard when he invaded Mughal territory;[108] yet Safdar Jang, a noble of the Mughal empire, assured them of his friendship. Evidently the nobles' own interests had precedence over any other considerations, including the security of the empire. This is further illustrated from Burhan-ul-Mulk's attitude toward the problems of the defence of the empire against the Persian invader in

---

[104] *T. Ahmad Shahi*, ff. 18b and 35; *Bayan-i Waqi* f. 104a; see also A. L. Srivastava *First Two Nawabs*, pp. 173–6.

[105] *Maktubat*, p. 150. The nature of the relationship between the governor of Awadh and the Bundela chief is further illustrated by the following incident. Two persons, Mir Khuda Yar Khan and Khwaja Hafizullah, were carrying some animals and goods from Delhi to Awadh. On their way at *Sarai* Akbarpur they were deprived of everything by robbers who apparently belonged to the Bundela country. Subsequently, Safdar Jang wrote to Jagat Raj, emphasizing his association with the victims, to recover the robbed goods and despatch them through Khwaja Muhammad Khan specially deputed by Safdar Jang for this purpose. Ibid., p. 154.

[106] *Maktubat*, pp. 159–60.   [107] Ibid., p. 159.

[108] Cf. S. Chandra, *Parties and Politics*, pp. 206–7.

1739, as well as from the details of the relationship between the court and the new *subadars* during the last phase of the period of our study.

Invasion of Nadir Shah and Burhan-ul-Mulk

In 1739, on the eve of Nadir Shah's invasion, Burhan-ul-Mulk's obeisance to the centre was little more than formal and only to legitimize his moves to establish himself firmly in Awadh. But significantly enough a special letter with the emperor's own signature (*shuqqa*) had to be sent to him inviting him to assist the emperor in the latter's campaign against Nadir Shah. Moreover, Murid Khan, an important noble of the court was specially ordered to accompany the couriers to convey the emperor's personal message to Burhan-ul-Mulk. In view of Burhan-ul-Mulk's lack of concern for events at the imperial centre which did not affect Awadh the emperor perhaps feared he would be reluctant to come to the court.[109]

Burhan-ul-Mulk was invited on account of his military capability. It is, however, possible that the emperor considered Burhan-ul-Mulk as the best person to mediate between him and the Persian invader. It seems that Burhan-ul-Mulk, very probably on account of his Iranian origin, had been contacted by Nadir Shah to help his envoy explain the Persian morarch's message to Muhammad Shah.[110] It was also alleged that Burhan-ul-Mulk and Nizam-ul-Mulk, in order to humiliate Samsam-ud-Daulah at the hands of Nadir Shah, had written to Zakariya Khan the governor of the Punjab, not to resist the Persian invader.[111] In view of the evidence of Zakariya Khan's stand against Nadir Shah, this cannot be accepted.[112] But

---

[109] Mubarak, f. 139a.

[110] Shaikh Ali 'Hazin' in his autobiography, *Tazkirat-ul-Ahwal* mentions that Nadir Shah had sent a letter and an envoy to Burhan-ul-Mulk, Cf. F. C. Balfour's English translation, London 1830, p. 285.

[111] Shakir, f. 41b. According to the author of the *Risala*, Zakariya Khan, in league with Nizam-ul-Mulk and Sa'adat Khan, invited Nadir Shah and admitted him to Lahore, f. 100a.

[112] We, however, know that the governor of the Punjab was not happy with Samsam-ud-Daulah. The latter did not respond to his repeated appeals for help from the centre to defend the province. Compare *Jahan Kusha-i Nadiri*, p. 231.

contemporary evidence, of whatever nature, reflects the new *subadar*'s alienation from the Mughal centre.

Samsam-ud-Daulah fully appreciated the disadvantages of the presence of Nizam-ul-Mulk and Burhan-ul-Mulk together at the court at this juncture. He, therefore, spared no effort in preventing the emperor from inviting Burhan-ul-Mulk to the court.[113] On the other hand, it is not without significance that, according to some historians, Burhan-ul-Mulk was summoned at Nizam-ul-Mulk's suggestion.[114] However, Burhan-ul-Mulk came by slow marches up to Etawah, motivated, as it was rumoured, by a desire to see Samsam-ud-Daulah defeated before his arrival.[115]

What happened afterwards is known to us. We need not repeat the familiar story of the responsibility of Burhan-ul-Mulk or for that matter of Nizam-ul-Mulk for the humiliation of the Mughal Emperor in 1739. Who occupied the throne in Delhi was of little significance to the new *subadar*, provided he was allowed to rule his province with a free hand. But there is some evidence to indicate Burhan-ul-Mulk's personal loyalty to the Mughal Emperor.[116] This may be a naive attempt at portraying him as a superb example of the time-honoured value of being true to the salt and may in fact be apocryphal.

But significantly enough when he feared that Nadir Shah might stay in Delhi the new *subadar* revived his active interest in offices at the court. Burhan-ul-Mulk's attempt to secure a high office at the court and his anguish over the appointment of Nizam-ul-Mulk as the *mir bakshi*[117] can be seen as evidence of his belief in the possibility of the re-emergence of a strong centre.

Burhan-ul-Mulk's successor, Safdar Jang obtained the gov-

---

[113] *Risala*, f. 106b.   [114] Compare S. Chandra, *Parties and Politics*, p. 250.

[115] Mubarak, f. 138b. In this connection may also be noted the conduct of the soldiers of Burhan-ul-Mulk in the *chakla* of Etawah which was the *jagir* of Samsam-ud-Daulah. They ravaged the *chakla* and its people.

[116] On the eve of the battle of Karnal, for example, Burhan-ul-Mulk, is reported to have stated his relations with the Mughal Emperor as follows: 'I have a chronic disease and death has shown [me] its face. As I have risen from an ordinary (lit. of one horse) position to [the rank of] 7000 in the service of the Lord of the World and become master of 50,000 horsemen and a huge treasury, I wish I may sacrifice myself for His Majesty and pass away from this world cheerfully and triumphantly.' *Risala*, f. 108a.

[117] Compare A. L. Srivastava, *First Two Nawabs*, p. 87.

ernorship of Awadh virtually on account of heredity. In a measure, he acted more independently and took stronger steps to establish his authority firmly in the province. Yet, he could not afford to remain indifferent to the centre, even though his interest in court politics was merely to defend and augment his authority in Awadh.

Safdar Jang and the imperial court

After Burhan-ul-Mulk's death, his two young relatives, Safdar Jang and Sher Jang, petitioned the court for the governorship. As the language and the contents of their petition show, both the petitioners treated the governorship of Awadh as the personal property of Burhan-ul-Mulk.[118] Nobody, not even the emperor disputed the validity of such an assumption. This signified that the legitimization of an otherwise illegally asserted claim (Burhan-ul-Mulk's defiance in sticking to the *subadari* of Awadh in spite of an imperial order transferring him to Malwa) had already taken place. It also highlighted that Burhan-ul-Mulk's stay in Awadh after 1726 was exclusively by the virtue of his own strength. Yet, Sher Jang and Safdar Jang referred their cases to the centre and unlike the Nawabs of Bengal[119] refrained from settling the dispute among themselves. This shows the limitation of the new *subadari* in Awadh. Nadir Shah's presence in Delhi and the fear that he might stay in India was a crucial factor in this context. Nadir Shah is

---

[118] Sher Jang petitioned the emperor that being the son of Burhan-ul-Mulk's brother he was the rightful heir to the office of the deceased and that so long as he was available it would be unjust to confer it on Safdar Jang, the other claimant, who was merely a son of the late governor's sister. On the other hand, Lachhmi Narayan, the *vakil* of Burhan-ul-Mulk at the court, pleaded the case of Safdar Jang on the strength of the confidence that the late governor had reposed in him. He argued that Burhan-ul-Mulk did not have full confidence in the capacity of Sher Jang nor was he well-disposed towards him. Otherwise he would not have given his favourite daughter in marriage to Safdar Jang. 'In actuality', he added, 'neither Abul-Mansur nor Sher Jang have claim to the office and property of Burhan-ul-Mulk. They belong first to the emperor who might confer them on any body he pleases and according to the *Sharia* and the order of His Majesty to the daughter of the deceased. *Imad*, pp. 30–1; *Hadiqat*, p. 135; *Siyar*, II, 485; *Tarikh-i Shahiya Nishapuriya*, pp. 19–20.

[119] Compare K. K. Datta, *Alivardi Khan and His Times*, Calcutta, 1939, pp. 17–40 for the details of the dispute between Sarfaraz Khan and Alivardi Khan.

reported to have cast his greedy eye on the treasury of Awadh as well.[120] The attempt of Burhan-ul-Mulk's relatives to appropriate the *subadari* and the treasury of Awadh, disregarding the authority of the Delhi court could have brought the Persian invader to the province.

The award of the *subadari* was consequently for life and the province became the *subadar's* home country (*dar-ul-mulk*).[121] The new governor, Safdar Jang paid two crores of rupees from the provincial treasury as a *peshkash* for his governorship. This again showed the governor's personal claims over the treasury of Awadh.

However, the *jagirs* of Burhan-ul-Mulk, those which were outside Awadh, were not regarded as a part of the inheritance. The late governor's *jagirs*, according to the Mughal convention, were resumed and we find Safdar Jang repeatedly petitioning for their reassignment.[122] In his petitions nowhere did he mention his relation with Burhan-ul-Mulk as grounds for his claim to the *jagirs* of the deceased.

Thus, by the time Burhan-ul-Mulk died his family's claim over Awadh had been largely established. But the *jagir*, with all its modifications, still tied together the divergent parts of the nominal Mughal empire. In other words the Mughal court was not yet prepared to equate the new *subadar*, however independent he be, with the traditional indigenous chiefs.

With the coming of Safdar Jang to power in Awadh, there was yet another major development. Safdar Jang appropriated the imperial prerogative of conferring titles and *mansabs*. Although the formal approval of the emperor was sought, they

---

[120] Burhan-ul-Mulk following Nadir Shah's demand, sent Sher Jang to Awadh. Two thousand Persian troopers also accompanied him. Sher Jang later brought a sum of Rs 1,80,00,000. Compare Mubarak, f. 153b. This amount should not be mixed up, as Srivastava has done (p. 90n), with the *peshkash* of rupees two crore which Safdar Jang promised to pay to Nadir Shah on his appointment to the governorship of Awadh. The amount of the *peshkash* was brought from Awadh not by Sher Jang but by the people of *diwani* (*yasawalan-i diwan*), Cf. *Durra-i Nadira*, p. 198.

[121] Compare *Siyar*, II, 487.

[122] In one of his *arzdashts* to the emperor, Safdar Jang complained of financial losses and his inability to meet the challenges in the *suba* with the existing resources. He, therefore, asked for the grant of the *jagirs* of his uncle. Later when he knew of the *wazir's* opposition, he despatched a personal letter to the *wazir* explaining condition in the *suba* and sought his help in securing the *jagirs*. *Maktubat*, pp. 19 and 48.

were initially conferred by the governor himself. Besides, the nature of the emperor's approval was merely confirmatory and could be conveniently set aside if it did not accord with the governor's interests. It was the governor's responsibility to provide *jagirs* against such *mansabs*. The imperial consent to such *jagirs* was merely to add grace and dignity to the act.[123] Also, in 1745, in the wake of a famine, Safdar Jang managed the resumption, as we have seen earlier, of the *jagirs* of a large number of the nobles and *mansabdars* posted outside Awadh. The extent of independence Safdar Jang assumed in provincial matters is further illustrated from the details of his relations with the centre and the principalities in the neighbourhood. On more than one occasion, he clashed, for example, with the *wazir* on matters which had a bearing on the province.

In 1740 when Nadir Shah left Delhi, the 'Mughal nobles' and their associates held the most important offices and constituted the most powerful group at the centre. Qamar-ud-Din Khan was the *wazir*, Nizam-ul-Mulk had lately been appointed the *mir bakshi* while Khwaja Sad-ud-Din and his son, Khwaja Hafiz-ud-Din Khan held the offices of the *khan-i saman* and the *mir atish* respectively. But in view of their role in the battle of Karnal and also on the plea for the urgency of a strong and independent monarchy, the other group headed by Amir Khan attempted to take the emperor into confidence and hatch a plot against them. The emperor was persuaded to sack Qamar-ud-Din Khan and make Amir Khan the *wazir* of the empire.[124] The plot, however, failed and Amir Khan had to withdraw to Allahabad, following a strong protest by the 'Mughal' group.[125]

---

[123] There are three such instances which illustrate this. Since the beginning of Muhammad Shah's reign, Qutb-ud-Din Ali Khan was in the service of Burhan-ul-Mulk and then of Safdar Jang. After his death, his son, Azam Khan was given a rank of 1000/500 and a title of Azam Ali Khan. Mir Nasir-ud-Din, a maternal cousin of Safdar Jang, came to India in the time of Burhan-ul-Mulk. His rank and position under Burhan-ul-Mulk is not known to us. Safdar Jang, however, promoted him to 3000/2000 with a title of Nasir-ud-Din Khan Haidar. Muhammad Baqar Beg, described as young, polite, useful and serviceable was given a *mansab* of 500. These *mansabs* and titles were subsequently approved by the emperor through Lachhmi Narayan. *Maktubat*, pp. 40 and 186.

[124] Kalyan Singh, *Khulasat-ut-Tawarikh*, Patna MS., f. 50a.

[125] Their protest over the plot flared up when Amir Khan suggested that the principle of escheat be employed in the case of the properties of Badr-ud-Din Khan, son of the

Amir Khan's appointment as governor of Allahabad was not well received by Safdar Jang. Being the successor of Burhan-ul-Mulk who had held the provinces of Awadh and Allahabad on his death, Safdar Jang presumably aspired for the governorship of Allahabad as well. Yet he avoided a conflict with Amir Khan,[126] for, in the recent regrouping, the governor of Awadh had been gradually isolated from Qamar-ud-Din Khan. The breach had commenced with Burhan-ul-Mulk's resentment over the conferment of the office of the *mir bakhshi* on Nizam-ul-Mulk. The *wazir* had also opposed Safdar Jang's bid to secure the *jagirs* of Burhan-ul-Mulk. The breach between the *wazir* and Safdar Jang widened owing to their conflicting interests in the Moradabad-Bareilly region. Safdar Jang thus found it necessary to ally himself with Amir Khan. Moreover, with a large part of the province of Allahabad, e.g., the *sarkars* of Jaunpur, Ghazipur, Chunar and Benaras being under his control, Safdar Jang thought it inadvisable to antagonize Amir Khan as long the latter did not attempt to wrest these *sarkars* from his control.

Safdar Jang was not unaware of the possible consequences for him of the presence of a noble with close links with the emperor as the governor in Allahabad. It could well impose serious constraints on his control over, at least, these four *sarkars*, all the more because Mir Rustam Ali Khan who had held them on *ijara* for about fifteen years, and Balwant Singh, the powerful *zamindar* of Benaras, had their own grievances against him. Following a dispute with the governor of Awadh over the rate of the *ijara* in 1738, Mir Rustam Ali had been divested of the *ta'ahhud* of these *sarkars* and had been left with only the deputy *faujdari* of Benaras.[127] In the case of Balwant Singh, Mansa Ram's successor as the *ijaradar* and *faujdar* of Benaras, Chunar and Jaunpur, Safdar Jang insisted on the

wazir. The *wazir* and Nizam-ul-Mulk strongly resented the move. They left the capital and threatened to set out for the Deccan. A compromise, apparently at the suggestion of Ishaq Khan, was then arrived at. Accordingly, Nizam-ul-Mulk left for the Deccan leaving his son Ghazi-ud-Din Khan Firoz Jang as deputy *mir bakshi* at the court while Amir Khan had to go to Allahabad. Compare Shakir, f. 77a; *Siyar*, III, p. 847.

[126] *Imad*, p. 32; *Ma'dan*, ff. 150b–151a.

[127] In 1736 when Burhan-ul-Mulk obtained the *suba* of Allahabad he retained Mir Rustam in his existing position. But the amount of *ijara* was raised from Rs 5,00,000 to

payment of a heavy *peshkash* of Rs 5,00,000 and an increase of Rs 2,00,000 over the existing amount.[128] Mir Rustam and Balwant Singh approached the emperor through Amir Khan, in a bid to come into direct contact with the centre and thus challenge the position of the governor of Awadh. As Qamar-ud-Din Khan, an old rival of Safdar Jang, was still the *wazir* of the empire, they succeeded not inconsiderably in their bid.[129] But they could not upset Safdar Jang's scheme, since Amir Khan's prime interests lay in the centre.

Safdar Jang's efforts to befriend Amir Khan were thus guided by his interests in the province. His attempt to obtain an important office at the centre was again to gain ascendancy over his potential rivals in the region. For the same reasons, as we shall see below, later he turned against Amir Khan, to finally become the *wazir* and to wield unshared authority over the entire province of Allahabad.

In August 1743, Amir Khan was back at the court. Immediately after this, on his suggestion, the emperor invited the governor of Awadh as well. Amir Khan hoped that Safdar Jang's presence in Delhi would strengthen his hands against his enemies whereas if he were to remain in Awadh Amir Khan's position in Allahabad could be threatened. On the other hand, Safdar Jang also seems to have realized that he could not secure ground even in Awadh unless he held an important position at the court. For the province was theoretically a part of the

---

Rs 8,00,000. This was resented by Mir Rustam who then began to collude with the refractory *zamindars*. In 1738 therefore with a view to chastising the Mir, Safdar Jang reached Jaunpur. The Mir was not prepared for this. He sent Mansa Ram, the sub-*ijaradar* and the *zamindar* of Benaras, to negotiate with Safdar Jang on his behalf. In the meanwhile, however, *sarkar* Ghazipur was taken away from the Mir and was assigned to Burhan-ul-Mulk's associate, Shaikh Abdullah. Mansa Ram, who had his own grievances against the Mir, then manipulated to get the remaining three *sarkars* for himself on the payment of an annual sum of Rs 13,00,000. Cf. *Tuhfa*, 10a–11b and *Maktubat*, pp. 60 and 175.

[128] Kamboh, f. 65b; see also Korwi, *Tarikh-i Benaras*, p. 124–5.

[129] Balwant Singh secured a *farman* from the emperor awarding the *zamindari* of the Benaras region and the title of raja. After that he is reported to have stopped the revenue to Safdar Jang. Mir Rustam tried to obtain the deputy governorship of Allahabad along with the *faujdari* of the *sarkars* Benaras and Jaunpur. Before he could get a response to his *arzdasht*, however, he was captured by Safdar Jang for his failure to clear the account of a huge sum of *ijara*. He was put into prison where he died. Kamboh, ff. 48b–49b and Korwi, *Tarikh-i Benaras*, p. 130.

empire and forts all over the country including Awadh were still under the control of the centre.[130]

Safdar Jang arrived at the court on 17 November 1743 and within a few months on 21 March 1744 the office of *mir atish* which had eluded Burhan-ul-Mulk twice in 1727 and 1739 was conferred upon him.[131] As Safdar Jang replaced Khwaja Hafiz-ud-Din Khan, an associate of the *wazir* and Nizam-ul-Mulk, his appointment was a major gain for Amir Khan too. The office gave its holder an authority to supervise the major arsenals and the forts all over the empire[132] and included the responsibilities of looking after the person, the assets and the honour of the emperor as well.[133] Safdar Jang was thus in close touch with the emperor. Besides, he and Amir Khan were now in a position to strengthen themselves militarily against the 'Mughal' group.[134] The province of the Punjab was one of the strongholds of the 'Mughal' group. Amir Khan, therefore, had managed to keep at least one contiguous province, i.e., Kashmir under the control of his own man, Asad Yar Khan. In the absence of Amir Khan from the court, however, Asad Yar Khan's loyalty to Amir Khan was questioned. On 4 October 1744 therefore, Safdar Jang replaced him as the governor of Kashmir.[135]

But, while Safdar Jang and Amir Khan acted in unison against the 'Mughal' group, their interests and views in matters of the regions, as we have seen above, were not identical. This was one reason why Mir Rustam and Balwant Singh expected

---

[130] This is illustrated by the fact that in 1742 when Safdar Jang was ordered by the emperor to march towards Bengal to assist Ali Vardi Khan against the Marathas, Safdar Jang wanted the fort of Rohtas. Cf. A. L. Srivastava, *First Two Nawabs*, pp. 93–7. Again, even though he held the *faujdari* of the *sarkar* of Chunar, the fort of Chunar was not under his control. He could secure the fort only in 1744. Cf. *Tarikh-i Shahiya Nishapuriya*, p. 23.

[131] *Siyar*, III, pp. 849 and 852–53; Mubarak, f. 163b; *Maktubat*, p. 32. Muhammad Ali Khan's statement that Safdar Jang obtained the office of the *mir atish* in lieu of his governorship of Awadh is obviously wrong. Cf. *T. Muzaffari*, f. 257b.

[132] Compare *Ausaf*, f. 42a which eulogizing Safdar Jang states that in the wake of Safdar Jang's assumption of the office of the *mir atish* (*topkhana-i mu'alla*) the forts of Hindustan, e.g., Akbarabad, Gwalior, Ilahabad, Chunar, Kalinjar, Rohtas, Alwar, Tijara and Daulatabad stood on a firm and stable footing.

[133] Compare *Siyar*, III, p. 852.

[134] 'The fort of Delhi had been vacant after the return of Nadir Shah. Now within a day Safdar Jang filled it with his own soldiers'. Cf. *Ausaf*, f. 42a.

[135] *Siyar*, III, p. 853; Mubarak, f. 163b.

Amir Khan to mediate, as indeed he did, while recommending their cases to the emperor.[136] Safdar Jang apprehended a threat to his position in Awadh if Amir Khan was allowed to combine his governorship of Allahabad with the office of the *wazir* at Delhi. He was thus gradually alienated from Amir Khan too, and aspired to build his own group at the centre. In achieving this quickly he was also assisted by Amir Khan's temperament. Amir Khan was arrogant and cared little for 'the decency that the nobles should maintain while conferring with the Kings' during the period when he held the office of the *wazir* for over seven months in 1746 owing to the illness of Qamar-ud-Din Khan.[137] Safdar Jang together with Najm-ud-Daulah Muhammad Ishaq Khan II whose sister had been married to his son, Shuja-ud-Daulah[138] (then Jalal-ud-Din Haidar), thus emerged as the leader of a new group of the emperor's favourites, followed by the death of Amir Khan in mysterious circumstances.[139]

After the death of Amir Khan, Safdar Jang became a pre-eminent noble at the court, next only to the *wazir* who was senior to him in age and service. In Rajab 1160/June-July 1747, Najm-ud-Daulah who was now his closest associate was appointed *diwan-i khalisa.*[140] In January 1748 when Safdar Jang was de-

---

[136] Kamboh, f. 49b and Korwi, *Tarikh-i Benaras*, pp. 129–30.

[137] Compare *Siyar*, III, pp. 857–8.

[138] Since Najm-ud-Daulah was the son of the late Mutamad-ud-Daulah Muhammad Ishaq Khan I who owed his fortunes to the patronage of Amir Khan, the latter treated him and his brothers with contempt. The emperor therefore wanted to strengthen Najm-ud-Daulah's position by negotiating a marriage between his sister and the son of Safdar Jang in 1745. Cf. *Siyar*, III, p. 858 and *Tarikh-i Shahiya Nishpuriya*, pp. 24–5.

[139] Amir Khan then grew apprehensive of the emperor's intentions and in desperate haste even plotted to depose Muhammad Shah and place on the throne one of the princes imprisoned in the Salimgarh fort. When he failed there, he insisted on replacing the existing *nazir-i darbar* (chief watchman of the court) by one of his own associates. In consequence, an aggrieved servant of Amir Khan was allegedly instigated to stab him to death. (25 December 1746). And nobody, not even Safdar Jang, took the responsibility of performing the last rituals for the deceased immediately. Amir Khan had not paid his troopers' salaries for fourteen months. They, therefore, immediately after his death, demanded the payment of their arrears and did not allow his burial to take place. On the fifth day apparently after the jewellery and the treasury of the deceased had been valued, Safdar Jang took it upon himself to discharge the debt. Amir Khan's assets worth 50 to 60 lakhs of rupees were valued at Rs 1,00,000 only. Compare *Siyar*, III, pp. 850–1 and 860–1.

[140] *Siyar*, p. 860. Najm-ud-Daulah succeeded Yahya Khan who was appointed to the

puted to fight under Prince Ahmad Shah against Ahmad Shah
Abdali, he was given Ambala and some other *parganas* from the
province of the Punjab in *jagir,* and also an amount of Rs
8,50,000 towards the expenditure of his troops.[141] In the meanwhile, Qamar-ud-Din Khan, the *wazir,* died in the battle
against Abdali. Subsequently, on 28 April, on the occasion of
his accession, Ahmad Shah, the new emperor, promised him
the office of the *wizarat* which he virtually held till 29 June when
he was formally appointed the *wazir* of the empire. His son,
Jalal-ud-Din Haidar, now entitled as Shuja-ud-Daulah, succeeded him as the *mir atish.*[142]

With the death of Amir Khan also emerged a situation in
which Safdar Jang ensured his undisputed control over the
province of Allahabad. Amir Khan's nephew, Baqaullah Khan
who had every chance to succeed him in the province obtained
only the *niyabat,* Safdar Jang himself acquiring the full-fledged
subadari.[143] In 1748, in the wake of the new appointments and
promotions at Ahmad Shah's accession to the throne, Sa'adat
Khan Zulfiqar Jang was appointed the governor of Allahabad
while Safdar Jang got the *suba* of Ajmer. An unprecedented

---

office of the *diwan-i khalisa* in 1744–5 after the dismissal of Abd-ul-Majid Khan
Kashmiri. He was a poet and a good prose writer (Cf. Qayam ud-Din 'Hairat':
Maqalat-ush-Shu'ra MS. Rampur, f. 80b) and was presumably a friend of Amir Khan
whose friends and supporters according to our sources were mainly the artists and the
men of letters.

[141] A. L. Srivastava, *First Two Nawabs,* p. 116.

[142] *Siyar,* III, pp. 868–9; *T. Ahmad Shahi,* f. 14b. Safdar Jang had been nominated to
the *wizarat* on the day of Ahmad Shah's accession at Panipat. But in fear of Nizam-ul-
Mulk it was kept secret and to ascertain his views, the emperor and Safdar Jang wrote
to him to come to Delhi and take over the responsibilities of the *wizarat.* Nizam-ul-
Mulk, however, excused himself on account of old age and ill-health and advised Safdar
Jang to accept the office. Yet, the formal appointment was delayed till Nizam-ul-Mulk
died on 31 May 1748. See for details A. L. Srivastava, *First Two Nawabs,* pp. 122–4;
J. N. Sarkar, *Fall of the Mughal Empire,* I, pp. 212–13.

[143] *T. Muzaffari,* f. 268b; *Khizana-i Amira,* p. 78; *Tabsira,* f. 107b; *M. U.,* I, pp. 60–1.
Only *M. U.* mentions Baqaullah Khan as the deputy of Safdar Jang in Allahabad.
Also, according to *M. U.,* Safdar Jang got the *subadari* of Allahabad in 1743 much before
the death of Amir Khan.

I could not find any evidence for Sir Jadu Nath Sarkar's opinion that after the death
of Amir Khan, Baqaullah Khan (whom he has wrongly identified as the son of the
deceased), was appointed the *subadar* of Allahabad. See his note on the lead page of the
Tarikh-i Suba-i Ilahabad (anonymous) MS., Allahabad University Library.

incident took place at this juncture. Without publicly defying
the emperor's order Safdar Jang accepted the reshuffle and then
exchanged his new assignment in Ajmer with Zulfiqar Jang's in
Allahabad. Zulfiqar Jang perhaps recognized the difficulties of
governing Allahabad without Safdar Jang's cooperation. The
exchange highlighted the nobles' attempt to adjust the distribution of administrtive power with the nominal authority of the
emperor.

The new *subadar* was thus involved in court politics even in the
last phase of our period. But at this stage, his involvement in
court politics had as its objective an attempt at reinforcing his
well-entrenched authority in the province, while earlier it had
been intended to provide him with a base at the centre where he
could return in case of failure in the province.

II THE PUNJAB

Abd-us-Samad Khan, the new *subadar* of the Punjab, like his
counterpart in Awadh, treated the province as his personal
domain, making every possible effort to secure his authority
there. When his rivals at the court, in a bid to weaken his power
in the Punjab, secured his transfer to Kabul, he refused to leave
the Punjab to take up his new assignment.

However, the differences in the respective positions of the
new *subadars* in Awadh and the Punjab are unmistakable.
Burhan-ul-Mulk and Safdar Jang's involvement in court politics was guided by their interests in the province; they held
premier positions in their factions, and their association with
the court had little bearing on their decisions in provincial
matters. On the other hand, since Abd-us-Samad Khan and
Zakariya Khan, the new *subadars* in the Punjab, belonged to the
close 'Mughal' kin group, led by no less a person than the *wazir*
himself, factional strife at the court affected developments in the
Punjab. While association with a court faction, in the case of
Burhan-ul-Mulk and Safdar Jang, in a measure helped them
strengthen their gains in Awadh, in the case of Abd-us-Samad
Khan and Zakariya Khan it tended to limit their freedom.
These factors by themselves carried enough weight to influence,
but, of course, not to determine, the course of political formations in Awadh and the Punjab. They also acquired particular

import as there was a glaring contrast in the social and
economic conditions of the two provinces. The continued
growth in and around Awadh from the seventeenth through the
eighteenth century lent strength to the governor to act independently; while the steadily increasing instability in the economy
of the Punjab, its links with the north-west frontiers of the
empire, the invasions and the magnitude of its internal problems was a serious setback to the process of growth of the new
subadari in the province.

Abd-us-Samad Khan and the
neighbouring provinces

From the developments of this phase of the period of our study,
it is evident that the governor of the Punjab aspired for control
over almost the entire Indus region.[144] From 1717 onwards,
Inayatullah Khan with Mir Ahmad Khan as his *naib* was the
governor of Kashmir. In 1720, in the wake of a serious civil
disturbance Mumin Khan Najm-i Sani replaced Mir Ahmad
Khan as the deputy governor and imperial orders were sent to
the *faujdars* of the Punjab to deploy half their retainers in
Kashmir to assist him in suppressing the rebels.[145] We have no
evidence of the *faujdars'* response to the imperial orders.
Mumin Khan, however, did not succeed in restoring peace in
Kashmir. This was the best opportunity for Abd-us-Samad
Khan to extend his control over the province of Kashmir.
Subsequently, his son, Zakariya Khan replaced Inayatullah
Khan as the governor of Kashmir.[146]

The extension of the power of Abd-us-Samad Khan into
Kashmir seems to have been resented and also resisted by at·
least Inayatullah Khan and his friends. As soon as Zakariya
Khan returned from Kashmir, Mumin Khan Najm-i Sani who
was still in Kashmir, began to create difficulties, in collusion

[144] See Chapter II, Section II.

[145] Kamwar, ff. 371a and 377a; K. K., II, p. 867; Shivdas, f. 76a and *T. Muzaffari*, 171a.
According to tne *Asrar-i Samadi* (p. 33) Abd-us-Samad Khan, in addition to his existing
governorship of the Punjab, was made governor of Kashmir with Zakariya Khan as his
naib.

For the disturbances in Kashmir see Kamwar, p. 300 and *M. U.*, III, pp. 761–5.
[146] Kamwar, f. 377a.

with the rioters, for the new deputy governor and the latter, unable to counter the threat, was forced to remain in his house. Then Abd-us-Samad Khan himself together with a strong detachment arrived in Kashmir and broke their strength by resuming their *jagirs*, their *a'immas* and their daily allowances (*yaumiyas*).[147]

Again, though Qamar-ud-Din Khan the *wazir* was Abd-us-Samad Khan's friend at the court, Samsam-ud-Daulah, the *mir bakhshi* and the Koki group which had been in possession of real authority was by all accounts hostile to him. They believed that if the governorship of two contiguous provinces remained in Abd-us-Samad's hands it would mean the strengthening of an important element of the new *subadari* in the Punjab. Under the plea for the necessity of a strong man on the disturbed northwest frontiers,[148] they managed to secure an order from the emperor for Abd-us-Samad Khan's transfer to Kabul. A sum of Rs 10,00,000 was despatched to him to raise an army for Kabul. In addition, Rs 20,00,000 were promised to him on his arrival at Kabul. Later, the total amount (Rs 30,00,000) was paid to him even before his departure for Kabul. A number of imperial orders spreading over a period of six months are said to have been despatched to him. But Abd-us-Samad Khan did not pay any attention to these orders. It was about seven months after the order of his transfer that his letter was received at the court, stating his refusal to leave Lahore.[149]

Abd-us-Samad Khan's defiance showed his strength and also signified, as in the case of Awadh, an important departure from the conventional pattern of the relations of the centre with the governor of the Punjab. However, he maintained rapport with the emperor by sending his son and also *arzdashts* to him, probably to explain his inability to go to Kabul.[150] His refusal to

[147] *T. Muzaffari*, ff. 182b–183a; *Bahr-ul-Mawwaj*, f. 284a.

[148] For disturbances on the north-west frontiers at this time see *M. U.*, III, pp. 703–6.

[149] *Mirat-ul-Haqaiq*, f. 294b. Abd-us-Samad Khan was appointed the governor of Kabul on 15 Jumada I, 1136/30 January 1724, and an entry dated 26 Zi Hijja 1136/4 September 1724, in the *Mirat-ul-Haqaiq* records his refusal.

[150] Ibid., ff. 297b, 306a and 351b for the *arzdashts* dated 12 Muharram 1137/20 September 1724; 26 Rabi I, 1137/2 December 1724 and 9 Zi Hijja 1137/8 August 1725; 299a for Zakariya Khan's arrival near Delhi on 22 Muharram 1137/30 September 1724.

comply with the imperial order could hardly impair his position either in the province or at the court, for the *wazir* was always there to fight his case by exaggerating his difficulties. It was under these circumstances that Abd-us-Samad Khan managed to secure the governorship of Multan in 1726 while retaining the governorship of the Punjab and Kashmir for his son, Zakariya Khan who was now promoted to 7000/7000.[151] It may be noted that he was reluctant to go to Multan without having been assured of his hold over the Punjab.[152]

But while Abd-us-Samad Khan's close association with the *wazir* buttressed his position, it enmeshed him in court politics and sometimes threatened his authority in the province as well. Abd-us-Samad Khan had to face opposition not only from his rivals but also from the opponents of the *wazir* at the court. This is illustrated from the way he had to forego the governorship of Kashmir. It appears that Lutfullah Sadiq and his brothers who hailed from Panipat had also begun to aspire for the governorship of any of the north-west provinces on a permanent basis. Since 1721 Lutfullah Sadiq and his brother, Sher Afgan Khan had been governing the province of Multan alternately and one of their brothers, Diler Dil Khan was still the governor of Thatta.[153] After 1726 when Abd-us-Samad Khan secured Multan, they combined with Amir Khan, an avowed enemy of the *wazir*. Subsequently, in 1731, Diler Dil Khan replaced Zakariya Khan as the governor of Kashmir, while Amir Khan secured the governorship of Thatta for himself with Diler Dil Khan's son, Himmat Diler Khan as his *naib*. Since his strength in the region also meant the strength of the *wazir* as the leader of the faction he was associated with, the new *subadar* had to govern the province under certain constraints. Diler Dil Khan thus chose Abul-Barakat Khan, a native of Kashmir as his deputy and himself preferred to stay at Lahore at Amir Khan's instance. This obviously imposed a check on the governor of the Punjab.[154] After that till the end of our period, the province

---

[151] Ibid., ff. 403, 412a, 433b and 435b.   [152] Cf. *Asrar-i Samadi*, p. 41.

[153] Shivdas, f. 67a; *T. Muzaffari*, f. 190a.

[154] *T. Muhammadi*, p. 95 and *T. Muzaffari*, f. 80b. Abul-Barakat Khan was the son of Muhammad Kazim Khan who had earlier held the *niyabat* and the *diwani* of Kashmir in the time of the *subadari* of Inayatullah Khan, K. K., II, p. 867; *T. Muhammadi*, pp. 82 and 131. Later Diler Dil Khan was replaced by Ataullah Khan, son of Inayatullah Khan, out the *niyabat* remained with Abul-Barakat Khan.

of Kashmir was in the possession of one or the other associate of
the rival of the *wazir* and thus of the governor of the Punjab as
well.

However, Abd-us-Samad Khan's rivals even in combination
with the opponents of the *wazir* could not dispossess him from
the governorship of Multan, notwithstanding their special endeavour to regain the province which they had held for over five
years consecutively. Towards the end of his governorship, the
unity of the Punjab and Multan seems to have been widely
recognized. Even though there is no direct evidence for the
emergence of this unity, there are strong grounds to believe
that it was based on the Punjab's close social and commercial
links with the northern tracts of *suba* Multan, as well as with
chakla Sirhind in the cis-Sutlej area. After the decline of imperial
control over the region, therefore, it was perhaps generally
appreciated that Multan and Sirhind had to be under the
administrative jurisdiction of Lahore, if the Punjab, the buffer
between the north-west borders and Delhi, was to function as
an independent province. It is not unlikely that Lahore's connections with the regions in the area also contributed to Diler
Dil Khan's decision to stay there and govern Thatta through
his deputy, particularly when he too along with his brother,
Lutfullah Sadiq aspired for control over the Indus basin. At any
rate, by the time of Abd-us-Samad Khan's death in 1738, the
provinces of Multan and the Punjab had become one political
unit. His son, Zakariya Khan who held the Punjab, therefore
succeeded to the governorship of Multan on grounds of hereditary rights,[155] while *chakla* Sirhind seems to have been in the
faujdari of the *wazir*. Ali Muhammad Khan Rohilla deputized
for the *wazir* in Sirhind for about five years after his 'exile' from
the Moradabad-Bareilly region.

The governor of the Punjab and the north-western frontier

The diminished imperial authority over the Punjab also implied a serious threat to the north-western borders and thus to
the whole of the Mughal empire. As Roshan-ud-Daulah and

---

[155] *M. U.*, II, p. 517; *Siyar*, II, p. 477; and *T. Muzaffari*, f. 80b.

Samsam-ud-Daulah, the *wazir*'s opponents, had the charge of Kabul affairs at the centre, the revenues from the *parganas* of the Punjab meant for the maintenance of the army in Kabul were often withheld by the governor.

Since the beginning of our period, the revenue of *chakla* Gujarat and the *parganas* of Eminabad, Pasrur and the Salt Range in the Punjab were earmarked for the pay-claims of the Mughal army in Kabul. But the amount seems to have, not infrequently, been withheld in the Punjab itself. As early as the reign of Bahadur Shah, it was reported that the governor of Kabul could not pay the army as he had not received a single penny from the *mahals* of the Punjab. Subsequently, the *mahals* assigned to the *mansabdars* in command of the contingents in Kabul were resumed into *khalisa*, with a view to eliminating the conflict between the individual *mansabdars* and the local officials of these *mahals*.[156] Even then, the governors of the Punjab and Kabul sometimes seem to have had disputes over the revenue of these *mahals*.[157] But no serious complaint from the governor of Kabul is recorded till the beginning of Muhammad Shah's reign. A measure of the new *subadar*'s independence from the centre was that he arbitrarily stopped the practice of despatching the revenue of these *mahals* to Kabul at a time when Kabul needed it most.[158]

The centre could not effect any change in the attitude of the governor of the Punjab. Consequently, 'owing to the negligence of the imperial officials and the contumacy of the governor of

---

[156] *Akhbarat*, BS, 5th R. Y., II, pp. 399, 439–40 and 459.

[157] Sometimes cultivation in the villages seems to have been disturbed due to some extraneous reasons such as the tyranny of the local officials. Cf. *Akhbarat* FS, 6th–8th R. Ys., p. 104.

[158] The magnitude of the defiance can be seen from a letter from the court to the governor of Kabul in response to the latter's desperate *arzdasht* to the emperor. '[your petition] in regard to the expenditure of the *suba* [of Kabul] and the request for issuing a strict order to Abd us-Samad Khan was put before the emperor. All at once, an instruction was sent to the *vakil* of the aforementioned Khan [Abd-us-Samad Khan] stating "that the *pargana* of Eminabad, etc., as per the former practice is a frontier. God forbid, if any disturbance occurs, your client will be asked for explanation". He [the *vakil*] said that he would present to the emperor the *razinama* from the agent of the governor of Kabul within the period of a month. Accordingly, a *muchalka* [bond] has been taken from him [the *vakil*]. You do not worry there will not be any delay in the despatch of the sum from the above mentioned *mahals*.' *Dastur-ul-Insha*, ff. 54.

Lahore', as a contemporary chronicler observes in 1737 'the Afghans of that district who were in the service of the emperor and were deputed in Kabul, and whose salaries were fixed from the *mahals* of *suba* Lahore, did not receive their emoluments for the last few years. Perforce, they gave up imperial service and took up their own way [left for their homes and resorted to robbery]'.[159]

There is a possibility that Abd-us-Samad Khan became indifferent to the problems of the borders after he had failed in his bid to combine the governorship of Kabul together with that of the Punjab and Multan. An undisturbed Kabul was, however, evidently a must for stability in the Punjab. In the face of the financial and military bankruptcy of the Mughal court, the governor of the Punjab had to take note of political developments on and beyond the north-western frontiers. This was probably one reason why Zakariya Khan was extremely courteous to the Persian envoy at Lahore and his *mutasaddi* then accompanied the embassy to Delhi.[160] Similarly, it was essential for the governor of the Punjab to contain the Afghan tribes on the frontier. Disruption and independent rule in Kabul had always conditioned the fortunes of Lahore. But unfortunately by the time the Mughal emperor became aware of the repercussions of his indifference to the Persian embassy and issued orders to Abd-us-Samad Khan in this regard, the latter had died.[161] Zakariya Khan who had succeeded him and combined the governorship of Lahore with the governorship of Multan was too preoccupied in dealing with the forces which threatened his authority in these provinces to go to the frontier.

The major question before Zakariya Khan was to safeguard his position in the Punjab and Multan. As long as he was able to govern them with the privileges that governorship had by then begun to entail, the question of who was on the throne of Delhi was of little concern to him. Thus, when Nadir Shah had entered Mughal territory Zakariya Khan, who had little in the way of resources to defend his possessions against the Persian invader, had no option but to submit. His submission to Nadir Shah was a useful device to save his power and interests in the

---

[159] *Chahar Gulzar*, f. 355b.   [160] Ashub, f. 136a.
[161] Ibid., f. 160a.

provinces.[162] An eighteenth-century historian writes of the whole episode—Zakariya Khan's preparation, initial fight and then compromise—as the war and peace of the fools.[163] Nadir Shah not only retained Zakariya Khan in his existing position, but also helped him, though primarily in his own interest, by leading an expedition against Nur Muhammad Leti, an important *zamindar* of Multan. The expedition obviously strengthened Zakariya Khan's authority and placed a check on some internal threats to his *subadari*.[164] Zakariya Khan, however, could not avoid having to bear the financial loss. He was promoted by Nadir Shah to the coveted rank of 8000/8000, but he had also to part with the revenue of a substantial part of the Punjab and Multan. Gujarat, Sialkot, Pasrur and Aurangabad and a few *mahals* of the *zamindari* of Khuda Yar Khan and Ghazi Khan in Multan were for all practical purposes annexed to the empire of Nadir Shah and Zakariya Khan was made an *ijaradar* of these *mahals* at Rs 20,00,000.[165] Although it is not possible to say that the amount was highly inflated, some kind of dual government in these *mahals* did undoubtedly create difficulties for Zakariya Khan. In 1743 it was reported that the people (traders?) of Wazirabad and Sialkot and some other towns, reduced to distress by Nadir Shah's deputy, Tahmasp Quli Khan, had decided to flee to Lahore,[166] and from there further to the east of Delhi and south of Multan.

Close on the heels of the steadily deteriorating economy of the region, came the devastations in the wake of the Persian inva-

---

[162] Zakariya Khan, though unsupported by the court, had made what defensive arrangements he could within his limited resources. Eventually he decided to surrender, but he could not save the *suba* from being plundered by the troops of Nadir Shah. Besides, every person in the province seems to have tried to take advantage of the disturbances and 'put forth his hand to plunder and pillage'. Cf. W. Irvine, *Later Moghuls*, II, pp. 331 and 333–4.

[163] Cf. *Siyar*, II, p. 482.

[164] *Siyar*, II, pp. 482 and 487. Nur Muhammad Leti, entitled Khuda Yar Khan was a powerful chief of Multan. His father Yar Muhammad had earned the title of Khuda Yar Khan and a *mansab* from Farrukh Siyar. In 1149/1736–7 Nur Muhammad was appointed the governor of Thatta and *sarkar* Bhakkar. The nature of his relations with Zakariya Khan at this juncture is not known to us. A powerful *zamindar's* rise to such position in and around Multan was, however, unwelcome to Zakariya Khan, Cf. *M. U.*, I, pp. 825–9.

[165] *Tazkira Mukhlis*, p. 78.   [166] Mubarak, f. 158b.

sion, causing a serious setback to the process of the consolidation of the new *subadari* in the Punjab. The province could not
recover from the shocks of the invasion and in 1748 it received
yet another grievious blow from the plunders of Abdali. The
jagirs of a number of important nobles (some of them were the
governor's relations and associates at the court), also restricted
the growth of the new *subadari* in the Punjab; and the governor
of the Punjab unlike Nizam ul-Mulk did not have the advantage
of geographical distance. He was thus never in a position to
assert the degree of independence equal to that of the governor
of Awadh. On many an occasion, he had to comply with imperial directives against his judgement. This is illustrated, for
instance, from an incident of 1742. A Mughal noble, Azimullah
Khan who had been reproved for his failure against the
Marathas and had been dismissed from his office of the *sadr*,
retired to Lahore. Since this was done without the emperor's
permission, the *wazir*'s sons at the head of over 2000 horsemen
were deputed to bring him back to the court. A sister of
Zakariya Khan's wife was married to Azimullah Khan. The
governor of Lahore therefore treated him well and apparently
was reluctant to hand him over to the imperial party. But he
had to make the fugitive over to them even though he knew that
Azimullah Khan would be imprisoned.[167]

Political developments in the Punjab after 1745

By 1745 when Zakariya Khan died, the hereditary claim of his
family over the Punjab and Multan had been established. But
the claim extended to the entire 'Mughal' group, owing to their
kinship with the governor. The Punjab thus had become the
homeland of the Mughals, and hence the non-'Mughal' faction's bid to retrieve these provinces from the family of Zakariya
Khan. This is vividly borne out from Anand Ram Mukhlis's
account in his *Tazkira*. According to Mukhlis the services of
Abd-us-Samad Khan and Zakariya demanded that following
the latter's death the provinces of the Punjab and Multan be
given to the sons of the deceased. 'Indeed the province of
Lahore', he adds, 'had been the Balkh and Bukhara of the

---

[167] *Siyar*, III, pp. 848–9.

Mughals where they had their mansions, orchards and grave-yards . . . . The appointment of anyone else (as the governor of the Punjab) would amount to the province's ruin and desolation.'[168]

Mukhlis's account showed how much the province of the Punjab had begun to be treated by the Mughals as their personal domain like a *watan* of an autonomous *zamindar*. He comments on the emperor's refusal to concede the claim of the sons of Zakariya Khan 'while Raja Isar Singh, son of Rajadhiraj [Sawai Jai Singh] after the death of his father had been honoured with [the award of] the *zamindari* of Amber and the governorship of Akbarabad [Agra] together with the *jagirs* that his father had held.'[169] Mukhlis, however, noted with satisfaction that ultimately at the *wazir*'s great insistence, the emperor ignored 'the others' proposal and conferred both the provinces to him [*wazir*]'. This appointment according the Mukhlis was in actuality the appointment of the sons of Zakariya Khan.[170]

The *wazir*'s effort was apparently aimed towards retaining, for his group, the resources of the power and authority they had gained in the Punjab and Multan. In view of the emperor's reluctance and the resistance of Safdar Jang and Amir Khan to the appointment of the sons of Zakariya Khan, he tried to secure these provinces for himself. For, the control of these provinces by the group and not the governorship of any particular individual was the issue at stake. The *wazir*, as Mukhlis reports, intended to go to Lahore to set things right, but an accident in which he broke his leg prevented him from doing so. Since Safdar Jang and Amir Khan were ever apprehensive of their opponents having a strong base in proximity to Delhi at Lahore and Multan they wanted to take full advantage of Zakariya Khan's death to break their opponents' control over the Punjab. Safdar Jang's governorship of Kashmir formed part of this plan.

The circumstances that followed the death of Zakariya Khan in the Punjab made the position of the governor *vis-à-vis* the imperial court meaningless. Once Kabul broke away from

---

[168] Cf. *Tazkira Mukhlis*, p. 134. Balkh and Bukhara were the towns in Central Asia from where the 'Mughal' nobles (Turanis) hailed.

[169] Ibid., p. 135.   [170] Ibid.

Delhi, the governor of the Punjab encountered difficulties from those in control of the erstwhile north-western borders of the Mughal empire. Nonetheless, Zakariya Khan remained loyal to Delhi, evidently because of his old personal ties with the Mughal Emperor and the *wazir*. But his sons had no such consideration for Delhi.

Yahya Khan and Shahnawaz Khan, who were then the deputies of the *wazir* in the Punjab and Multan, had serious differences over the left-over assets of Zakariya Khan. The dispute eventually led to the eruption of civil war in 1746 in Lahore. Yahya Khan, the lawful deputy governor of Lahore was overpowered and imprisoned by Shahnawaz Khan who deputized for the *wazir* in Multan. Although later he sent his envoy to the emperor to seek legitimization of his conduct, the emperor, at the suggestion of the *wazir*, was reluctant to recognize him as the lawful *naib* in Lahore. When Shahnawaz Khan feared reprisals from the Mughal centre, he did not hesitate to break even nominal relations. Shahnawaz Khan then sought legitimacy from those in control of Kabul and beyond, only to further confirm the politico-military importance of the north-west frontiers in relation to Delhi's control of the Punjab.[171]

---

[171] Compare Sujan Rai Bhandari, *Khulasat-ut-Tawarikh*, p. 88; J. N. Sarkar, *Fall of the Mughal Empire*, I, pp. 119–21; Ganda Singh, *Ahmad Shah Durrani*, pp. 40–3.

Conclusion

The stresses resulting in the disintegration of the Mughal empire towards the last phase of the period of our study, were first reflected in the crisis of the relations between the emperor and the nobility. When the *zamindars* in the regions resisted the authority of the centre effectively, the nobles in control of provinces began to see this as a threat to their fortunes and sought more powers. The emperor did not view this as a systemic crisis but as a mere extension of the old problem of the entrenched position of dominant sections of the nobility and tried to counter this by encouraging the newer elements.

However, the problem of the nobility at this stage was no longer linked to one or other group of the nobles. It concerned the organization and the emoluments of the entire class of the nobility and percolated down to officials on lower rungs as well. It was closely linked to the challenges that the emperor and the state officials began to face in the regions. The emperor believed wrongly that by reasserting his position as the source of all power and patronage he could recover the waning prestige of the empire. While, on the one hand, the emperor was unable to evolve innovative solutions outside the well-established framework of the emperor-noble equations, the nobles' urge for additional powers, on the other, indicated that the principle of the emperor as the source of all authority was no longer tenable.

The provincial governor's attempt to combine his authority, ultimately, with all powers and offices in the province marked a virtual rejection of the authority of the imperial centre. The process of change began when the old and established nobles (the *khanazads*) tried to make up for the loss of their prestige at the centre by seeking additional powers in the provinces. They were allowed this privilege in consideration of their eminent position in the hierarchy of the nobility. But this did not represent the aspiration of the *khanazads* alone; it was part of a wider problem of the provincial administration, reflected in the second phase of our period in the changing position of the governor. At the beginning of this phase, the governors of Awadh enjoyed some additional authority, even though they could not claim the eminence and the influence of their predecessors. Soon the governor sought a major break from established Mughal convention in Farrukh Siyar's reign when he made an effort to maintain a longer term of office, to extend his authority to a province in the neighbourhood and, above all, to control provincial finance. In 1716, the governor even resisted the conferment of executive and military powers by the imperial centre on the provincial *diwan*. This was obviously incompatible with the imperial control of the province and the Mughal system of 'checks and balances'.

The appointment of Girdhar Bahadur in 1719 perhaps amply illustrates the change in the attitude of the nobles posted in the province towards imperial authority. Girdhar himself chose the province. This was in keeping with developments at the court where nobles and not the emperor had come to dictate the course of state action. It eroded the very basis of imperial authority. To such governorships we can trace the beginnings of the new *subadari* and provincial independence in the eighteenth century.

This change was, however, also conditioned by the nature of relations between the nobles in control of provinces and the central authorities. The emperor, during the first phase, saw the governors' plea for extended powers as a threat to imperial power founded on their claims to high position as *khanazads*. He allowed them to govern the provinces with special privileges in order to keep them at a distance from the court. But the emperor was unable to resist the erosion of his power, since his authority rested on support from the nobles. The emperor was compelled to reconcile with one or the other faction of the nobility, whom he considered to be less ambitious and who, to him, appeared to be willing to help him keep, at least, the myth of the imperial aura intact. During the second phase in Farrukh Siyar's time when the *wazir* aspired and threatened to take over the central position from the emperor, the latter allowed the governor of Awadh to control provincial finance. The governor

in this particular case was Chhabele Ram, a supporter of Farrukh Siyar in his battle against the *wazir*, and the purpose was
simply to increase his strength *vis-á-vis* the *wazir* and his faction
and not to enable him (the governor) to meet the extraordinary
situation in the province. Chhabele Ram also sought the *subadari* for a long term in order to build a base in case of his and his
master's defeat against the *wazir* at the centre. The case of
Chhabele Ram set a precedent. Yet in 1719 when Girdhar
Bahadur, the governor of Allahabad, was allowed to take the
charge of Awadh with extended powers, it was not in consideration of the problems of administration in the province. The
wazir, at this stage, was keen that Girdhar should leave Allahabad where he had revolted and had thus threatened the
passage from the eastern provinces to the centre.

The process is also illustrated from the case of the Punjab. As
the governor did not belong to the faction of the *wazir*, he
received little support from the centre. Instead, the *wazir* tried
to replace him by a man of his own faction, incited the local
chiefs to rise against him and, if possible, to eliminate him. The
governor survived, in a large measure, due to his association
with a kin group, opposed to the faction of the *wazir*, at the
centre. In return, however, the governorship with extended
powers in the Punjab came to be virtually shared with those
leaders of his group who held offices at the centre.

In the governor's struggle for additional powers there was a
case for a political framework flexible enough to accommodate
the interests and aspirations of the different components of the
ruling class in the province together with a lose imperial unity.
But with the centre unable to guarantee provincial security, the
governor had to work it out himself in alliance with emerging
local forces. In fact, the emperor and central authorities,
vulnerable as they were to factional politics at the court, had
become the channel for extending such politics to the provinces.
The centre now acted as a force for destabilization rather than
stabilization in the provinces.

Thus, there was a rapid decline in control of the centre over the
various departments of local administration following invariably the governor's estrangement with central authorities. Not

only was the governor utterly disrespectful of the centre during the second phase, but the persons in charge of the provincial and local offices that he aspired to control had to encounter his hostility. On the other hand, the central authorities overlooked cases of dereliction, irregularities and even serious offences by those local officials who were intended or were posted in the province to be a check on the governor. Accordingly, the composition of the local officials kept changing to suit the interests of one or the other party in power at the centre, often in total disregard of the requirements of the offices in the province.

Crippled imperial control over local administration manifested itself in the misappropriation of revenue by local officials which resulted in a conflict, for instance, with the agents of the *jagirdars* and the *amils* of *khalisa*. Again, the *faujdar's* indifference to the difficulties of the news-writers, which posed a problem in obtaining details from the *mahals*, seriously affected the working of local administration. As a result, in a number of cases, the centre was either uninformed or ill-informed. Moreover, in a number of instances from the Punjab, the news-writers took the side of the governor in the latter's clashes with the centre; they remained in office in spite of imperial orders to the contrary.

The office of the *qazi* operated until the end of our period, but it tended to become hereditary in Awadh from almost the beginning of the eighteenth century. In some cases, the *qazis* complied with the orders of their transfer, but they illegally retained the *madad-i ma'ash* granted to them against their services.

The *jagirdars* became primarily concerned with the protection and promotion of their own interests. They resisted implementation of imperial regulations and defied the practice of frequent transfers. The extension of *watan jagir* to non-*zamindar mansabdars* created more difficulties for the functioning of the administration. Most of such *mansabdars* in Awadh obtained positions in or around their *watans* and they remained idle, hardly attending to their work. Some of them retained their *jagirs* and collected revenue even after they had become physically disabled and of no use to the state. It would appear that the *jagirdars* were not content with the terms and conditions of their service. Their resistance of imperial principles was evident in their attempt to hold on to their *jagirs* and treat them as hereditary rights. The tendency was seen at work not only in and around the provinces under review but also in the areas dominated by the Marathas and the Rajputs.

The local and organized regional resistance against the centre expressed itself in widespread agrarian uprisings, mounted in Awadh by the dominant Rajput *zamindars*; while in the Punjab, socially and politically, an increasingly important community took over the leadership of these revolts. The agrarian risings were not a new phenomenon in our period. The *zamindars* who were in control of rural production and producers, had never welcomed the state extraction of almost the entire surplus from the villages, leaving them only a marginal share. There was always a lurking fear, as indeed often the reality, of the *zamindars*' resistance to the local officials. But a notable feature of the *zamindar* risings in our period was the remarkable speed with which they recovered from a defeat and re-engaged themselves against the Mughals. In Farrukh Siyar's reign a number of military expeditions against *zamindars* in Awadh reportedly ended in the victory of the Mughals. Yet the prime concern of Girdhar Bahadur and later of Burhan-ul-Mulk was to suppress the rebel *zamindars* or, at least, to seek a strategy to arrive at some kind of accommodation with the dominant landed communities in the province. This indicated the wide popular base of resistance and also the extent of the resources at the command of their leaders. The strength of the armed bands under their command and also the fortresses they had under their control is to be particularly noted in this connection.

The intensity of the *zamindars*' resistance in our period followed economic growth and the prosperity in our regions in the seventeenth century together with an imperial decline. A number of old settlements in southern Awadh appear to have become notable for trade and artisanal production, while a number of others were emerging as new centres of important *zamindaris*. By the middle of the eighteenth century the central and southern districts of Awadh were apparently linked with the towns on the south banks of the Ganga in the provinces of Agra and Allahabad. The entire area was endowed with rich soil and good natural irrigation, favouring a particularly productive agriculture. The available *jama* figures suggest a remarkable rise in revenue from the end of the sixteenth century.

There is a possibility that the swollen *jama* figures showed merely the magnitude of state demand and that they represented a readjustment following the increase in prices in the seventeenth century. There is, however, enough evidence to lead us to believe that the rise in *jama* figure in our region cannot be explained simply in terms of the price hike of the seventeenth century. We have reports that the intermediaries' collections from the peasants had risen more substantially in proportion to their payments to the state. The *jama* seems to have borne some relationship with the performance of agriculture.

Two different processes which complemented and gained momentum from each other in the course of the seventeenth century proved to be of enormous profit to the *suba* of the Punjab and the adjoining areas. One was the impressive agriculture following the Jat settlements in the areas which combined regular rainfall, rich soil and extensive fields of river basins. These Jat settlements were connected with the great route which carried the trade of the country east and south of Delhi with the Punjab and beyond with Persia and Central Asia. The region also had an opening through the Indus to Lahari Bandar. The second process was the emergence in the Punjab on and around the trade routes of a number of towns with the merchants who specialized both in inland and foreign trade. All this resulted in the prosperity of the province in the seventeenth century which the contemporary Punjab historians speak of so boastfully and which is reflected in the fantastic increase in revenue, in particular, from the bazaar levies and tolls.

The growth in these regions led to a dislocation of existing agrarian relationships. In some cases, the dominant *zamindar* and the peasant castes emerged from their original settlements and began to make encroachments into the *zamindari* areas of the others, while in the others a *zamindar*-peasant clan struggled to bring under their control the entire territory around their area of residence. Their resistance in such cases was not necessarily directed against the state, but certainly against the rule, the order and the class positions the state protected and promoted. At any rate, the *zamindar* risings predominantly signified a challenge to the imperial power from regional and local communities.

The Mughal imperial power rested on a balance between the interests of different regional and local magnates on the one hand and the ambitions of the Mughal emperor and his nobles and the other *mansabdars* on the other. This coordination or the alliance between the two with the emperor as the dominant partner was possible due to the social conditions of the country, which never allowed local and regional elements to act in unison. They were divided among themselves on caste, community and territorial lines and were perpetually at war with each other. Their strength was limited even though each of them tried to subjugate the other. There were certain traditions which guided and regulated their actions and inter-caste and community relationships, while most of them also had a history and memory of having served as intermediaries under the Sultans of Delhi. These factors minimized the possibility of rising above the narrow limits of their communities and territories. They were thus not only weak enough to be vanquished by a power above community and limited territorial considerations, but were also in need of a 'paramount' power under whose umbrella their individual positions were guaranteed.

The Mughals on the other hand were not bound by any such considerations which prevented them from building an empire that allowed for these local loyalties. And, as they came from an area which had long social and trade contacts with the subcontinent, they could also appreciate the implications of and respond accordingly to an extraordinary phenomenon of the time, namely the expansion of India's external trade following the advent of the Europeans with the precious white metal from the New World. The empire responded to the widening network of money and commerce connecting the peripheries with the heartland of Hindustan. The traders and the money dealers welcomed a system which could reinforce, augment and regulate the economic integration of the territories and the communities under the jurisdiction of their operations. Artisans and the producers also were in need of stable extended markets.

However, the same factors eventually provided nourishment to the process of political 'decentralization'. The Mughal alliance with the local and the regional magnates had been uneasy. The conflict between the two had not been resolved entirely. Whenever the *zamindar* found an opportunity he raided and tried to demolish the bastions of imperial power in the region. In a highly differentiated society, the expansion of **artisanal production, urban development and the region's integ-**ration into a wider market network in the seventeenth century was to the obvious benefit of the upper strata of the local communities. The strength acquired following the prosperity of their regions enabled them to challenge Mughal claims in the face of declining imperial authority. They were now rich enough to afford the weapons and the provisions necessary to wage a long war against the Mughals. The *zamindar* uprisings in the early-eighteenth century were widespread, demonstrating the breakdown of the alliance between them and the Mughals as well as the region's resistance against control by the centre.

But the *zamindars* fought for a very limited cause, and their strength was often impaired by their internal social differences. The agrarian revolts were often organized on caste and community lines and were a threat to those rural sections which did not belong to the caste or creed of the rebels. A large number of the *zamindars* and peasants were constrained to seek help from the Mughals. There is also evidence of the support of some *zamindars* and peasants to the Mughals in their military expeditions against the rebels. This is amply illustrated from the case of Mansa Ram, a Bhumihar *zamindar* of Gangapur, who mobilized his community behind the Mughals against the turbulent Rajputs to eventually found a raj in Benaras. It is also not unlikely that the rebels in Awadh, for instance, submitted after they won some privileges from the nawab. Their social conditions did not allow them to fight beyond a point, lest the others join hands with the Mughals and crush them and take over the leadership of the locality.

Again, within the village and the *zamindari* centres there were social groups, namely the *madad-i ma'ash* holders, with interests, attitudes and objectives sharply different from those of the rebel *zamindars*. The *madad-i ma'ash* holders were the ideologues and traditional supporters of the Mughal state and subsisted in principle on the revenues alienated from the states' share in the produce. By the beginning of the eighteenth century they constituted a considerably strong social force, being in control of large land-holdings and sometimes were assertively present in local *zamindari* and money transactions. By the virtue of their ideological position they were in conflict with the *zamindars*, but now that they had become rich and powerful while also enjoying the full support of the state, their position was anomalous. They not only provoked but also restrained the strength of the rebels. As symbols and representatives of imperial power, they became victims of the wrath of the *zamindar*. The *madad-i ma'ash* holders were, however, a local social group and were vulnerable to the shifting fortunes of the region. For instance, they were a source of trouble for the imperial authority in Awadh in the early-eighteenth century.

The merchants and the other urban sections also suffered at the hands of the rebel *zamindars*. Long distance trade and money transactions were closely linked with political stability which, in the prevailing circumstances when economic integration had followed the political unification, could be thought of only through the maintenance of imperial authority. The traders and also some artisans sided with the Mughals and thus invited the hostility of the rebels. Trade and urban properties like the offices of the *qazi* and *kotwal* became targets of their raids since they were believed to represent the Mughal power in the region.

The *zamindars* thus could rarely think beyond the limited goal of a greater share in political power and revenues for themselves and their communities, even if their actions became part of a larger regional endeavour to become independent of the political control of the centre.

The feeling of uncertainty and apprehension among the officials posted in the region was inevitable. As the support from the centre, if available, was of little value, most of them rejected imperial authority and in some cases even colluded with the rebels.

In these circumstances, the Mughal governor sought additional powers and as he earned these through a course of confrontation with the central authorities, his success depended more on his ability to meet the demands of the region, including the *zamindars*, the *madad-i ma'ash* holders and the local and provincial officials. The governor aspired to establish his dominance over them which often led to virtual rebellion against the centre. By bringing the powers of the *diwan* and the *faujdars* under his control, the governor tried to strengthen himself to tackle the problems of local administration. And as he could arrive at some arrangement with the leaders of the rebels, and protected and promoted with some success the interests of the different local elements, he saw the possibility of refurbishing the Mughal power in the region through some changes in the existing political alignments including his own relations with the centre. This meant a longer if not a permanent tenure of his office, which was denied to him as the centre still insisted on the old pattern of its relations with the province.

The governor thus defied the directives from the centre and refused to leave the province, as he built and mobilized the resources of the region which enabled him to survive independently of the centre. Burhan-ul-Mulk remained in Awadh in spite of the emperor's order of his transfer to Malwa. Later, after his death, Safdar Jang succeeded him by the virtue of his blood relations with the deceased. In the Punjab Abd-us-Samad Khan, the governor, appropriated the revenues of the *khalisa mahals* earmarked for the maintenance of the army on the borders. Abd-us-Samad Khan refused to leave Lahore to take over his assignment in Kabul. Instead, he and his son, Zakariya Khan, together managed to control the Mughal Punjab and the *suba* of Multan towards the third phase of our period. This, in a measure, indicated their appreciation of the social and commercial links of the two provinces. Later, after his father's death, Zakariya Khan combined the governorship of both the provinces virtually on account of hereditary rights.

In all matters relating to the province, the governor did what he thought would further his interests in the region. Burhan-ul-Mulk showed no regard for the legitimate possession of the office of governorship of Allahabad, since he aspired to hold the province as a buffer zone between Awadh and the Baghela and Bundela chieftaincies. He added to the difficulties of Muhammad Khan Bangash against the Bundelas, as the Bangash chief had a base in the neighbourhood. The governor of Awadh was friendly towards the Bundelas even when they had entered into an offensive alliance with the Marathas against the Mughals. Relations between Awadh and the Marathas were independent of any regard for the centre. Political alignments in the region came to be guided by the factors which threatened or were believed to promote the position of the governor. Safdar Jang thus financed an imperial campaign against Ali Muhammad Khan of Anola, his potential rival in the region, while the *wazir* of the empire, who also had his *jagirs* in the area, was kept in the dark about the objectives of the expedition.

Yet, it was not possible for the governor to be completely free from the centre. The imperial tradition was not totally forgotten. The emperor was the source of all claims to authority, even though he himself was effectively divested of power. The nobles, including those in control of virtually independent provinces, defended him, provided he did not imperil their interests in the regions. As late as 1739, Burhan-ul-Mulk and Nizam-ul-Mulk arrived at the centre from Awadh and the Deccan respectively to defend the emperor against Nadir Shah. Safdar Jang refused to act on an imperial order to defend the Raja of Jaipur against the Marathas; he went half-heartedly to Patna to help Ali Vardi Khan of Bengal; but he could not avoid taking active interest in court politics.

Again, the *jagirs* of the nobles posted at the centre or in any other provinces, restricted the freedom of the governor. Together with the agents of their *jagirs*, these nobles also had their associates among the local rural and urban gentry. Indeed, the *jagir* system had added considerably to the problems of the governor in the earlier phases of our period. The practice of the *jagirdar* having *faujdari* right over his *jagir mahal* had amounted to legitimizing dual authority in the province. It had imposed limitations on the exercise of powers by the regular provincial officials. Similarly the recently modified *jagir* set-up encouraging and creating a long-term interest of the nobles in their *jagirs* jeopardized the governor's endeavour to build a base in the province.

The governor thus had to be in touch with the developments at the centre. Burhan-ul-Mulk developed and maintained political equations with some nobles at the court, whose response to his overtures showed little concern for the damage he had caused to the emperor's authority in Awadh. His attempt to establish links with one or the other faction at the centre was evidently because he appreciated that it was necessary for his independence in the province. When the road passing through Allahabad, Bindki, Kora to Delhi was disturbed, he readily undertook the responsibility of the safe passage of the Bengal treasury through Awadh to the centre. This, he hoped, would compensate for his defiance of the imperial order, increase his prospects of bargaining for greater power and also enable him to show formal obeisance to the emperor. Burhan-ul-Mulk also envisaged an increase in the financial base of the *nawabi* rule when the imperial highway between Buxar and Delhi was diverted from the Allahabad-Bindki route to the one that passed through Lucknow and Bareilly.

The cases of the attempts of the new governor to continue his association with the centre highlighted the necessity of maintaining the imperial frame. The semblance of empire had to be sustained, for it suited the individuals and the groups who had hitherto constituted the empire and were now in power in the regions. He who had greater ambitions in the regions aspired to a higher and stronger position at the court. This brought the regional powers including the Marathas and later the British into direct contact with court politics.

The kind of power politics that emerged in different parts of the Mughal empire in the eighteenth century explains in part the need of emphasizing the imperial symbols. In order to survive and thrive in the absence of the long accepted legitimate and fairly effective imperial organization of the Mughals, each of the newly emerged regional powers looked for and seized the opportunities to subordinate the others, at least, in its neighbourhood. But each of them also resisted, or, at least, had the ambition or ability to fight any such endeavour of the other. To the victorious among them when they sought institutional arrangement of their spoils, it was convenient to accept and maintain the legitimizing authority of the Mughal centre which had in fact collapsed and come to coexist with their ambitions and positions in the regions.

The necessity of maintaining the symbols of the political unity of the regions of the erstwhile empire may perhaps be sought more in the realm of the economy of the period. By the 1720s when the symptoms of political disintegration were all too evident, the different parts of the empire were economically integrated by inter-regional trade along the coastal as well as the inland routes. The economic and monetary institutions of the seventeenth century which had led to the expanded network of commerce and the distant credit markets survived the collapse of the Mughal empire, and amid the political turmoils of the eighteenth century, kept a large part of the erstwhile empire inter-connected.

The decline of the Mughal empire was thus manifested in our regions in a kind of political transformation, in the emergence and configuration of the elements of the new *subadari*. However, as the beginnings of the new *subadari* are to be seen more in the context of the history of the region, the devlopments in and around Awadh and the Punjab provide explanation for its stability or weakness in these provinces. The genesis for the emergence of 'the successor state' was present in both the provinces, but in the Punjab it ended with chaos at the close of our period while Awadh saw a stable dynastic rule.

Geographical continguity of the Punjab with the frontier province and the emergence of a strong power beyond Kabul in the face of the rapidly collapsing Mughal centre together with the actuality and the lurking dangers of foreign invasions influenced the political developments in the province. Zakariya Khan's special equation with the centre also mattered considerably. Almost the entire 'Turani' kin group had a claim to whatever independence and stability these provinces had acquired under Abd-us-Samad Khan and Zakariya Khan.

Burhan-ul-Mulk and Safdar Jang, however, did not allow the interests of any court party to determine the course of the developments in Awadh, even though they were involved in court politics in varying measures during their tenures as governors. In this they were facilitated also by the fact that they were not ethnically tied with any dominant faction at the court. They assessed the problems of the province and experimented with solutions almost independently.

Since the nobles influenced provincial politics and administration through the local agents in their *jagirs* in the province, an attempt to change the *jagir* administration was among the first measures Burhan-ul-Mulk took to establish his rule in Awadh.

Even though *jagir* was still a symbol of imperial control over the region, it had in actuality come to signify the extent of the nobles' strength, sometimes threatening to emerge as a *quasi zamindari*. Due to the pecuniary benefits and influence that their position and continued association with the noble *jagirdars* implied, these agents, not infrequently local people, often endangered the strength of the governor. To convert the entire *jagir* into *khalisa* was not possible, for it amounted to inviting the hostility of the nobility. Burhan-ul-Mulk therefore brought their agents under his control by taking over the right of collection of revenue of the *jagirs* from the *jagirdars*, and he minimized interference in his schemes by non-Awadhi sections of the nobility. He was now able to distribute patronage to the local service gentry and also to hold in check revenue defalcators. An important feature of the new *subadari* in Awadh was thus realization of the revenues and then payment to the *jagirdars* by the officials who were in direct control of the governor. By the end of our period, the governor in Awadh also succeeded in reducing to the minimum the number of the large sized *jagirs* of outside nobles; quite a considerable number of the officials and military men who had *jagirs* in Awadh were in the service of the governor himself.

On the other hand, the *jagirs* in the Punjab remained very large in size, assigned to the powerful nobles including those belonging to the governor's kin group. In addition, a considerable amount from the revenues of the Punjab was earmarked for the imperial hospitals, imperial food houses and, above all, for the imperial armed forces posted on the north-west frontiers. This implied constant outside interference, even when the centre was weak and the governor had virtual control over the finance of the province.

The governor in Awadh also integrated local groups into the provincial administration and army. There is sufficient evidence to suggest the emergence of regional elements in various positions in the Awadh administration and army. A large number of Awadhis, specially from urban areas, were in Mughal service, posted in different regions of the empire. With the decline of imperial authority in these regions and the inevitable decrease of avenues of promotion in the empire, we can legitimately presume, that these Awadhis sought their fortunes at home. Our sources convincingly show their reluctance and even refusal to accept offers outside Awadh. There is also evidence to suggest a definite and positive response from local groups to the political stability and opportunities that *nawabi* rule in Awadh ensured. This the Shaikhzadas demonstrated effectively in their defence of the *nawabi* against the invasion of the Farrukhabad Afghans and, subsequently, in their invitation to Safdar Jang, to come and take possession of Lucknow despite an imperial *farman* to the contrary. The Shaikhzadas, the Afghans and certain sections of the Hindus can be said to have formed a very loosely organized 'regional ruling group' in Awadh. But we must note that Burhan-ul-Mulk and Safdar Jang were outsiders and that the Qazilbash formed substantial part of the Awadh army in the middle of the eighteenth century.

In providing a firm foundation to the new *subadari* in Awadh, equally important was the governor's success in reducing, if not totally removing, the rural tension that ensued with the changes in the position of the *madad-i ma'ash* holders. The strength and the impact of the *madad-i ma'ash* holders are indicated in the shifts in Burhan-ul-Mulk's policy towards the *madad-i-ma'ash* holding. He began with an uncompromising sternness, but ended with nominal assessment, lending legitimacy to their behaviour as virtual *zamindars*. The insignificance of the size of their shares in the revenues notwithstanding, they had close social links with the Shaikhzadas in imperial service and thus with the nobility and the imperial court. The new *subadar* perhaps eventually recognized the necessity of using their influence in the furtherance of the state's interests. Even though we have not discussed it, the context of the foundation and the configuration in Awadh in our period of the Sunni *madrasa* syllabi (*Dars-i Nizami*) which was to bring to its fold the future *madrasa* system in India needs careful analysis. The claims of the *madad-i ma'ash* holders in the late-seventeenth and eighteenth centuries may be seen in the light of their authority and ability to legitimize or otherwise social and political actions. Azad Bilgrami's observation (which typified their reaction) on the rise of Maratha power indicated their enthusiasm to contribute, as also their response, to the stability implied by *nawabi* rule in Awadh.

The arrangement with the *zamindars*, however, was a singular achievement of the Awadh government. Until the end of our period, the provincial government was opposed by one or the other *zamindar*, nevertheless its victory over the local problems was, in a large measure, due to the support of the *zamindars*. Baiswara, a centre of constant threat to Mughal power, appears to have turned into a base of *nawabi* power in Awadh. The *zamindars* were reconciled through a contract (*ta'ahhud*) which empowered them to engage in the collection of revenue and the payment of the stipulated sum to the government together with some kind of military and administrative authority over the territories under their jurisdiction. The contract combined in it the elements of the earlier Mughal attempt of both conceding some autonomy to the *zamindars* as well as absorbing them in the imperial service. To such *ta'ahhuds* can be traced the rise of some of the rich *ta'alluqadaris* of eighteenth-century Awadh.

Such *ta'ahhud* also contributed, in a certain measure, to the decay of the institution of *faujdari*. The decay of the *faujdari* as a bulwark of imperial authority had set in with the new *subadar*'s acquisition of *faujdari* rights over the province. The new *subadar* began to appoint his own men as his deputies, not infrequently from among the local elements in different areas of the province. These deputies, often referred to as *naibs* and *nazims*, were different from the Mughal *faujdars* in that they combined both executive and financial powers.

The governor of the Punjab, unlike Burhan-ul-Mulk and Safdar Jang, could not reach accommodations with any section of the rural magnates. His failure stemmed, to a great extent, from the nature of the problems in the province. The problems in Awadh emanated from the movement and uprisings of the regional and *quasi*-regional magnates to secure, at least, a greater share in political power and revenues. The governors in Awadh made use of their weaknesses and planned to take over the leadership of the resistance against the centre. In this they were helped a great deal by the continued growth in and around Awadh from the seventeenth to the eighteenth century. Not only did the revenues of the province almost double in our period, but the governor was also able to augment his strength by adding to his domain a large rich area of the neighbouring provinces of Allahabad and Agra.

Indeed, the entire region of Awadh and the adjoining districts experienced remarkable growth in the eighteenth century. In the Benaras region, Benaras city was particularly noted for its wealth and money. Azamgarh, Bhadohi and Mirzapur flourished in this region amidst a number of bazaars and *ganjs*. The *jama* in the region rose by over 107 per cent and continued to rise under the Benaras raj in the mid-eighteenth century. In the early 1730s, Burhan-ul-Mulk collected twenty-five to thirty lakh rupees in *sarkar* Kora which had earlier seen one of the severest rural uprisings in the Gangetic plain under Bhagwant Udaru. No governor or *faujdar* could subjugate Bhagwant Udaru and realize state dues from the *zamindars*. In 1745 the Mughal emperor demanded one crore rupees from Ali Muhammad Khan, an *ijaradar*-cum-*zamindar* of a few *parganas* in the Moradabad-Bareilly region. Ali Muhammad Khan did not pay the amount on the strength of the *wazir*'s support to him, but the sum demanded of him indicated his capacity and the riches he had accumulated from *ijara* and his military adventures in the region. The rise in *jama* in this region was almost incredible—over 247 per cent. In 1745 when Amir Khan, the erstwhile governor of Allahabad, died his assets were assessed at fifty to sixty lakh rupees. In the same year, Safdar Jang is reported to have spent forty lakh rupees on the marriage of his son, Shuja-ud-Daulah, while according to one report he paid more than three crore rupees to Nadir Shah from the Awadh treasury to obtain the *subadari* in 1739–40 and to prevent him from attacking Lucknow.

In a measure, the problems in Awadh represented administrative breakdown and a dislocation of the political and social balance at the local level. The legend that on Burhan-ul-Mulk's query, the *qanungo* indicated the gap between what the *zamindars* actually collected from the peasants and what they paid to the state is significant.

The Sikh uprisings, on the contrary, which spearheaded the local and regional resistance to the Mughal rule in the Punjab, were fraught with weaknesses. The Sikh movement reflected a deep-rooted antagonism between the Mughal state and its beneficiaries on the one hand and the various categories of smaller *zamindars* and the peasants on the other at a stage where any attempt at reconciliation and compromise failed to operate effectively. The Sikhs had also begun to put forward a claim to rulership and were not to be contented with less than the total overthrow of Mughal rule and the establishment of their power in the province. The high sounding title of *Sachcha Badshah* and the symbols of *degh, tegh* and *fath*, therefore, continued to inspire the Sikh leaders even after the ruthless execution of Banda and his seven hundred comrades in 1715. The chiefs of the Punjab also looked for an opportunity, which they seized in the wake of foreign invasions, to totally throw off their obeisance to Mughal authority. The new *subadar* in the Punjab was, thus, unable to make any arrangements with the *zamindars*, nor there is any evidence to suggest that he could effect any changes in the administrative set-up of the province.

Zakariya Khan did try to build a base for the new *subadari* by associating the Khatris, a dominant trading community of the Punjab, with the provincial government. The Khatris and the Turanis, the faction to which the governor of the Punjab belonged, seem to have been in association with each other even at the centre. But the Khatris themselves suffered heavily in the wake of the decline of trade and urban centres in the Punjab by the middle of the eighteenth century. Trade had contributed a great deal to the prosperity of the Punjab in the seventeenth century. The trading centres and towns concentrated on and around the great land route which linked the Mughal empire through Kabul and Qandahar with Persia and Central Asia. These towns were, in turn, connected with the rich agricultural settlements in the Indo-Gangetic plains and the sub-Himalayan zones of the province. The trade of the Punjab also had an opening through the Indus to Lahari Bandar.

The trade with the countries beyond the north-western frontiers was brisk and made up for the loss of what may have accrued to the economy of the region due to the silting of the Indus in the seventeenth century. The Punjab appears to be in a flourishing state even in the early eighteenth century. Banda's concentration on the townsfolk showed the wealth in the cities for which our sources contain incontrovertible evidence. The Sikhs under Banda could plunder Rs 60,000 from Garhi Pathanan. In 1714, the deputy *faujdar* of Jammu misappropriated Rs 33,000 of the collection of the *mahals* of the *walashahis* in the *chakla*. In 1716, the *rabi* collection of *pargana* Sialkot amounted to Rs 6,00,000 out of which Rs 2,50,000 were reportedly misappropriated by the *faujdar*. The Shalharias of the *pargana* readily offered to pay Rs 5,000 for the release of two of their *zamindars* who had been imprisoned by the local *amil* for non-payment of revenue. Mirza Muhammad's evidence for the end of Farrukh Siyar's reign clearly shows that the office of the *amini faujdari* in Jalandhar was keenly sought and was still profitable, but, of course, only for those who could muster sufficient strength to collect the revenue.

However, political developments beyond the north-west frontiers, as well as the Maratha inroads into western and upper India, disturbed this trade. The revenues of the province fell sharply in Muhammad Shah's reign, the decline being the heaviest in the income from the bazaar levies and tolls. The dislocation of the economy led to great sufferings to the urban communities including the Khatris and thus shattered one source of social support for the new *subadari* in the Punjab. The governor did not possess enough resources to make arrangements with any other groups of local magnates. The Sikh movement continued to challenge the Mughal power, now, greatly reinforced by the dipossessed *zamindars*, impoverished peasants and the pauperized lower urban classes.

There were variations in the regions of our study in the nature and growth of the conditions in which set in the process of the formation of the new *subadari* in the early-eighteenth century. Conditions emerged in Awadh favouring the foundation and consolidation of a regional state under the aegis of a Mughal noble. On the other hand, the dislocation of the economy of the Punjab led to a change in the character of popular uprisings against the Mughals in the province, with the liquidation of all prospects, whatsoever, of accommodation between the provincial government and the Sikhs. One can speculate that the narrow religious and caste bond of the Sikh movement, absence of a positive political programme and hostility to urban communities must have also had their own share in the political chaos in the Punjab in the mid-eighteenth-century.

It is therefore difficult to find a single explanation commonly applicable to the problems of the Mughal empire in all its regions and provinces. It is also difficult to accept the view that by the end of the seventeenth century the Mughal empire was faced with an insurmountable crisis owing to the very nature of the Mughal mechanism of administration. We may perhaps look more profitably to the conditions in the early-eighteenth century in which the empire disintegrated into the regional principalities in north India. In some regions the land still yielded riches if it was collected either by show of strength or tactful dealings with the intermediaries. The growing tendency among the nobles and officials to hold *jagirs* on a permanent/ *quasi*-permanent basis, the struggle to convert the *madad-i ma'ash* holding into *milkiyat*, the emergence of the *ta'alluqa*, *ta'ahhud* and *ijara* contract as the most acceptable forms of government, and the consensus among the regional powers to maintain the Mughal imperial symbols to obtain legitimacy and thus stability and security of their spoils—all indicated the eighteenth-century endeavour to make use of the possibilities for growth within existing social structures.

Bibliography

The majority of sources used for this work are unpublished and preserved in different collections of the oriental manuscripts. The manuscripts have been identified in the bibliography by their library or catalogue numbers. The documents and administrative records are rarely available in duplicates, but a number of reliable MSS of the other works exist. C. A. Storey has mentioned many of them in his *Persian Literature–a Bio-bibliographical Survey*. I have noted and described only those MSS which I have consulted or seen for my purpose, indicating, where it was necessary, the MS/MSS I have cited in this work. I have also mentioned if a translation or analysis in English is available in print.

A word is perhaps needed about the historical works of the late-eighteenth and early-nineteenth centuries. Many of the authors of these works write about my period from the memory of their childhood days, supporting their accounts from the reports of the actual participants of the events of this period. They also write on the basis of a large number of official and private papers which have not survived. These works, thus, are notable as sources for the study of the eighteenth century history, even if they do not fall strictly under the category of contemporary evidence. For this reason, European works, including reports and travelogues written by Indians in English, are listed in a category separate from modern works.

PRIMARY SOURCES

A. ADMINISTRATIVE RECORDS AND DOCUMENTS

Documents in the Uttar Pradesh State Archives, Allahabad. The Persian records in this collection consist of *farmāns*, *ḥasb-ul-ḥukms*, *parwānchas*, *maḥẓars* and other documents concerning land grants, sale deeds, land disputes, judgements, *jāgīr* assignments, etc. They date from the sixteenth century. I have used the following documents (cited as Allahabad, followed by No.) pertaining to the late-seventeenth and the earlier half of the eighteenth centuries: Nos. 1, 4, 5, 7, 11, 12, 14, 95–7, 117, 128, 136, 192, 194, 286, 288, 431, 505, 514, 524–5, 536, 577, 607, 609, 626, 787–8, 791, 802, 872, 882, 918–21, 923,–4, 936–7, 942, 998, 1002, 1009, 1018, 1280, 1283–5, 1291, 1295, 1309–11, 1314–16, 1318, 1321–3, 1565, 2031, 2086, 2204, 2560–1, 2743, 11430–1, 11641, 11971, 11992, 12023–4, 12034, 12036, 12124, 12132, 12139–40, 12227, 12249.

Revenue records of the Mughal provinces in the late-seventeenth and eighteenth centuries, in London. These statistical details which in a number
of cases include both *jama'* and *ḥāṣil* figures of different years, are parts of
copies of the reports submitted to the East India Company Revenue
Department by local revenue officials of Bengal, Bihar and Orissa. The
purpose of the Company after it obtained *dīwānī* in 1765, seems to have
been to understand the Mughal system in order to arrive at an agreement
with the *zamīndārs* about the magnitude and method of assessment of the
revenue. These papers are rich in information on Bengal, Bihar and
Orissa, but as the Company and the *zamīndārs* rarely agreed with each
other, both felt the necessity of obtaining details of other provinces to
illustrate and support their viewpoints. Thus, the volumes entitled the
Jama' ḥāṣil-i ṣūbajāt Bangāla, Bihār wa Orissa often contain pages on the
other provinces. Besides, there are a large number of papers in this series
bound in separate volumes for the different provinces. Information about
the regions under this study is scattered in numerous volumes, but is
available largely in I. O. 4471 (Part III as *Kaifiyat-i Maḥālāt-i Sarkārāt Ta
'alluq Rāja Chait Singh az 'ahd-i 'amaldārī Rāja Mansā Rām wa Rāja Balwant
Singh)*, 4485 (Part III as *Goshwāra Sarkārāt-i Ṣūba Ilāhabād: 'ahd-i Bādshā-
hān wa 'ahd-i Muḥammad Shāh)*, 4487 (*ṣūba Shāhjahānabād waghairah*), 4488
(*Kaifiyat-i Jama'dāmī wa ḥāṣil-i Ṣūba Panjāb wa Multān waghairah*), 4489
(*Kaifiyat-i Jama'dāmī wa ḥāṣil-i Ṣūba Awadh ta'alluqa-i Nawāb Shujā'-ud
Daulah)*, 4491 (*Kaifiyat-i Jama'-i Maḥālāt-i Khāliṣa)*. These papers, extremely valuable for the scholars of eighteenth-century agrarian history
in India, are not properly catalogued.
I. O. 4506. This is an extremely important volume containing in Part I a list of
the *jāgīrdārs* of the Punjab of Muḥammad Shāh's times with details of the
jama'dāmī of their *jāgīrs* in different *parganas* of the five Doabs of the
province. Part II of the volume enlists the *jāgīrdārs* who had their *jāgīrs* in
Awadh while Part III records the *manṣabs* of Ṣafdar Jang and his 191
companions/associates (*hamrāhiyān*) with details of *jama'dāmī* of their
jāgīrs in different parts of the empire, namely, Kashmir, the Punjab,
Multan, Delhi, Agra, Awadh, Allahabad, and Bihar, under three heads:
ṭalab, muqarrara ṭalab and *mawājib*.
Sale-deeds, gift-deeds, legal dispositions and judgements concerning the town
of Batala in the Punjab. Texts printed with photographic reproductions
of the originals, translated and annotated with a comprehensive Introduction by J. S. Grewal, *In the By-Lanes of History: Some Persian Documents from
a Punjab Town*, Simla, 1975.
Documents relating to a land dispute in *pargana* Laharpur, *Sarkār* Khairabad
preserved at the Lucknow University Library under the title of *Kaghazāt-
i pargana Lāharpūr*.
Farmāns, parwānas, ḥasb-ul-ḥukms, etc., relating to the times of Jahāngīr to Shāh
'Alam II (originals) bound together under the title of *Majmū'a-i Farāmīn*,
Rampur MS, No. 2879.
Farmāns concerning *madad-i ma'āsh* grants in the Punjab. Rampur MS.
Farmāns and other documents concerning *madad-i ma'āsh* grants in the Punjab.
Texts printed with photographic reproductions of the originals, trans-

lated and annotated by J. S. Grewal and B. N. Goswami under the titles of *The Mughals and the Jogis of Jakhbar* and *The Mughals and the Sikh Rulers and the Vaishnavas of Pindori*, Simla, 1969.

Documents reproduced with translation and comments by J. S. Grewal in 'Some Persian Documents from Nurpur' *Miscellaneous Articles*, Guru Nanak Dev University, Amritsar, 1972.

Farmāns pertaining to land grants and appointments of *manṣabdārs* and *qāẓīs* covering the period between the reign of Akbar and that of Shāh 'Alam II. Texts printed in Bashir-ud-Din Ahmad, *Farāmīn-i Salāṭīn*, Delhi, 1926.

Farmān of Bahādur Shāh conferring *āl-tamghā* grant, A. D. 1710, Br. M. Or. 2285.

Farmāns of Muḥammad Shāh relating to *madad-i ma'āsh* grants in *pargana* Gopamau, *sarkār* Khairabad. Texts printed with translations and notes in M. A. Ansari, *Administrative Documents of Mughal India*, Delhi, 1984.

A *maḥẓar* dated 1153 A. H./1740 concerning a *zamīndārī* dispute and two sale-deeds dated 1130 A. H./1717 and 1147 A. H./1734 of *pargana* Muhammada-bad, *sarkār* Ghazipur. Originals available in the personal collection of Prof. M. A. Ansari, Jamia Millia, New Delhi.

Documents relating to Awadh preserved at the National Archives of India, New Delhi.

Bilgram Documents, transcripts, Department of History Library, Aligarh.

Firangi Mahal Documents, transcripts, Department of History Library. These documents relate to the areas, e.g., *Ḥavelī* Bahraich, Sadrpur, Amethi Dongar, etc., where descendants and relatives of Mullā Quṭb-ud-Dīn of Sahali had their *madad-i ma'āsh*. An unpublished edition of these documents with English translations by Dr Iqbal Husain is available in Department of History, AMU, Aligarh.

Jais Documents, transcripts, Department of History Library, Aligarh. This collection also includes documents pertaining to Sultanpur, *sarkār* Awadh, Kishni, *sarkār* Lucknow, Nasirabad, *sarkār* Manikpur in Allahabad and *Ḥavelī* Moradabad, *ṣūba* Delhi.

Khairabad Documents, transcripts, Department of History Library, Aligarh. For a description and translation of this collection see Iqbal Husain, 'A Calendar of Khairabad Documents: Sixteenth-Nineteenth Century', *Islamic Culture*, January, 1979.

Akhbārāt-i Darbār-i Mu'allā: Newsletters from the Imperial Court, (Sitamau Malwa Collection). The Sitamau transcripts (of the Rajasthan State Archives, Bikaner and Royal Asiatic Society Library, London) are ar-ranged in chronological order according to the *san-i julūs* (regnal year) of the emperors in numerous volumes. Twenty-three volumes pertain to the post-Aurangzeb period (1707–19). Besides, there is a volume entitled 'Miscellaneous Papers' which consists of *waqāi'*, *wakīl* reports, etc., of Farrukh Siyar's reign. For a description of the collection see Raghubir Sinh, *Handlist of Important Historical Manuscripts in the Raghubir Library*, *Sitamau*, Sitamau, Malwa, 1949.

Cited as *Akhbārāt*, followed by abbreviation of the name of the emperor (BS, JS, or FS), specific regnal year, volume number where the same

year's papers are bound in more than one volume and page: e.g. *Akhbārāt*,
FS, II, 5th R. Y., p. 74

No regular *akhbārāt* are available for the third and the fourth phases of
the period of my study. But some folios of *akhbārāt* of Muḥammad Shāh's
reign (25th R. Y.) are preserved at the Bibliotheque Nationale (Supplement Persian 313), Paris, Blochet, 613.

Jaipur Records (Sitamau transcripts) 7 volumes of the Sarkar Collection
Series and 7 other volumes of the Sitamau Collection under the titles of
'Miscellaneous' and 'Additional Series'. For a description see Raghubir
Sinh, *Handlist of the Important Historical Manuscripts.*

B. *INSHĀ'* COLLECTIONS

'Ajā'ib-ul-Āfāq, Br. M. Or. 1776. A collection of letters of Chhabele Rām,
Gridhar Bahādur and the Saiyid Brothers. The Rampur MS, a transcript
copy of which is available at the Department of History Library, Aligarh,
also includes copies of the *Akhbārāt* containing information about
Chhabele Rām and Gridhar Bahādur.

'Azīz-ul-Qulūb, by Munshī Bhagwān Dās, M. A. L., Aligarh MS. 'Abd-us-
Salām 188/54 F. A collection of letters of Muḥammad Khān Bangash.
The work is divided into five sections (*faṣls*): (a) Muḥammad Khān's
'arẓdāshts to the emperor (b) Muḥammad Khān's letters to nobles (c)
farmāns and the nobles' letters to Muḥammad Khān (d) congratulatory
letters drafted by Bhagwān Dās, and (e) other drafts of Bhagwān Dās.

Bhagwān Dās was a native of Hisar Firoza (a district town in modern
Haryana) who compiled this work in 1748. The Aligarh MS was transcribed in 1813.

Bahār-i Khayāl, Rampur MS No. 2857. Contains letters exchanged between
the nobles and minor officials, drafted apparently by different *munshīs* of
the time.

Bālmukand Nāma, by Mehta Bālmukand. A collection of letters of Saiyid
'Abdullāh Khān to the important nobles of the time, edited with translation, notes and a critical introduction by Satish Chandra, Bombay 1972.

Dastūr-ul-Inshā', by Munshī Yār Muḥammad Qalandar, Patna MS No. 3682.
Divided into two parts. Part one contains the letters of Nawāb Amīn-ud-
Daulah to various nobles, while part two includes two long letters of the
compiler (Yār Muḥammad Khān) giving interesting details about his
association with Burhān-ul-Mulk and about his itinerary to the Kumaon
hills.

Inshā'-i Mādho Rām, edited by Maulawī Qudrat Aḥmad, Nawalkishore, Lucknow, 1260 A. H. Contains important information about expeditions
against the Sikhs.

Inshā'-i Roshan Kalām, by Bhūpat Rāi. A collection of letters written on behalf
of Ra'd Andāz Khān, *faujdār* of Baiswara, 1698–1702. M. A. L., Aligarh
MS, 'Abd-us-Salām 109339; I. O. 4011; Jalsa-i Tahzib Library,
Lucknow MS, now preserved in Lucknow University Library. I have
cited from the lithographed edn, Nizami Press, Kanpur. For an analysis
of this collection see Zahir Uddin Malik, *PIHC*, 34th Session, Chandi-
garh, 1973, pp. 211–15.

Khujasta Kalām, by Ṣāḥib Rāi. A collection of letters of Muḥammad Khan Bangash. I have cited from Sitamau Rotograph Copy of I.O. MS.

Manṣūr-ul-Maktūbāt, by Lāla Awadhī Lāl, Jalsa-i Tahzib Library, Lucknow MS, now preserved in the Lucknow University Library. A collection of *'arẓāshts* of Ṣafdar Jang to the emperor, his letters to Nizam-ul-Mulk, Qamar-ud-Dīn Khān, Ṣamṣām-ud-Daulah and to other nobles of the time, and his *parwānas* to local officials in Awadh. Most of these were drafted by Santokh Rāi, father of Awadhī Lāl. The fourth section of the book contains some letters drafted by Lāla Hirday Rām, a *dīwān* of Nawāb Shujā'-ud-Dīn at Orissa. In the end the compiler adds some letters he drafted for notables of his time. Compiled in 1210/1795–6.

Nigārnāma-i Munshī, by Malikzāda, a collection of letters and administrative documents of late 17th century. Or. 1735; Or. 2018; Bodleian MS Pers. e-1, lithographed edn. Nawalkishore, Lucknow, 1882. I have cited from M. A. L. Aligarh MS, 'Abd-us-Salām 362/132. For an analysis of this collection see Shaikh Abdur Rashid, *PIHC*.

Ruq'āt-i Lachhmī Narāyan, by Lachhmī Narāyan Shafīq, Lucknow, 1882. Lachhmī Narāyan, associated with the Deccan administration, was a disciple of Ghulām 'Alī Āzād Bilgrāmī, the famous author, poet and scholar of the eighteenth century.

Ruq'a-i Mutafarriqāt, by Bechū Rām, Patna MS No. 2535. Bechū Rām's letters to Lāla Lāl Bihārī, apprising him of developments in Bihar after 'Alī Vardī came to power at Murshidabad, provides information about Ṣafdar Jang's visit to Patna. This collection is bound with another collection entitled *Majmū'a Ruq'āt-i Bhāramal waghairah* in the catalogue.

C. CHRONICLES

'Abd-ul-Karīm Kashmīrī, Khwāja, *Bayān-i Wāqi'*, an eye-witness account of the period between 1739 and 1779. 'Abd-ul-Karīm joined the service of Nādir Shāh in 1739 and accompanied him to Persia. Chapters I and II describe Nādir Shāh's rise, his invasion of Hindustan, his return to Persia, Chapter III is an account of the author's journey from Qazwin to Mecca, and back to Hugli, Chapter IV is an account of the reign of Muhammad Shāh from 1740 to '48, and Chapter V describes the details of the time of Ahmad Shāh and after. Edited with a brief Introduction and notes by K. B. Nasim, Lahore, 1970. Francis Gladwin published a translation of this work under the title of *Memoirs of Khojeh Abaul-Kurreem*, Calcutta, 1798. H. G. Pritchard's translation in part is incorporated in Elliot and Dowson's *History of India as told by its own Historians*, Vol. VIII.

Anonymous, *Account of the Rohillas in the 18th Century*, Jawaharlal Nehru University Libary MS. The MS which was compiled and transcribed some time in the late eighteenth century corroborates the information of the better known contempoary sources on Afghān activities in the eighteenth century.

———, An account of the daily activities of the Rohilla Chiefs. Br. M. Or. 12886 (Meredith–Owen) this work includes a letter from Ṣafdar Jang.

———, *Asrār-i Samadī*, an account of 'Abd-uṣ-Ṣamad Khan's military campaigns against the Sikhs, 'Isā Khān Meʾin, Husain Khān Khweshgī, Sharf-ud-Dīn Kashmīrī and the *zamīndārs* of Jammu and Multan. Edited with notes and introduction in Urdu by Muhammad Shuja-ud-Din and Muhammad Bashir-ud-Din, Lahore, 1965.

———, *Iqbālnāma*, Rampur MS, ascribed to Shivdās Lakhnawī, the author of *Shahnāma Munawwar Kalām*. The book provides details of the events of the times of Farrukh Siyar and Muhammad Shāh. For a description see S. H. Askari, Introduction to his English translation, Patna, 1983.

———, *Risāla-i Khān-i Daurān wa Muhammad Shāh*, Br. M. Or. 180. Extremely subjective and highly exaggerated account of Samsām-ud-Daulah Khān-i Daurān. In the end, however, there is an interesting account of some *kārkhānas* innovated by Samsām-ud-Daulah.

———, *Sahīfa-i Iqbāl*, Br. M. Or. 1900. A large part of the book is devoted to an unconnected and chronologically defective account of the daily activities of Muhammad Shāh.

———, *Tārīkh-i Ahmad Shāhī*, Br. M. Or. 2005. Useful for details of court politics and conflict of Safdar Jang with the other nobles and later with the Emperor Ahmad Shāh.

———, *Tārīkh-i Shāh ʿĀlam I*, National Archives of India, New Delhi transcript. This appears to be heavily based on Niʿmat Khān ʿAlī's *Bahādur Shāh Nāma*.

———, *Tārīkh-i Sūba-i Ilāhabād*, Allahabad University Library MS.

Ansārī, Muhammad ʿAlī Khān, *Tārīkh-i Muzaffarī*, M. A. L., Aligarh MS. Subhānallāh 364/134.

———, *Bahr-ul-Mawwāj*, Patna MS No. 544 (Fārsī No. 87). This is to be distinguished from the *Tārīkh-i Muzaffarī*; is second volume of Ansārī's bigger history under the title of *Akhbār us-Salātīn*. Account of the later Mughals begins on f. 196-a.

Ashūb, Mirzā Muhammad Bakhsh, *Tārīkh-i Shahādat-i Farrukh Siyar wa Julūs-i Muhammad Shāh*, Br. M. Or. 1832; Patna MS No. 2608. An important and intelligent but prejudiced account of the developments following Muhammad Shāh's accession. The title of the book is misleading, there is nothing in the book on or about the *shahādat* (assassination) of Farrukh Siyar. The book ends with the death of Zakariyā Khān, the governor of the Punjab, in 1745.

Bhīmsen, *Nuskha-i Dilkushā*, Br. M. Or. 23. For an account of the author and the work see Majida Khan, *PIHC*, 41st Session, Bombay, 1980, pp. 386–94.

Ghulām Husain Khān, *Zikr-us-Siyar*, Br. M. Or. 6652. A history of Benaras in the eighteenth century. For a description see G. M. Meredith-Owen, *Handlist of Persian Manuscripts in the British Museum, 1895–1966* (Meredith-Owen).

Ghulām Husain Salīm, *Riyāz-us-Salātīn*, Bib. Ind., Calcutta, 1898.

Ghulām Muhī-ud-Dīn Khān, *Futūhātnāma-i Samadī*, Br. M. Or. 1870. An account of the military achievements of ʿAbd-us-Samad Khān, the governor of the Punjab.

Harcharan Dās, *Chahār Gulzār-i Shāh Shujāʿī*, Br. M. Or. 1732. An account of the period from Muhammad Shāh to ʿĀlamgīr II with emphasis on the activities of the nawābs of Awadh. The work, dedicated to Nawāb Shujā-'ud-Daulah, contains information on administration as well.

Ijād, Muḥammad Aḥsan, *Farrukh Siyar Nāma*, Br. M. Or. 25. A detailed history of the early life of Farrukh Siyar and of the first year of his reign following his coronation in Patna.

Irādat Khān (?), *Tārīkh-i Mubāraknāma*, M. A. L., Aligarh MS 345/115 F. The authorship of this work is wrongly ascribed to Irādat Khān (d. 1717). Very likely it is an extension of the better-known *Tārīkh-i Irādat Khān* by a member of his family, down to the middle of the eighteenth century.

Jahāngīr, Nūr-ud-Dīn Muḥammad, *Tūzuk-i Jahāngīrī*, edited by Saiyid Ahmad, Aligarh, 1864.

Kalyān Singh, *Khulāṣat-ut-Tawārīkh*, Patna MS No. 594.

Kamboh, Ghulām Ḥusain, *Tarīkh-i Banaras*, Patna MS No. 608. It is a history of the family of Mansā Rām, the founder of Benaras Rāj down to the time of Chait Singh.

Kāmrāj bin Nayan Singh, *A'zam-ul-Ḥarb*, Br. M. Or. 1899. A detailed account of Prince Muḥammad A'zam's preparations for the War of Succession at Jaju (15 March 1707–17 June 1708).

———, *'Ibratnāma*, I.O. MS, Ethe, 391. A political history from 1707 to 1719.

Kāmwar Khān, Muḥammad Hādī, *Tazkirat-us-Salaṭīn Chghtā*, a general history of the Mughals in India in two volumes. The book ends abruptly in 1724. Portion dealing with the post-Aurangzeb period edited with notes and a critical Introduction by Muzaffar Alam, Bombay, 1980. Cited mainly from the M. A. L., Aligarh MS, citations in pages are from the published copy.

Khāfī Khān, Muḥammad Hashim, *Muntakhab-ul-Lubāb*, a history of the Mughals in two volumes. A useful eye-witness account of Aurangzeb and his successors is in Vol. II. Edited by K. D. Ahmad and Woseley Haig, Bibl. Ind. Calcutta, 1869. A. J. Syed (Bombay, 1977) and S. Moin ul-Haq (Karachi 1977) published two separate translations of the portion dealing with Aurangzeb's reign.

Khair-ud-Dīn Muḥammad Khān *Tuhfa-i Tāza or Balwant Nāma*, Patna MS No. 607. It is a detailed history of the ruling house of Benaras from Mansā Rām to 1195 A. H./1780, gives a valuable account of the relations between Burhān-ul-Mulk and Ṣafdar Jang on the one hand and the first two rājas of Benaras.

Khush-ḥāl Chand, *Nādir-uz-Zamānī*, Br. M. Or. 1844. General history up to 1735, contains useful information on prices in Delhi in the early-eighteenth century.

Khwāja Muḥammad A'zam Shāh, *Waqi'āt-i Kashmīr*, lithographed edn., Lahore, 1303 A. H./1885–6.

Khwāja Muḥammad Khalīl, *Tārīkh-i Shāhanshāhī*, Buhar MS No. 79, National Library, Calcutta.

Mirzā Muḥammad bin Mu'tamad Khān, *Tārīkh-i Muḥammadī*, records in chronological order the dates of the deaths of the nobles and notables with their *manṣabs* and offices. Vol. II, Part 6, which deals with the post-Aurangzeb period has been edited with Introduction and extensive notes in Persian by Imtiaz Ali Khan 'Arshī', Aligarh, 1960.

Mirzā Muhammad Mahdī Astarabadī, *Durra-i Nādira*, Bombay, 1293 A. H./ 1876, contains a useful account of Nadir Shah's invasion of Hindustan. The author served as a secretary to Nādir Shah.

Muḥammad Qāsim Aurangabadī, *Aḥwal-ul-Khwāqīn*, Br. M. Add. 26, 244. The author was in the service of Nizam-ul-Mulk and the work is devoted principally to the history of his relations and conflict with the Mughal court, nobles, the Marathas and his arrangements in the Deccan.

Muḥammad Qāsim 'Ibrat Ḥusainī Lāhorī, *'Ibratnama*, Br. M. Or. 1934. An account of the period from 1707 to 1719, with valuable information about the Sikhs. His account of the court politics is highly prejudiced in favour of the Saiyid Brothers.

Mukhliṣ, Anand Rām, *Badā'i' Waqā'i'*, Rampur MS Loharu Collection B 5; Aligarh MS records in detail invasions of Nadir Shāh and Aḥmad Shāh Abdālī. The Aligarh MS incorporates also a section on Muḥammad Shāh's expedition against the Rohilla Chief (*aḥwāl-i safar-i Bangaṛh*). But Mukhliṣ treats his account of this expedition as a separate work. Mukhliṣ is a famous writer of the eighteenth century. He composed over a dozen works of prose and poetry including the famous glossary, *Mir'āt-ul-Iṣṭilāḥ*. For a description and analysis of *Badā'i' Waqā'i'* in Urdu see Muhammad Shafi, *Oriental College Magazine*, Lahore, February, 1941.

Murtaẓā Ḥusain Ilah Yar Usmanī Bilgramī, *Ḥadīqat-ul-Aqālīm*, Nawalki-shore, Lucknow, 1879. Though a geographical work, it contains signific-ant information about the nobles (Sarbuland Khān, Burhān-ul-Mulk, Ṣafdar Jang and Aḥmad Khan Bangash) with whom he was associated before he joined the service of Jonathan Scott as his *munshī* in 1776.

Ni'mat Khān, 'Alī, (also known as Dānishmand Khān) *Bahādur Shāh Nāma*, Br. M. Or. 24. A detailed official history of the first two years of Bahadur Shāh's reign.

Nūr-ud-Din Faruqi, *Jahandar Nāma*, Br. M. Or. 3610. A brief but reliable eye-witness account of the Civil Wars at Lahore (1712) and Agra (1713), of the reign of Jahāndār Shāh and the developments attendant to Far-rukh Siyar's coming to power. The author along with his father was in the service of Prince Jahāndār Shāh and took part in the two wars.

Qudrat, Muḥammad Ṣāliḥ, *Tārīkh-i 'Alī*, Patna MS No. 581. A general history of the eighteenth century, with useful information about the Saiyids of Bārha, compiled some time in the 1780s.

Rustam 'Alī Shāhabādī, *Tārīkh-i Hindī*, Br. M. Or. 1628, was compiled in 1742, is a brief history of India from before the Turkish conquest, but with details of the events of the post-Aurangzeb period.

Salīmullāh, *Tārīkh-i Bangāla*, edited with notes and introduction by S. Imam-ud-Din, Dacca, 1981.

Sāqī Musta'id Khān, *Ma'āṣir-i 'Ālamgīrī*, Bib. Ind., Calcutta, 1871. Trans-lated by J.N. Sarkar, Calcutta, 1947.

Shākir Khān, *Tārīkh-i Shākir Khānī*, Br. M. Add. 6585, Shākir Khān belonged to the family of Luṭfullāh Khān Ṣādiq of Panipat, and hence his account suffers from certain obvious prejudices. Though chronologically defec-tive, his history is of immense value for developments at the court of Muhammad Shāh, especially for the period after the Karnal debacle.

Shākir Khān gives a list of *manṣabdārs*, *ṣūfīs*, theologians, musicians, dancers, astrologers, *peshkārs* and some merchants, and also records *jama'* figures of the empire together with copies of some official documents.

Shivdās Lakhnawī, *Shāhnāma Munawwar Kalām*, Br. M. Or. 26; A. S. B. MS Ivanow 25/1/33, contains copies of official letters and *farmāns*, and gives a day-to-day account of events under *waqā'i'*. An English translation has been published by S. H. Askari from Patna in 1980.

Ṣiddīqī, Muḥammad Muḥsin, *Jauhar-i Ṣamṣām*, Br. M. Or. 1898; A. S. B. MS, compiled in 1740, provides details of invasion of Nādir Shāh and a brief account of the Mughal Empire from Bahādur Shāh to Muḥammad Shāh. Highly prejudiced in favour of Ṣamṣām-ud-Daulah to whom the author dedicates this work.

Ṭabāṭabā'ī, Munshī Ghulām Ḥusain, *Siyar-ul-Muta'akhkhirīn*, Vols. 2 and 3, Nawalkishore, Lucknow, one of the most regular and authentic histories of the period under review. The author (b. 1727) was closely associated with many important men and events of the time. An English translation by M. Raymond also known as Haji Mustafa, even though not very accurate, was published from Calcutta in 4 volumes in 1902.

Wārid, Muhammad Shafi', *Mir'āt-i Wāridāt or Tārīkh-i Chaghtāi*, Rampur MS 2120; M.A.L., Aligarh MS. Compiled in 1734, provides significant details about the Marāthas, court politics, shoesellers' riot in Delhi and the activities of Sarbuland Khān, the patron of many Shaikhzādas of Awadh, Wārid also mentions Bhagwant Udāru's revolt.

Yaḥyā Khān, *Ṭazkirat-ul-Mulūk*, I. O. No. 409, a general history of India from the Arab conquest of Sindh down to 1736–7. The author has been a *mīr munshī* (secretary) at the court of Farrukh Siyar.

D. BIOGRAPHIES & MEMOIRS

Anonymous, *Aḥwāl-i Ādīna Beg*, transcript, personal copy of Prof. Ganda Singh, Patiala, contains interesting, but not always dependable, account of the famous *faujdār* of Beth Jalandhar under Zakariyā Khān.

Arzū, Sirāj-ud-Dīn 'Alī Khān, *Majma'-un-Nafā'is*, Rampur MS, a biographical dictionary of poets and men of letters. Account of Ārzū's contemporaries has been edited and published by Abid Raza Bedar, Patna, n.d.

Āzād, Bilgrāmī, Ghulām 'Alī, *Khizāna-i 'Amira*, lithographed edn., Kanpur.

———, *Ma'āṣir-ul-Kirām*, 2 volumes, lithographed edn., Hyderabad, 1913. This work together with *Khizāna-i 'Amira* are among the best and the most authentic accounts of the period, as a member of the contemporary intelligentsia saw it. Āzād Bilgrāmī (1705–85) was associated with Niẓām-ul-Mulk and therefore he is prejudiced against Burhān-ul-Mulk and Ṣafdar Jang. His view about the confiscation of all *madad-i ma'āsh* by Burhān-ul-Mulk shows his bias.

Both *Khizāna-i 'Amira* and *Ma'āṣir-ul-Kirām* are biographical dictionaries of poets, scholars, ṣūfīs and theologians.

———, Bilgrāmī, Ghulām Ḥusain Ṣiddīqī Firshorī, *Sharā'if-i Uṣmānī*, Department of History Library, Aligarh MS No. 63. An important biographical dictionary of the important families of Bilgram, compiled sometime in the mid-eighteenth century.

Bilgrāmī, Saiyid Muḥammad, *Tabṣirat-un-Naẓirīn*, M. A. L., Aligarh MS, Fārsiya Akhbār 204; A. S. B. MS. Primarily a *taẓkira*. The book is divided into three parts (a) *Muqaddima* deals with the biographies of the notables of Bilgram (b) *Maqāla* I deals with the history of the period between 1690 and 1767 (c) *Maqāla* II is an account of saints, *'ulamā*, rulers and nobles, etc. To most of the events mentioned in the book, the author was an eye-witness. For the remaining portion, he obtained information from his elders and from his friends through correspondence. The author was born in Bilgram in 1689 and the work was completed in 1767.

Ḥazīn, Muḥammad 'Alī, *Taẓkirat-ul-Aḥwāl*, edited and translated by F. C. Balfour, London, 1830. Ḥazīn (1692–1766) completed this account of his life, which contains biographical sketches of many of his contemporaries and sheds light on prevailing social and political conditions in 1752.

Irādat Khān, Mīr Mubārakallāh, *Tārīkh-i Irādat Khān*, M. A. L., Aligarh MS University 69/3 F. A well-known memoir, completed in 1714. Irādat Khān held several important offices and was closely associated with the Mughal court politics. Jonathan Scott's *History of the Deccan* incorporates an English translation of this work.

'Khushgo', Bindrāban Dās, *Safīna-i Khushgo*, edited by Ataur Rahman Kakwi, Patna, 1959, a biographical dictionary of poets and men of letters.

Mirzā Muḥammad bin Mu'tamad Khān, *'Ibratnāma*, Patna MS, Catalogue, vii, 623. Memoir of an important Mughal official under Farrukh Siyar. Besides developments at the court and significant biographical notices of some important nobles, the book throws light on the working of some aspects of local administration as well.

———, *Chār Chaman*, Rampur MS No. 2870. Primarily a literary work, but contains some references to the events unnoticed in the other works of Mukhliṣ.

Mukhliṣ, Ānand Rām, *Safarnāma*, edited with a critical Introduction and extensive notes in Urdu by M. Azhar Ali, Rampur, 1946, is an eyewitness account of Muḥammad Shah's expedition against the Afghān chief, 'Alī Muḥammad Khān Rohilla in 1743.

———, *Taẓkira*, cited from the Sitamau transcript of Patna MS. This work, almost the same as *Badā'i' Waqā'i'*, is divided in three parts. Part one describes Nādir Shāh's invasion, in part two is mentioned an expedition of Bangarh while part three records the details of Abdālī's invasion.

Qāzī Aḥmadullāh, *Al-Musajjalāt Fī Tārīkh-al-Quẓāt*, Department of History Library, Aligarh. MS No. 87. A history of the *qāẓīs* of Bilgram. The author was the son of the famous Qāzī Muḥammad Iḥsān who came into conflict on a *madad-i ma'āsh* issue with Burhān-ul-Mulk.

Shafīq, Lachhmī Nārāyan, *Ma'āsir-i Āṣafī*, A. S. B. MS; Osmania University Library, Hyderabad MS. Primarily a history of the ruling family of Hyderabad. Contains useful information about Niẓām-ul-Mulk's relations with the governors of Awadh and the Punjab.

Shāhnawāz Khān, Ṣamṣām-ud-Daulah, *Ma'āsir-ul-Umarā*, 3 vols., edited by Maulawi Abd ur-Rahim and Ashraf Ali, Bib. Ind., Calcutta, 1888–95.

Translated by H. Beveridge with a volume of Index by Baini Prasad, Calcutta. A well known and oft-cited biographical dictionary of the Mughal nobles. The author held an important office at the court of the Niẓām in Hyderabad. He began this voluminous work on the basis of contemporary MSS in 1767 and completed it in 1780.

E. ADMINISTRATIVE MANUALS, GLOSSARIES AND OTHER HISTORICAL WORKS

Abul Faẓl 'Allāmī, Ā'īn-i Akbarī. edited by Blochman, Bibl. Ind. Calcutta, 1867–77 (also Saiyid Ahmad's edn., Delhi, 1855 and Nawalkishore edn., Lucknow, 1869); English translation by Blochmann, revised by Phillot, Vol. I, Calcutta, 1927 and 1939 and by Col. H. S. Jarrett, revised by J. N. Sarkar, Vols. II & III, Calcutta, 1949 and 1948 Repr., Delhi, 1978.

Dastūr-ul-'Amal, A. S. B. MS No. 381. Part of it contains some valuable information based on the akhbārāt. The remaining portion is like the usual Dastūr-ul-'Amals giving details about the jama'dāmī and topography of the empire and the emoluments of the manṣabdārs, etc.

I'timād 'Alī Khān, Mir'āt-ul-Haqā'iq, Bodleian MS. Fraser Collection No. 124. Though it mainly comprises information on administrative and economic conditions in Gujarat, this work throws some interesting light on the developments at Delhi and in other parts of the empire as well.

Khulāṣat-us-Siyāq, A. D. 1703, M. A. L., Aligarh MS, Subḥānallāh Collection (ẓamīma), F. 900/15.

Bahār, Munshī Tek Chand, Bahār-i 'Ajam, A. D. 1739–40. Lithographed edn., Nawalkishore, Lucknow, 1916. A comprehensive Persian dictionary.

Mukhliṣ, Anand Rām, Mir'āt-ul Iṣṭilaḥ, Br. M. Or. 1813; a glossary of idioms, proverbs and technical terms.

————, An album containing autographed notings and some letters by Mukhliṣ, pertaining to the court and the Punjab in the 1740s. Br. M. Or. 9236 (Meredith-Owen).

Dabistān-i Maẓāhib, a work on the religions of the world, written during 1653–6 by an unknown author, ascribed to Muḥammad Muḥsin Fānī, edited by Nazr Ashraf, Calcutta, 1809. An English translation by Anthony Troyer and David Shea as Schools of Religions in 3 vols. was published from London 1843.

A Hindi Poem by Trilok Dās, giving the popular view of Nādir Shāh's invasion and the conditions of the empire under Muḥammad Shāh. Text and translation in English by W. Irvine, Journal of Asiatic Society of Bengal, 1897. See also an eighteenth-century Urdu translation as Hālāt-i Nādir Shāh wa Muḥammad Shāh, I. O. U29.

Jangnāma of Sri Dhar Murlī, Text and English translation by W. Irvine, Journal of the Royal Asiatic Society of Bengal, 1900, pp. 1–30.

F. LATER HISTORICAL WORKS

Anonymous, Tārīkh-i Jāis (a local history of the leading families of Jais compiled possibly in the late-18th century) MS. Dr. Abdul Ali Collection, Nadwat-ul-'Ulamā, Lucknow.

Bhatnāgar, Bahādur Singh, Yādgār-i Bahāduri, Uttar Pradesh State Archives, Allahabad MS. A voluminous memoir-like work, compiled in 1249

A. H./1833–34. Historical narrative in this work is based largely on *'Imād* and *Ma'dan*. But it also contains a useful topographical account of Awadh, its products, industries and trade and a description of Hindu religious. sects and biographical notices of poets and scholars.

Bilgrāmī, Saiyid 'Abbās 'Alī Khān, *'Ibrat-ul-'Alam*, Patna MS No. 2612. Compiled in 1287 A. H., but an interesting family history based on a number of family papers and treatises. The work is primarily a history of Saiyid Nūr-ul-Ḥasan of Bilgram who built an estate in Shahabad, Bihar in the late-eighteenth century, and who had been portrayed rather hostilely in Mīr Sakhāwat Bilgrāmī's *Tārīkh-i Nūr-ul-Ḥasan Khān*. Nūr-ul Ḥasan was son of Saiyid Muḥammad Muḥsin who died fighting with Burhān ul-Mulk against Nādir Shāh in 1739. He was brought up under the care of Ṣafdar Jang.

Bilgrāmī, Saiyid Ibn Ḥasan, *Burhān-i Awadh*, M. A. L., Aligarh MS. Subḥānallāh 954/14. Compiled sometime in the mid-nineenth century.

Faiẓ Bakhsh, Munshī Muḥammad, *Tārīkh-i Farḥ Bakhsh*, M. A. L., Aligarh MS. A history of Faizabad, but contains information regarding the developments at the Mughal court in the early-eighteenth century. The work was completed in 1817. W. Hoey has translated this work as *Memoirs of Delhi and Faizabad*, Allahabad, 1889.

Gaur Sahāi, Munshī, *Tārīkh-i Awadh*, M. A. L., Aligarh MS.'Abd-us-Salam 489/1 F., Compiled in 1242 A. H./1826–27.

Ghulām 'Alī Khān, *Shāh 'Alam Nāma*, edited by Al-Mamun Suhruwardi and Aqa Muhammad Kazim Shirazi, Bib. Ind., Calcutta, 1874.

Hamdānī, Qāsim 'Alī, *Tārīkh-i Shāhiya Nishapuriya*, Rampur MS No. 2148. Compiled sometime in the earlier half of the nineteenth century.

In'āmullāh bin Khurram Shāh, Munshī, *Auṣaf-ul-Āṣaf*, M. A. L., Aligarh MS, Abd us-Salam 480/1 F. A verbose account of *nawābī* rule in Awadh, written in 1795.

Kishan Sahāi 'Aẓīmabādī, *I'jāz-i Arsalānī*, Bibliotheque Nationale, Paris MS Blochet 713–4. A collection of letters of Major Polier dated 1187–93 A. H./1773–9, throws interesting light on social life and trade in northern India in the eighteenth century. For a description see G. Colas and Francis Richard's article on Polier's papers in *Bulletin De l'École Francais D'Extreme Orient*, Paris, LXXIII, 1984.

Mīr Muḥammad Walīullāh, *Tārīkh-i Farrukhabād*, M. A. L., Aligarh MS. A History of Muḥammad Khān Bangash, the founder of Farrukhabad, and his contemporaries.

Mirzā Abū Ṭālib Khān, *Tafzīh-ul-Ghāfilīn*, translated by William Hoey as *History of Aṣaf-ud-Daulah*, Allahabad, 1885, reprinted, Lucknow, 1971. Abū Ṭālib, better-known as Abū Ṭālib *Londonī*, was a revenue officer in Āṣaf-ud-Daulah's service. This work, compiled in 1797, is a history of the time of Āṣaf-ud-Daulah, but also notes some important facts about Burhān-ul-Mulk and Ṣafdar Jang.

Ma'āṣir-i-Ṭālibī, translated by Charles Stewart as *Travels of Mirza Abu Taleb Khan*, London, 1810, reprinted, New Delhi, 1972.

Munawwar 'Alī Khān, *Lauḥ-i Tārīkh*, I. O. MS. No. 4243. A mid-nineteenth century history of the Bangash nawābs of Farrukhabad, provides useful information about towns in the territory of the Bangash chief.

Nāmī, Harnām Singh, *Tārīkh-i Sa'ādat-i Jāwīd*, Br. M. Or. 1820. A history of Awadh up to 1805–6.

Naqawī, Saiyid Ghulām 'Alī Khān, *'Imād-us-Sa'ādat*, Nawalkishore, Lucknow. A regular and extremely valuable history of the nawābs of Awadh from Burhān-ul-Mulk to Sa'ādat 'Alī Khān, compiled in 1808 and named after Sa'ādat 'Alī Khān, the fifth nawāb.

Qāzī Muhammad Sharīf, *Tārīkh-i Bhadohīn*, I. O. MS. No. 437. An Urdū history of the family of the author who belonged to the town of Bhadohin in *sarkār* Chunar, compiled in 1847.

Safawī, Saiyid Sultān 'Alī Khān, *Ma'dan-us-Sa'ādat*, A. S. B. MS, Ivanow 181 (Society Collection), composed between 1798 and 1802 at Lucknow and dedicated to Nawāb Sa'ādat 'Alī Khān, is a general history of the Mughals in four volumes. Volume IV begins with the reign of Bahādur Shāh and ends with 1802, the seventh year of Sa'ādat 'Alī Khān's rule in Awadh. Often repeats *Siyar*, but provides some useful information about the nawābs of Awadh.

Saiyid Roshan 'Alī Khān Bārha, *Saiyid-ut-Tawārīkh* I. O. MS No. 423. A mid-nineteenth century family history, throws interesting light on the family customs and kin organization of the Bārha Saiyids.

Sāqib, Jai Gopāl, *Zubdat-ul-Kawā'if*, Lucknow University Library MS; Br. M. Or. 6632 (Meredith-Owen). A history of the rulers of Awadh, compiled in the mid-nineteenth century.

Shauq, Qudratullāh, *Jām-i Jahān Numā*, Rampur MS No. 1858.

Sūrī, Sohan Lāl, *'Umdat-ut-Tawārīkh*, Lahore, 1885–9, Vols. I and II.

Tārīkh-i A'zamgarh, I. O. MS No. 4038. This is an important work on the history of the rise of the Gautam *zamīndārī* of Azamgarh. Two earlier versions of the same, one by Saiyid Amīr 'Alī Rizwī as *Sarguzasht-i Rājahā-i A'zamgarh* (No. 237), and the other by Gridhārī as *Intizām-ul-Rāj* or *Intizām-i Rāj-i A'zamgarh*. (No. 238) are preserved in the Edinburgh University Library. See also pp. 247–8n.

Tārīkh-i Khāndān-i Mahārāja Karam Singh wa Khāndān-i-Phūlkiyān, transcript. Personal copy of Prof. Ganda Singh, Patalia.

Tārīkh-i Khāndān-i Rājahā-i Phūlkiyān, transcript. Personal copy of Prof. Ganda Singh, Patalia.

Vadera, Ganesh Dās, *Chār Bāgh-i Panjāb*, (ed.), Kripal Singh, Amritsar, 1965. A part of this work has been translated by J. S. Grewal and Indu Banga as *Early Nineteenth Century Panjab*, Amritsar, 1975.

EUROPEAN WORKS

Archer, Maj. Edward, *Tours in Upper India and in Parts of the Himalayan Mountains*, London, 1833.

Angusta, Deare, *A Tour Through the Upper Provinces of Hindustan: 1804–1814*, London, 1823.

Barr, William, *March from Delhi to Peshawar and from thence to Cabul*, with the mission of Lt. Col. Sir. C. M. Wade, including Travels in the Punjab, a visit to the city of Lahore and a narrative of operations in the Khyber Pass undertaken in 1839, reprint, Patiala, 1970.

Browne, James, *History of the Origins and Progress of the Sicks in Indian Tracts*, London, 1788.

Burnes, Alexander, *Cabool, Being a Narrative of a Journay to and Residence in that City*, London, 1842.

————, *Travels into Bokhara with a Narrative of a Voyage on the Indus*, 3 Vols., reprint, OUP, 1973.

Butter, Donald, *Topography and Statistics of the Southern Districts of Awadh and Sultanpur*, Calcutta, 1839.

Forbes, James, *Oriental Memoirs*, 2 Vols., London, 1813.

Foster, George, *A Journey from Bengal to England, through the Northern Part of India, Kashmere, Afghanistan and Persia and into Russia by the Caspean Sea*, Vol. I, London, 1798.

Hamilton, Walter, *A Geographical, Statistical and Historical Description of Hindoostan and the Adjacent Countries*, 2 Vols., London 1820.

Hodges, William, *Travels in India, 1780–83*, London, 1793.

Jacquemont, Victor, *Letters from Inida describing a Journey in the British Dominions of India, Tibet, Lahore and Cashmere—During the Year 1828–1831*, London, 1835.

Lumsden, Lt. Thomas, *A Journay from Meerut in India, to London through Arabia Persia . . . during the years 1819 and 1820*, London, 1822.

Maulawi Abdul Kadir Khan, 'Memorandum of the Route between Delhi and Cabul, 1797 A. D.', *Panjab Past and Present*, XII, Part I, 1978.

Mohan Lal, *Travels in the Panjab, Afghanistan and Turkistan to Balkh, Bokhara and Herat*, reprint, Patiala, 1971.

Moorcraft, W. and C. Trebek, *Travels in the Himalayan Provinces of Hindustan and the Panjab: in Ladakh and Kashmir in Peshawar, Kabul, Kunduz and Bokhara*, 2 Vols., reprint, New Delhi, 1971.

Orme, Robert, *Historical Fragments of the Mogul Empire*, 2nd reprint, New Delhi, 1978.

Prinsep, Henry T., *The Origins of the Sick Power in the Punjab*, Calcutta, 1834 (reprint 1970).

Rennell, James, *Memoirs of a Map of Hindustan*, reprint, Patna, 1975.

Sleeman, William Henry, *A Journey through the Kingdom of Oude*, 2 Vols., London, 1885.

Thornton, Edward, *Gazetteer of the Territories under the Government of the East India Company and the Native States on the Continent of India*, 2 Vols., London, 1854.

Tieffenthaler, Joseph, *Historische-geographische Beschreibung von Hindustan, 1785–87* in English tr. as *Mid-Gangetic Region in the Eighteenth Century*, by S. N. Sinha, New Delhi, 1977.

Twinning, Thomas, *Travels in India a Hundred Years Ago*, London, 1893.

MODERN WORKS

Ahmad, Iftikhar, 'Medieval Jatt Immigration into the Punjab' *PIHC*, 43rd Session, Kurukshetra, 1982, pp. 342–50.

Akhtar, Shirin, *The Role of the Zamindars in Bengal, 1707–1772*, Dacca, 1982.

Ali, M. Athar Ali, *The Mughal Nobility under Aurangzeb*, Bombay, 1966.

———, 'Provincial Governors under Aurangzeb', *Medieval India: A Miscellany*, Vol. I, Bombay, 1969

———, 'The Mughal Empire in History' Presidential Address to the Medieval Indian Section, *PIHC*, 33rd Session, Muzaffarpur, 1972, pp. 175–88.

———, 'The Passing of Empire: The Mughal Case', *Modern Asian Studies*, Vol. 9, No. 3, 1975, pp. 385–96.

———, 'The Eighteenth Century—An Interpretation' *The Indian Historical Review*, V, Nos. 1–2, July 1978–January, 1979, pp. 175–86.

Ashraf, K. M., 'Presidential Address to the Medieval Indian Section', *PIHC*, 23rd Session, Aligarh, 1960, pp. 143–52.

Askari, S. H., 'Baba Nanak in Persian Sources', *Journal of the Sikh Studies*, II, No. 2, August, 1975, pp. 112–16.

Atkinson, Edward, *Statistical, Descriptive and Historical Account of the North-Western Provinces of India*, Allahabad, 1875–1876.

Bal, S. S., 'Early Years of the Pontificate of Guru Gobind Singh', *Proceedings of the Punjab History Conference*, 1966 (Patiala 1968), pp. 63–78.

Banerjee, I. B., *Evolution of the Khalsa*, 2 Vols., Vol. II, Calcutta, 1947.

Banga, Indu, *Agrarian System of the Sikhs*, Delhi, 1978.

———, 'Religious Land Grants under Sikh Rule', *Proceedings of the Panjab History Conference*, Patiala, 1971, pp. 144–51.

———, State Formation under Sikh Rule', *Journal of Regional History*, Department of History, Guru Nanak Dev University, Amritsar, I, 1980.

Barnett, Richard B., *North India Between Empires, Awadh, the Mughals and the British, 1720–1801*, Berkeley, 1980.

Bayly, C. A., *Rulers, Townsmen and Bazaars: North Indian Society in the Age of British Expansion, 1770–1870*, Cambridge, 1983.

———, 'Indian Merchants in Traditional Setting, 1780–1830', in Clive Dewy and A. G. Hopkins (eds.), *The Imperial Impact : Studies in the Economic History of Africa and India*, London, 1978.

———, 'The Pre-History of 'Communalism'? Religious Conflict in India, 1700–1860', *Modern Asian Studies*, 19, 2, (1985), pp. 177–203.

Benett, W. C., *A Report on the Family History of the Chief Clans of the Roy Bareilly District*, Lucknow, 1870.

Bhadra, Gautam, 'Two Frontier Uprisings in Mughal India', in Ranajit Guha (ed.), *Subaltern Studies, II, Writings on South Asian History and Society*, Delhi, 1984.

Bhatnagar, V. S., *Life and Times of Sawai Raja Jai Singh*, Delhi, 1974.

Bhattacharya, S., 'Towards an Interpretation of the Pre-Colonial Economy', review of T. Raychaudhuri and Irfan Habib (eds.), *The Cambridge Economic History of India, I*, in *Economic and Political Weekly*, October 1, 1983, pp. 1707–11.

Bilgrami, Rafat M., *Religious and Quasi-Religious Departments of the Mughal Period, 1556–1707*, Delhi, 1984.

Bingley, A. H., *History, Caste and Culture of Jats and Gujars*, New Delhi, 1978.

Calkins, C. Philip, 'Formation of a Regionally Oriented Ruling Group in

Bengal, 1700–1740, *Journal of Asian Studies*, XXIX, August, 1970, pp. 799–806.

———, 'The Revenue Administration in Bengal', mimeographed.

Carnegy, Patrick, *Notes on the Races, Tribes and Castes, Inhabiting the Province of Avadh*, Lucknow, 1868.

Catanach, I. J., 'Some Continuities in Indian History in the Eighteenth and Early Nineteenth Centuries', *New Zealand Journal of History*, 3, No. 1, 1969, pp. 1–13.

Chandra, Bipan, *Communalism in Modern India*, New Delhi, 1984.

Chandra, Satish, *Parties and Politics at the Mughal Court, 1707–1740*, Third edn. Delhi, 1982.

———, *Medieval India: Society, the Jagirdari Crisis and the Village*, Delhi, 1982.

———, 'Early Relations of Farrukh Siyar and the Saiyid Brothers', *Medieval India Quarterly*, Vol. I, 1957, pp. 135–46.

———, '*Jizya* in the Post-Aurangzeb Period', *PIHC*, 1946.

———, '*Jizya* and the State in India during the Seventeenth Century', *Journal of the Economic and Social History of the Orient*, XII, Part III, 1969.

Cohn, Bernard, 'Political Systems in Eighteenth Century India : The Banaras Region', *Journal of the American Oriental Society*, 82, No. 3, September 1962, pp. 312–19.

Crooke, William, *The Tribes and Castes of the North-Western Provinces and Oudh*, 4 Vols., Calcutta, 1896.

———, *The North-Western provinces of India : Their History, Ethnology, and Administration*, London, 1897, reprinted, Delhi, 1971.

Cunningham, J. D., *A History of the Sikhs, from the Origin of the Nation to the Battle of the Sutlej*, London, 1849, reprinted, Delhi, 1955.

Darogha, Haji Abbas Ali, *An Illustrated Historical Album of the Rajas and Taalluqdars of Oudh*, Allahabad, 1880.

Dasgupta, Ashin, *Indian Merchants and the Decline of Surat*, c. *1700–1750*, Wiesbaden, 1979.

———, 'Trade and Politics in Eighteenth Century India', in D. S. Richards (ed.), *Islam and the Trade of Asia*, Philadelphia, 1970.

Datta, K. K., *Alivardi Khan and His Times*, Calcutta, 1939.

———, *Survey of India's Social Life and Economic Conditions in the Eighteenth Century (1707–1813)*, Calcutta, 1961.

De, Barun (ed.), *Perspective in the Social Sciences, I : Historical Dimensions*, Calcutta, 1977.

———, 'Some Implications of Political Tendencies and Social Factors in Eighteenth Century India' in O. P. Bhatnagar (ed.), *Studies in Social History*, Allahabad, 1964.

Deol, G. S., *Banda Bahadur*, Jullunder, 1972.

Dighe, V. G., *Peshwa Baji Rao I and the Maratha Expansion*, Bombay, 1944.

District Gazetteers, United Provinces of Agra and Oudh, and of the Punjab.

Duff, I. G., *A History of the Mahrattas*, London, 1912.

Elliot, Charles Alfred, *Chronicles of Oonao*, Allahabad, 1862.

———, *Chronicles of Gujrat*, reprint, Patiala, 1970.

Faruqi, Burhan Ahmad, *Mujaddid's Conception of Tauhid*, Lahore, 1960.

Fisher, Michael H., 'The Imperial Court and the Province : A Social and

Administrative History of Pre-British Awadh, 1775–1856', unpublished Ph. D. thesis, University of Chicago, 1978.

Fox, Richard G., *Kin, Clan, Raja and Rule : State-Hinterland Relations in Pre-industrial India*, Berkeley, 1971.

Fraser, James, *History of Nadir Shah*, London, 1742.

Friedmann, Yohnan, *Shaykh Ahmad Sirhindi, An Outline of His Thought and a Study of His Image in the Eyes of Posterity*, Montreal, 1971.

Frykenberg, R. E. (ed.), *Land Control and Social Structure in Indian History*, Madison, 1969, reprint, New Delhi, 1979.

———, 'Traditional Process of Power in South India : An Historical Analysis of Local Influence', *IESHR*, I, No. 2, 1963.

Fukazawa, Hiroshi, 'Land and Peasants in the Eighteenth Century Maratha Kingdom', *Hitotshubashi Journal of Economics*, VI, 1 June 1965.

———, 'State and Caste System (*Jati*) in the Eighteenth Century Maratha Kingdom', in M. R. Sinha (ed.), *Integration in India*, 'Bombay, 1971.

———, 'Rural Servants in the Eighteenth Century Maharashtrian Village—Demiurge or *Jajmani* System?', *Hitotshubashi Journal of Economics*, XII, 2, 1972.

Goetz, Hermann, *The Crisis of Indian Civilization in the Eighteenth and Early Nineteenth Centuries*, Calcutta University—Series, Chowkhamba Sanskrit Series, reprint, 1938.

Gordon, Stewart N., 'Legitimacy and Loyalty in Some Successor States of the Eighteenth Century', in J. F. Richards (ed.), *Kingship and Authority in South Asia*, University of Wisconsin, Madison 1978.

Grewal, J. S., *From Guru Nanak to Ranjit Singh : Essays in Sikh History*, Amritsar, 1972.

———, *Studies in Local and Regional History*, Amritsar, 1974.

———, *Miscellaneous Articles*, Amritsar, 1976.

Griffin, L. H., *The Rajas of the Panjab*, Lahore, 1870, reprint, Delhi, 1977.

———, *The Panjab Chiefs—Historical and Biographical Notes of the Principal Families in the Panjab*, Vol. I, London, 1869, Vol. II, Lahore, 1890.

Gupta, H. R., *Studies in the Later Mughal History of the Panjab*, Lahore, 1944.

———, *History of the Sikhs*, 5 Vols., Delhi, 1978–82.

Gupta, S. P., 'The System of Rural Taxation in Eastern Rajasthan', *c.* 1665–1750', *PIHC*, 33rd Session, Muzaffarpur, 1972, pp. 283–90.

———, 'The *Jagir* System during the Evolution of the Jaipur State, *c.* 1650–1750', *PIHC*, 35th Session, Jadavpur, 1974, pp. 171–9.

———, 'New Evidence on Agrarian and Rural Taxation in Eastern Rajasthan (17th and 18th Centuries)', *PIHC*, 36th Session, Aligarh, 1975, pp. 229–42.

———, 'Evidence for Urban Population and Its Composition From 17th–18th Century Rajasthan' *PIHC*, 37th Session, Calicut, 1976, pp. 179–84.

———, and Shirin Moosvi, 'Weighted Price and Revenue Rate Indices of Eastern Rajasthan', *IESHR*, XII, No. 2, 1975.

Habib, Irfan, *The Agrarian System of Mughal India (1556–1707)*, Bombay, 1963.

———, *An Atlas of the Mughal Empire*, Delhi, 1982.

———, 'Political Role of Shaikh Ahmad Sirhindi and Shah Waliullah', *PIHC*, 1960 (Aligarh), pp. 209–23.

————, 'Currency System of Mughal India, 1556–1707', *Medieval India Quarterly*, IV, 1961, pp. 1–22.

————, 'The *Mansab* System 1595–1637', *PIHC*, 29th Session, Patiala, 1967, pp. 221–42.

————, 'Potentialities of Change in the Economy of Mughal India', *The Socialist Digest*, No. 6, September, 1972.

————, 'Presidential Address' in the *Proceedings of the Panjab History Conference*, 1971, (Patiala 1972), pp. 49–54.

————, 'Forms of Class Struggle in Mughal India' mimeographed, paper presented at the 41st Session of IHC, Bombay, 1980.

Hardy, P., 'Comments and Critique', *Journal of Asian Studies*, XXXV, No. 2, February, 1976, pp. 257–63.

Hasan, Ibn, *The Central Structure of the Mughal Empire*, reprint, New Delhi, 1970.

Hasan, S. Nurul, *Thoughts on Agrarian Relations in Mughal India*, Delhi, 1973, reprint, 1984.

————, 'New Light on the Relations of Early Mughal Rulers with their Nobility', *PIHC*, 1944.

————, 'Shaikh Ahmad Sirhindi and Mughal Politics', *PIHC*, 1945 (Annamalainagar), pp. 248–57.

————, 'Du Jardin Papers: A valuable Source for the Economic History of Northern India, 1778–1787', *Indian Historical Review*, V, Nos. 1–2, July 1978–January, 1979, pp. 187–99.

————, and S. P. Gupta, 'Price of Foodgrains in the Territories of Amber', *PIHC*, 29th Session, Patiala, 1967, pp. 345–68.

Husain, Iqbal, 'Some Afghan Settlements in the Gangetic Doab, 1627–1707,' *PIHC*, 31st Session, Benaras, 1969.

————, 'Pattern of Afghan Settlements in India in the Seventeenth Century', *PIHC*, 39th Session, Hyderabad, 1978, pp. 327–36.

Husain, Yusuf, *The First Nizam : Life and Times of Nizam-ul-Mulk, Asaf Jah I*, Second edn., Bombay, 1963.

Hutchison, J. and J. Ph. Vogel, *History of the Panjab Hill States*, 2 Vols., Lahore, 1933.

Ibbetson, Denizel, *The Punjab Castes*, reprint, Patiala, 1970.

Imperial Gazetteer, (Punjab), 2 Vols., Calcutta, 1908.

India North-Western Provinces and Oudh, *Gazetteer of the Provinces of Oudh*, 3 Vols., Allahabad, 1877.

Irvine, William, *Later Moghuls*, reprint, Delhi, 1971.

————, *Army of the Indian Moghuls*, reprint, Delhi, 1962.

————, 'The Bangash Nawabs of Farrukhabad : A Chronicle (1713–1857)', *Journal of the Asiatic Society of Bengal*, 47, No. 1 (1878), pp. 259–383; 48, No. 1 (1879), pp. 49–170.

Jafari, S. Z. H., 'The Land Controlling Classes in Awadh, 1600–1900', paper presented to the 43rd Session of IHC, Kurukshetra, 1982.

————, 'Two *Madad-i Ma'ash farmans* of Aurangzeb from Awadh', *PIHC*, 40th Session, Waltair, 1979, pp. 302–14.

Karim, A., *Murshid Quli Khan and His Times*, Dacca, 1963.

Keen, H. G., *The Fall of the Moghul Empire*, London, 1876.

Kessinger, Tom G., *Vilyatpur, 1848–1968, Social and Economic Change in a North Indian Village*, New Delhi, 1979.

Khan, Iqtidar Alam, *Mirza Kamran, A Biographical Study*, Bombay, 1964.

———, *Political Biography of a Mughal Noble : Mun'im Khan, Khan-i Khanan, 1497–1575*, New Delhi, 1973.

———, 'The Turko-Mongol Theory of Kingship', *Medieval India—A Miscellany*, Bombay, 1972, Vol. II, pp. 8–18.

———, 'Middle Classes in the Mughal Empire', Presidential Address to the Medieval Section, *PIHC*, 36th Session, Aligarh, 1975, pp. 113–41.

———, 'Shaikh Abdul Quddus Gangohi's Relations with Political Authorities : A Reappraisal', *Medieval India : A Miscellany*, Vol. IV, Bombay, 1977, pp. 73–90.

Khan, A. R., *Chieftains in the Mughal Empire during the Reign of Akbar*, Simla, 1977.

Kudryavtsev, M. K., 'The Role of the Jats in Northern India's Ethnic History', in J. N. Singh Yadav (ed.), *Haryana : Studies in History and Politics*, New Delhi, 1976, pp. 95–103.

Kulkarni, G. T., 'Banking in the Eighteenth Century : A Case Study of a Pune Banker', *Artha Vijnan*, XV, 2 June 1973, pp. 180–200.

Kumar, Dharma and Meghnad Desai (eds.), *The Cambridge Economic History of India, II*, Cambridge, 1983.

Latif, S. M., *History of the Panjab*, Calcutta, 1891, reprint, New Delhi, 1964.

Leonard, Karen, 'The Hyderabad Political System and its Participants', *Journal of Asian Studies*, 30, No. 2, May 1971, pp. 569–82.

———, 'The "Great Firm" Theory of the Decline of the Mughal Empire', *Comparative Studies in History and Society*, 21, No. 2, April, 1979, pp. 161–7.

Lockhart, L., *Nadir Shah*, London, 1938.

———, *The Fall of the Safavid Dynasty and the Afghan Occupation of Persia*, Cambridge, 1958.

Luard, C. E. (ed.), *Rewa State Gazetteer*, Lucknow, 1907.

Macauliff, M. A., *The Sikh Religion, Its Gurus, Sacred Writings and Authors*, 6 Vols., Oxford, 1909, reprint, Delhi, 1963.

Mahmud, S. Hasan, '*Yasin's Glossary:* Edition, Translation, Annotation and Analysis', unpublished Ph. D. thesis, Jamia Millia, New Delhi, 1984.

Malik, Zahir Uddin, *A Mughal Statesman of the Eighteenth Century: Khan-i Dauran, Mir Bakhshi of Muhammad Shah, 1719–1739*, Bombay, 1973.

———, *The Reign of Muhammad Shah : 1719–1748*, Bombay, 1977.

———, 'Financial Problems of the Mughal Government during Farrukh Siyar's Reign', *IESHR*, 4, No. 3, September, 1967, pp. 265–75.

Marshall, P. J., 'British Expansion in India in the Eighteenth Century : A Historical Revision', *History*, 60, February 1975, pp. 28–43.

———, 'Economic and Political Expansion: The Case of Oudh', *Modern Asian Studies*, 9, No. 4, 1975, pp. 465–82.

McLeod, W. H., *The Evolution of the Sikh Community*, Delhi, 1975.

Massy, Col. Charles Francis, *Chiefs and Families of Note in the Panjab*, 3 Vols., Lahore, 1890, reprint, 1940.

Mehta, Makrand, 'Indian Bankers and Political Change : A Case Study of the Travadis of Surat, *c.* 1720–*c.* 1820', *Studies in History*, IV, No. 1, January–June, 1982, pp. 41–55.

Mishra, K. P., *Banaras in Transition, 1738–1795*, New Delhi, 1975.

Mitra, R., 'The Bisen Talukdars of Northern Oudh', *Calcutta Review*, LXXIV, 1882.

Muhammad Umar, 'Indian Towns in the Eighteenth Century—Case Study of Six Towns in Uttar Pradesh', *PIHC*, 37th Session, Calicut, 1976, pp. 208–18.

Mohammad Yasin, *A Social History of Islamic India, 1605–1748*, Lucknow, 1958.

Moosvi, Shirin, 'Suyurghal Statistics in the *Ain-i Akbari*' *Indian Historical Review*, II, No. 2, January, 1976, pp. 282–9.

Mukherji, Rudrangshu, 'Trade and Empire in Awadh', *Past and Present*, No. 94, February, 1982.

Mukhia, Harbans, 'Illegal Exactions from Peasants, Artisans and Menials in Eighteenth Century Eastern Rajasthan', *IESHR*, XIV, No. 2, April-June 1977, pp. 231–45.

———, Om Prakash and S. Arsaratnam, 'Review Symposium on T. Raychaudhuri and I. Habib (ed.), *The Cambridge Economic History of India I, IESHR*, 21, No. 1, 1984, pp. 112–27.

Naqvi, H. K., *Urban Centres and Industries in Upper India 1556–1803*, Bombay, 1968.

———, *Urbanization and Urban Centres under the Great Mughals*, Simla, 1972.

Narayan, Brij, *Indian Economic Life, Past and Present*, Lahore, 1929.

Nijjar, B. S., *Panjab under the Later Mughals*, Jullunder, 1972.

Nizami, K. A., 'Shah Walliullah Dehlavi and Indian Politics in the Eighteenth Century' *Islamic Culture*, XXV, Jubilee Number, 1951.

———, 'Naqshbandi Influence on Mughal Rulers and Politics', *Islamic Culture*, XXXIX, 1965, pp. 41–52.

Owen, S. G., *The Fall of the Moghul Empire*, London, 1912.

Pearson, Michael, *Merchants and Rulers in Gujarat*, Berkeley, 1976.

———, 'Political Participation in Mughal India', *IESHR*, IX, No. 2, 1972, pp. 113–31.

———, 'Shivaji and the Decline of the Mughal Empire', *Journal of Asian Studies*, XXXV, No. 2, February 1976, pp. 221–35.

Perlin, Frank, 'Proto-Industrialization and Pre-Colonial South Asia', *Past and Present*, No. 98, February, 1983, pp. 30–95.

———, 'The Pre-Colonial Indian State in History and Epistemology : A Reconstruction of Social Formation in the Western Deccan from the 15th to the Early 19th Century', in H. J. M. Classen and Peter Skalnik (eds.), *The Study of the State*, the Hague, Mouton, 1981, pp. 275–302.

Prasad, Ishwari, *India in the Eighteenth Century*, Allahabad, 1973.

———, *The Mughal Empire*, Allahabad, 1974.

Qaisar, Ahsan Jan, *The Indian Response to European Technology and Culture, 1498–1707*, Delhi, 1982.

Qanungo, K., *History of the Jats*, Calcutta, 1925.

Raghuvanshi, V. P. S., *Indian Society in the Eighteenth Century*, New Delhi, 1969.

Rana, R. P.. 'Agrarian Revolts in Northern India during the Late 17th and Early 18th Century', *IESHR*, 18, Nos. 3 & 4, July-December, 1981, pp. 287–326.

————, 'Social and Economic Background of the Rise of Bharatpur Kingdom', unpublished Ph. D. thesis, Jawaharlal Nehru University, 1984.

Ray, Niharranjan, *The Sikh Gurus and the Sikh Society*, New Delhi, 1968.

Raychaudhuri, Tapan and Irfan Habib (eds.), *The Cambridge Economic History
of India, I*, Cambridge, 1982.

Raza, Moonis, 'Delimiting *Suba* Avadh, 1550–1605', *The Avadh Geographer*, I,
1975, pp. 1–5.

Richards, J. F., *Mughal Administration in Golconda*, Oxford, 1975.

————, 'The Imperial Crisis in the Deccan', *Journal of Asian Studies*, XXXV,
No. 2, February 1976, pp. 237–56.

————, 'Mughal State Finance and the Premodern World Economy', *Comparative Studies in Society and History*, 23, No. 2, April, 1981, pp. 285–308.

————, (ed.), *Kingship and Authority in South Asia*, Madison, 1978.

————, and V. N. Rao, 'Banditry in Mughal India : Historical and Folk
Perceptions', *IESHR*, XVII, No. 1, January-March, 1980.

Rizwi, Najmul Raza, 'A Zamindar Family of Eastern Uttar Pradesh, 1609–
1771', *PIHC*, 41st Session, Bombay, 1980, pp. 239–47.

Rose, H. A., *A Glossary of the Tribes and Castes of the Punjab and North-West
Frontier Province*, 3 Vols., reprint, Patiala, 1970.

Ross, David, *The Land of the Five Rivers and Sind*, reprint, Patiala, 1970.

Sanyal, Hiteshranjan, *Social Mobility in Bengal*, Calcutta, 1981.

Saran, P., *The Provincial Government of the Mughals*, reprint, Bombay, 1973.

Sardesai, G. S., *New History of the Maratha People*, 2 Vols., Bombay, 1946–8.

Sarkar, J. N., *History of Aurangzeb*, 5 Vols., Calcutta, 1912–30, reprint,
Bombay, 1971–2.

————, *Fall of the Mughal Empire*, 4 Vols., Calcutta 1932–50, reprint, Bombay,
1971–5.

————, *The India of Aurangzeb (topography, Statistics and roads) compared with the
India of Akbar;* with extracts *from the Khulasat ut Tawarikh and the Chahar
Gulshan*, tr. and annotated, Calcutta, 1901.

————, *Mughal Administration*, reprint, Bombay, 1972.

————, *History of Bengal*, 2 Vols., reprint, Dacca, 1972.

Sarkar, Jagdish Narayan, *A Study of Eighteenth Century India*, Calcutta, 1976.

Savory, Roger, *Iran under the Safavids*, Cambridge, 1980.

Schwartzberg, Joseph E., 'Caste Regions of the Northern Plain', in Milton
Singer and Bernard S. Cohn (eds.), *Structure and Change in Indian Society*,
Chicago, 1968, pp. 81–115.

————, 'The Evolution of Regional Power Configurations in the Indian
Subcontinent', in Richard G. Fox (ed.), *Realm and Region in Traditional
India*, New Delhi, 1977, pp. 197–233.

————, 'Prolegomena to the Study of South Asian Regions and Regionalism',
in Robert I. Crane (ed.), *Regions and Regionalism in South Asian Studies: An
Explotary Study*, Durham, 1967, pp. 89–111.

Sen, S. N., *Administrative System of the Marathas*, Calcutta, 1928.

Shah, A. M., 'Political System in Eighteenth Century Gujarat', *Enquiry*, New
Series, I, No. 1, 1964, pp. 83–95'.

Shhaikh, Abdur Rashid, 'Suyurghal Lands under the Mughals' in H. R.

Gupta (ed.), *Essays Presented to Sir Jadu Nath Sarkar*, Panjab University, 1958, pp. 313–22.

Sharma, G. D., *Rajput Polity*, Delhi, 1977.

———, '*Vyaparis* and *Mahajans* in Western Rajasthan during the Eighteenth Century', *PIHC*, 41st Session, Bombay, 1980, pp. 377–85.

Sharma, S. R., *The Religious Policy of the Mughal Emperors*, Oxford, 1940, 2nd edn., Bombay, 1962.

Siddiqi, N. A., *Land Revenue Administration under the Mughals, 1700–1750*, Bombay, 1970.

———, 'The *Faujdar* and *Faujdari* under the Mughals', *Medieval India Quarterly*, IV, 1961, pp. 22–35.

———, 'Pulls and Pressures on the *Faujdar* under the Mughals', *PIHC*, 29th Session, Patiala, 1967, pp. 242–55.

Singh, Chetan, 'Socio-Economic Conditions in Panjab during the Seventeenth Century', unpublished Ph. D. thesis, Jawaharlal Nehru University, New Delhi, 1984.

———, 'Irrigation in Panjab: Persian Wheel Reconsidered', *IESHR*, 22, No. 1, 1984, pp. 74–87.

Singh, Dilbagh, 'Local and Land Revenue Administration in Eastern Rajasthan, *c.* 1750–1800', unpublished Ph. D. thesis, Jawaharlal Nehru University, New Delhi, 1975.

———, 'Ijarah System in Eastern Rajasthan, 1750–1800', *Proceedings of Rajasthan History Congress*, 6, 1973, pp. 60–9.

———, 'The Role of the *Mahajans* in the Growth of Rural Economy in Eastern Rajasthan during the Eighteenth Century', *Social Scientist*.

———, 'Caste and Structure of Village Society in Eastern Rajasthan during the Eighteenth Century', *Indian Historical Review*, II, No. 2, January, 1976, pp. 299–311.

Singh, Ganda, *Life of Banda Singh Bahadur*, Amritsar, 1935.

———, *Ahmad Shah Durrani*, Bombay, 1959.

———, *Bibliography of the Punjab*, Patiala, 1966.

———, and Teja Singh, *A Short History of the Sikhs*, Bombay, 1950.

Singh, Gurbux, '*Haqiqat*' on Sikh Polity during the Eighteenth Century', *Proceedings of Panjab History Conference*, Patiala, 1978.

———, 'Banda Singh Bahadur, His Achievements and Place of His Execution', *Proceedings of the Panjab History Conference*, Patiala, 1975.

Singh, Gurtej, 'Bhai Mani Singh in Historical Perspective', *Proceedings of the Panjab History Conference*, Patiala, 1968, pp. 120–7.

Singh, Khushwant, *A History of the Sikhs*, Vol. I, London, 1963.

Singh, Sohan, *Banda, the Brave*, Lahore, 1915.

Sinh, Raghuvir, *Malwa in Transition*, Bombay, 1936.

Sinha, H. N., *Rise of the Peshwas*, Allahabad, 1931.

Sinha, N. K., *Rise of the Sikh Power*, Calcutta, 1936.

Sinha, S, N., *Subah of Allahabad under the Great Mughals : 1580–1707*, New Delhi, 1974.

———, *The Mid-Gangetic Region in the Eighteenth Century : Some Observations of Joseph Tieffenthaler*, Allahabad, 1976.

Smith, W. C., 'Lower Class Risings in the Mughal Empire', *Islamic Culture*,
     1946, pp. 21–40.

Spear, P., *Twilight of the Moghuls*. Cambridge, 1951.

Srivastava, A. L., *The First Two Nawabs of Awadh*, Second edn., Agra, 1954.

Thapar, Romila, Irfan Habib and P. S. Gupta, 'The Contributions of Indian
     Historians to the Process of National Integration', *PIHC*, 24th Session,
     1961, Delhi, 345–61.

———, Harbans Mukhia and Bipan Chandra, *Communalism and the Writing of
     Indian History*, New Delhi, 2nd edn., 1977.

Trivedi, K. K., 'The Mughal Province of Agra during the Seventeenth
     Century', unpublished Ph. D. thesis, Aligarh Muslim University, 1978.

———, 'Commerce at Agra in the Seventeenth Century' (mimeographed),
     paper presented to the 34th Session of IHC, Chandigarh, 1973.

———, 'Changes in Caste-Composition of the *Zamindar* Class in Western
     Uttar Pradesh, 1595–*circa*–1900', *Indian Historical Review*, II, No. 1, July
     1975, pp. 47–67.

———, 'Non-Ruling Rajput Families in the Mughal Nobility in *Suba* Agra',
     PIHC, 39th Session, Hyderabad, 1978.

Trivedi, Madhu K., 'Cultural History of the Kingdom of Awadh', unpub-
     lished Ph. D. thesis, Aligarh Muslim University, 1977.

Varady, R. G., 'The Diary of a Road: A Sequential Narration of the Origins of
     the Lucknow-Kanpur Road (1825–1856)' *IESHR*, XV, No. 2, April-
     June 1978.

Varma, V. K., '*Suba* of Allahabad, 1707–1765', unpublished Ph. D. thesis,
     University of Allahabad, 1969.

Wink, Andre, 'Land and Sovereignty in India under the Eighteenth Century
     Maratha Swarajya', unpublished Ph. D. thesis, University of Leiden,
     1984.

———, 'Maratha Revenue Farming', *Modern Asian Studies*, 17, 4, 1983,
     pp. 591–628.

———, 'Sovereignty and Universal dominion in South Asia' *IESHR*, XXI,
     No. 3, July-September, 1984, pp. 265–92.

Wolfe-Murray, Col. J., *Dictionary of the Pathan Tribes*, Calcutta, 1899.

Zafarul Islam, 'Nature of Landed Property in Mughal India : Views of an
     Eighteenth Century Jurist', *PIHC*, 36th Session, Aligarh, 1975,
     pp. 301–9.

Zaidi, Sunita, 'Problems of the Mughal Administration in Sind during the
     First-half of the Seventeenth Century', *Islamic Culture*, April 1983,
     pp. 153–62.

URDU WORKS

Abbasi, Muhammad Hasan, *'Abbāsiyān-i Kākorī* (History of the 'Abbāsī
     Shaikhs of Kakori), Lucknow, 1945.

Ahmad, S. M., *Tārīkh-i Ilāhabād* (History of Allahabad), Allahabad, 1938.

Alavi, Muhammad Ali Haidar, *Tazkira-i Mashāhīr-i Kākorī* (Account of the
     Eminent Persons of Kakori), Lucknow, 1927.

Ansari, Muhammad Raza, *Bāni-ye Dars-i Nizāmī, Mullā Nizam-ud-Dīn Firangī
     Maḥali*, (History of Mullā Nizām-ud-Dīn), Aligarh, 1973.

Bilgrami, Qazi Sharif ul-Hasan and Munshi Muhammad Mahmud, *Tanqīḥ ul-Kalām Fī-Tārīkh-i Bilgrām* (History of Bilgram).

Brejbhogan Lal, *Tārīkh-i Daryābād* (History of Daryabad), Lucknow (n.d.).

Diwan Ramjas, *Tawārīkh-i Riyāsat-i Kapurthala* (History of Kapurthala State), Lahore, 1897.

Ghulam Nabi, *Tārīkh-i Jhajjar* (History of Jhajjar), Delhi, 1865.

Ghulam Sarwar, *Tārīkh-i Makhzan-i Panjāb*, Lucknow, 1877.

Gyani, Gyan Singh, *Tawārīkh-i Gurū Khālṣa* (History of Sikh Religion), 3 vols., Amritsar, 1923–5.

Haider, Kamal-ud-Din, *Sawāniḥāt-i Salāṭīn-i Awadh* (History of the Rulers of Awadh), Lucknow, 1879.

Khalifa Saiyid Muhammad Hasan Khan, *Tārīkh-i Patiāla* (History of Patiala State), Amritsar, 1878.

Korwi, Saiyid Mazhar Husain, *Tārīkh-i Banāras* (History of Banaras), Vol. I, Banaras, 1916.

Maulawi Inayatullah, *Tazkira-i 'Ulamā-i Firangī Maḥal* (Account of the *'Ulamā* of Firangi Mahal), Lucknow 1930.

Mirza Muhammad Azim Beg, *Tārīkh-i Gujrāt*, (History of Gujrat in the Punjab), Lahore, 1870.

Najm-ul-Ghani, *Tārīkh-i Awadh* (History of Awadh), Vol. I, Lucknow, 1919.

———, *Akhbār-uṣ-Ṣanādīd*, (A history of the Eminent Persons of North India), 2 Vols., Lucknow, 1918.

Pramanand, Bhai, *Bairāgī Bīr* (History of Banda Bahadur), Lahore, (n.d.).

Prasad, Durga, *Tārīkh-i Sandīla* (History of Sandila), Lucknow, (n.d.).

Ram Kishan, Munshi, *Qaum-i Kāyasth Kī Taraqqī* (A history of the Kayasthas), Lucknow, 1875.

Sabihuddin, Md., *Tārīkh-i Shāhjahānpūr* (History of Shahjahanpur), Lucknow, 1932.

Saiyid Iqbal Ahmad, *Tārīkh-i Shīrāz-i Hind, Jaunpūr* (History of Jaunpur), Jaunpur, 1963.

Singh, Ranzor, *Tārīkh-i Simūr* (History of Sirmur hill state), Allahabad, 1910.

Varma, Brij Narain, *Phūlnāma* (A history of the Jind State), Lahore, 1914.

Index